DECISIVE BATTLES

OF THE U.S.A.

✭

Other books by
MAJOR–GENERAL FULLER

Julius Caesar: Man, Soldier, and Tyrant.

The Conduct of War, 1789-1961.

The Generalship of Alexander the Great.

A Military History of the Western World (in three volumes).

How to Defeat Russia.

The Second World War, 1939-1945.

Armament and History.

Thunderbolts.

Watchwords.

Warfare Today.

Armoured Warfare.

Machine Warfare.

Decisive Battles: Their Influence on History and Civilisation.

The Generalship of Ulysses S. Grant.

Grant and Lee: A Study in Personality and Generalship.

The Memoirs of an Unconventional Soldier.

The Last of the Gentlemen's Wars: The Journal of a Subaltern during the War
in South Africa.

India in Revolt.

The Dragon's Teeth: A Study of Peace and War.

The First of the League Wars, Its Portents and Omens.

On Future Warfare.

The Foundations of the Science of War.

Tanks in the Great War.

The Reformation of War.

War and Western Civilisation: A Study of War as a Political Instrument and the
Expression of Mass Democracy.

Towards Armageddon.

Empire Unity and Defence.

Lectures on F.S.R. III, Operations between Mechanised Forces, etc., etc.

DECISIVE BATTLES
OF THE U.S.A.

By

J. F. C. FULLER

With Maps and Plans

Da Capo Press • New York

Library of Congress Cataloging in Publication Data

Fuller, J. F. C. (John Frederick Charles), 1878-1966.
  Decisive battles of the U.S.A. / by J.F.C. Fuller.
    p.   cm.
  Originally published: New York: Harper & Brothers, 1942.
  Includes index.
  ISBN 0-306-80532-4
    1. United States—History, Military. 2. Battles—United States—History. I.
  Title.
  E181.F95   1993   93-23004
  973—dc20   CIP

First Da Capo Press edition 1993

This Da Capo Press paperback edition of *Decisive Battles of the U.S.A.*
is an unabridged republication of the edition first published in New York in
1942. It is reprinted by arrangement with HarperCollins Publishers, Inc.

Published by Da Capo Press, Inc.
A Subsidiary of Plenum Publishing Corporation
233 Spring Street, New York, N.Y. 10013

To

HOFFMAN NICKERSON
Student of War and Military Historian

PREFACE

On December 3, 1793, Washington, addressing both Houses of Congress, said:

I cannot recommend to your notice measures for the fulfilment of *our* duties to the rest of the world, without again pressing upon you the necessity of placing ourselves in a condition of complete defence, and of exacting from *them* the fulfilment of *their* duties towards *us*. The United States ought not to indulge a persuasion that, contrary to the order of human events, they will for ever keep at a distance those painful appeals to arms, with which the history of every other nation abounds. There is a rank due to these United States among nations, which will be withheld, if not absolutely lost, by the reputation of weakness. If we desire to avoid insult, we must be able to repel it; if we desire to secure peace, one of the most powerful instruments of our rising prosperity, it must be known, that we are at all times ready for war.

The wisdom of these words must be apparent to every thinking American. Yet, strange to say, as late as 1936, in his book *The American Army in France 1917–1918,* General Harbord could still write: "We have learned nothing as a nation from our experiences in any of our wars."

Accepting these words as true, it occurred to me, when the present Anglo-German conflict arose, that it might be of interest to Americans—civilians as well as sailors, soldiers, and airmen—to have presented to them in a single volume a history of their past wars, not only because these struggles have made the U. S. A. what they are, but also because, in my opinion, it is war above all other activities which will make them what they will become. Should this be accepted, then logically it follows that a nation which studies its past military history will not only be the better prepared to defend its liberties, but also the better placed to turn war to its advantage.

On account of the conditions of war under which I have been living, the writing of this book has been no easy task. Literally, much of it has been written under gunfire and the crash of bursting bombs. Yet such inconveniences are slight when compared to the destruction or closing of public libraries, and particularly so because, as a historian I have always preferred to consult the writings of participants in and eyewitnesses of events, rather than those of the commentators, and these are hard to come by even in good libraries. I have adopted this course, not because such writings are the more accurate, but, in my opinion, the more real. Real·in the sense that, as history is so largely fiction, those who make it bring their readers into closer contact with the emotions, sentiments, and feelings of their day than do subsequent historians, who live and work in totally different surroundings.

As regards the book itself, I have followed the same lines I adopted in my *Decisive Battles: Their Influence on History and Civilisation,* of which an American edition was published in 1940. That is to say, so far as condensation allows, it is written as a continuous story, each battle chapter being linked to the next by a synopsis covering the intervening period. The reason for this is that I have never held the opinion that the understanding of battles *per se* is sufficient in the study of war. Instead, as in my opinion war should be looked upon as a whole, just as life is a whole, its activities must be related to the cycles of peacefulness out of which each conflict arises and into which it sinks. In brief, there is a rhythm between peace and war, as well as between the last war and the next war, and unless it is measured there can be no true understanding of either peace or war: both springing as they do from the same source—the life force.

As regards the battle chapters, though in Chapter II I have drawn upon Chapter XIX of my *Decisive Battles,* it has been recast and written more from the American angle than the British; whereas Chapter VIII follows closely Chapter VII and VIII of my *The Generalship of Ulysses S. Grant,* because on rereading them I found that I had little now to add.

Finally, though in a work covering so many important and debatable events, there are bound to be errors both of judgment and fact, I hope that this book will not only appeal to my readers, but will also in some small way lead them to appreciate the wisdom of Washington's words, spoken so long ago.

J. F. C. Fuller.

TABLE OF CONTENTS

LIST OF MAPS AND PLANS

DECISIVE BATTLES

OF THE U.S.A.

☆

1763–1776

THE CAUSES OF THE WAR OF INDEPENDENCE

THE destruction of the power of France in Canada during the Seven Years' War cleared the ground for a straight fight between the colonists and Great Britain, a fact foreseen by the Duke of Bedford as early as May 9, 1761; for on that day he wrote to the Duke of Newcastle, "Indeed, my lord, I don't know whether the neighborhood of the French to our American colonies was not the greatest security for their dependence on the mother country, which I feel will be slighted by them when their apprehension of the French is removed."

Though this was true enough, nevertheless, during the years immediately following the expulsion of the French, the colonists not only made no attempt to protect themselves against the sole remaining menace—the Indian forays—but relied almost entirely on England to do so. As this cost money, and as the national debt had been doubled since 1755, the government in London considered it only right that the colonists should contribute toward the cost of their own security. The means proposed was the tightening up of the Acts of Trade and Navigation, which, so far, had been systematically disregarded.

Historically the Navigation Acts may be traced back to the reign of Richard II (1377–1400), when they were introduced in order to prevent the country being drained of specie. But, so far as the American colonies are concerned, it was not until 1647, when the Rump Parliament in England passed an ordinance authorizing duty-free shipments to Virginia, so long as that colony traded exclusively with England, that trouble arose. This meant free trade within the Empire and protection against the trading activities of all other nations. Then, four years later, in order to strike a blow at Holland, Parliament enacted that all merchandise would in future be carried in English bottoms, which en-

3

abled the Puritan merchants to gain a monopoly of the colonial trade and in consequence stabilize their profits. Next, in 1660–1661 further restrictions were introduced, and, in 1663, an Act for the Encouragement of Trade became law, which, as one writer suggests, might with greater propriety have been called "An Act for the Enrichment of English Merchants."

As it was not possible to police the seas sufficiently, most of these acts, and notably the Molasses Act of 1733, were never fully enforced, and in consequence a premium was put on smuggling. In turn this open violation of the law brought the British government into contempt, which alienated the colonists as much as attempts to enforce it. In short, evading the law became the law of the colonies.

Besides this obvious cause of perpetual friction, there were deeper and more obscure ones.

First, the English of America, unlike the English of England, were intellectually not of the Georgian period; instead they were Stuart Englishmen, who believed that Parliament made laws for England, and that the Crown made laws for the colonies. They "preferred to be ruled by . . . royal prerogative rather than by Parliament, partly because the powers of the Crown were less definite and were more easily resisted than were those of Parliament, but chiefly because they were familiar with those powers and dreaded the new, unknown authority of the English legislature." They looked upon the Crown as the government and on Parliament as but one means by which the king governed.

Secondly, life on the fringe of the New World wilderness had divorced the colonists from Old World restraint, and had roused within them, as Channing says, "a spirit of self-independence, and invited to liberty of utterance and of action." Further still, by 1763 the colonists had become a mixed race recruited from the peoples of many countries— French, German, Swiss, Dutch, Swedes, and Finns who brought over with them a way of life totally unknown in England. Again, the Great Awakening had, after a spell of fervor, closed rather than invigorated the religious period in American history, and had resulted in political discussion replacing theological controversy.

Thirdly, the conceptions of government held in America and England were diametrically opposed: in America the governing instrument was an agricultural democracy, whereas in England it was a commercial oligarchy. In America, democracy sprang directly from Calvinism, and was tempered by the ideas of Locke, Grotius, Pufendorf, Beccaria, Montesquieu, and Burlamaqui; the last-mentioned—a Swiss publicist and author of *Principes du droit naturel* and *Principes du droit politique* —declaring that "Natural society is a state of equality and liberty, a state in which all men enjoy the same prescriptive rights, and an entire independence of any other power than God, for by nature every man is master of himself and equal to his fellows. . ." In England it was otherwise, for as a democratic assembly the House of Commons was a fiction, certainly in so far as the representation of the people was concerned, because only a fraction of the electors was represented in Parliament. For instance, though in 1765 there were 160,000 electors out of a total population of 8,000,000, the majority of the members of Parliament was elected by less than 15,000 voters. "Owing to the prevalence of rotten boroughs, in which there were few or no elections, one hundred and fifty-four individuals, among them the king and members of the House of Peers, named three hundred and seven members of the House of Commons." Thus was the king, by means of the national funds and by gifts of places and pensions, enabled to enforce his personal rule.

It was these three causes, stimulated and irritated by the Trade Acts, which not only precipitated the rebellion, but rendered war inevitable. Two opposing ideas were in conflict, Nevertheless, on both sides the contending parties were small; in America, but a fraction of the people; in England, but a group of oligarchs. The former were contending with the latter and not with the English people, and the latter were contending with the former and not with the colonists in bulk. When war came, the fight was not against England, but against the vested political interests of that country led by the king, who, by becoming a party leader—a Parliamentarian—had in the eyes of the colonists abdicated his throne so far as they were concerned. They did not attack the monarchy, but the king as the leader of a system of government they feared, abhorred, and despised.

To return now to the question of taxation. When, in 1763, Lord Bute, succeeding William Pitt, undertook to direct affairs, his Chancellor of the Exchequer—George Grenville—determined that in future the colonists should shoulder the larger part of the cost of maintaining the garrison in America—some 10,000 officers and men. To accomplish this, he decided to tighten up the customs service and introduce stamp duties which would bring in £100,000 a year. Thereupon, in March, 1764, he introduced into the House of Commons twenty-two resolutions upon which the Stamp Act and Revenue Act of that year were based; acts which greatly increased the price of imported commodities. Not only did the colonists object to these laws in principle, but they also feared that they would drain the colonies of gold and silver. A vigorous agitation followed, to be still further stimulated when that same year the Quartering Act was passed. By it the provinces were required to provide barracks for the troops as well as supply them with salt, vinegar, rum, beer, etc. Royal assent was given to the Stamp Act on March 22, 1765.

Thus the match was set to the train; for the colonists, refusing to obey the law, brought into existence radical associations known as the "Sons of Liberty," and a general agreement was arrived at to refuse all goods "which are, or shall hereafter be taxed by act of parliament for the purpose of raising a revenue in America." The result of this boycott was a vast loss of trade, exports to America falling from £3,000,000 yearly to half that figure. The distress in England became so great that, all over the Kingdom, merchants and tradesmen petitioned Parliament to repeal or modify the Act. This led to the fall of the government in July, 1765, when the Rockingham Ministry came into power and repealed the Stamp Act. But in order to salve the wounded pride of Englishmen, it passed a Declaratory Act, whereby the authority of Parliament over the colonies was upheld without any reservation.

In July, 1766, the Rockingham Ministry was succeeded by yet another under William Pitt—now the Earl of Chatham—who was so crippled by gout that the supreme direction of affairs passed into the hands of his Chancellor of the Exchequer—Charles Townshend. When opening the budget address for 1767, that minister estimated that the cost of the colonial military establishments would be £400,000; further, he decided to extract a proportion of this sum from the colonists by laying new duties on imported goods, such as paper, glass, and tea. By this means he also proposed to maintain a colonial civil list which would be outside the jurisdiction of the Assemblies. This meant that the judges and governors of each province would be freed from colonial control, and that a large number of jobs would be created for a swarm of office-holders. Townshend died in September and a few months later these new duties came into force.

The Customs Commissioners at once set to work stationing revenue cutters at Philadelphia and other American ports. The main result was a stimulation of smuggling.

So great was the discontent in Boston that, in July, 1768, the commissioners requested General Gage to send troops to that city in order to assist the revenue officers in enforcing the law. When he refused to comply with this demand, two regiments were sent out by the home government, whereupon an attempt to enforce the Quartering Act caused further disturbances and a return to the boycott of English goods. At length, on March 5, 1770, came the inevitable clash; in a riot between the troops and the crowd four citizens were shot dead and seven wounded. This affray was at once christened the "Boston Massacre," sensational reports sweeping through the colonies and later on through England as well.

The Duke of Grafton, who had succeeded Lord Chatham in 1768, was followed by Lord North in 1770, who was little more than a stalking-horse for the king. Nevertheless he wisely initiated a policy of conciliation, and removed all the American import duties except that on tea. The retention of this single tax, which brought in only £40,000 a year, was as foolish as it was puerile. It was decided upon by a Cabinet majority of one, and was retained not only as a sop to the East India Company, but also as an assertion of Parliamentary right to tax the colonies, North saying: "To repeal the tea duty would stamp us with timidity."

The next incident was even more serious. On December 16, 1773, a band of some forty to fifty men disguised as Mohawk Indians, under the immediate direction of Samuel Adams, boarded some East India Company ships and threw their cargoes of tea overboard, an incident which has gone down to history as the "Boston Tea Party." This roused Lord North, and on March 7, 1774, he asked Parliament to provide means to put down disorder and secure the "dependence of the colonies upon the Crown and Parliament of Great Britain." A week later he moved that leave be given to bring in a bill for removing the customs house from Boston until £15,000 was paid to the East India Company for the tea which had been destroyed. This bill became known as the Boston Port Act, which, coming into operation on June 1, virtually meant the blockade of that city. The inhabitants of Boston appealed to the other colonies for aid. Simultaneously General Gage was appointed by the king as governor of the province, in spite of the fact that Gage had warned him and North that coercion would mean war, a war which it would require at least 20,000 British troops to wage. He was not listened to, and on taking over his governorship was at once obstructed, the citizens of Boston refusing to build barracks or supply his men with food. Thereupon, in order to secure his position, he started to fortify the narrow neck of land which connected the city, as it then was, to the countryside.

The psychosis created by these events went far to consolidate the rebellion, and led to a decisive step being taken by Samuel Adams, who, adopting the suggestion of the creation of a Continental Congress as expounded by the Sons of Liberty, in the autumn of 1773 launched a campaign in its favor. The upshot was the assembly of the first Continental Congress at Philadelphia on September 5, 1774, where, on October 14, a Bill of Rights was drawn up in which it was declared that the rights of the colonies rested upon the immutable laws of nature. Next, on September 20, an Agreement of Association was passed, by which the colonies bound themselves to boycott English goods and cease trading with England. This agreement should have warned Parliament that the rebellion was no local affair; yet Lord North failed to realize that fact, and, on November 18, he told the king that as "the New England Governments are in a state of rebellion, blows must decide whether they are to be subject to this country or independent."

As winter approached, Gage sent out agents to discover where military stores were being collected and on April 18, 1775, he ordered a detachment under Colonel Smith to proceed to Concord in order to seize and destroy the stores reported to be found there. When Lexington was reached there was a skirmish with the local militia in which eighteen men were killed. The troops then entered Concord and destroyed the stores, while the entire population turned out under arms. Reinforced by Lord Percy and 1,400 men, the British engaged in a running fight until they reached Boston, during which, out of 1,800 men in all, 359 were killed and wounded.

The immediate result of this first action of the War of American Independence was that the whole countryside rushed to arms and blockaded Gage in Boston, a wave of enthusiasm sweeping from the outworks of that beleaguered city to Savannah.

The Second Continental Congress, which assembled at Philadelphia on May 10, was a true revolutionary body. It took over the soldiers blockading Boston and formed them into the "Army of the United Colonies." Further, it appointed Washington commander in chief, not only on account of his reputation as a soldier, but because it was considered his influence would bring Virginia and the Southern Colonies to the aid of New England.

Simultaneously an extraordinary man steps into the arena—Captain Benedict Arnold: one of the greatest leaders of men this war revealed, and also, because of his eventual treason, one of the most despised. Seeing that the works which were being built round Boston lacked cannon, on May 10 with 83 men he took possession of Ticonderoga by a ruse, seizing 120 light and heavy pieces. Next he occupied Crown Point, overpowered the garrison at St. John, and there learning that General Carleton at Montreal had but two British battalions—the 7th and 26th Foot—he determined to reduce the whole of Canada.

While this expedition was being undertaken, Boston was reinforced, and with the troops despatched from England came Generals Sir William Howe, John Burgoyne, and Henry Clinton, all to play leading parts during the war. To secure his position and the harbor, Gage decided to occupy the Charlestown peninsula immediately to the north of Boston, upon which rose two hills—Bunker's and Breed's. But on June 16 he was forestalled by the rebels, whereupon he ordered Howe to storm their entrenchment on Bunker's Hill (actually Breed's) on the following day. The attack was badly conceived though gallantly executed. Two assaults were beaten back by the rebels, the third only succeeding because they ran out of ammunition. The cost of this Pyrrhic victory was devastating, for out of the 2,500 attackers 1,054 officers and men were killed and wounded; nor were the defenders' losses light—441 in killed, wounded, and prisoners.

The influence of this bloody engagement was prodigious. First, it convinced the rebels that a regular military organization was unnecessary, and so added enormously to Washington's difficulties. Secondly, its memory made an indelible impression on General Howe, who, as we shall see, henceforth failed to press his victories. Thirdly, the Battle of Bunker's Hill cleared the air and plainly showed to all who could see, that the rebellious colonists were determined to conquer or perish in the attempt.

Meanwhile, Arnold, with the full support of Washington, was maturing his audacious scheme. On September 5 with 1,050 men he sailed up the Kennebec River, and disembarking at the portage near Mount Bigelow, with 200 boats he plunged into the wilderness of Maine. Meanwhile Montgomery, at the head of 1,200 men, crossed Lake Champlain, captured Chambly, forced the surrender of St. John, and pressing on to Montreal occupied that city on November 12. General Carleton escaped by boat to Quebec.

Simultaneously Arnold pressed on, but most unfortunately for him a letter he sent by an Indian to General Schuyler was taken direct to Carleton, who, learning of the danger that threatened Quebec, at once collected every armed man he could.

Reaching the St. Lawrence, Arnold crossed the river in such boats as he could find, and landing at Wolfe's Cove he assembled his half-naked band—now reduced to 650 men—on the Heights of Abraham. When Carleton refused to surrender, Arnold, who was in no condition to assault the fortress, retired to Point aux Trembles to await Montgomery. When at length that officer arrived with 300 men, they advanced on Quebec, and, on December 31, in a driving snowstorm attempted to take the city by assault.

The attack that followed was a complete failure: Montgomery was killed, Arnold was severely wounded in the leg, and 500 men were lost, of whom 426 were captured. In April, Arnold was reinforced, but in the following month General Thomas, who had replaced him, was compelled to retire to Richelieu. There he died of smallpox and was succeeded by General Sullivan, who, on being badly defeated by Burgoyne at Three Rivers, retired to Crown Point. So ended one of the most audacious operations of war recorded in history: an operation which, though wildcat in character, might well have proved successful had the letter to Schuyler remained unwritten. "Had it succeeded," writes General Francis Vinton Greene, "it would probably have united Canada to the Thirteen Colonies, and changed the whole course and outcome of the war."

The fall of Ticonderoga led to the replacement of General Gage by Sir William Howe; and the Battle of Bunker's Hill spurred the English government to ransack Europe for mercenaries. A plan of campaign had to be decided upon, and Gage was of opinion that, were the line of the Hudson occupied, the rebellion would collapse. In England, the leading military authority, General Harvey, the adjutant general, thought otherwise. His opinion was that land operations would prove futile, and that instead the American coast should be blockaded until the rebels gave in. He also said: "Unless a settled plan of operations be agreed upon for next spring, our army will be destroyed by damned driblets . . . America is an ugly job . . . a damned affair indeed." Nevertheless the governors of the various provinces reported that, as large numbers of people were still loyal, a show of arms was all that was required.

Unfortunately for England, this view was accepted by Lord George

Germaine, who, in November, had been appointed secretary-at-war. He had disgraced himself at the Battle of Minden in 1759, and was held in high contempt by the army. This, together with the contempt which he had for the rebels, placed Howe in a difficult situation. Yet Howe's opponent—General Washington—was confronted by even greater difficulties. His men were enrolled only until January 1, 1776, and his ammunition was so scarce that he had but three rounds per musket.

"Nevertheless," writes Fortescue—the historian of the British Army, "by hook or by crook the indomitable Washington succeeded (to use his own words) in disbanding one army and raising another within distance of a reinforced enemy; so that by February, 1776, he was once more in command of nearly eighteen thousand men, with the cannon captured at Ticonderoga and a sufficiency of ammunition, ready to drive the British from Boston."

Meanwhile Howe remained inactive, and when, on March 2, Washington suddenly occupied Dorchester Heights to the south of Boston, Howe's position became untenable. Compelled to evacuate the city on the 17th, he carried his army—9,000 strong—to Halifax, where he arrived on April 2.

In May, the third Congress met again in Philadelphia to discuss the "Declaration of Independence" drafted by Thomas Jefferson, whose political theories were derived largely from John Locke. This Declaration was adopted on July 2 and proclaimed on the 4th of that month. In it may be read:

We hold these truths to be self-evident, that all men are created equal, that they are endowed by their Creator with certain inalienable rights; that among these are life, liberty and the pursuit of happiness; that to secure these rights, governments are instituted among men, deriving their just powers from the consent of the governed; that whenever any form of government becomes destructive to these ends, it is the right of the people to alter or abolish it, and to institute new government, laying its foundations on such principles, and organizing its powers in such form as to them shall seem most likely to effect their safety and happiness.

Thus did the Great Revolution spring to life, and thus did the rebellious colonists become Americans.

CHAPTER I

THE SURPRISE AT TRENTON AND THE
BATTLE OF PRINCETON, 1776–1777

THE Battle of Bunker's Hill and Arnold's invasion of Canada, by giving the rebellion the status of war, brought the British government face to face with the problem of conquest. How should it be undertaken? The correct answer to this question depended upon whether strategical conditions were read aright.

The first consideration was the theater of war; it was immense, stretching from the St. Lawrence to the St. Mary's river, which bounds the eastern end of the northern frontier of Florida. And though this long stretch of country was of no great width, it was not only generally roadless and undeveloped, but quite beyond the power of the British Army to occupy and hold in its entirety. Further, its size was indirectly multiplied by the length of the British communications across the Atlantic, over which the bulk of the military supplies came from England and the West Indies. Therefore from the first it should have been obvious—as we have seen it was to General Harvey—that success demanded oceanic and not continental strategy; in other words, blockade and not conquest and occupation, if only because: (1) all the American centers of population bordered the seacoast, and (2) the rebellious states were as much a sea power as Great Britain, depending on their export trade to provide their people with practically all their luxuries and not a few of their necessities of life. It was for this reason that Harvey, when he heard that conquest was decided upon, exclaimed "As wild an idea as ever controverted common sense." [1] Nevertheless, strategy was misread, not only what may be called the strategy of geography, but above all the strategy of politics, which split the theater of war into three well-defined sections—namely: (1) New England; (2) New York City, New Jersey, Delaware, and Pennsylvania; and (3) Maryland, Virginia, the Carolinas, Georgia, and Florida.

As the first section was violently anti-British, the second moderately so and the third semiloyal, three courses of action offered themselves—namely: (1) to subdue the first, whereupon the second and third were likely to collapse; (2) to subdue the second, in which case, though the third might collapse, the first would continue to hold out; and (3) to subdue the third, with the chance that the first and second sections would continue the struggle. Therefore to subdue and hold New England—and the British Army was powerful enough to do this—was the only practical course to take. Another point in its favor was the fact that the Hudson River provided the main thoroughfare for an invading force based on one of the two key positions—Quebec and New York. As I will show in my next chapter, this strategy was attempted and bungled; nevertheless, as General Greene writes: "The Hudson played (or should have) the same part in the Revolution as the Mississippi in the Civil War"; because "If the British could take and hold this line it would cut off New England from the other colonies." [2]

Simultaneously to attempt more than one of these courses meant disaster, not only because the British Army could not possibly hold all three sections, but because the tactical conditions of all three favored the defensive. This is admirably explained in *The Annual Register* as follows:

Among the principal of these [difficulties] may be considered the vast extent of that continent, with its unusual distribution into great tracts of cultivated and savage territory; the long extent of sea coast in front, and the boundless wastes at the back of the inhabited countries, affording resource or shelter in all circumstances; the numberless inaccessible ports, and strong natural barriers, formed by the various combinations of woods, mountains, rivers, lakes and marshes. All these properties and circumstances, with others appertaining to the climates and seasons, may be said to fight the battles of the inhabitants of such countries in a defensive war . . . To these may be added, the people's not being bridled by strong cities, nor fettered by luxury to those which were otherwise, so that the reduction of a capital had no effect upon the rest of the province, and the army could retain no more territory than what it occupied, which was again lost as soon as it departed to another quarter.[3]

From this strategical base two very different armies operated, in most ways so different that in order to understand the tactics of this war it is necessary to examine and compare them.

The British Army, like the American, was a heterogeneous assembly of soldiers, royal instead of democratic, comprising Englishmen, Irish, Scots, and Germans hailing from Hesse-Cassel, Anspach, Brunswick, and other petty states; the American adding to its Anglo-Saxon stock Negroes,[4] French, Poles, Germans, Jews, and Dutchmen. Whereas the British Army came under Parliament, which knew nothing about war, the American Army came under Congress, which knew too much about politics. Instead of taxing the people and enlisting an army of regular soldiers, Congress largely depended upon patriotism and enthusiasm to act as recruiting sergeants, and, when they failed, upon Sergeant Major "Bounty."

In the army, the men were enlisted for twelve months and then were disbanded, whereas the militia, up to the end of 1776, appointed its officers by ballot, and they in turn would frequently pool their pay with that of their soldiers and rely on parish-pump committees for command. "Can it then be wondered at," writes General Reed on July 4, 1776, "that a captain should be tried and broken for stealing his soldiers blankets? or that another officer should be found shaving his men in the face of characters of distinction?"[5] A man of one state would not serve under an officer of another state, neither would any state really serve Congress, for state rights and individual rights were sacrosanct. Well may Washington with asperity have exclaimed that his men regarded their officers "no more than broomsticks."

The bounty system led to endless discontent and lack of discipline. Frequently these enticements were not paid or the men were swindled out of them. Elijah Fisher, who experienced this, informs us: "They will promise them that they will give them so and so, and after they have got them to enlist they are Cheated out of one-half they ought to have by one or other of the offisers."[6] Again, this system encouraged desertion, "bounty-jumping" becoming quite a lucrative profession, though at times a dangerous one. On August 17, 1778, Fisher jots down in his *Journal:* "There was a man shot Near Head Quarters for Enlisting seven times and taken bountys," and again the next year on July 26: "There was two men shott for Enlisting severill times and for Deserting . . . "[7] Of the militia Washington writes: "They come in you cannot tell how; go out you cannot see when; act you cannot tell where; consume your provisions; exhaust your stores; and leave you at last in a critical moment." [8] Yet there was a saving clause: though they seldom were in being for long, they could generally be rapidly mobilized for brief periods and in defensive actions were often formidable fighters.

As may be supposed, discipline in the American Army was lacking, though individually the men were brave soldiers. The punishments meted out to defaulters were quite as barbarous as in the British Army. Though the ragamuffins of Boston had shouted "bloody-backs" at the English redcoats, this did not prevent Washington on several occasions ordering up to five hundred lashes. Also the camp gallows was a standing article of furniture as were the wooden horse and the strappado.[9]

Administration kept close heel to discipline, or, in other words, it was generally nonexistent. For instance, the scale of diet laid down by Congress was generous, consisting as it did of a pound of bread, a pound and a quarter of beef, a pint of milk, a quart of beer, a gill of peas or beans, and weekly six ounces of butter and half a pint of vinegar. But unfortunately for the soldier the schedule ended with the words: "if the goods may be had," and they seldom could be without means to pay for them. Lack as well as depreciation of money were the standing bugbears of the army.

Again, should a man be wounded or fall sick, the chances were that he would be killed by the surgeon or physician. In December, 1776, Wayne, writing to Gates, says: "Our hospital, or rather House of Carnage, beggars all description and shocks humanity to visit." [10]

The bulk of this free, easy, pugnacious, and at times panicky army was the infantry arm, clad in a variety of uniforms and frequently in rags. At the battle of Eutaw Springs, in 1781, we are told that many of the men had as clothing only their belts and clumps of moss. Washington himself preferred Indian dress to regimental uniform, and undoubtedly he was right, for not only was it practical, but most becoming, consisting of fringed deerskin embroidered with scarlet needlework.

Of artillery there was little, the bulk consisting of captured cannon; and the cavalry arm was negligible. The universal weapon was the firelock of the British brown Bess pattern, which weighed about fourteen pounds; rifles were few but though slow to load most deadly in skilled hands; the men frequently made their own powder and nearly always molded their own bullets. In brief, their tactics were to kill without being killed, and though they were often unstable fighters in a field attack, behind walls, fences, and entrenchments they could seldom be dislodged except at high cost.

Let us turn to their opponents. In 1776 the British and German forces in America numbered approximately 36,000 all told, the former being enlisted and the latter bought.[11] These figures, however, do not include regiments of American Loyalists (Tories)[12] and bands of Indians.[13] I say "enlisted," but in fact the British soldiers were conscripted by press gangs or by kidnaping.[14] When these means failed the jails were opened; but as in 1776 there were nearly two hundred offenses incurring the death penalty,[15] it frequently happened that these "criminals" were men of initiative and character, not a few being poachers and excellent shots.[16]

Though some of the officers were able soldiers many were utterly worthless, having been commissioned from the riffraff of the aristocracy instead from the offscourings of the proletariat. In these days commissions were not infrequently given to infants in arms, whose half-pay was pocketed by their parents,[17] as the following well-known jest makes clear: "Which of the children is crying?" asked an anxious mother of her Irish maid. "Faix, ma'am, it's the major tumbled out of his cradle," she replied.

Whereas the American Army was frequently underdressed, the reverse was the case with the British, which, copying the Germans, was garbed as for a masquerade and laced up with crossbelts and other trappings. A leather stock forced the soldier to keep his head up, curl papers were provided for his hair, his legs were squeezed by long gaiters, and his feet cramped by overtight shoes. Though heelball and pipe clay kept him well occupied, seldom did he fire a shot in training; his musketry exercises consisted in learning how to load and which eye to shut when aiming.

Again, administration was utterly defective. If the regimental colonel happened to be honest, interior economy went up in quality as his command went down in numbers. Or to put it more clearly, as he drew pay for a stated number of men—about five hundred—at the rate of £9 for each N.C.O. and £3[18] for each private a year, should this number fall, let us suppose, to four hundred, he found himself with some £400 in hand to spend on the remainder or else to put into his pocket. Also, as may be expected, the medical services were of the crudest. A surgeon was qualified as such so long as he had learned to bleed a patient, give a clyster, prepare a potion and spread a plaster. For these acquirements he received four shillings a day, out of which he had to pay for his drugs, bandages, lint, plasters, splints, and his tools—the most important of which was a butcher's handsaw.[19]

Such were the armies which faced each other, when, early in June, Howe set out from Halifax at the head of 32,000 men, carried in more than 400 transports and escorted by thirty warships commanding 1,200 guns—the largest expedition ever sent abroad by England up to that time—to cast anchor off Sandy Hook at the mouth of the Hudson. Disembarking on July 3 on Staten Island, he pitched his camp, while Washington, with 20,000 men fit for duty, watched him from Long and Manhattan Islands.[20]

I will now turn briefly to the campaign that followed, because without an outline of it it is not possible to plumb the darkness of the background which before the year closed was to throw into brilliant relief Washington's remarkable counterattack.

On August 22, Howe landed with 20,000 men and 40 cannon at Gravesend Bay, Long Island. Five days later he launched a frontal attack, followed by a most skillful maneuver by which he turned Washington's left flank and came down upon his rear. Had he ordered an assault then, it is difficult to see how his enemy could have escaped.[21] This, however, he did not do, because, as he says, it might have cost him from a thousand to fifteen hundred men.[22] As a result, although at a cost of 377 officers and men, killed, wounded, and missing he killed and wounded about 1,000 of his enemy and took 1,097 prisoners and 32 cannon, Washington skillfully slipped away during the night of August 29, and aided by a dense fog[23] withdrew his demoralized men to Manhattan Island. Next, he decided to abandon New York,[24] while Howe sat down for a fortnight to enjoy his victory.

At length Howe bestirred himself and, under cover of a naval bombardment, on September 15, he landed his army on Manhattan Island at Kip's Bay. This undertaking proved too much for the nerves of his enemy, who took panic, and though Washington galloped amongst his men firing his pistols, he could not stay their flight.[25] By nightfall the remnants of his broken army were gathered together north and west of Harlem, having lost 17 officers and 350 men, killed, wounded, and missing. Rightly Washington stigmatized their conduct as "disgraceful and dastardly."[26]

Once again, had Howe only pushed on, his enemy must have been completely routed. Instead, he accepted an invitation from a Tory lady —a Mrs. Murray—to lunch, and after a skirmish on the 16th he spent the following four weeks in throwing up entrenchments to cover New York from the north.[27] Six days later—that is on the 22d—a third of

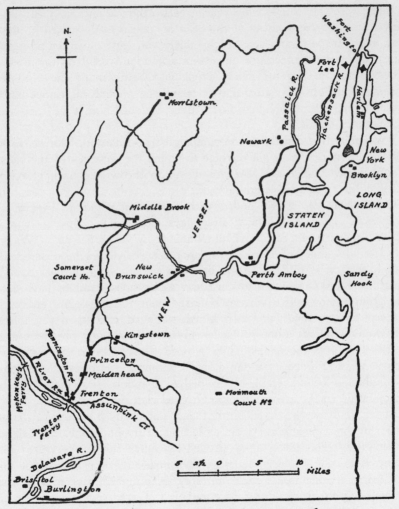

1. Campaign of Trenton and Princeton, 1776–1777

New York was destroyed by fire, started, either accidentally or more probably intentionally, by the Americans.[28]

The next move did not take place until October 12, when Howe, leaving a detachment to observe the Harlem position, embarked the rest of his army and landed at Pell's Point on the mainland, for his intention was to outflank Washington. Advancing slowly, on the 25th he encamped in the Bronx, four miles from White Plains, to where Washington moved to block his way. There, on the 28th, an abortive frontal attack was launched on the American lines, in which the British lost 214 men killed and wounded. Next, two days later, when Washington fell back, Howe, instead of following him up, withdrew to Dobb's Ferry on the Hudson. This time his reason was, as he says, "Political . . . and no other." [29]

Whatever this may mean, strategically Howe had a very good reason for not pursuing, because his enemy's withdrawal in a northerly direction had uncovered Fort Washington, which lay some ten miles south of Dobb's Ferry, and should it still be held its garrison lay at his mercy. Though Washington did not want to hold it, Congress did,[30] and so did General Nathanael Greene and most of Washington's senior officers,[31] because it and Fort Lee commanded the left and right banks of the Hudson, and also because its evacuation would still further demoralize the army. Washington should have said "no!" However he did not; therefore Greene, who lay close to Fort Lee, continued to hold it, and though Washington joined him on November 14 he left things as they were.

Howe was too good a soldier to miss such an opportunity. On the 15th he summoned the fortress to surrender, and, this demand being refused, he carried it by storm the following day under cover of a naval bombardment, the Hessians greatly distinguishing themselves. Though he lost 458 officers and men in killed and wounded, the cost was cheap, for he took 2,818 prisoners, 146 pieces of artillery, 1,200 shot, 2,800 muskets, and 400,000 musket cartridges as well as other stores.[32] For once, losing no time, Howe ordered Lord Cornwallis to land eight miles above Fort Lee on the Jersey shore; whereupon Greene withdrew its garrison and the fort was occupied by Cornwallis.

For the British this was the first important victory since the war opened. For Washington it was a terrible disaster, as may be gathered from the following extracts taken from a letter he wrote on the 19th to his brother, John Augustine:

"This is a most unfortunate affair, and has given me great mortification; as we have lost not only two thousand men that were there, but a good deal of artillery, and some of the best arms we had. And what adds to my mortification is, that this post, after the last ships went past it, was held contrary to my wishes and opinion . . . I did not care to give an absolute order for withdrawing the garrison, till I could get round and see the situation of things, and then it became too late, as the fort was invested. . . ."

"I am wearied almost to death with the retrograde motion of things, and I solemnly protest that a pecuniary reward of twenty thousand pounds a year would not induce me to undergo what I do . . ." [33]

When Cornwallis crossed the Hudson, but one course was open to Washington—to retire. Falling back on the Raritan, where he destroyed the bridges, he then withdrew behind the Delaware, after having taken the precaution to remove all boats on that river for seventy miles above Philadelphia.[34] There he halted to find that his army had melted away to a residue of 3,153 officers and men,[35] whose enlistment was due to expire by the end of the year. His situation was indeed desperate, as may be gathered from his correspondence. On the 10th to Mr. Lund he wrote: "I tremble for Philadelphia," and two days later again to Congress: "The inhabitants of this State [New Jersey], either from fear or disaffection, almost to a man refused to turn out," [36] while to his rear the Quakers in Philadelphia were rejoicing at his discomfort.[37]

As Washington fell back, Cornwallis pushed on to New Bridge, Newark, Elizabeth Town, and Brunswick, where he arrived on December 1. There, as Howe wrote to Germaine on the 20th, "the enemy went off most precipitately to *Princeton,* and had they not prevented the passage of the Raritan, by breaking a part of *Brunswick* bridge, so great was the confusion among them, that their Army must inevitably have been cut to pieces." [38] Yet, instead of obtaining material from the houses to mend the bridge—he had no pontoon train [39]—he halted his advance, an action which Stedman considers, "saved the panic-struck and fleeing army of the Americans from utter ruin." [40] Here, on the 6th, he caught up with Cornwallis, and the advance was continued, a halt of seventeen hours being made at Princeton on the 7th. Then he "marched at nine o'clock in the morning of the eighth, and arrived at Trenton at four o'clock in the afternoon; just when the last boat of General Washington's embarkation crossed the river, as if he had calculated, it was observed, with great accuracy, the exact time necessary for his enemy to make his escape." [41] No boats being available on the Delaware, the pursuit was abandoned and by what seemed a miracle Washington's doomed army was saved.[42]

What induced Howe to miss such an obvious and supreme opportunity? This was no case of a Bunker's Hill assault, so that excuse may be set aside. The reason appears to be that he had received instructions not to bring the war to a close by military means if peaceful ones could possibly be substituted for them.[43] Also in November he had asked for 15,000 reinforcements, and imagining that he would receive them, it seems to me that, being an indolent and pleasure-loving man, he considered the next campaign such a certainty that it was not worth his while prolonging the present one into the winter.[44] Anyhow he decided, as some say, to halt until the Delaware was frozen, when it could be crossed without bridging. Therefore he issued orders for his army to go into winter quarters, and granting Cornwallis leave to return to England for the winter—which does not look as if he intended anything serious until the spring—he hied back to his mistress in New York.

General Grant, who was selected on account of his gallant behavior at the storming of Fort Washington, was left in command of some 12,000 men. Before his departure Howe had instructed him to quarter six brigades—fifteen regiments—in Princeton and Brunswick and post six regiments of Hessians, under von Donop, along the Delaware from Bordentown (Burdenton) to Burlington, with Rall's brigade—between 1,300 and 1,500 strong—at Trenton.[45] The line of posts, which in its entirety stretched from the Delaware to the Hackensack River—that is 80 miles—was overextended, a fact which von Donop, a good soldier, pointed out to Howe, and which he, a good tactician, fully realized;[46] yet he held to it in order to cover the Loyalists who were now flocking into his camps.[47]

The weakest point in this distribution was the village of Trenton, not only because it was half a day's march from the neighboring posts of Bordentown and Princeton, but because it lay at an angle to them—that is, in a salient. Worse still, Rall, though brave, was a parade soldier and intensely stupid.[48] Though directed by von Donop to entrench the village, fortify the ferry, and erect redoubts to cover the roads, he willfully disregarded these instructions and instead harassed his men with parades and band-playings. Again and again his officers approached him with requests to place his post in a state of defense: "Let them come," said Rall. "We want no trenches. We will go at them with the bayonet." "Colonel," answered von Donop, "an entrenchment costs nothing. If it does not help, it can do no harm."[49]

To render conditions still more difficult, the Hessians who came from petty autocratic states in which the rights of the common people were not respected during wartime, proceeded to plunder the surrounding country so effectively that in a few days most of the Loyalists regretted their loyalty. Washington's troops had behaved badly enough. According to one writer "The infamous and cruel ravages which have been made on the wretched distressed inhabitants of this unfortunate island [New York] by many of our soldiers must disgrace and expose our army to detestation";[50] now the Hessians stepped into their shoes, and not only reduced hundreds of families to ruin, but encumbered themselves with loot. A journalist writes: "The Hessians plunder all indiscriminately, Tories as well as Whigs; if they see any thing they want they seize it, and say, 'Rebel good for Hesse man.' "[51] Though Howe rebuts these charges,[52] stating that they were grossly exaggerated, this very exaggeration and the excuses for it went far to consolidate his enemy and render the name of "Hessian" an anathema throughout the land.[53]

Meanwhile Washington's situation was daily growing worse, a fact which may be gleaned from his correspondence. On the 14th he wrote to General Charles Lee, giving him the British distribution and mentioning that Congress had "adjourned from Philadelphia to meet at Baltimore,"[54] and then the next day he heard that Charles Lee had been captured. In the letter notifying the Council of Safety of Pennsylvania of this, he writes: "Instead of giving any assistance in repelling the enemy, the militia have not only refused to obey your general summons . . . but, I am told, exult at the approach of the enemy, and on our late misfortunes."[55] On the 16th he informs Congress that many of his men are "entirely naked and most so thinly clad as to be unfit for service,"[56] and on the 17th: "The unhappy policy of short enlistments and a dependence upon militia will, I fear, prove the downfall of our cause, though early pointed out with an almost prophetic spirit . . . In short, your imagination can scarce extend to a situation more distressing than mine. Our only dependence now is upon the speedy enlistment of a new army. If this fails, I think the game will be pretty well up. . . ."[57] Then, again on the 20th: "But I rather think the design of General Howe is to possess himself of Philadelphia this winter, if possible, and in truth I do not see what is to prevent him, as ten days more will put an end to the existence of our army."[58]

That day Generals Sullivan and Gates joined him at his camp above Trenton Falls, bringing with them their small demoralized forces. Well might a Tory journalist write: "The Rebels are mouldering away like a rope of sand. With the most impotent bravadoes they have not had the spirit to make anything like a stand in a single encounter . . . Mr. *Washington,* with about two thousand poor wretches who can get no subsistence except by following him, has fled to *Lancaster,* in Pennsylvania." [59]

Though the American Army was miserable, Washington's intelligence service was admirable. On the 14th he had written to four of his major generals entreating them "to find out some person, who can be engaged to cross the river as a spy, that we may, if possible, obtain some knowledge of the enemy's situation, movements, and intention." [60]

The man selected was one John Honeyman, a butcher and cattle dealer by profession, who had served in Wolfe's bodyguard at Quebec. Disguised, he entered Trenton, purchasing slaughter cattle for the Hessians, and then allowing himself to be captured by some American scouts, he was taken to Washington's headquarters at Newton, where he informed the commander in chief of Colonel Rall's situation. [61]

Honeyman's tidings convinced Washington that he could now carry out what had been in his mind ever since the 14th, when he had written to General Charles Lee suggesting the possibility of "a stroke upon the forces of the enemy, who lay a good deal scattered, and to all appearance, in a state of security. A lucky blow in this quarter would be fatal to them, and would most certainly raise the spirit of the people, which are quite sunk by our late misfortunes." [62]

Then, on the 21st, General Dickinson sent in information regarding the Hessians, [63] and on the following day Colonel Joseph Reed at Bristol wrote:

We are all of opinion, my dear General, that something must be attempted to revive our expiring credit, give our cause some degree of reputation, and prevent a total depreciation of the Continental money . . . In short, some enterprise must be undertaken in our present circumstances, or we must give up the cause . . . Will it not be possible, my dear General, for your troops . . . to make a diversion, or something more, at or about *Trenton?* The greater the alarm the more likely success will attend the attacks. If we could possess ourselves again of *New-Jersey,* or any considerable part of it, the effect would be greater than if we had never left it . . . I will not disguise my own sentiments, that our cause is desperate and hopeless, if we do not take the opportunity of the collection of troops at present to strike some stroke. Our affairs are hasting fast to ruin, if we do not retrieve them by some happy event. Delay with us is now equal to defeat. [64]

This courageous letter and the fact that the Delaware would be frozen over after the middle of January convinced Washington that the moment to strike had come, and so, on the 23rd, he wrote to Reed (the adjutant general) and to Colonel John Cadwalader at Bristol: "The bearer is sent down . . . to inform you, that Christmas day at night, one hour before day, is the time fixed upon for our attempt on *Trenton*. For Heaven's sake keep this to yourself, as the discovery of it may prove fatal to us; our numbers, sorry I am to say, being less than I had any conception of; but necessity, dire necessity, will, nay must, justify my attack." Then he informed him that all ferries and fords would be picketed.[65]

On the 22d Washington had at his immediate disposal 10,106 rank and file, of whom no less than 5,399 were sick, which left him with an effective force of 4,707 men, representing thirty small Continental regiments. These he organized into eight brigades and two divisions, one under Sullivan and the other under Greene. To these troops must be added some 3,000 men brought in by Sullivan, four regiments sent south from the Northern Army (1,200) and the Pennsylvanian Militia under Cadwalader (1,800),[66] which goes to show how rapidly an army of considerable size, though of doubtful efficiency, could be assembled by the Americans in this war.

Though his men were clad like scarecrows, in three respects Washington's army was superior to his enemy's. First, his artillery, under Colonel Henry Knox, was thoroughly efficient. Secondly, he possessed a rudimentary pontoon train, whereas his adversary had none. Thirdly, he had under his command a number of exceptionally able officers, such as Greene, Sullivan, Knox, and Alexander Hamilton, Lord Stirling, John Stark, Haslet, and James Monroe.

On Christmas Eve a conference of the principal officers was assembled in General Greene's lodgings, and the plan of attack was finally decided upon. It may be summarized as follows:

(1) Colonel Cadwalader and some 2,000 men, mostly militia, were to cross the Delaware near Bristol and by beating up von Donop's cantonments at Bordentown, keep him engaged.

(2) General Ewing and 1,000 militia men were to cross at Trenton Ferry and by occupying the southern bank of the Assunpink Creek, cut off the line of retreat of Rall's men should they break away to the south.

(3) Meanwhile Washington and 2,400 Continental veterans under Greene and Sullivan, accompanied by ten cannon, were to cross the

Delaware at McKonkey's Ferry (now Taylorsville) nine miles above
Trenton. Sullivan's division was to take the Lower or River Road and
Greene's the Upper or Pennington Road, so that both might rapidly
converge on Trenton.

Each column was to be provided with a reliable guide; all watches
were to be synchronized with Washington's; a piece of white paper was

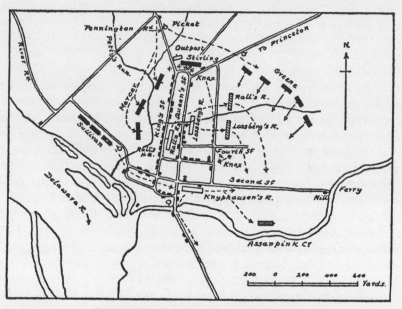

2. Battle of Trenton, December 26, 1776

to be worn in every man's hat; three days cooked rations were to be
carried and each man provided with a new flint and forty rounds of
ammunition. The countersign was "Victory or Death."

At two o'clock on Christmas afternoon Washington's column set out
from its quarters and by sunset reached the Delaware. The night was
pitch dark, for though it was the time of the full moon, the weather was
frightful, a blizzard of rain and snow beating down on the half-frozen
men. At McKonkey's Ferry the river was found to be full of block ice
driven up into heaps by the inflowing tide. Nevertheless the troops set
to work and began to cross. Meanwhile Ewing found it quite impossible
to cross at Trenton Ferry, and at Dunn's Ferry Cadwalader was so
long delayed that he was too late to be of any use.[67]

These failures were reported to Washington as his men were cross-ing. Nevertheless he determined to push on in spite of the fact that, although he had hoped to be on the left bank by midnight, the terrific weather and the ice prevented him from completing this movement until 4 A.M. on the 26th, when he still had nine miles to march to Trenton. Of this delay he writes:

"This made me despair of surprising the town, as I knew well we could not reach it before the day was fairly broke. But as I was certain there was no making a retreat without being discovered and harassed on repassing the river, I determined to push on at all events." [68]

What, meanwhile, of their enemy?

Confident of himself and contemptuous of Washington's rabble, Rall had not troubled to send out spies, although two deserters from the Continental Army, as well as a Tory farmer, had informed him that an attack was probable. Then, a little before midnight on Christmas Eve, Grant sent word to von Donop that "Washington has been in-formed that our troops have marched into winter quarters and that we are weak at Trenton and Princeton . . . so that I need not advise you to be upon your guard against an unexpected attack at Trenton." [69] This information was passed on to Rall, but he took no notice of it. He sat up late that night over a game of cards, drank heavily, and as his enemy was approaching he retired to rest.

His outposts had been posted as follows: (1) Covering the ferry on the north bank of the Delaware one officer and thirty men; (2) on the River Road half a mile from the village, one officer and fifty Jägers; (3) on the Pennington Road, a company of Lossberg's regiment a quarter of a mile from Trenton, with twenty-four men under Lieutenant Wiederhold a quarter of a mile in advance of it, and (4) two officers and seventy-five men a quarter of a mile up the Princeton highroad.

At eight o'clock on the morning of the 26th, as Wiederhold stepped out of his quarters he saw 200 men emerging from a wood to the west of him; they were Greene's advanced scouts. A minute or two later, they opened fire on the Hessian picket, and three minutes later still Sullivan's scouts appeared on the River Road.[70] Then Greene extended his two leading brigades and, driving the Hessian pickets in, formed a continuous front extending from the junction of the Pennington and Princeton Roads to a little west of the Mill on the Assunpink Creek. His third brigade, under Mercer, extended immediately west of the village, its right linked to Sullivan's left, and its left covered by Stirling.

Thus, by the time Rall, awakened by the firing, had flung on his uniform, Trenton had been enveloped on its northern and western sides and Sullivan was pushing along its southern side to cut off his enemy's retreat to the ferry.

Rushing out of his quarters, Rall ordered his own regiment to fall in along King's Street and Lossberg's to clear the north end of Queen's Street; Knyphausen's, under Colonel Dechow, he turned in the opposite direction in order to drive Sullivan's advancing men into the river. Though these orders were logical, the proximity of the enemy reduced them to a series of muddled movements. Knox, bringing up his leading battery, opened fire, throwing Rall's men into confusion, which became worse confounded when the American sharpshooters, under cover of the cannon smoke, rushed the houses—where they could keep the pans of their muskets dry—to open fire on the disorganized mass. As the fighting caught hold, Stirling doubled his men down King's and Queen's Streets, capturing the Knyphausen battery, which had come into action immediately north of the Queen's Street and Fourth Street junction. This assault threw Rall's regiment back upon the left of Lossberg's, whereupon Knyphausen's broke away in rout before Sullivan's advance led by John Stark. The men streamed toward the ferry, where some hundreds accompanied by Rall's small detachment of cavalry effected their escape to Bordentown. Thus closed the first phase of this small battle, as the shot fell and clouds of smoke rolled over the village amidst the roar of cannon and musketry, the shouting of orders, the cheering of men, and, as one participant relates, "a good deal of swearing in two languages."

In spite of the overwhelming surprise, Rall, a staunch fighter, did not lose his presence of mind. Seeing the impossibility of maintaining his position in the streets, he withdrew the Rall and Lossberg regiments into the fields east of the houses, and there facing them about ordered a bayonet assault on the enemy.

Gallantly accepting the deadly risk, the von Lossbergers moved forward, but Rall's own regiment refused to face the fire. As he was urging it on, he was struck by two bullets and rolled from his horse mortally wounded. Then the two regiments broke back toward Second Street, where huddled together, unable to use their muskets on account of the sleet and the rain, and deprived of their artillery, which alone could have supported them in such weather, they ceased to be fighting men.

The end now came quickly. Knox, hurrying forward his cannon from the Princeton-Pennington Road junction, brought them into action immediately south of Fourth Street, from where he opened fire on the Hessians. This action ended the fight. The Hessians lowered their standards and grounded their muskets; whereat the Continentals tossed their hats into the air and a great shout resounded over the battlefield.

According to Bancroft, the action lasted for no more than thirty-five minutes.[71] In killed and wounded the losses were insignificant, the Americans having two officers and one or two privates wounded, and the Hessians some twenty to thirty killed and wounded as well as 23 officers and 886 men made prisoners.[72]

Wisely Washington did not press a pursuit; his men were worn out and in no condition for such an operation; besides he had no reserves at hand, and with his back to the river his position was a dangerous one. Therefore, as soon as he had collected his prisoners, he set out on his return,[73] to learn that Congress, ignorant of his victory, had, on the 27th, vested him with powers which virtually raised him to the position of dictator for a period of six months.[74]

I doubt whether throughout the history of war any general in chief in the middle of a decisive operation has been placed in so anxious and difficult a situation as Washington now was. Seventy-two hours stood between him and utter ruin, for in three days' time the enlistment period of his army would expire. In a fortnight to three weeks the Delaware would be frozen over and already Howe's army was on the move. As time did not permit the recruiting of a new army, salvation rested in raising sufficient money, so that by means of a bounty men might be persuaded to remain with the colors. Therefore on the last day of the year we find Washington writing as follows to Robert Morris, delegate in Congress for Pennsylvania:

I wish to push our success to keep up the panick and in order to get their [his men's] assistance, have promised them a bounty of ten dollars, if they will continue for one month. But here again a new difficulty presents itself: We have not money to pay the bounty, and we have exhausted our credit by such frequent promises that it has not the weight we could wish. If it is possible, sir, to give us assistance, do it. Borrow money where it can be done. We are doing it upon our private credit . . . No time, my dear sir, is to be lost.[75]

On New Year's morning Mr. Morris roused the Philadelphians from their beds, and borrowing $50,000 from them, sent it by express to

Washington, who thus was able to persuade half his men to extend their service for six weeks. The van of his army having recrossed the Delaware on the 30th, he reoccupied Trenton, and gathered in his militia levies, none of which had been embodied for more than a fortnight. Thus, within three days, he collected around him 5,000 men supported by 40 cannon.

In the meanwhile Howe was rousing himself from his lethargy. Cornwallis—who had not yet sailed for England—was hurried south with a picked force to gather in the garrisons stationed along his line of march. By nightfall on January 1, he had arrived at Princeton at the head of 8,000 men and a formidable train of cannon. On the 2d, he hurried forward to Trenton, leaving behind him a strong detachment which was under orders to catch up with him on the 3d.

Fortunately for Washington, on the 30th he had ordered Reed to reconnoiter the British posts as far as Princeton. In the course of his reconnaissance, Reed had captured a dispatch revealing the movements of Cornwallis. Thereupon Washington, leaving strong guards to hold the fords over Shabbacunk (or Shabbakong) Creek, withdrew from Trenton and posted his army along the southern bank of the Assunpink Creek. The guards accomplished their task so well that, though Cornwallis reached the Shabbacunk at noon, he was delayed there for two hours and yet again at Trenton; it was not until late in the afternoon that he was able to open his cannonade on Washington's main position. When twilight set in he broke off the engagement, determined to renew the conflict in the morning. Of this cannonade Washington writes: "We were drawn up on the other side of the creek. In this situation we remained till dark; cannonading the enemy, and receiving the fire of their fieldpieces . . ." [76] And General Wilkinson says: "If ever there was a crisis in the affairs of the Revolution, this was the moment. Thirty minutes would have sufficed to have brought the two armies into contact, and thirty minutes more would have decided the combat." [77]

Washington's position was indeed critical; his levies were raw, his opponent's troops highly disciplined, and the next day they would be reinforced. Furthermore, the Delaware, which flanked his position, was uncrossable, even by boats, on account of the pack ice. Should his position be forced it meant annihilation.

Again Washington rose to the occasion. Realizing that to retire southwards would demoralize his men and that to hold his present position meant ruin, he decided to abandon his communications, march round

Cornwallis's left flank, scatter such of his rear guard as might be found at Princeton and then make for Brunswick in order to destroy his supply base and so force him to abandon his advance on Philadelphia. Therefore, as he writes: "I ordered all our baggage to be removed to Burlington soon after dark; and at twelve o'clock after renewing our fires, and leaving guards at the bridge in Trenton, and other passes in the same stream above, marched by a roundabout road to Princeton, where I knew they could not have much force left, and might have stores. One thing I was certain of, that it would avoid the appearance of a retreat." [78] With his army of 3,600 men he marched by way of Sandtown along the Quaker Road.

At Princeton, Cornwallis had left Colonel Marwood with the 17th, 40th, and 55th Foot, two guns, and a small force of dragoons, whom he now ordered forward at top speed, in order that they might reinforce him on the 3d. Therefore, early that morning, Marwood set out with the 17th—his own regiment—followed a mile in rear by the 55th, the 40th standing fast at Princeton to guard the stores. At daybreak, when he was halfway to Maidenhead—where yet another of Cornwallis's brigades was preparing to move—the advanced guard of Washington's army struck the Princeton highway a few hundred paces in advance of him. To the astonishment of the Americans they saw moving towards them through the morning mist a column of redcoated infantry; and simultaneously their opponents, seeing a ragged host to their front "were as much astonished as if an army had dropped perpendicularly upon them from the clouds."

The American van was led by General Mercer, who as a surgeon had served in Prince Charles's army at Culloden. Moving forward, he raced Marwood's leading troops for an orchard, the property of a Mr. William Clark. The English, gaining it first, poured three volleys into their enemy and charged home with the bayonet, Mercer falling a victim to that weapon. The Americans gave ground and Marwood was following up when he was faced by the leading troops of Washington's main body who, on hearing the firing, had turned off the highway and were now wheeling toward the orchard. Seeing the redcoats approaching, the van—composed of Philadelphia Associators—was thrown into confusion, whereupon Washington galloped forward between them and their enemy and restored order. Then other units rapidly formed line. The British, who were but 224 strong, must inevitably have been annihilated had not Marwood abandoned his guns and, placing himself at the head of his men, cut his way through the enemy's ranks and gained the Trenton Road. "This," writes Stedman, "was one of the most gallant

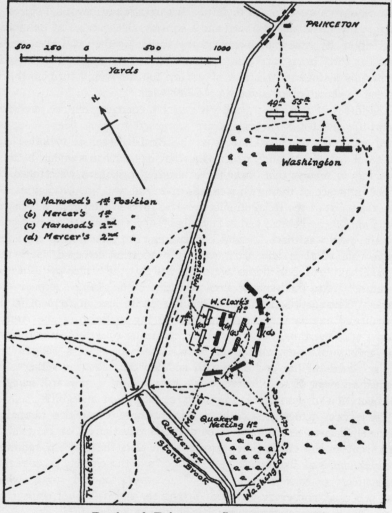

3. Battle of Princeton, January 3, 1777

exploits during the whole war." [79] In all, this action lasted twenty minutes, the 17th Foot losing 66 in killed and wounded and 35 prisoners. Meanwhile the 55th Regiment, now followed by the 40th, instead of falling back on Princeton, advanced south. At no great distance from the scene of Marwood's defeat they were confronted by the whole of Washington's army with Sullivan leading the right wing. Almost at once both regiments were forced to fall back through and beyond Princeton, losing a few killed and wounded and a considerable number of prisoners. Thereupon the Americans occupied the town. As they had been under arms for forty hours, and also because Washington feared that directly Cornwallis discovered the trick played on him he would turn north, he decided to abandon his advance on Brunswick.

The losses of these two small yet decisive engagements are variously given. Those of the Americans are supposed to have been about 40 killed and 100 wounded. Howe puts the British losses at 17 killed and 200 wounded and missing, which is an obvious understatement, because Washington reports that "near three hundred prisoners were taken." [80]

The influence of these two victories upon the war was prodigious. At once the spirit of the Revolutionists revived, and Washington was hailed as a Camillus, a Fabius, and a Hannibal.[81] Everywhere there had been despair; now was there joy and hopefulness. As their spirits rekindled the morale of their adversary was in proportion lowered, Germaine exclaiming: "All our hopes were blasted by the unhappy affair at Trenton." As to this there is ample evidence. *The Annual Register* remarks: "The surprise at Trenton did not excite less amazement in the British and auxiliary quarters than it did joy in those of the Americans. . . . That three old established regiments, of a people who make war their profession, should lay down their arms to a ragged and undisciplined militia, and that with scarcely any loss on either side, seemed an event of so extraordinary a nature, that it gave full scope to the operation of conjecture, suspicion, censure, and malignity . . . " [82]

These two victories, as if by magic, changed the entire campaign. Philadelphia was temporarily saved and the moral effect of Howe's advance cut to the quick. The Jerseys were lost, the English retaining "only the posts of Brunswick and Amboy," and those solely because they were linked to New York by sea.[83] ". . . every load of forage which was procured, and every article of provision, which did not come from New York, was sought or purchased at the price of blood . . . the whole country, with too few exceptions, became hostile; those who were incapable of arms acting as spies and keeping a continual watch for those who bore them . . ." [84] But above all these victories added immensely to Washington's prestige. In fourteen days he had "snatched victory out of the the jaws of defeat," and had established once and for all both in America and in Europe his reputation as a general and as a leader of men. Of him Frederick the Great said: "The achievements of Washington and his little band of compatriots between the 25th of December and the 4th of January, a space of ten days, were the most brilliant of any recorded in the annals of military achievements." [85] Finally, it is pleasant to record that, after the capitulation of Yorktown, at a dinner given by the American headquarters, Cornwallis, in response to a toast proposed by Washington, said: "When the illustrious part that your Excellency has borne in this long and arduous contest becomes matter of history, fame will gather your brightest laurels rather from the banks of the Delaware than from those of the Chesapeake." [86]

REFERENCES

[1] *Correspondence of George III with Lord North*, W. B. Donne, vol. II, p. 7.

[2] *The Revolutionary War*, Francis Vinton Greene, p. 30.

[3] *The Annual Register*, 1777, p. 20.

[4] In 1778 in Washington's army a return shows 54 Negroes to each battalion. Alexander Hamilton recommended their enlistment.

[5] Quoted from *The History of the Origin, Progress, and Termination of the American War*, C. Stedman, vol. I, p. 206 (1794).

[6] Elijah Fisher's *Journal*, 1775–1784, p. 14 (Augusta, 1880).

[7] *Ibid.*, pp. 9 and 15.

[8] Quoted by Henry Belcher in *The First American Civil War*, vol. II, p. 202.

[9] The wooden horse was a ridged, studded device on which soldiers were condemned to sit astride. The strappado consisted in hoisting a soldier by a rope, sometimes fastened to his wrists behind his back, and letting him fall to the length of the rope.

[10] Quoted by *Belcher*, vol. II, p. 85.

[11] To the Duke of Brunswick the "levy money" paid was £4-4-4½ᵈ a man; also the same sum for each man killed and half for each man wounded, and when the men were in the field he received an annual subsidy of £11,517-17-1½ᵈ. Under these agreements, 30,000 German soldiers in all were sent out to America. (See Channing's *A History of the United States*, vol. III, pp. 214–215.) For these troops, see *The Hessians*, Edward J. Lowell, and *The German Soldier in the Wars of the United States*, J. G. Rosengarten. It is customary to belittle the Hessians; nevertheless they produced a number of remarkable troop leaders, such as Colonel von Ewald, whose admirable *Abhandlung vom Dienst der leichten Truppen*, translated into English under the title of *A Treatise upon the Duties of Light Troops*, became a textbook in Sir John Moore's training camp at Shorncliffe in 1804–1805. (See my *British Light Infantry in the Eighteenth Century* and my *Sir John Moore's System of Training*.)

[12] The total number of Loyalists serving in the British Army has been estimated at from 30,000 to 50,000. (See *Loyalists in the American Revolution*, C. H. Van Tyne, p. 183.) The greatest number at any one time was 9,000 in December, 1780.

The most efficient regiments were Ferguson's American Riflemen, Simcoe's Queen's Rangers, and Tarleton's Legion.

[13] Though the Americans were the first in this war to employ Indians—namely, during the blockade of Boston—the use made of them by the British as raiders was as impolitic as it was atrocious. (See Winsor's *History of America,* vol. VI, pp. 605–684 and *English Historical Review,* vol. II, p. 709.)

[14] This infamous trade had been thoroughly commercialized, boys being kidnaped in England for the colonial markets of Boston and Williamsburg. (See *Social Life in the Eighteenth Century,* H. G. Graham.)

[15] In 1773, Mary Jones, whose husband had been seized by the press gang, was hung at Tyburn for stealing a bit of coarse linen from a shop in Ludgate Hill. The sensation of her execution was that the hangman dragged her infant out of her arms before adjusting the rope round her neck.

[16] The British penal code of this period was not the least of the factors in British overseas expansion.

[17] See *Military Forces of the Crown,* C. M. Clode, vol. II, p. 93.

[18] This compared favorably with civil wages, as thirty shillings a year with all found was the hiring fare for an indoor hand at Doncaster or Stourbridge; and in Scotland, twenty shillings a year. (See *Work and Wages,* Thorold Rogers, p. 410.)

[19] Lint being expensive, sponges were used for scores of wounds and blood poisoning resulted. When a limb was removed the patient was given a draught of rum and a bullet to chew. During the Seven Years' War in Canada, though only 1,512 men were killed in action, 13,400 died of disease or badly tended wounds.

[20] See *The Writings of George Washington,* Worthington Chauncey Ford, vol. IV, pp. 200–204.

[21] General Putnam wrote to the governor of Connecticut on September 12: "General Howe is either our friend or no general. He had our whole army in his power at Long Island . . . Had he followed up his victory the consequence to the cause of Liberty must have been dreadful." (*History of New York during Revolutionary War,* T. Jones, vol. I, p. 119.)

[22] *The Narrative of Lieut.-Gen. Sir William Howe,* p. 5 (1780).

[23] Stedman, vol. I, p. 197.

[24] *American Archives,* Fifth Series, vol. II, col. 326–329.

[25] Ford, vol. IV, p. 407.

[26] *Ibid.,* vol. IV, p. 408.

[27] His excuse was the difficulty of the ground—a fictitious one. (See Howe's *Narrative,* p. 6.)

[28] *The New York Mercury* of September 30 says: "It is not inferior to the Gunpowder Plot" (*Diary of the Revolution,* Frank Moore, vol. I, p. 313). The water supply of New York was very lacking. In 1776 there was but one pump which supplied water of a quality fine enough to make tea. Hence it was called the "Tea Water Pump."

[29] Howe's *Narrative,* pp. 6–7.

[30] *Journals of the Continental Congress,* vol. VI, p. 866.

[31] Ford, vol. V, p. 33.

[32] *American Archives,* Fifth Series, vol. III, cols. 1058–1059. See also *Ford,* vol. V, p. 44.

[33] Ford, vol. V, pp. 37–40.

[34] *American Archives,* Fifth Series, vol. III, col. 1120.

[35] *Ibid.,* vol. III, cols. 1035–1036; *Ford,* vol. V, p. 86.

[36] Ford, vol. V, pp. 78 and 86.

[37] "But the Quakers, abhorring the new form of government, at their meeting

held at Philadelphia . . . refused 'in person or by other assistance to join in carrying on the war'; and with fond regret they recalled to mind 'the happy constitution' under which 'they and others had long enjoyed peace.' " (*History of the United States of America,* George Bancroft, vol. V, p. 89, 1885.)

[38] *American Archives,* Fifth Series, vol. III, col. 1316.

[39] "How provoking it is" (exclaimed Colonel Enoch Markham) "that our army, when it entered the Jerseys, was not provided with a single pontoon! . . . If we had six flat-bottomed boats, we could have crossed the Delaware" (Sir George Otto Trevelyan, *The American Revolution,* Part II, vol. II, p. 24).

[40] Stedman, vol. I, p. 219.

[41] *Ibid.,* vol. I, p. 220.

[42] *American Archives,* Fifth Series, vol. III, cols. 1316–1317.

[43] See Belcher, vol. II, pp. 170–171.

[44] See his dispatch to Germaine of November 30, 1776, *American Archives,* Fifth Series, vol. III, col. 926. Bancroft goes so far as to write: "Howe fired his sluggish nature with wine and good cheer; his mistress spent his money prodigally, but the continuance of the war promised him a great fortune" (vol. V, p. 94). See also *The Cambridge Modern History,* vol. VII, p. 211.

[45] Distributions are given in *The Annual Register,* 1777, p. 14 and in Stedman, vol. I, pp. 224–225.

[46] See his letter to Germaine of December 20, 1776 (*American Archives,* Fifth Series, vol. III, col. 1317).

[47] Howe's *Narrative,* p. 7.

[48] Stedman writes of him: "He was obstinate, passionate and incessantly intoxicated with strong liquors" (vol. I, p. 234).

[49] Trevelyan, Part II, vol. II, p. 96.

[50] *History of the Rise, etc. of the Independence of the United States,* W. Gordon, vol. II, p. 332 (1788). See also A. Graydon's *Memoirs,* p. 193. Nevertheless, when possible, Washington did attempt to stop these brutalities; for Fisher informs us in his *Journal* of men being shot for robbing the Tories. (See pp. 10, 11, and 13.)

[51] Moore, vol. I, p. 320. See also pp. 378–380 for lurid accounts.

[52] Howe's *Narrative,* pp. 58–60.

[53] See also *The Annual Register,* 1777, p. 13.

[54] Ford, vol. V, p. 97.

[55] *Ibid.,* vol. V, p. 98.

[56] *Ibid.,* vol. V, p. 103.

[57] *Ibid.,* vol. V, p. 79.

[58] *Ibid.,* vol. V, p. 113.

[59] *New York Mercury,* December 23, 1776. See *American Archives,* Fifth Series, vol. III, col. 1377.

[60] Ford, vol. V, p. 93.

[61] For Honeyman's movements see W. S. Stryker's *Battles of Trenton and Princeton.*

[62] *American Archives,* Fifth Series, vol. III, col. 1215.

[63] *Ibid.,* col. 1343.

[64] *Ibid.,* col. 1361.

[65] *Ibid.,* cols. 1376–1377. Also, see Ford, vol. V, pp. 126–128.

[66] See footnote, Ford, vol. V, p. 130.

[67] For his difficulties, see *American Archives,* Fifth Series, vol. III, col. 1486.

[68] Ford, vol. V, pp. 132–133.

[69] Quoted from Bancroft, vol. V, p. 93.

[70] Ford, vol. V, p. 133.

[71] Bancroft, vol. V, p. 99.

[72] These are Washington's figures (Ford, vol. V, p. 133). Winsor (vol. VI, p. 376) says two American privates were killed, one frozen to death, and two officers and four men wounded, and Bancroft (vol. V, p. 99)—"the Americans lost not one man." The return of Hessians captured, as given in *American Archives* (Fifth Series, vol. III, cols. 1445–1446), is 918 in all and six 3-pounders.

[73] Ford, vol. V, p. 135.

[74] For powers, see Ford, vol. V, p. 140.

[75] *American Archives,* Fifth Series, vol. III, col. 1514.

[76] Ford, vol. V, p. 147. See also *Life and Correspondence of J. Reed,* W. B. Reed, vol. I, pp. 282–288.

[77] Winsor, vol. VI, p. 377.

[78] Ford, vol. V, p. 148.

[79] Stedman, vol. I, p. 237. See also *The Annual Register,* 1777, p. 19; Lamb's *An Original and Authentic Journal,* p. 133, and Moore's *Diary,* vol. I, p. 372.

[80] Ford, vol. V, p. 148.

[81] See Moore's *Diary,* vol. I, pp. 380–381.

[82] *The Annual Register,* 1777, p. 17.

[83] Stedman, vol. I, p. 239.

[84] *The Annual Register,* 1777, p. 21.

[85] *Field Book of the Revolution,* B. J. Lossing, vol. II, p. 33; also *Battles of Trenton and Princeton,* W. S. Stryker, p. 464.

[86] Quoted from Trevelyan, Part II, vol. II, p. 155.

1777

SYNOPSIS OF BACKGROUND EVENTS

WHILE Howe was engaged on his New York and New Jersey campaigns, Sir Guy Carleton, commanding the British forces in Canada, which John Burgoyne was with, set out to invade the State of New York by way of Lake Champlain. Moving forward in October, 1777, he appeared before Ticonderoga, and then, considering the season too advanced, decided to take his army back to Canada. Bitterly disappointed by this decision, Burgoyne sailed for England in November, having made up his mind how the war might be brought to a speedy end.

Howe knew of Burgoyne's idea, and when, on November 30, he wrote to Germaine setting forth his plan for 1777, it was accepted. In brief, it was as follows:

The army from Canada was to move via Lake Champlain to Albany, reaching that town by September. Then, "in order, if possible, to finish the war in one year," Howe proposed the following operations with his own army: (1) 10,000 men under Clinton to move on Boston and reduce that city; (2) 10,000 men to move from New York up the North River (Hudson) to Albany; (3) "A defensive Army of eight thousand men to cover Jersey, and to keep the Southern Army [Washington's] in check, by giving a jealousy to *Philadelphia*, which," he writes, "I would propose to attack in the autumn" provided the other operations succeeded. For these movements he asked for an additional 15,000 men. This communication was received by Germaine on December 30.

Then, on December 20, Howe changed this plan as follows:

. . . the opinions of people being much changed in *Pennsylvania*, and their minds in general, from the late progress of the Army, disposed to peace, in which sentiment they would be confirmed by our getting possession of *Philadelphia*, I am for this consideration fully

37

persuaded the principal Army should act offensively on that side . . .

By this change, the offensive plan towards *Boston* must be deferred until the proposed reinforcements arrive from *Europe,* that there may be a corps to act defensively upon the lower part of Hudson's river, to cover *Jersey* on that side, as well as to facilitate, in some degree, the approach of the Army from *Canada.*

"We must not look for the Northern [Canadian] Army to reach Albany before the middle of September. Of course the subsequent operations of that corps will depend upon the state of things at the time."

This letter was received by Germaine on February 23, 1777.

Meanwhile Burgoyne landed in England on December 13. He frequently discussed the situation with Germaine and the king, and, on February 28, submitted a project entitled, *"Thoughts for Conducting the War from the Side of Canada."* In brief his scheme was as follows:

(1) To assemble at least 8,000 men at Crown Point, as well as artillery, "a corps of watermen, two thousand Canadians including hatchetmen and other workmen and one thousand or more savages." This column to move on Ticonderoga.

(2) Simultaneously, Howe was to send an army up the Hudson, "the only object of the Canada army" being "to effect a junction with that force." And again, a little further on: "These ideas are formed upon the supposition that it be the sole purpose of the Canada army to effect a junction with General Howe, or after co-operating so far as to get possession of Albany and open the communication to New York, to remain upon the Hudson's River, and thereby enable that general to act with his whole force to the southwards."

(3) Simultaneously, a force was to move from Oswego down the Mohawk River in order to join hands with the above two forces at Albany.

Although the distance to be traveled by the Canadian Army was about 200 miles through most difficult country, Burgoyne's plan was a sound one. His aim was to operate against the heart of the rebellion, to cut off the New England States by occupying the Ticonderoga-Hudson line and holding it by blockhouses. Next, to conquer New England, and then, should the Southern States still remain in arms, to fall upon them. Strategically, the plan's greatest recommendation was that, except for a break of a few miles between Lake George and the Hudson, water transport could be used all the way from Quebec to New York.

This plan was accepted both by the king and Germaine, who, nevertheless, also held to Howe's plan of December 20. On March 26 he wrote to Sir Guy Carleton, as follows: While he (Carleton) held Quebec with 3,770 men, Burgoyne with 7,173 men was "to proceed with all possible expedition" to join General Howe at Albany. There Burgoyne would come under Howe's command. Simultaneously Lieutenant Colonel St. Leger and 675 men were "to make a diversion on the Mohawk river," and also proceed to Albany. Then he writes: "I shall write to Sir William Howe from hence by the first packet; but you will nevertheless endeavour to give him the earliest intelligence of this measure, and also direct Lieutenant-General Burgoyne, and Lieutenant-Colonel St. Leger to neglect no opportunity of doing the same, that they may receive instructions from Sir William Howe . . . they must never lose view of their intended junction with Sir William Howe as their principal object."

This dispatch having been posted, a copy of it was handed to Burgoyne who set out on his return to Canada, considering that all was arranged. Yet this was not so. Germaine had instructed his clerk to draft a somewhat similar letter to Sir William Howe, in which positive orders were given to him to move up the Hudson, but it was not ready when he called at his office to sign it. Instead of waiting until it had been penned, he left it unsigned, and it was pigeonholed or mislaid.

To make matters worse, on April 2, while Burgoyne was at sea, Howe again changed his plan, because only 2,900 of the 15,000 reinforcements he had asked for were available. He informed Germaine that he had relinquished the idea of all the expeditions "except that to the Southward and a diversion occasionally upon Hudson's River" and, that instead of moving overland on Philadelphia, the Southward Army would proceed there by sea. To this letter Germaine replied on May 18, agreeing with the new proposal, but, apparently having discovered that his unsigned letter had never been sent to Howe, he added that he trusted "whatever he [Sir William Howe] may meditate, it will be executed in time to co-operate with the army ordered to proceed from Canada." Where Howe was when this letter was received, and what Burgoyne was doing, will be related in the following chapter.

Meanwhile, at Morristown, Washington was addressing himself to his annual task of raising a new army, and in May, convinced that Howe would advance on Philadelphia, he moved to the vicinity of Brunswick and Princeton. Then followed a period of interesting maneuvering. On June 30, Howe withdrew to Staten Island and embarked his army for the Chesapeake. Washington countered by marching south, at the head of 14,000 men, halting in the neighborhood of Philadelphia. As nothing was heard of Howe for three weeks, Washington returned to the Delaware, imagining that Howe must have sailed for Charleston. Learning on August 23 that the British Fleet had cast anchor in the Chesapeake, he hastened back to Philadelphia, and, on the 25th, with the Marquis de Lafayette, his nineteen-year-old major general, he watched Howe land his men at the Head of Elk.

Another period of maneuvering followed, which, on September 10, ended in the neighborhood of Chad's farm on the Brandywine River. Here Howe attempted to repeat his Long Island tactics but failed, losing 576 men in killed, wounded, and missing. The American casualties totaled some 900. After this battle Washington withdrew to Germantown, Howe following him. Then, crossing the Schuylkill, Washington determined to bring the English to battle at Warwick Tavern—some twenty miles west of Philadelphia—but was prevented from doing so by a rainstorm. Falling back, Howe countermarched and, placing himself between Washington and Philadelphia, he occupied that city on September 25. There Howe left 3,000 of his men and encamped 9,000 at Germantown.

Washington with some 11,000 men was then on Skippack Creek. Leaving his camp under cover of darkness and adopting a plan somewhat similar to the one which had proved so successful at Trenton, on October 4 he fell upon his enemy, and was driving him through the village when the American fighting line took panic and retired. In this battle Howe's losses were 535 killed, wounded, and missing, and Washington's 1,073. Washington then withdrew to his camp on Skippack Creek and later on to Valley Forge, Howe going into winter quarters in and around Philadelphia.

CHAPTER II

THE BATTLES OF BENNINGTON AND FREEMAN'S FARM AND THE CAPITULATION OF SARATOGA
1777

O N May 6, Burgoyne arrived at Quebec, and immediately wrote to Howe, saying "that under the present precision of my orders, I should really have no view but that of joining him [Howe] nor think myself justified by any temptation to delay the most expeditious means I could find to effect that purpose." [1] Then, on the 12th, he proceeded to Montreal, where Carleton, who had been abominably insulted by Germaine, welcomed him. "Had that officer been acting for himself, or for his brother," writes Burgoyne, "he could not have shown more indefatigable zeal than he did, to comply with and expedite my requisitions and desires." [2] Next, Burgoyne wrote another letter to Howe, once again mentioning the juncture of the two armies at Albany.

In spite of Carleton's unselfish assistance, Burgoyne was at once faced by all but insuperable difficulties. Nothing could be kept secret. On May 19 he wrote to General Harvey in London: "I had the surprise and mortification to find a paper handed about at Montreal, publishing the whole design of the campaign, almost as accurately as if it had been copied from the Secretary of State's letter," [3] and he attributed the leakage to people in England. Worse still, the Canadians hung back; a paralyzing shortage of transport was discovered; and there were not enough horses to haul the guns. [4] Five hundred two-wheeled carts had to be made at once, out of green wood. Thus began Burgoyne's crucial problem—supply; for it should be remembered that eighteenth-century armies seldom lived on the country. Foraging, in any case, would prove all but impossible in so sparsely inhabited a land as lay along his line of march.

Unfortunately for Burgoyne, he, like many other British officers, held his enemy in contempt. It is true that, throughout the country and particularly in the New England states, men of military age were loth to enlist except in the militia, and, unless danger immediately threatened them, would seldom leave their home localities or remain for any length of time under arms.[5] Nevertheless, as I have already mentioned, they could mobilize rapidly, and in so broken a country as New England, the protection afforded them by the woods, mountains, and ravines went far to compensate for their lack in discipline. Madame de Riedesel calls the New Englanders "natural soldiers," and Lord Balcarres, who commanded Burgoyne's light infantry, rightly says, "they fought at all times with courage and obstinacy," [6] which is all the more remarkable because they were shockingly equipped. Nevertheless, this disadvantage was more than offset by the fact that they knew the terrain and instinctively adapted their tactics to the nature of the country.[7] Many were unsurpassed as marksmen, and when armed with rifles they completely outclassed their enemy; for though this weapon was slow to load, it was out of all comparison more accurate than the smoothbore musket.

As the rebels possessed little artillery, and, as Balcarres informs us, "were always indefatigable in securing themselves by entrenchments, and in general added an abbatis," [8] the importance of cannon on the British side was considerable. Bunker's Hill had been an eye opener, and its significance was fully appreciated by Burgoyne, who never attempted to apply European tactics to forest and bush fighting. In one place we read: "The Major-General desires the utmost Alertness and Dispatch in all the different Movements of the Army, and particularly upon coming to fresh Ground, and in a Campaign such as this, that officers act, from their own lights, and not tediously wait for first Intelligence, and new Orders . . ." [9]

Having trained his army in a common-sense tactics, early in June, Burgoyne, then in his fifty-sixth year, began to assemble it on the Richelieu River, to the north of Lake Champlain. It consisted of the 9th, 20th, 21st, 24th, 47th, 53rd, and 62nd Regiments and the Grenadiers and Light Infantry Companies of the 29th, 31st, and 34th Regiments, all British, and numbering 3,724 men; five regiments of Germans (mostly Brunswickers)—3,016 strong; gunners, 357; recruits, 154; Canadians, 148 and Indians 500; making a total of 7,899, and with

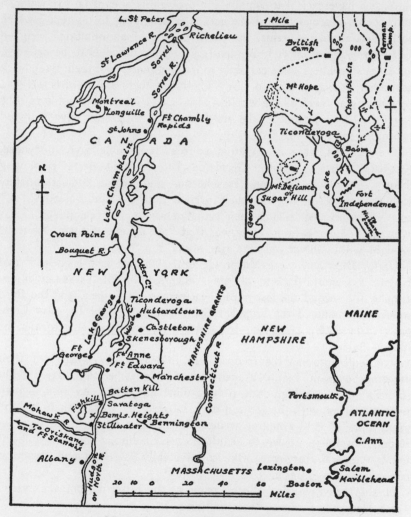

4. Map of the Saratoga Campaign, 1777

officers about 8,200.[10] The ordnance for the field army consisted of thirty-eight pieces of field artillery, two 24-pounders, six 12-pounders, and four howitzers.[11]

It is interesting here to note what the British soldier of that day carried with him in campaign. Anburey tells us: ". . . a knapsack, a blanket, a haversack that contains his provisions, a canteen for water, a hatchet and a proportion of the equipage belonging to his tent," which with "accoutrements, arms, and sixty rounds of ammunition" weighed about sixty pounds.[12] A heavy load; yet, if Stedman is to be believed, the English soldiers were certainly more fortunate than their Brunswick comrades; for, according to him, "Their very hats and swords weighed very nearly as much as the whole equipment of one of our soldiers. The worst British regiment in the service would with ease have marched two miles for their one."[13]

The Indians were a perpetual source of trouble and annoyance. Against Carleton's advice Germaine had insisted upon employing them.[14] They were as usual treacherous and brutal, indiscriminately scalping friend or foe. On their arrival Burgoyne addressed them,[15] and did his utmost to curb their cruelty, but to no great purpose. His estimate of their fighting value was that "not a man of them was to be brought within the sound of a rifle shot."[16]

Under Burgoyne were Major Generals Phillips and Riedesel[17] and Brigadier General Fraser, all able officers. The first was an expert gunner, the second the leader of the German contingent, and the third was in command of the brigaded Grenadier and Light Infantry Companies, the latter being led by Lord Balcarres and the former by Major Acland.

From all accounts the troops were in every way worthy of their officers. Sergeant Lamb, a member of this expedition, says: "The soldiers were in a high state of discipline and had been kept in their winter quarters with the greatest care, in order to prepare them for this expedition."[18] And Anburey writes: "As to our army, I can only say if good discipline, joined to health and spirit among the men at being led by General Burgoyne, who is universally esteemed and respected, can ensure success, it may be expected."[19]

In short, this was no ordinary army, as the following notes, extracted from Hadden's *Orderly Book,* will show:

The Men are to clean and oil their Feet and Shoes, and take every means to re-fresh, and be prepared for long marches (p. 185).

The clothing of such men as have not been properly fitted, are to be immediately completed (193).

Artillery training to be carried out, "an Examination will be held before the Campaign on the Lakes, which the Second Lieutenants are to prepare themselves for" (pp. 219–222).

As the Rain laying upon the surface of the Ground in Camp is extremely prejudicial to the Health of the men, drains are to be made . . . to carry it off . . . The Carpenters, etc., . . . are to be employed in collecting any materials to lay at the bottoms of the Tents, that may tend to keep the ground dry (p. 240).

New and convenient Necessaries are to be made in the Rear of every Cantonment and Encampment every week, and the old ones filled up; at least six inches depth of Earth should also be thrown into the Necessaries in use every Morning (p. 356).

All orders to be most Carefully read to the men every day, and the particulars explained to them by an officer (p. 309).

From these various quotations it will be seen that Burgoyne's army was "modern" in the extreme, even more so than some armies of today.

On June 20, from his camp at Bouquet Ferry, Burgoyne issued a pedantically worded proclamation to the civil inhabitants,[20] and, on the 30th, a general order to his troops in which he informed them that "the Services required of this particular Expedition are critical and conspicuous. During our progress occasions may occur, in which nor difficulty, nor labour, nor life are to be regarded. THIS ARMY MUST NOT RETREAT." [21]

At dawn the next day the "General" was beaten and the doomed adventure set out for Ticonderoga.

The advance up Lake Champlain was as spectacular as Alexander's down the Indus. First in their canoes came the Indians in full war paint; next the advanced guard of little warships, followed by the 1st, 2nd, and German Brigades, with the camp followers, sutlers, and women in rear. It must have been a splendid spectacle; the British infantry in scarlet, the artillerymen and the Germans in blue, the Jägers in green, the British Grenadiers in their bearskins, and the light infantry with their small caps of black leather.

Ticonderoga had been named the Gibraltar of America, yet it was nothing of the kind, for though its works were extensive enough to hold 10,000 men, they were indifferently sited. In March, Congress had sent General Gates to repair them; now they were held by Colonel St. Clair, who had under his command 2,546 Continentals and 900 militia. In his turn St. Clair came under the orders of Major General Philip Schuyler, who also commanded troops scattered in small detachments at Skenesborough (now Whitehall), Fort Ann, Fort Edward, and Albany. Unfortunately for the American cause, Schuyler was a gentleman by nature and inclination, and too well bred either for Congress [22] or the New Englanders, whose officers were peculiarly democratic. After Burgoyne's capitulation, Madame de Riedesel relates: "Some [of the American officers] had been shoemakers, who on our halts made boots for our officers, and sometimes even mended our soldiers' shoes." [23] On August 4, this year, Schuyler wrote to Washington: "Too many of our officers would be a disgrace to the most contemptible troops that ever collected, and have so little sense of honour that cashiering them seems no punishment. They have stood by, and suffered the most scandalous depredations to be committed upon the poor, distressed, ruined, and flying inhabitants." [24] Such outspokenness did not render him popular.

When Burgoyne's army landed some four miles north of Ticonderoga, St. Clair was taken by surprise. He had not expected so formidable an expedition and was short of supplies, and therefore in no position to withstand a siege. On July 3, his enemy occupied Mount Hope, immediately north of the fortress.

The position held by St. Clair was a weak one. It consisted of three fortified localities separated by water and dominated by Mount Defiance (Sugar Hill), which, because of the difficulty of its ascent, had not been entrenched. At once Burgoyne recognized it to be the key to the position, and on the 4th, he sent out Lieutenant Twiss to reconnoiter it. As this officer's report was favorable, General Phillips remarked: "Where a goat can go a man can go, and where a man can go he can drag a gun." [25] Consequently, by daybreak on the 6th, the hill was occupied and guns posted on it. Convinced that his position was now untenable, St. Clair forthwith ordered his boats and such cannon as they could carry to fall back on Skenesborough (named after Philip Skene). Simultaneously he withdrew with the garrison by way of Hubbardtown, where he left his rearguard, to Castleton, arriving there the same day, after a magnificent march.

Directly Burgoyne discovered St. Clair's withdrawal, he set out in pursuit, his boats rowing down Wood Creek, Fraser and his brigade, followed by Riedesel, moving by the Hubbardtown Road. They came up with the Americans early on the morning of the 7th, and a fierce engagement resulted. Fraser was heavily outnumbered until Riedesel arrived, when St. Clair fell back on Skenesborough. Attacked there by Burgoyne, he fell back on Fort Ann, and from there was ordered by

General Schuyler to withdraw to Saratoga, evacuating Fort Edward on the way.

It was now that Burgoyne committed the error which, even more than Howe's delinquency, ruined his campaign. Instead of returning to Ticonderoga and sailing down Lake George to Fort George, whence a wagon road led to Fort Edward, he decided to press straight on. "Had he," writes Stedman, "returned to Ticonderoga, and crossed Lake St. George, he would have reached Fort Edward at least ten or twelve days sooner. He should have detached General Fraser from Skenesborough to Fort George, by which means a quantity of provisions and stores, destined by the Americans for Ticonderoga, would have been secured, as well as a supply of carts, wagons and draft bullocks. This conduct would have enabled him to have penetrated to Albany before the enemy were sufficiently powerful to oppose him." [26]

Be this as it may, Burgoyne was so elated by his initial success that he decided to plunge on into an all but trackless wilderness,[27] keep up the pursuit, occupy Albany without a serious battle, and there entrench his army and await the arrival of Sir William Howe. This plan, however, fell through, for he was unable to occupy Fort Edward until July 30, during which time his enemy recovered.

For this long halt Burgoyne was blamed, not only by Germaine, but by most historians ever since. Yet, accepting this line of advance, an impartial examination of the conditions he had to work under convinces me that Fortescue is right when he says that, though Burgoyne assembled his army at Skenesborough on the 10th, "it was no small feat that" he "should have reached Fort Edward on the 30th of July." [28] What were these conditions? I will let Sergeant Lamb answer this question:

"The British were now obliged to suspend all operations for some time, and wait at Skeensborough for the arrival of provisions and tents; but they employed this interval clearing a passage for the troops, to proceed against the enemy. This was attended with incredible toil. The Americans, now under the direction of General Schuyler, were constantly employed in cutting down large trees on both sides of every road, which was in the line of march. The face of the country was likewise so broken with creeks and marshes, that there was no less than forty bridges to construct, one of which was over a morass two miles in extent." [29]

Coupled with these difficulties were Burgoyne's deficiencies in transport. On the 10th he wrote: "The army very much fatigued (many parts of it having wanted their provisions for two days, almost the whole of their tents and baggage) . . ." [30] The five hundred Canada carts seem to have broken up rapidly; for, according to Captain Money, when asked by the Parliamentary Committee, "How many carts and ox-teams could be mustered at any one time?" his answer was, "I think only 180 carts . . . the number of ox-carts I really forget, but I believe between 20 and 30." [31] Though a garrison of 910 men was left at Ticonderoga to protect the line of communications, it was imperative for Burgoyne to collect supplies before plunging into the forest. He says: "In the first place, it was necessary to bring forward to Fort Edward four score or a hundred boats, as mere carriage-vessels for the provisions, each boat made a hard day's work for six or more horses . . . At the next carrying place . . . it was necessary to place a considerable relay of horses to draw over, first, a portion of carriage-boats, and afterwards the provisions . . ." as well as a "great number of other boats . . . to form bridges, to carry baggage and ammunition, and the number of carriages framed to transport the boats themselves at the ensuing carrying places. . . ." [32] Horses and oxen were unobtainable from the countryside and it rained continually.

On July 24, supplies having been collected, the main body marched to Fort Ann and encamped there; Fraser and the advanced guard moving on to within two miles of Fort Edward. Then, on the 29th, the army set out again, arriving at the Hudson the next day. Lieutenant W. Digby writes: "We moved on further to a rising ground, about a mile south of Fort Edward, and encamped on a beautiful situation, from whence you saw the most romantic prospect of the Hudson's River interspersed with many small islands." [33]

Meanwhile much was happening to the south of these gleaming little islands, which it was not possible for either Digby or Burgoyne to see. They knew that in armies consisting principally of militia, a setback is nearly always magnified into an overwhelming disaster, and this is what actually happened on the fall of Ticonderoga, consternation overwhelming Congress and roaring through the land. But Burgoyne did not know that Washington, scores of miles to the south, was concerned not so much by this loss as by conflicting reports on Howe's movements. Schuyler, meanwhile, had rightly fallen back to Stillwater, although not without further disaster. Not only did two of his Massachusetts' regiments at once desert him, but worse still John Adams impeded him in every way, while General Gates was hard at work convincing Congress that he alone could bring victory to the American arms. In this welter of panic and intrigue one man alone kept his balance and his nerve, and that man was Washington, who once again saved the situation.

Three days before Ticonderoga fell, he had gauged the British plan. Writing of Burgoyne's advance to Governor Trumbull on July 2, he said: "If it is not merely a diversion, but a serious attack, of which it bears strongly the appearance, it is certain proof, that the next step of General Howe's army will be towards Peekskill, and very suddenly, if possible to get possession of the passes in the Highlands, before this army can have time to form a junction with the troops already there." [34] On the 18th, directly after he had learned of the evacuation of the fortress, he sent Arnold to Schuyler, recommending his bravery, and at the same time wrote to the brigadier generals of militia in the western parts of Massachusetts and Connecticut, pointing out the danger should Howe join Burgoyne, and urging them to come to the aid of Schuyler and Arnold.[35]

Nine-tenths of Washington's difficulties were due to the fact that his enemy had absolute command of the sea. This may be gathered from his letter of the 25th to Congress, in which he wrote: "The amazing advantage the Enemy derive from their ships and the command of the Water, keeps us in a state of constant perplexity and the most anxious conjecture . . ." [36] Howe's conduct puzzled and embarrassed him "beyond measure." [37] On the day he wrote this letter, Washington decided to go north, but on receiving an intercepted letter of Howe's addressed to Burgoyne, which he recognized to be a blind, he wrote: "I am persuaded more than ever, that Philadelphia is" Howe's "place of destination." [38] On the 30th he informed General Gates that Howe was probably going to the Delaware, and adds: "General Howe's in a manner abandoning General Burgoyne is so unaccountable a matter, that, till I am fully assured it is so, I cannot help casting my Eyes occasionally behind me," and the next day he informed Trumbull that Congress had notified him that "the enemy's fleet consisting of two hundred and twenty-eight sail were at the Capes of Delaware yesterday in the forenoon." [39] Nevertheless, he was still in doubt, for on August 1 he wrote to General Putnam: "The importance of preventing Mr. Howe's getting possession of the Highlands by a *coup de main* is infinite to America . . . The possibility of his going eastward is exceedingly small, and the ill effects that might attend such a step inconsiderable in comparison with those, that would inevitably attend a successful stroke upon the Highlands." The same day he ordered Governor George Clinton to "call in every man of the militia that you possibly can to strengthen the Highland posts." [40] At length, on the 11th, he again wrote to Putnam that Howe's fleet had been seen on the 7th "sixteen Leagues to the southward of the Capes of Delaware"; but that General Sir Henry Clinton would now probably move from New York to the support of Burgoyne.[41] Finally, on the 22d he learned that his enemy's fleet had entered Chesapeake Bay, and on the 25th that Howe had begun to land his army about "Six miles below Head of Elk." [42]

From the above correspondence it will be seen not only how clearly Washington fathomed his enemy's plan, but how dangerous he considered it to be, which is as flattering to Burgoyne as it is unflattering to Howe, whose lack of strategical perception ruined it. Further, Washington's advice to Schuyler was pre-eminently sound. On July 22 he wrote: "From your accounts he [Burgoyne] appears to be pursuing that line of conduct, which of all others is most favorable to us; I mean acting in Detachments. This conduct will certainly give room to Enterprise on our part, and expose his parties to great hazard. Could we be so happy, as to cut one of them off, supposing it should not exceed four, five, or six hundred men, it would inspirit the people and do away much of their present anxiety. In such an Event . . . they would fly to arms and afford every aid in their power." [43] Again, two days later: "As they can never think of advancing, without securing their rear by leaving garrisons in the fortresses behind, the force with which they can come against you will be greatly reduced by the detachments necessary for the purpose . . ." [44] This, as we shall see, is what actually occurred, and to assist in bringing it about, on August 16, Washington sent Colonel Daniel Morgan and his five hundred riflemen [45] north to the aid of Schuyler.

Meanwhile, what of Burgoyne? From now on the question of supply was his dominant problem, and as is usual it was closely related to the problem of transportation. Arriving at the Hudson, he determined to collect all the animals he could, if possible sufficient to mount his German dragoons as well as make good his casualties in draft horses. Persuaded by Major Skene, a brave but unreliable Loyalist who had gained his confidence, he reluctantly determined to raid the country on the Connecticut River for cattle and horses. He was however gravely misinformed by that officer, who, exaggerating the sympathy of the local inhabitants, led him to understand that a small show of arms would bring them flocking to his standard. The upshot was that, on August 9,

Burgoyne selected Lieutenant Colonel Baum to lead the expedition to the Connecticut, in spite of the fact that Baum could speak only German. To make matters worse, Burgoyne gave him the most detailed instructions,[46] and then, on the 11th, when Baum set forth from Fort Miller, galloped up to him and changed his destination from Manchester to Bennington, because, as he informed him, a large depot of horses and cattle was established there. Bennington lies at the foot of the Green Mountains, some thirty miles to the southeast of Fort Edward.

Baum's force was not only too small for such a risky enterprise, but also internally weak on account of its make-up. It consisted of 170 unmounted Brunswick dragoons, about 100 German infantry, a detachment of gunners with two 3-pounders, and 50 of Fraser's marksmen; in all 374 regular soldiers accompanied by some 300 Loyalists, Canadians, and Indians.

Moving off with no appreciation that speed was necessary and misled by Skene's optimism, that night and the following Baum "allowed people to go and come from his camp, readily believing the professions of sympathy with the royal cause, and imparting to them most fully and completely all information as to his strength and designs." [47] Be this as it may, one thing is certain—that his Indians behaved in a most disgraceful way. Not only did they plunder everything and everybody, but they completely nullified the purpose of his raid by slaughtering herds of fine cattle, bringing nothing back with them except the cowbells.

Slowly the advance continued until the 14th, when, hearing that the Americans were in strength at Bennington, Baum sent back to Burgoyne for reinforcements. Colonel Breyman and 550 German dragoons, accompanied by two 6-pounders, were sent out on the 15th; but, on account of the rain and their ponderous equipment, they failed to cover much ground that day. Meanwhile Baum, who had advanced to the Walloomsac River, entrenched his men on its northern bank and awaited the arrival of Breyman.

Shortly before Baum set out, John Stark—one of those many intractable Americans who could command, but who could not be commanded, and who had fought against Gage at Bunker's Hill and with Rogers and Abercromby during the Seven Years' War—was gathering in the men of New Hampshire. On August 8, he marched into Bennington at the head of some 1,500 followers. From there, on the morning of the 16th, he came into contact with Baum, who at first mistook his men for a party of Loyalists on their way to tender their services to the king,[48] and instead of opening fire on them, he allowed them to wander round his position.

Having thus peacefully picketed his enemy, Stark divided his command into three small columns. The central one under himself, supported by Colonels Stickney and Hubbard, was to move up the Walloomsac and

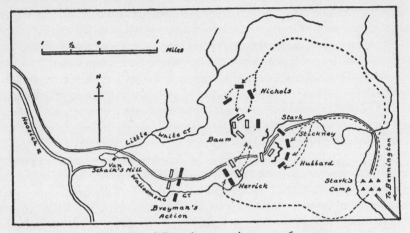

5. Battle of Bennington, August 16, 1777

launch a frontal attack on Baum, while the other two—the right under Colonel Nichols and the left under Colonel Herrick—were to move out to the flanks and then close in on the enemy's rear. The result of this distribution was that Baum was surrounded before he realized it; whereupon his Indians fled, clanging their cowbells.

With a shout of "We will gain the victory, or Molly Stark shall be a widow to-night," [49] Stark launched his attack with the greatest impetuosity. It was now between three and four o'clock, and an eye-witness writes:

The action was extremely hot for between one and two hours; the flanking parties had carried their points with great ease, when the front pressed on their breastwork with an ardor and a patience beyond expectation. The blaze of the guns of the contending parties reached each other, the fire was so extremely hot, and our men easily surmounting their breastworks, amidst peals of thunder and flashes of lightning from their guns, without regarding the roar of their field-pieces, that the enemy at once deserted their covers and ran: and in about five minutes their whole camp was in the utmost confusion and disorder, all their battalions were broken in pieces, and fled most precipitately; at which instant our whole army pressed after with redoubled ardor, pursued them for a mile, made considerable slaughter amongst them, and took many prisoners.[50]

Had Breyman been present, events would undoubtedly have been different, for he was an able soldier; but for some reason, though he was within six miles of Bennington early on the 16th, he did not approach the scene of action until after Baum's force had been destroyed. When he did, he found Stark's men plundering their enemy's camp; whereupon he extended his own and swept them out of it. Most fortunately for Stark, as his men were breaking back, Colonel Seth Warner, at the head of a battalion of Green Mountain Boys—who had been roughly handled at Hubbardtown—suddenly appeared on the field. The courage of Stark's militiamen revived, and Breyman was forced to retire under cover of darkness.

The British losses in these two encounters were extremely heavy, amounting to 596 men killed and missing, Baum being mortally wounded. Stark lost thirty killed and forty wounded, and for his gallant action was presented by the Board of War of New Hampshire with "a compleat suit of clothes . . . together with a piece of Linen."

Stark deserved better than that, for the effect of his small yet dramatic victory over the dreaded Germans was electric. Every newspaper throughout the states simultaneously glorified him and ridiculed his enemy. Thus, for example, the *Pennsylvania Evening Post* of August 28 exclaimed: "They say poor General Burgoyne is gone STARK MAD." [51]

Nor was Burgoyne under any illusion as to the meaning of Baum's defeat. Not only did it teach him how formidable the Americans could be, but it made him realize that, should he press on, his communications would have to be abandoned, and that he could not burn his boats until he had accumulated at least a month's supplies. This, with his wretched transport, would take a long time, and while he was thus employed his adversary would daily become numerically and morally more formidable. On August 20 he wrote a despondent letter to Germaine stating that he had heard from Howe that he intended to go to Pennsylvania. "Had I latitude in my orders," he wrote, "I should think it my duty to wait in this position . . . I little foresaw that I was to be left to pursue my way through such a tract of country, and hosts of foes, without any co-operation from New York . . ." [52]

The difficulty of his situation was enormously aggravated by the frenzied campaign of propaganda which swept over America. From the opening of the war an intense feeling had existed because the British employed Indians, in spite of the fact that the Americans did the same.[53] Most unfortunately for Burgoyne, on July 27 a Miss Jane MacCrea, the daughter of a clergyman, was brutally murdered and scalped by one of his Indians—the Wyandot Panther [54]—and though Burgoyne was in no way to blame,[55] very naturally a howl of indignation was let loose. *Saunders' News Letter* of August 14, 1777, proclaimed that Burgoyne's Indians "conjointly with the English Light Infantry" had "scalped 700 men, women and children," in an area which, incidentally, possessed "not more than ten human dwellings." [56]

Here is a more poetic example, signed "John Burgoyne":

> I will let loose the dogs of hell,
> Ten thousand Indians, who shall yell
> And foam and tear, and grin and roar,
> And drench their moccasins in gore:
> To those I'll give full scope and play
> From Ticonderog to Florida. . . .[57]

While this propaganda was stimulating recruiting, Congress, on August 1, ordered Washington to remove General Schuyler and replace him by General Gates. This man, whom Burgoyne calls "an old midwife," arrived at Stillwater on August 19, at the moment when another reverse was to overwhelm the British.

It will be remembered that the second part of the plan of invasion was an advance down the Mohawk Valley, which was to be carried out by Colonel St. Leger, who, after reducing Fort Stanwix (near the present city of Rome), was to advance to the Hudson and link up with the main army. This fort, which had been built at the portage between Wood Creek and the Mohawk River, was held by Colonel Gansevoort and Lieutenant Colonel Willett, who had renamed it Fort Schuyler. Setting out on July 25 from Oswego, St. Leger arrived before the fort on August 3, at the head of a mixed force of 850 Regulars, Tories, and Canadians accompanied by 1,000 Indians under Sir John Johnson—son of Sir William who had died in 1774—and the celebrated Mohawk Chief Joseph Brant (Thayendanega).[58] Meanwhile General Herkimer, then sixty-four years old, roused the militia of Tryon county to rally to the rescue, and, on the 6th, tumbled headlong into an ambush laid by Brant at Oriskany. There the Americans would in all probability have met with the fate of Braddock's army, had not the contest suddenly been interrupted by a drenching rainstorm. Meanwhile Willett was sent out from the fort to fall upon the Indian camp, now denuded of men. Brant's Indians, hearing the firing in rear of them, at once fled the field. Then St. Leger surrounded the fort, but because of his inadequate artillery could make little impression on it.[59]

Hearing that Gansevoort was hard pressed, Schuyler sent out Benedict Arnold and 1,200 men—mostly Continentals—to his relief. Advancing rapidly to German Flats, some fifteen miles east of Fort Stanwix, he captured a Mohawk Dutchman, a semi-imbecile named Hon Yost, sentenced him to death, and then promised to reprieve him if he would proceed to St. Leger's camp and inform his Indians[60] that the Americans were advancing in overwhelming numbers. Yost carried out his orders with such effect that the Indians took panic and abandoned St. Leger, who in consequence was compelled on the 22d to raise the siege and retire to Oswego.

On this same day, as we have seen, Sir William Howe cast anchor in Chesapeake Bay, having on the 15th notified General Clinton, in command at New York, that should he "see occasion to act offensively," he was to do so. On the 25th he received Germaine's letter of May 18 and again wrote to Clinton saying: "If you can make any diversion in favour of General Burgoyne approaching Albany . . . I need not point out the utility of such a measure."[61]

After the disaster at Bennington, Burgoyne was compelled to remain encamped on the Hudson in order to accumulate supplies, because he saw that, once a forward movement was made, he would be forced to abandon his line of communications. Still believing that Howe would support him, by September 11 he had accumulated "5 weeks' Provisions for the Army," all "forwarded from *Quebec* upwards of four hundred Miles by Land or water."[62] Finally, on the 13th, he set out on his last lap, leaving but two posts behind him—at Ticonderoga and Diamond Island in Lake George. His army consisted of 2,633 British rank and file, 1,711 Germans and 300 reinforcements, in all 4,646 combatants, not counting gunners, Tories, and Indians.[63] They crossed the Hudson, by a bridge of boats; then used the boats to augment the supply of transport vessels.

Meanwhile Gates had been reinforced by Arnold and 1,200 men, triumphantly returned from the Mohawk, and by Morgan and his 500 riflemen, who had been sent north by Washington. On September 12 the whole American Army occupied Bemis Heights at Stillwater, which Kosciusko, the Polish engineer, at once proceeded to fortify. Gates immediately sent out James Wilkinson and some scouts, who soon discovered Burgoyne's approach. A series of outpost actions followed, with results much to the advantage of the Americans.

Having to all intents and purposes burned his boats, Burgoyne was left with no alternative but to fight his way southwards; so he moved slowly down the track which skirted the western bank of the Hudson towards his enemy's position at Stillwater.

Reconnoitering it and discovering that to the immediate west lay a height which dominated it and which was neither fortified nor occupied, he decided, under cover of a demonstration against Gates's right and center to occupy this height and drive his opponent into the river. In spite of the fact that this meant a division of his small army, his plan, though daring, was tactically sound; Gates's on the other hand was decidedly indifferent. It consisted in concentrating the whole of his force, now some 12,000 strong, behind his fortifications and awaiting attack.

On the 15th, Burgoyne issued his orders, and the army moved forward to Dovecote, halfway between Saratoga and Stillwater. On the 17th it reached Sword Farm, and on the morning of the 19th the whole force was organized in three groups—a right wing, a center, and left wing, under Generals Fraser, Hamilton, and Phillips, with Riedesel supporting Phillips.

As the three columns advanced, the glitter of their weapons and the scarlet of their uniforms could be seen between the trees by the American scouts. Yet Gates sat tight behind his entrenchments, and, as Lossing says, "gave no orders and evinced no disposition to fight." [64] His officers were impatient; Arnold "urged, begged and entreated" to be allowed to advance. At length he obtained permission to send forward Morgan's riflemen and Dearborn's infantry. A little later, according to Gates's adjutant general, Wilkinson: "Gates and Arnold were together in front of the camp. Major Lewis came in from the scene of action, and announced that its progress was undecisive. Arnold immediately exclaimed: 'By G-d! I will soon put an end to it'—and clapping spurs to his horse galloped off at full speed." [65] Gates in consternation sent Wilkinson after him to order him back. Of Arnold, Samuel Downing, who fought with him at Bemis Heights, says: "He was dark-skinned, with black hair and middling height; there wasn't any waste timber in him, he was our fighting general, and a bloody fellow he was. He didn't care for nothing; he'd ride right in. It was 'Come on boys'—'t wasn't 'Go, boys.' He was as brave a man as ever lived." [66]

Arnold reached the front not far from Freeman's Farm, to find Morgan's riflemen hard pressed by Fraser's light infantry. Flinging himself at Fraser, he drove in his skirmishers, then lost control, regained it, swung his men to the right and flung himself on Hamilton's column. I will let Sergeant Lamb, an eyewitness, describe what followed:

Here the conflict was dreadful; for four hours a constant blaze of fire was kept up . . . Men, and particularly, officers dropped every moment on each side. Several of the Americans placed themselves in high trees, and as often as they could distinguish a British officer's uniform, took him off by deliberately aiming at his person . . . Major General Phillips, upon hearing the firing, made his way through a difficult part of the wood to the scene of action, and brought up with him Major Williams and four pieces of artillery; this reinforcement animated our troops in the centre, which at that moment were critically pressed by a great superiority of fire, and to which the major general led up the 20th Regiment at the most personal hazard. Major General Riedesel then brought forward part of the left wing, and arrived in time to charge the enemy, with regularity and bravery. [67]

Victory was now to the general who could bring up the last reserves. Burgoyne had none; Gates had approximately 9,000. Of his astonishing reticence in grasping victory, Fortescue writes: "Had Gates sent to Arnold the reinforcements for which he asked, Arnold must certainly have broken the British center," [68] and Lossing says: "Had he [Arnold] been seconded by his commander, and strengthened by re-inforcement . . . he would doubtless have secured a complete victory." Then he adds: "But for Arnold, on that eventful day, Burgoyne would doubtless have marched into Albany at the autumnal equinox a victor." [69] Darkness at length put an end to the conflict, when "large packs of wolves made night hideous by their howls. Indians prowled through the surrounding forest, scalping the dead and dying who had fallen among the brushwood, and were with difficulty restrained from invading that open space, covered with English bodies, where the prey they coveted was to be found in the greatest abundance." [70]

In this stubborn and well-contested battle, in which "the British Troops were not a little surprized at the boldness of their adversaries," [71] the British losses were heavy, some 600 killed and wounded—that is about 33 per cent of those engaged. Comparatively speaking, the American losses were light, numbering 65 killed, 218 wounded, and 33 missing, or less than 10 per cent of the total engaged.

In spite of these paralyzing losses, Burgoyne's first intention was to renew the attack on the 20th; but finding that this was out of the question, he postponed it until the 21st. Gates, now intensely jealous of Arnold, after a stormy interview with him deprived him of his command. Then, instead of attacking on the 20th, which he should have done, he contented himself with merely sniping at his enemy and pushing out posts onto the left bank of the Hudson. Meanwhile, Stark once again appeared and took Fort Edward. On the 21st, two unexpected factors caused Burgoyne again to postpone his advance. The first was a letter from General Clinton, and the second, news that on the 18th General Lincoln had surprised and occupied Sugar Hill at Ticonderoga and had captured the greater part of the supply fleet on Lake Champlain. This meant that Burgoyne's communications were definitely cut.

Clinton's letter, dated September 12, was in cypher,[72] and informed Burgoyne that it was his intention to attack Fort Montgomery (near Peekskill on the narrows of the lower Hudson) in about ten days' time. Burgoyne at once answered, describing his situation and asking Clinton to hasten his advance. This reply was secreted in a silver bullet, but unfortunately the messenger was caught and shot.[73]

When Howe had sailed for the Delaware, Clinton had been too weak to act upon his vague hints to proceed north. His circumstances did not improve until September 24, when 3,000 reinforcements arrived from England, bringing his total force up to some 7,000 men. He at once set out with a force of 3,000, and, on October 5, nearing Peekskill, had received a message from Burgoyne informing him that his provisions would last until October 29. "He asked for orders as to whether he should attack or retreat. He desired Clinton's positive answer whether the latter could reach Albany . . . If no answer was received by October 12, he would retreat." [74] On the 6th, Clinton took Forts Clinton and Montgomery, cut his way through the boom, and sent Burgoyne the following message: *"Nous y voici* and nothing now between us and Gates . . . I heartily wish you success." [75]

This advance decided Burgoyne to attack. On October 3 rations had been reduced, and as forage was growing scarce a move was imperative. Added to this, the sniping of the enemy's riflemen had become intolerable. On the 4th, Burgoyne summoned a council of war, and on the 5th it met again, when both Riedesel and Fraser proposed an immediate withdrawal, while Phillips offered no opinion. Burgoyne, however, stood out for an advance, because, as he said, should they remove the pressure on Gates, that general would be in a position to lead 14,000 men to Washington's support, which might easily result in Howe's defeat. He proposed to leave 800 men in camp and with 4,000 once again attempt to turn his enemy's left flank. As his officers objected to this plan, he modified his proposal to a reconnaissance in force by 1,500 men, in order to discover the best place to attack. Should none be found, then a retreat would take place on the 11th. This plan was radically unsound, because the enemy was not only strongly entrenched, but now numbered nearly 20,000. It was, in fact, the blind throw of a gambler.

So it came about that, between ten and eleven o'clock on the morning of the 7th, Burgoyne moved out of his entrenched camp accompanied by Fraser, Phillips, Riedesel, and Balcarres. Halting in a field of corn he deployed his small force; Balcarres with the Light Infantry on the right, the 24th Regiment, and some weak German battalions in the center, and on the left Acland's Grenadiers.

When this approach was reported to Gates, he ordered Morgan with 1,500 men to turn the enemy's right, while Poor and 1,000 attacked the left and Learned and 2,000 the center. A hot engagement took place, Morgan driving in the British Light Infantry under Balcarres, and Poor decimating Acland's Grenadiers. Thereupon Burgoyne ordered a withdrawal.

Meanwhile Arnold, now without a command and totally ignored by Gates, was fretting behind the works on Bemis Heights. As the roar of battle grew louder and louder, he could restrain himself no longer. Turning to his aide-de-camp, he exclaimed: "No man shall keep me in my tent to-day. If I am without command, I will fight in the ranks; but the soldiers, God bless them, will follow my lead. Come on," he shouted, "victory or death!" [76] and leaping into his saddle he galloped toward the battle.

Catching up with Learned's brigade he rushed it forward, leading it against the Germans, who, nevertheless, withstood his frenzied attack. Next he galloped to the American left and led on Morgan's riflemen against Balcarres, whose men, when Fraser was mortally wounded by a sharpshooter, fell back to their works near Freeman's Farm. Thereupon Arnold attempted to storm them.[77]

Next, he galloped towards the British right "exposed to the cross fire of the contending armies," and once again meeting Learned's

Brigade, he led it forward. Driving back his enemy's center he rode direct
for a redoubt on the right, which was held by Colonel Breyman, stormed

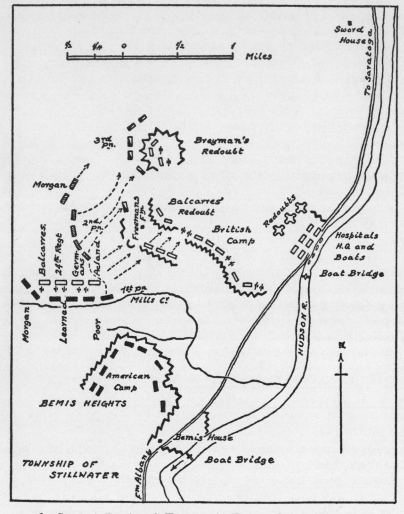

6. Second Battle of Freeman's Farm, October 7, 1777

and carried it. During this action his horse was killed and he himself
severely wounded in the leg.

With his fall and the closing in of night the battle ended. The most

astonishing thing about it is that, though the British were outnumbered
by three to one, it had lasted for over five hours. Of it Anburey writes:
"In order that you may form some idea with what obstinacy the enemy
assaulted the lines, from the commencement . . . till they were repulsed, there was a continual sheet of fire along the lines, and in this
attack we were fully convinced of what essential service our artillery
was." [78] It was undoubtedly the British gunners who saved Burgoyne
from annihilation, and it was undoubtedly Arnold and his frantic leadership which in both these battles of Freeman's Farm saved Gates. During
it that general did nothing, or rather, he sat arguing on the merits of
the American Revolution with a wounded British officer—Sir Francis
Clarke. "Losing his temper in the discussion, Gates called his adjutant—
Wilkinson—out of the room and asked him, 'Did you ever hear so
impudent a son of a b——h?' And this seems to have been all that the
commanding general contributed to the crowning victory of Saratoga." [79]
"It is a curious fact," writes one American historian, "that an officer
who really had no command in the army, was the leader in one of the
most spirited and important battles of the Revolution." [80]

The losses in this battle are not exactly known. According to Winsor,
the Americans lost 50 killed and 150 wounded, and the British 176 killed,
250 wounded, and 200 prisoners. Among the prisoners was Acland,
badly wounded, and among the dead were the gallant Fraser, who died
of his wound, and Colonel Breyman, who was shot while defending
his redoubt.

Burgoyne now knew that the game was up, and that nothing short of
a miracle could save him. When dawn broke on the 8th, he found that
during the night his enemy had entrenched himself on the high ground
east of the Hudson; he was left no option but to withdraw. Soon after
sunset the beaten army set out, slowly moving northwards over the
sodden ground, impeded by its supply barges, which moved snakelike
through the darkness upstream. Yet, the morale of the men was as high
as ever. Sergeant Lamb says: "The men were willing and ready to
face any danger, when led on by officers whom they loved and respected
and who shared with them in every toil and hardship." [81]

To make matters worse, it rained in torrents.[82] So exhausting became
the retreat that, at 5 A.M. on the 9th, Burgoyne called a halt, resting his
men for eleven hours; this also gave "time to the batteaux loaded with
provisions to come a-breast." [83] At 10 P.M. the army reached Schuyler's
Farm, and next morning crossed the Fishkill.

Though Gates now had under his command 1,698 officers and 18,624 men, of whom 14,914 were present for duty,[84] he did not attempt to follow up, and as Elijah Fisher remarks, he "gave the Enemy three Days to git off with themselves." [85] True, he was short of supplies and Arnold's victory had disorganized his half-disciplined men. At length he set out, and, on the afternoon of the 10th, caught up with the British rear guard. Thereupon Burgoyne prepared to attack him, drawing up his men on the rising ground overlooking Fishkill Creek. But on the 12th, finding himself now three-quarters surrounded, Burgoyne summoned a council of war, which decided to abandon all transport and guns, and, loading six days' rations on each soldier, to retreat that night. It was, however, too late. While the council was debating, the trap closed and retreat became impossible.

As the result of another council of war on the 13th, a flag of truce was sent to Gates. The answer received was, "Unconditional surrender." Burgoyne immediately rejected this reply and demanded that his troops should march out of their camp with the honors of war.[86] To this Gates agreed, probably because Clinton was now moving toward his rear, and he wanted to be free to meet him. Further, it was agreed: "A free passage to be granted to the Army under Lieut.-General Burgoyne, to Great Britain, on Condition of not serving again in North America during the present Contest . . ." [87] This was the vital clause of the Convention of Saratoga, signed on October 16.

This Convention concluded, Burgoyne asked for an interview with Gates. Gates received him courteously and behaved with the highest chivalry, as also did General Schuyler.[88] With marked delicacy Gates confined his troops to their camps when,[89] on the 17th, Burgoyne's 3,500 men marched to their appointed place to pile their arms.

However, the terms of the Convention were not honorably kept, for, in spite of Washington's protests, they were repudiated by Congress. So disgraceful was this act that I will leave it to an American writer to comment on it. The conduct of Congress, writes John Fiske, "can be justified upon no grounds save such as would equally justify firing upon flags of truce." [90] The troops were never restored to their native lands.

Reviewing this decisive campaign, one of the most fateful in history, it is apparent that, though, as a general, Burgoyne does not stand in the front rank, few British overseas expeditions have been commanded by an abler man. When summing up his adventure, Fortescue says: "That no more honourable attempt of British officers and men to achieve the impossible is on record," [91] and, "but for Arnold," he "might have made his way to Albany."

Throughout those perilous months—June to October, 1777—his loyalty to his men was unbroken, and was only equaled by their loyalty to him. After the Convention had been signed, Lamb still could write: "He possessed the confidence and affection of his army in an extraordinary degree, that no loss or misfortune could shake the one, or distress or affliction the other . . . not a voice was heard through the army, to upbraid, to censure or blame their general . . ." [92] Very different was the attitude of the politicians in England, who heaped abuse on him. Germaine, who more than any other man was responsible, remained in office.[93] Burgoyne's reputation was finally cleared; yet when he died, on August 4, 1792, and was buried in the Cloister of Westminster Abbey, but one coach followed his body, and from that day to this no stone marks the spot where his remains are interred.

Consequences more important than his victimization arose from his defeat, for the surrender at Saratoga was the unbottling of the jinn. With the loss of Ticonderoga and the Highlands, all the British had to show for a strenuous year's campaigning was the occupation of Philadelphia, a city empty of military or political significance, and Gates was free to reinforce Washington. More important, France reinforced America, and still more important, France soon dragged into the war the greater part of Europe.

On November 1, a fast sailing ship cleared Boston, and in thirty days cast anchor at Nantes. On December 4, Franklin had the news of Burgoyne's surrender, and the next day it rocked Paris to its political foundations. On the 6th, Louis XVI approved an alliance with the United States, and by the 17th it was known that France would support the insurrection. A treaty with the United States was signed on February 6, 1778, and on March 11, Great Britain and France were at war. Thus, at Saratoga, the sword of Damocles fell, not only on Great Britain, but, because of the fervor of the American Revolution, upon the whole of the Western World.

REFERENCES

[1] *A State of the Expedition from Canada as laid before the House of Commons,* Lieut.-General Burgoyne, Appendix, p. XXVI (1780).

[2] *Ibid.,* p. 6.

[3] *Ibid.,* Appendix, pp. XXI–XXII. (See also *Travels through the Interior Parts of America,* Captain Thomas Anburey, vol. I, p. 181.)

[4] Anburey (p. 188) writes: "Another great disadvantage which we experience in the prosecution of this war, and which the Americans avoid is, that we have to transport all our provisions with us, whereas they have magazines stored with great abundance, every thirty or forty miles . . . Added to this, the Americans are by much our superiors at wood fighting . . ."

[5] General Schuyler writes: "Nothing can surpass the impatience of the troops from the New England colonies to get to their firesides. Near three hundred of them arrived a few days ago, unable to do any duty; but as soon as I administered that grand specific, they instantly acquired health; and, rather than be detained a few days to cross Lake George, they undertook a march from here of two hundred miles with the greatest alacrity." (Quoted from *The American Revolution*, Sir George Otto Trevelyan, Part III, p. 101.)

[6] *A State of the Expedition, etc.*, p. 36.

[7] Captain Anburey writes: "This war is very different to the last in Germany; in this the life of an individual is sought with as much avidity as the obtaining a victory over an army of thousands" (vol. I, p. 293); and "In this action [Hubbard-town] I found all manual exercises is but an ornament" (p. 295).

[8] *Ibid.*, p. 30.

[9] Hadden's *Journal and Orderly Book*, James H. Hadden, p. 308 (1884).

[10] These figures are extracted from Burgoyne's *A State of the Expedition, etc.*, Appendix, pp. XXVII–XXVIII, dated July 1. More information may be obtained from Hadden's *Orderly Book*, pp. 44–46, and from Fonblanque's *Political and Military Episodes*, Appendix D.

[11] ". . . the brass train that was sent out upon this expedition, was perhaps the finest, and probably the most excellently supplied as to officers and private men, that has ever been allotted to second the operations of any army . . ." (*The Annual Register*, 1777, p. 143.) Stedman considered it too large, *The History of the Origin, Progress, and Termination of the American War* (vol. I, p. 337).

[12] Anburey, vol. I, p. 335.

[13] Stedman, vol. I, p. 331.

[14] Anburey writes: ". . . our employing Indians in the war is reprobated in England . . ." (vol. I, p. 248).

[15] *A State of the Expedition, etc.*, Appendix, pp. XII–XIII.

[16] *Ibid.*, p. 122.

[17] Count von Bernstorff, German ambassador to the U.S.A. in 1917, was descended from one of his daughters.

[18] *An Original and Authentic Journal of Occurrences during the late American War from its Commencement to the Year 1783*, R. Lamb, p. 135 (1809).

[19] Anburey, vol. I, pp. 180–181.

[20] See Hadden's *Orderly Book*, pp. 59–62.

[21] Burgoyne's *Orderly Book*, p. 17.

[22] "Congress ousted Schuyler, insulted Greene and Knox, reprimanded Stark, snubbed Benedict Arnold, court-martialled Sullivan, St. Clair, Wayne, and Matthews, and Promoted a cabal against Washington himself" (*The First American Civil War*, Henry Belcher, vol. II, p. 322).

[23] *Letters and Journals relating to the War of the American Revolution*, Baroness von Riedesel, p. 194 (1827).

[24] *Washington Letters*, Sparks, pp. 392–395.

[25] Quoted from *The Turning-Point of the Revolution*, Hoffman Nickerson, p. 144.

[26] Stedman, vol. I, p. 354. See also *History of America*, Justin Winsor, vol. VI, p. 313.

[27] See *The Annual Register,* 1777, p. 152. The difficulties of the country are clearly described in *The Gentlemen's Magazine* for October, 1777, in an article entitled "Some of the Circumstances which inevitably retard the Progress of the Northern Army through the uninhabited countries of America."

[28] *A History of the British Army,* Hon. J. W. Fortescue, vol. III, p. 226.

[29] Lamb's *Journal,* p. 144.

[30] *A State of the Expedition, etc.,* Appendix, p. XIX.

[31] *Ibid.,* p. 41.

[32] *Ibid.,* p. 14. See also *Fortescue,* vol. III, p. 226, and *Anburey,* vol. I, p. 340.

[33] Lieutenant Digby's *Journal,* p. 240.

[34] *The Writings of George Washington,* Worthington Chauncey Ford, vol. V, p. 459.

[35] *Ibid.,* vol. V, pp. 490 and 492. On the 24th, General Lincoln was also sent north (p. 511).

[36] *Ibid.,* vol. V, p. 515.

[37] *Ibid.,* vol. V, p. 506.

[38] *Ibid.,* vol. V, pp. 513–514.

[39] *Ibid.,* vol. V, pp. 518, 521.

[40] *Ibid.,* vol. VI, p. 2.

[41] *Ibid.,* vol. VI, p. 28.

[42] *Ibid.,* vol. VI, pp. 49, 52.

[43] *Ibid.,* vol. VI, pp. 504–505.

[44] *Ibid.,* vol. VI, p. 508.

[45] Certainly the finest light infantry of that day. Though frequently called "Morgan's Virginians" they were largely composed of men from the western frontier of Pennsylvania of Scotch-Irish stock. They marched exceedingly light, refusing all wheeled transport, and on one occasion covered 600 miles within three weeks. They were armed with a long-barreled flintlock rifle.

[46] See Hadden's *Orderly Book,* pp. 111–117; also *Diary of the American Revolution,* Frank Moore, vol. I, pp. 488–489, in which these orders are heavily criticized by the *Pennsylvania Evening Post* of August 28, 1777.

[47] *The Centennial History of the Battle of Bennington, 1877,* F. W. Coborn, p. 88.

[48] See *The Annual Register,* 1777, p. 159.

[49] *Life of Stark,* Edward Everett, p. 86.

[50] Moore's *Diary,* vol. I, p. 480. Extracted from the *Pennsylvania Evening Post,* September 4, 1777.

[51] *Ibid.,* vol. I, p. 491. (See also *The Annual Register,* 1777, p. 163.)

[52] *A State of the Expedition, etc.,* Appendix, pp. XXIV–XXVI.

[53] Burgoyne's *Orderly Book,* p. 123. Under date September 30, 1777, we read "that seven men of those who deserted have been scalped by the Enemy's Indians."

[54] For a full account of this murder see *The Annual Register,* 1777, p. 117.

[55] Washington Irving exculpates him in his *Life of George Washington,* vol. III, p. 191; so also does Miss MacCrea's brother (Fonblanque, p. 259). The Indians were quite impossible to restrain. General Heath quotes the following incident: "A British officer sending his waiter to a spring for some cool water, in a few minutes an Indian came in with the scalp of the waiter smoking in his hand" (*Memoirs of Major-General Heath,* p. 135, 1904).

[56] See Fonblanque, p. 224, and Lamb's *Journal,* p. 158.

[57] Quoted from the Introduction to Burgoyne's *Orderly Book,* p. XXII.

[58] See *Life of Joseph Brant, Thayendanega,* William L. Stone.

[59] See Stedman, vol. I, p. 335.

[60] Among the Indians lunatics were always treated with great respect.

[61] *The Narrative of Lieut.-General Sir William Howe*, p. 22.

[62] Hadden's *Orderly Book*, p. 143.

[63] *A State of the Expedition, etc.*, p. 78. For September 17, according to Hadden, Burgoyne's strength was 6,000, or in effectives, including officers, "nearly 5,000." (See his *Orderly Book*, p. 153.)

[64] *Life of Philip Schuyler*, B. J. Lossing, vol. II, p. 344.

[65] Wilkinson's *Memoirs*, vol. I, p. 245, quoted by Isaac N. Arnold in *Life of Benedict Arnold*, p. 173.

[66] Quoted from Arnold's *Arnold*, p. 29.

[67] Lamb's *Journal*, pp. 159-160.

[68] Fortescue, vol. III, p. 233.

[69] Lossing's *Schuyler*, vol. II, p. 348.

[70] Trevelyan, Part III, pp. 181-182.

[71] *The Annual Register*, 1777, p. 165.

[72] *A State of the Expedition, etc.*, Appendix, p. XLIX. (Trevelyan, p. 184.)

[73] Lamb's *Journal*, p. 162.

[74] *The Turning-Point of the Revolution*, Hoffman Nickerson, pp. 344-345.

[75] *Ibid.*, p. 352.

[76] Quoted from Arnold's *Arnold*, p. 198.

[77] See *Field Book of the Revolution*, B. J. Lossing, vol. I, p. 63.

[78] Anburey, vol. I, p. 391.

[79] *The American Revolution*, John Fiske, vol. I, p. 333. Sparks writes: "Gates was not on the field, nor did he leave his encampment during either of the battles of Bemis Heights" (*Life of Arnold*, p. 119).

[80] *Life and Treason of Benedict Arnold*, Jared Sparks, p. 118 (1835).

[81] Lamb's *Journal*, p. 166. Anburey (p. 413) also praises Burgoyne.

[82] Anburey does not altogether agree, he writes: "The incessant rain during our retreat was rather a favorable circumstance, for though it impeded the army in their march, and increased its difficulties, it served at the same time to retard, and in a great measure prevented, the pursuit of the enemy . . . The heavy rain offered another consolation . . . which was, in the case the enemy had attacked us, the fate of the day would have rested solely upon the bayonet" (vol. I, p. 401).

[83] *A State of the Expedition, etc.*, p. 126.

[84] *Ibid.*, Appendix, p. CIV.

[85] Fisher's *Journal*, p. 6.

[86] For details see Burgoyne's *Orderly Book*, pp. 132-151.

[87] *Ibid.*, p. 145.

[88] See *Life of Joseph Brant*, pp. 276 and XLVIII-XLIX.

[89] Stedman (vol. I, p. 352) writes: "General Gates's conduct in this melancholy event was peculiarly generous and humane. It is said that when the British troops piled their arms he would not suffer his own men to be witness to the sad spectacle."

[90] *The American Revolution*, Fiske, vol. I, p. 342.

[91] Fortescue, vol. III, pp. 241-242.

[92] Lamb's *Journal*, p. 183.

[93] Walpole records in his *Last Journals* (vol. II, p. 160): "Lord George Germaine owned that General Howe had defeated all his views by going to Maryland instead of waiting to join Burgoyne"; nevertheless he did all in his power to deny Burgoyne justice. (See *A State of the Expedition, etc.*, pp. 116-118.)

1778–1781

SYNOPSIS OF BACKGROUND EVENTS

A T Valley Forge the American Army passed a terrible winter.
Most fortunately, it was joined by Baron von Steuben, who
during the Seven Years' War had served on the personal staff of
Frederick the Great. An exceptionally able administrator, he was appointed inspector general by Washington, and at once set to work to
organize, discipline, and train all branches of the service.

Meanwhile events were progressing rapidly in Europe. After the
American-French alliance, the British Ministry offered the rebellious
colonies everything they had asked for short of independence. Next, a
peace commission, headed by the Earl of Carlisle, was dispatched to
Philadelphia, but it failed ridiculously. Early in June, 1778, Sir William
Howe was succeeded by Sir Henry Clinton, who on the 18th of that
month evacuated Philadelphia. Thereupon Washington broke up his
camp at Valley Forge and marched toward his enemy. On the 27th, contact between the two armies was made at Monmouth Court House, and
the following day an indecisive engagement was fought in such intense
heat that many men died of sunstroke. When the last British assault
failed, Clinton retired to Sandy Hook and from there transported his
army by sea to New York.

While this negative operation was in progress, Comte D'Estaing,
who had sailed from Toulon with 4,000 French soldiers, escorted by
twelve sail of the line and five frigates, was approaching the American
coast. On July 8 he arrived off the Delaware, and on the 12th was faced
by Lord Howe, who, though his fleet was inferior to D'Estaing's, at
once maneuvered for battle. Unfortunately for the British cause, the
French ships were scattered by a storm. Thereupon Howe retired to
New York to refit and D'Estaing put into Newport, where he remained

67

until November 4, when he sailed for Martinique. Meanwhile, Washington cantoned his army in a semicircle of forty miles' radius round New York.

Germaine once again entered the picture. Checkmated in the north, he decided, without abandoning the Hudson, to turn his attention to the south. First, he intended to conquer Florida and Georgia, then the Carolinas, and lastly Virginia, assuming that the northern states could then be reduced by isolation and exhaustion.

Clinton at once fell in with his idea, if only because it renewed the abortive campaign he and Cornwallis had carried out against Charleston in 1776. In June he received instructions from Germaine to dispatch 5,000 men to St. Lucia, and 3,000 to Georgia and Florida. Next, on November 27, he sent south 3,500 more under Lieutenant Colonel Archibald Campbell, who arrived safely at Tybee Island, at the mouth of the Savannah River, on December 23.

This new campaign was opened by a startling success; for on the 29th, Savannah was captured and within six weeks the conquest of Georgia was complete. Meanwhile General Lincoln had arrived at Charleston on the 19th. Not disposed to surrender South Carolina, in February, 1779, he assumed the offensive, but on March 3, General Prevost (who had recently been operating in Florida) defeated him at Briar Creek. This victory destroyed all possibility of the Americans recovering Georgia. Next, Prevost advanced on Charleston, appearing before it on May 5, when Lincoln marched to its relief. Because of the intense heat little of importance happened until September. On the 4th of that month D'Estaing returned from the West Indies with 6,000 French soldiers, and on the 13th demanded the surrender of Savannah. His demand being refused, he laid siege to the city, and on October 9 attempted an assault, which was repulsed at a loss of 837 officers and men killed and wounded—six times the number of the British casualties. Eleven days later he raised the siege and sailed for France.

Meanwhile, Clinton, at New York, was finding it impossible to draw Washington into an engagement south of the Highlands. On hearing of D'Estaing's failure he decided to leave General Knyphausen in command of New York, and to proceed south accompanied by Lord Cornwallis as his second-in-command. He set out on December 26 with 8,500 men, carried in ninety transports, convoyed by Admiral Arbuthnot and five ships of the line and nine frigates. He met with such bad weather that one ship, carrying Hessians, was driven across the Atlantic to be beached on the coast of Cornwall. The remainder of his fleet arrived at Tybee Island on January 30, 1780.

He landed on John's Island—about thirty miles south of Charleston—on February 11, but did not lay siege to that city—then held by Lincoln—until March 29. On May 12 it capitulated, and 7 general officers, 290 other officers, and 5,169 rank and file were made prisoners of war.

Believing South Carolina to be fully conquered, Clinton left Cornwallis in command with 8,500 men, and returned to New York early in June. Congress, learning of this disaster, without consulting Washington, appointed Gates to take command of the Southern Army, which he did on July 25, at once setting out on a 120-mile march to seize the British post at Camden, then held by Lord Rawdon.

Hastening up from Charleston with some 3,000 men, 800 of whom were prostrated by the intense heat, Cornwallis arrived at Camden on August 13, to face Gates at the head of some 3,000. On the 16th he vigorously attacked and routed him, capturing all his artillery, baggage, supplies, and nearly all his muskets and ammunition. Two days after this American defeat, Colonel Tarleton, commanding the British Legion, surprised Sumter in his camp at Fishing Creek, and at a loss of six killed and nine wounded, killed and wounded 150 of Sumter's men, took 300 prisoners, and dispersed the remainder of his force.

In spite of these several disasters, the tide of defeat was about to turn, its ebb being heralded by two events; the appearance of one of the greatest of small war leaders and a perfect little victory won by those natural soldiers, the backwoodsmen of the Alleghanies.

In place of Gates, Washington selected Nathanael Greene, then thirty-eight years old, to command the Southern Army. John Fiske informs us: "in every campaign since the beginning of the war [Greene] had been Washington's right arm." With him went Steuben as his second-in-command. When he arrived at Charlotte (Charlottetown) on December 4, he found that the strength of his army was 2,307, of whom 1,482 were present for duty and 800 sufficiently well equipped to fight.

Meanwhile, between the defeat of Gates and Greene's appointment, the second event occurred. Cornwallis had marched to Charlotte, and Clinton had sent General Leslie and 3,000 men to the Chesapeake to act under his orders, when, some thirty miles west of Charlotte, Major Ferguson, a gallant and skillful officer, with 1,100 men, mostly Tory militia, was surrounded at King's Mountain by an equal force of backwoodsmen, and virtually annihilated. Two hundred and twenty-four men were killed, 163 wounded, and 716 taken prisoners; and Ferguson himself was shot dead.

The news of this small though most decisive victory set ablaze the back settlements, and at once brought out the militias of North Carolina and Virginia. Cornwallis, now finding himself surrounded by a hostile people, at once retired to Winnsborough, ninety miles to the south of Charlotte, a movement which rendered co-operation with Leslie impossible. Therefore they were brought round by sea to join him.

While these changes were taking place, Greene was assuming the offensive; but as battle was out of the question, he wisely opened a guerrilla war. Thus the year 1780 ended. No sooner had the New Year opened than Clinton sent Benedict Arnold, now in the British service (his treason had occurred in September, 1780), and 1,600 men to the Chesapeake, to support Cornwallis. Washington countered by sending Lafayette and a slightly smaller force there to oppose him.

As Greene split up his small army into guerrilla bands, Cornwallis followed suit instead of concentrating his forces, which now numbered over 11,000 in all. On January 2 he sent out Tarleton and his Legion —1,000 strong—to mop up Morgan and an equal force of men then operating in the vicinity of Ferguson's defeat. These two forces met at Cowpens on January 17, where Morgan, by means of an extremely able tactical distribution, at a loss of 12 killed and 60 wounded, all but wiped out his enemy, for Tarleton lost 100 killed, 229 wounded, and 600 unwounded prisoners. Thereupon Morgan fell back to the Catawba River, which Cornwallis crossed on February 1. Then, deciding to abandon South Carolina, Cornwallis moved northeast to Hillsborough to rest his exhausted troops.

Meanwhile Greene and Steuben, having built up a respectable little army of from 4,500 to 5,500 men, set out to follow Cornwallis's track. On March 2 the two armies came into contact on the Haw River, where a series of maneuvers took place which, on the 15th, led to the Battle of Guilford Court House. In this battle the Americans were numerically superior, for whereas Greene had 4,441 men present for duty, Cornwallis could bring but a little over half that number into action. Nevertheless, in spite of their numerical superiority, the militia, good as partisans, again proved their weakness when called upon to act as regulars, for soon after the battle was engaged they were seized by panic and bolted from the field. Greene then found himself faced by a numerically equal foe, more highly disciplined than his own men. Consequently, not wishing to risk a complete defeat, after some severe fighting he fell back behind the Haw River, having lost 78 killed, 183 wounded, and 1,046 in missing. Cornwallis's losses were not light, for they amounted in all to 532 officers and men.

Though Greene lost this battle he won the campaign, because Cornwallis's losses were so great that he now decided to abandon the interior and march to the coast at Wilmington—some 200 miles southeast of Guilford Court House. Rawdon, then at Camden, was left to confront Greene, who shortly after his defeat set out for South Carolina to regain that state. These two decisions bring us to the threshold of the Yorktown campaign, the greatest disaster which befell Great Britain from the commencement of her imperial history.

CHAPTER III

THE BATTLE OF THE CHESAPEAKE AND THE
SIEGE OF YORKTOWN, 1781

O NCE the French-American alliance was cemented, war ceased
to be purely a matter of land operation and became mainly a
matter of sea operation. This change became still more pronounced
when on April 12, 1779, Spain allied herself to France and two months
later declared war on England. From then onward, except in the case
of North America, England was forced to be on the defensive, and by
surrendering the initiative to Spain and France—which, in December,
1780, were joined by Holland—took a certain road to eventual disaster.

Of all men watching this change, Washington most clearly saw that
his cause would in the end prove a lost one unless command of the sea
could be gained, if only for a brief period. As early as July 15, 1780, he
had sent by Lafayette to the Marquis de Rochambeau a "Memorandum
for concerting a plan of operations with the French army" which read
in part: "In any operation, and under all circumstances, a decisive naval
superiority is to be considered as a fundamental principle, and the basis
upon which every hope of success must ultimately depend." [1] Then again,
six months later, when sending Lieutenant John Laurens to France, he
wrote to him a long letter outlining the situation at that moment—
indeed a desperate one—and among other things said:

That, next to a loan of money, a constant naval superiority on these
coasts is the object most interesting. This would instantly reduce the
enemy to a difficult defensive, and, by removing all prospect of extending
their acquisitions, would take away the motives for prosecuting the war.
Indeed it is not to be conceived how they could subsist a large force in

72

this country, if we had the command of the seas, to interrupt the regular transmission of supplies from Europe . . . With respect to us, it seems to be one of *two* deciding points; and it appears, too, to be the interest of our allies, abstracted from the immediate benefits to this country, to transfer the naval war to America.[2]

For a long time the French could not or would not see this, mainly, I think, because they came into the war on moral rather than on strategical grounds, to support revolution in general rather than the American revolutionaries in particular. "Liberty" was beginning to bubble on the lips of the many; nevertheless few as yet realized that this froth was the first symptom of the general insanity, which, within six years of this war's closing, was to sweep over France, and from France into the rest of Europe. This was the age in which the writings of Montesquieu, Voltaire, Rousseau, Diderot, and D'Alembert were intoxicating the intellectuals. This was the age in which newly born humanity was loved in the abstract, and in which enthusiasm for liberty was so great that no one noticed that the shadow it cast was in form of the guillotine. Yet all this worship of Liberty was as nothing without French naval power to implement it, and when 1781 dawned Washington's position was indeed desperate.

The year opened with a mutiny of the Pennsylvania line.[3] Then the Jersey line followed the example of the Pennsylvanians,[4] while in the south General Greene reported that his army was "literally naked."[5] Such was the situation Washington faced during the first three weeks of the New Year. His eventual victory was largely due to the divided nature of the British command, for though Sir Henry Clinton was commander in chief in America, he was nevertheless tied to the apron strings of Germaine—3,000 miles away. Also, because of distance and the length of time it took to communicate with Lord Cornwallis, who was under his orders, his link with this general was extremely slight. On the top of this, though all combinations depended on naval power, Arbuthnot, who commanded the British Fleet in American waters, was not under his orders nor Germaine's. On April 30, Clinton wrote to Germaine bitterly complaining of this, and then added: "For I must be free to own to Your Lordship, that I cannot place any Confidence in Vice Admiral Arbuthnot, who, from Age, Temper, and Inconsistency of Conduct, is really so little to be depended on . . ."[6] As in 1777, this lack of unity in command was the direct cause of the final British disaster.

To begin with, Germaine, assuming that the Carolinas had been conquered and that Greene's army was no more than a "contemptible" rabble, wrote to Clinton on March 7 saying: "I doubt not You will avail Yourself of his [Washington's] Weakness, and Your own great Superiority, to send a considerable Force to the Head of the Chesapeak as soon as the Season will permit Operations to be carried on in that Quarter . . ." [7] His aim, now that the Carolinas were assumed to have collapsed, was to push the war in Virginia. This was also Cornwallis's idea, for on April 18 he wrote to Germaine in the same strain, saying: "I take the liberty of giving it as my opinion, that a serious attempt upon Virginia would be the most solid plan, Because successfull operations might not only be attended with important consequences there; but would tend to the security of South Carolina, and ultimately to the submission of North Carolina." [8]

Clinton, adopting a diametrically opposite point of view, wrote to Cornwallis on the 13th: "except as a visitor, I shall not probably move to Chesapeak, unless Washington goes thither in great force." [9] Then, ten days later, he wrote to Germaine: "But I must beg leave, my Lord, in this place to observe that I cannot agree to the opinion given me by Lord Cornwallis in his last Letter, that the Chesapeak should become the Seat of War, even (if necessary) at the Expence of abandoning New York; as I must ever regard this post to be of the utmost Consequence, whilst it is thought necessary to hold Canada, with which, and the Northern Indians, it is so materially connected." [10] Undoubtedly this was a correct appreciation; nevertheless this letter crossed with one written to him by Germaine on May 5, in which Germaine mentioned "the vast Importance of the Possession of Virginia." [11]

While Cornwallis was marching towards Wilmington, Clinton had various conversations with Major General William Phillips—whom we first met under Burgoyne—which were destined to have an important influence on the campaign. These referred "to a station for the protection of the King's ships," Clinton suggesting to Cornwallis that there was "no place so proper as York Town," which he considered might be held by "one thousand men." Also he mentioned Old Point Comfort at the mouth of the James River. [12] Finally he decided to send Phillips south to reinforce Arnold. Accordingly that general and 2,600 men set out on March 10 and arrived on the Chesapeake sixteen days later. [13] Meanwhile Washington, who as early as February 6 had considered

the possibility that Clinton might establish a post in Virginia, on the
15th of that month decided to send Lafayette and 1,200 men "towards
the Head of Elk River" to operate against Arnold, whose capture
"would be an event particularly agreeable" and of "immense importance." [14]

Next, hearing of Cornwallis's arrival at Wilmington, Clinton, on
April 26, wrote to Phillips, pointing out that this unexpected move
had considerably changed the complexion of affairs, and that "all operations to the northward must probably give place" to Cornwallis's.
Further, that before he had heard from Cornwallis, he had hoped "that
his Lordship would have been in a condition to have spared a considerable part of his army from Carolina for the operations in Chesapeak." He informed Phillips that he proposed to send him a further
detachment, to render him strong enough to co-operate with Cornwallis
in Carolina. Then, suddenly, he switched to quite a different operation,
"which if successful would be most solidly decisive in its consequences."
This was to transfer the war to Virginia, Maryland, and Pennsylvania
and subdue those states. He wrote: "but the inhabitants of Pennsylvania
on both sides of the Susquehannah, York, Lancaster, Chester, and the
Peninsula between Chesapeak and Delaware, are represented to me to
be friendly. There or thereabouts I think this experiment should now
be tried." [15]

Meanwhile Cornwallis, then in camp "near Wilmington," put forward
a similar suggestion, for on April 10 he wrote as follows to Clinton: "I
cannot help expressing my wishes, that the Chesapeak may become the
Seat of War, even (if necessary) at the expence of abandoning New
York; untill Virginia is in a manner subdued, our hold of the Carolinas
must be difficult, if not precarious." [16] This view, as we have seen, he
communicated on the 18th to Germaine, with whom he corresponded
directly. Then, on the 23rd, in a letter to Clinton he hinted at "a junction with General Phillips," and the next day informed him that he intended to join him, enclosing a copy of a letter to Phillips in which he
said: "Send every possible intelligence to me by the Cypher I inclose,
and make every Movement in your power to facilitate our Meeting
which must be somewhere near Petersburg, with safety to your Army." [17]

As it would have taken weeks to get a reply, and as he had made up
his mind, he set out on a march of 223 miles to join Phillips and Arnold.
Arriving at Petersburg on May 20, he learnt that Phillips had died of

fever on the 13th. There, on the 24th, he received a copy of the "Conversations" Clinton had had with Phillips, also Clinton's letter to Phillips of April 26,[18] as well as his instructions to him of March 10, in which Phillips was bidden to occupy Yorktown or Old Point Comfort, should he be in a position to do so without risk.[19] Meanwhile, Clinton, knowing nothing of Cornwallis's march north, had written to Germaine on May 20th: "But should Lord Cornwallis persist in his intention of joining Major-General Phillips . . . I shall be under some apprehension for every part of South Carolina, except Charlestown, and even for Georgia . . ."[20] He wrote again on the 22nd, expressing his belief that such a move would be "replete with the worst Consequences to our Southern Possessions, in their present State."[21] Next, having received Cornwallis's letter of April 24, on May 29 he wrote to him saying: "I cannot therefore conceal from your Lordship the apprehensions I felt . . . that you should probably attempt to effect a junction with Major-General Phillips . . . I shall dread what may be the consequence of your Lordship's move, unless a reinforcement arrives very soon in South Carolina . . . "; and then adds "I have in the most pressing terms requested the Admiral's [Arbuthnot] attention to the Chesapeak, having repeatedly told him, that should the enemy possess it even for forty-eight hours your Lordship's operations there may be exposed to most imminent danger."[22]

When this correspondence is considered, it should be borne in mind that, between posting and receipt, not only days but weeks and sometimes months intervened; consequently, more often than not, this seesaw of letters confused the operations they were intended to assist. The truth is that in this war there was no actual commander in chief. Cornwallis was to all intents and purposes his own supreme head, therefore he had to decide for himself; yet, as we shall see, he failed to realize this.

On entering Petersburg he found himself at the head of 7,000 men, with Lafayette and 1,200 watching him from Richmond. The marquis was instructed by General Greene to take over the command of all troops in Virginia;[23] but, as they were few in number, all he could do, as he himself says, was "to skirmish" and "not to engage too far."[24] Therefore, on the 27th, he evacuated Richmond and headed for Fredericksburg, so that he might draw Cornwallis north and simultaneously augment his own strength. Meanwhile Cornwallis, realizing that he was not strong enough to conquer Virginia, had the day before written to Clinton saying that, after having dislodged his enemy and destroyed all stores in the neighborhood of Richmond, he intended to move to Williamsburg, and, as he wrote, "keep myself unengaged from operations, which might interfere with your plan for the Campaign untill I have the Satisfaction of hearing from you . . . At present I am inclined to think well of York; The objections to Portsmouth are, that it cannot be made strong, without an Army to defend it, that it is remarkably unhealthy, and can give no protection to a Ship of the Line." [25] Thereupon he crossed the James River, and on the 27th camped near White Oak Swamp, and, slowly following Lafayette, arrived in the neighborhood of Hanover Junction on June 1. On the 4th he sent his mounted units under Simcoe and Tarleton to destroy stores at Charlotteville,[26] where they nearly caught Jefferson. Then, having heard that Wayne and 1,000 men had reinforced Lafayette, he retired on the 15th from Elk Head—via Richmond—to Williamsburg, followed by his enemy, who by now had been reinforced also by Steuben.

Arriving at Williamsburg on the 26th, Cornwallis found there awaiting him a letter from Clinton dated June 11, which informed him that, as Washington was about to lay siege to New York, he should send forthwith to that city some 3,000 men.[27] Once this force was detached, Cornwallis decided that as he would not be sufficiently strong to hold Yorktown and Gloucester, he had better retire to Portsmouth, from where he could comfortably proceed south. Therefore, on the 30th, he informed Clinton that, as Lord Rawdon was sick, he was "willing to repair to Charlestown." [28] This meant the abandonment of the Virginia campaign.

Not awaiting Clinton's reply, which would have taken many days to arrive, Cornwallis set out from Williamsburg to Jamestown on his way to Portsmouth. On July 6, Lafayette, then following him up, was so severely handled by the British rear guard at Green Springs that Tarleton is of opinion that, had Cornwallis turned with his whole army on his adversary,[29] in all probability he would have annihilated him. However, except for a long distance raid on Bedford,[30] carried out by Tarleton, nothing but letter writing occupied the following month.

On the 8th, Clinton wrote to Cornwallis saying that the 3,000 men he had asked for need no longer be sent, and that Old Point Comfort should be occupied in order to secure Hampton Roads.[31] Also, on the same day, Cornwallis wrote to Clinton suggesting the abandonment of the campaign.[32] Clinton wrote to him again on the 11th, pointing out the absolute necessity of holding a station on the Chesapeake for ships of the line, and ended by saying: "I beg leave to request that you will without loss of time examine Old Point Comfort and fortify it." [33] The next day Admiral Graves—who had replaced Arbuthnot—made a similar request.[34] Then, receiving Germaine's letter of May 2—ordering him to hold fast to Virginia—as well as Cornwallis's letter of June 30, Clinton wrote on the 15th to the latter that he was mortified to hear he had crossed the James and retired to Portsmouth.[35] Meanwhile, Cornwallis sent Lieutenant Sutherland, an engineer, to examine Old Point Comfort. As he reported it unsuitable, Cornwallis wrote to Admiral Graves on the 26th that "I shall immediate seize and fortify the posts of York and Gloucester." [36] This decision he communicated to Clinton the next morning.[37]

In 1781 both Yorktown on the southern and Gloucester on the northern bank of the York River were but villages, the first consisting of "about 60 houses" and the second of twenty.[38] Cornwallis set out to occupy them a few days after he had written to Clinton.

Commenting on this correspondence, Fortescue writes:

The truth was that Clinton, Cornwallis and Germaine were all of them in favour of a campaign in the Middle Colonies. Clinton . . . wished to await the arrival of reinforcements and of a covering fleet, and meanwhile secure a naval base. Cornwallis was for evacuating New York, transferring the principal base of the British to the Chesapeake, and opening the campaign there at once. Germaine desired to combine both designs after some incomprehensible fashion of his own . . .[39]

And the result was a repetition of the muddle of 1777, when by favoring two variant plans Germaine precipitated the disaster of Saratoga.

Meanwhile, Washington's idea was still to drive the English out of New York. His main forces, posted at White Plains, were reinforced on July 6, 1781, by Lieutenant General Jean-Baptiste Donatian de Vimeur, Comte de Rochambeau, aged fifty-five, who brought with him four strong regiments of foot, a battalion of artillery, and the Duke de Lauzun's Legion. He had sailed from France on May 2, 1780, and had disembarked his army at Newport, Rhode Island, on July 11 of that year.

To Washington this reinforcement was most welcome, as was also the arrival of a small squadron under Admiral Count de Barras, who brought with him the good news that the Count de Grasse was on his way from France with a powerful fleet. Washington set out from his headquarters at New Windsor (Newburg) and met Rochambeau at Wethersfield (near Hartford, Connecticut) on May 22. There they drew up a dispatch for de Grasse, which would find him at Cape François (St. Domingo) on his arrival there. In it they suggested that he either sail for Sandy Hook, in order to support an attack on New York, or else to the Chesapeake. Washington favored the first and Rochambeau, somewhat doubtfully, the second destination.[40] On the following day a dispatch was sent to the Chevalier de la Luzerne to pass this information on to de Grasse. Doubt, however, seems to have been in the air, for, on June 1, de la Luzerne wrote to Rochambeau as follows:

The situation of the Marquis de Lafayette and that of General Greene is most embarrassing, since Lord Cornwallis has joined the English division of the Chesapeake. If Virginia is not helped in time, the English will have reached the goal which they have assigned to themselves . . . they will soon have really conquered the Southern States.[41]

That same day Washington wrote to Greene:

I have lately had an interview with Count de Rochambeau at Weathersfield. Our affairs were very attentively considered in every point of view, and it was finally determined to make an attempt on New York with its present garrison, in preference to a southern operation, as we had not the decided command of the water.[42]

Meanwhile, on May 27, Washington had written to the President of Congress informing him of the impending New York operation;[43] but the express carrying it was captured by the English. Clinton learning "of the enterprise in agitation . . . made a requisition of part of the troops under Lord Cornwallis's command in Virginia, and directed that they should be sent to New York."[44] Such was the origin of his letter of June 11.

Early in June, Washington received a letter from Rochambeau informing him that news of de Grasse had been received, and that he would appear in American waters about midsummer. Also he learned from Lafayette that there could be no doubt that Cornwallis had abandoned North Carolina. These developments persuaded the allied commanders to reconsider the question of how best to utilize the approaching fleet and their respective land forces for the relief of the South.

For a moment I must turn to de Grasse. Late in March he had sailed from Brest and made for the French colony of Haiti. Shortly after setting out he sent word to Rochambeau of his sailing, and on his arrival at Haiti secured 3,000 soldiers and a large sum of money. Then he sailed north through the Bahama Channel, as it was an unfrequented passage. Admiral Sir George Rodney, then commanding the British West Indies squadron, not suspecting that de Grasse would take his whole fleet northward, sent Admiral Sir Samuel Hood with only fourteen sail of the line to follow him up, while he himself returned to England to recuperate his health.

Meanwhile, on receipt of Rochambeau's letter, informing him of de Grasse's expected arrival, Washington, on June 13, replied as follows:

Your Excellency will be pleased to recollect that New York was looked upon by us as the only practicable object under present circumstances; but should we be able to secure a *naval superiority,* we may perhaps find others more practicable and equally advisable. If the frigate should not have sailed, I wish you to explain this matter to the *Count of Grasse* . . . In the letter which was written to the minister from Weathersfield, in which he was requested to urge the *Count* to come this way with his *whole fleet,* Sandy Hook was mentioned as the most desirable point . . . Should the *British fleet* not be there, he could follow them to the Chesapeak . . .[45]

The upshot of this change in point of view was that on July 20, Rochambeau asked Washington for a "definitive plan of Campaign."[46] Washington had three possible schemes in mind:

(1) Should Clinton reinforce Cornwallis, to attack New York.

(2) Should Cornwallis reinforce Clinton, to attack Virginia.

(3) Then, if conditions were favorable, to besiege Charleston.·

He adhered to the first plan until August 1, at which time all should have been ready to set on foot operations against New York. However the states again failed to support him. " . . . Not more than half the number [of men] asked of them have joined the Army and of 6,200 . . . continuously called for to be with the Army by the 15th of last Month, only 176 had arrived from Connecticut . . . " "Therefore," he continued, "I turned my views more seriously (than I had done before) to an operation to the Southward and, in consequence, sent to make inquiry, indirectly, of the principal Merchants to Eastward what number, and what time, Transports could be provided to convey a force to the Southward, if it should be found necessary to change our plan." [47]

Next, on the 11th, he heard that Clinton had been reinforced by a draft of 2,880 Germans, and three days later he received a dispatch from Count de Barras "announcing the departure of the Count de Grasse from Cape François with between 25 and 29 Sail of the line and 3,200 land Troops on the 3rd Instant for Chesapeake bay . . . Matters having now come to a crisis . . . I was obliged . . . to give up all idea of attacking New York; and instead thereof to remove the French Troops and a detachment from the American Army to the Head of Elk to be transported to Virginia for the purpose of co-operating with the force from the West Indies . . ." [48] The next day he wrote to Lafayette "to prevent if possible the Retreat of Cornwallis towards Carolina," [49] and on the morrow heard from him that Cornwallis had landed at "York and Gloucester Towns" on the 6th. [50] Whereupon a letter jointly signed by Washington and Rochambeau was sent to de Grasse notifying him that a Franco-American Army would march to the Chesapeake, and asking him on his arrival to send up to Elk River all the transports he could spare in order to carry the French and American troops down the bay. [51]

Speed now controlled everything, and a number of rapid measures were taken to prepare for what was destined to be one of the most epoch-shattering as well as epoch-making marches in the history of war.

Leaving old General Heath and some 3,000 men at West Point to amuse Clinton and his 16,000, on Monday the 20th the allied armies—2,000 American and 4,000 French soldiers—began to cross the Hudson at King's Ferry, some twelve miles south of West Point. [52] From there the advance was made in such a way that Clinton was induced to believe that these forces were making for Staten Island in order to threaten New York from the south. [53]

The next day Washington issued a "Circular Letter to the States," informing them of his plan, and pointing out that it would give them "the fairest opportunity to reduce the whole British force in the south, and to ruin their boasted expectations in that quarter." [54] Then the allies set out on their 400-mile march, the Americans taking the river road, and the French the way by Northcastle, Pine's Bridge, and Crompond.

On the 29th, when the Americans bivouacked at Brunswick and the French at Bullion's Tavern, it was no longer possible to hide their destination, so from there onward the march became an open movement.[55] The following day, Washington and Rochambeau rode on ahead of their men to Philadelphia, entering that city among "the universal acclamations of its citizens." From Philadelphia, having heard nothing further of de Grasse, Washington wrote to Lafayette on September 2:

But, my dear Marquis, I am distressed beyond expression to know what has become of the Count de Grasse, and for fear that the English fleet, by occupying the Chesapeake (towards which my last accounts say they were steering) may frustrate all our flattering prospects in that quarter. . . . Adieu, my dear Marquis, if you get anything now from any quarter, send it I pray you, *on the* spur of speed for I am almost all impatience and anxiety . . .[56]

On the 5th, having halted his troops at Elk Head, Washington at length heard of "the safe arrival of the Count de Grasse in the Bay of Chesapeake with 28 Sail of the line, and four frigates, with 3,000 land Troops . . ."[57] Thereupon, Washington left Philadelphia for Head of Elk, and by the 18th the troops were being carried down the Chesapeake to the landings nearest to Williamsburg where, on the 26th, all the forces of Washington, Rochambeau, and Lafayette were concentrated.

The *day* before this general assembly took place, Admiral Hood on his way north stood into Chesapeake Bay, and, on seeing or hearing nothing of de Grasse, made for New York.[58] There he joined Admiral Graves, who had at his disposal five ships of the line. He, also, had heard nothing of de Grasse, but informed Hood that de Barras, with eight sail of the line and a convoy of eighteen transports, had sailed from Rhode Island on the previous day. So, on the 31st, the two fleets put to sea under Graves—the senior admiral—and stood out for the Chesapeake to intercept Barras. Unfortunately for Graves, de Grasse had sailed into Chesapeake Bay the day before.

On his arrival, de Grasse at once disembarked his 3,000 soldiers, who were under the command of the Marquis de St. Simon, and ordered his transports to proceed up the Chesapeake to the Head of Elk. Then he cast anchor in Lynnhaven Bay, immediately to the west of Cape Henry, which lies about ten miles south of Cape Charles and is separated from it by a shoal called the Middle Ground. There he was when, at 8 A.M. on September 5, one of his lookout frigates signaled a fleet approaching. At first it was thought to be Barras, but soon nineteen sail of the line [59] were reported, from which de Grasse realized that it must be Admiral Graves. The wind was then north-northeast.

At noon, with the ebb tide, the French ships slipped their cables and got under way; but as many had to make several tacks in order to clear Cape Henry, their line was late in forming or, as Stedman writes, they were compelled to "form the line promiscuously as they could get up." [60] It was then, as Admiral Hood, who was leading the British van, says,

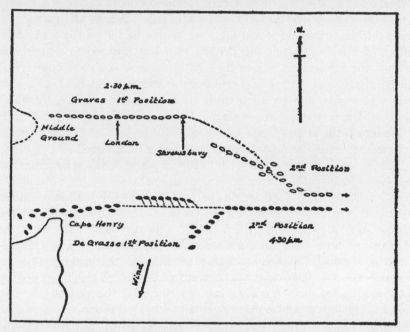

7. Battle of the Chesapeake, September 5, 1781

Graves should have attacked. He writes: "Soon after, they [the French] began to come out in a line of battle ahead, but by no means regular and connected, which afforded the British fleet a most glorious opening for making a close attack to manifest advantage, but it was not embraced." [61] According to Corbett, this is correct comment, for, he writes: "Graves, instead of signalling 'General Chase' or one of its modified forms, so as to attack the French before they could form, continued to stand in shore, so as to extend his line parallel with theirs." [62] However, Graves himself informs us: "My aim was to get close to form parallel, extend with them, and attack all together; to this end I kept on until the van drew so near a shoal called the Middle Ground as to be in danger." [63] He thereupon signaled for the whole fleet to wear together, by which it was put about on the same tack with the enemy, when Hood's division became the rear. This took place at 1 P.M. An hour later, the French van was three miles to the south of the *London*—Graves's flagship—and abreast the British center. Then, in order to allow it to come abreast of his, "At 2.30 P.M. Graves made the signal for the van ship (the *Shrewsbury*) to lead more to starboard—towards the enemy. As each ship in succession would take her course to follow the leader, the effect of this was to put the British on a line inclined to that of the enemy, the van nearest, and as the signal was renewed three-quarters of an hour later—at 3.17—this angle became still more marked . . . This was the original and enduring cause of a lamentable failure, by which seven of the rear ships, in an inferior force undertaking to attack, never came into battle at all." [64]

Then occurred the fatal misunderstanding of the signals.

When, on July 2, Arbuthnot left for England, Graves continued to use his signals and instructions with additional ones of his own, and it seems probable that Hood and his officers had not had sufficient time to assimilate them. Two were now flown simultaneously—namely, "close action" and "line ahead at half a cable," with the result that, while the British van bore down on the French, the British center and rear, instead of closing, followed it and so accentuated the distance between themselves and their enemy's center and rear. This happened at 3.45 P.M., when both the vans became engaged; the rest of the two fleets to all intents and purposes remained out of action. At 4.27 P.M. the signal of "line ahead" was hauled down; yet it was not until 5.20 P.M. that Hood at length bore down on the French, who by bearing up avoided close engagement. At sunset, the battle ended, the British having lost 90 killed and 246 wounded to the French 221.

That night Graves used his best endeavors to keep up the line, so as to renew the action in the morning; but the 6th was calm all day, and on the 7th and 8th the enemy bore to windward and refused to engage. On the 9th, Hood wrote: ". . . the French carried a press of sail, which proved to me beyond a doubt that de Grasse had other views than fighting." [65] The next day when he gained the Chesapeake he found that Barras and his fleet had arrived with eight line-of-battle ships and had brought with him the siege artillery and stores indispensable for the siege of Yorktown. This augmentation of his enemy's strength persuaded Graves to call a council of war on the 13th. Following the decision of the Council, the fleet returned to New York, arriving there on the 19th.

This indecisive and fatal engagment spelt the doom of Cornwallis, and consequently must take its place among the decisive battles of the world. As Captain Mahan, quoting Captain Thomas White, points out:

Had Admiral Graves succeeded in capturing "Barras's squadron" it would have greatly paralysed the besieging army [it had the siege train on board], if it would not have prevented its operations altogether; it would have put the two fleets nearly on an equality in point of numbers, would have arrested the progress of the French arms . . . and might possibly have created such a spirit of discord between the French and Americans as would have sunk the latter into the lowest depths of despair . . .[66]

Whatever Graves's failure, it cannot be denied that the outcome of the engagement was due also to Rodney's miscalculation of de Grasse's strength, as well as to Hood's pigheadedness during the battle.[67] In the eyes of Graves, "the fiasco was entirely due to the fact that his captains, and particularly Hood and his squadron," wrote Corbett, "were too hide-bound in the stereotyped tradition of the old Fighting Instructions to interpret his signals intelligently, or to act with a reasonable initiative." Then Corbett comments:

Why Hood of all people did not show more initiative, it is difficult to understand, but he chose to keep the line as it was formed, obliquely to the enemy. It may be he hoped still to see a concentration of de Grasse's centre and van, or that he was so much out of heart and temper at the chance that had been missed that he would do nothing but obey the order for the line literally . . .
. . . Had Hood but acted with one-half of the spirit that Nelson showed at St. Vincent, would de Grasse have been able to get back to the Chesapeake? And if he had not, what then?[68]

Four days before Admiral Graves sailed from Sandy Hook, Clinton wrote to Cornwallis: "I cannot well ascertain Mr. Washington's real intentions by this move of his army."[69] Not until September 2 did he at length discover what had happened, when he wrote to Cornwallis:

By intelligence which I have this day received, it would seem that Mr. Washington is moving an army to the southward, with an appearance of haste, and gives out that he expects the cooperation of a considerable French armament. Your Lordship, however, may be assured, that if this should be the case, I shall either endeavour to reinforce the army under your command by all the means within the compass of my power, or make every possible diversion in your favour.[70]

This same day Cornwallis also discovered his predicament, for he sent a cypher message to Clinton stating: "Comte de Grasse's fleet is within the Capes of the Chesapeak." [71]

True to his word, Clinton carried out a diversion. He sent Arnold to New London, and there, on the 6th, Arnold stormed two forts. The same day Clinton sent a dispatch to Cornwallis, saying: ". . . I think the best way to relieve you, is to join you as soon as possible, with all the Force that can be spared from hence, which is about 4,000 men. They are already embarked, and will proceed the Instant I receive Information from the Admiral that we may venture . . ." [72] It was a vain hope, for already the Battle of the Chesapeake had put a stop to the carrying out of this proposal. Not until six weeks later did this expedition sail.

When this proposal was made, Cornwallis lay at Yorktown with 7,000 men, Lafayette facing him with 5,000. Obviously Cornwallis could have attacked him and in all probability have beaten him before the arrival of Washington and Rochambeau. For not having done so, he has been severely censured by both Tarleton and Stedman, and also for not having withdrawn into North Carolina. [73] Even as late as the 16th and 17th, when he hinted at a withdrawal and informed Clinton that his position was desperate, he could have slipped away. [74] That he did not is difficult to explain, because he must have appreciated the seriousness of the naval situation. On the 29th he received a dispatch from Clinton saying that he hoped to set out on October 5 with a fleet of twenty-three sail. [75] Later, Clinton informed him that "repairs of the fleet" would detain him, and still later that he hoped to "pass the bar by the 12th of October." [76]

While these delays were taking place, in the enemy's camp all was activity. On the 17th, Washington had already visited de Grasse, [77] and on the 25th he successfully induced him to remain in Chesapeake Bay until Yorktown had surrendered, and not to proceed north, as he had intimated he intended to do. [78] On the 27th he assembled his army at Williamsburg. It consisted of 16,645 men [79] organized into three divisions under Lincoln, Lafayette, and Steuben. The following day the army advanced to within two miles of its goal, and on the 29th, as the anonymous American chaplain informs us, "Our troops lay on their arms the last night, and expected an attack from the enemy; but they did not disturb us." [80] Thus the famous siege opened.

The positions of Yorktown and Gloucester were not favorable to defense without command of the sea, and it cannot be doubted that Cornwallis would have abandoned them had he but realized, as he should have, that naval supremacy had for the time being passed to the French.[81]

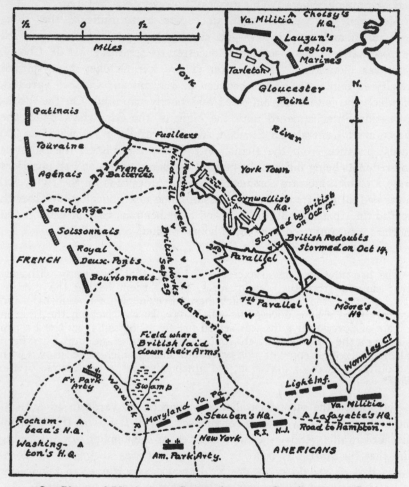

8. Siege of Yorktown, September 30—October 17, 1781

Beyond the immediate defenses of Yorktown lay an outer ring of works which Cornwallis, on receipt of Clinton's letter of September 24 notifying him that he would sail south on October 5, most foolishly abandoned [82] during the night of the 29th. The next day they were occupied by his enemy.[83] Thereupon Washington, suspecting that Cornwallis was attempting to escape, urged de Grasse to pass up the York River and so prevent him from seeking shelter between the Pamunky and Mattapony Rivers.[84] This request, however, was refused.

Meanwhile, to render such an escape more difficult, the Duke de Lauzun and his Legion—300 cavalry and 300 infantry—as well as 700 marines, were sent to Gloucester to reinforce M. de Choisy, who was blockading that position. There, on October 3, a spirited cavalry encounter took place between de Lauzun and Colonel Tarleton, in which the latter was unhorsed and nearly captured. On the Yorktown side little happened until the night of the 6th, when, under the direction of General von Steuben, the first parallel was opened at 600 yards' distance from the British left. Three days later, the batteries and redoubts being finished, "a general discharge of 24- and 18-pounders and of 10-inch mortars commenced by the Americans on the right, and continued all night without intermission. The next morning, the French opened their batteries on the left, and a tremendous roar of cannon and mortars was continued for 6 or 8 hours without ceasing." [85]

Of the 10th, Washington wrote:

The fire now became so excessively heavy, that the enemy withdrew their cannon from their embrasures, placed them behind the merlins [that part of the parapet which lies between two embrasures], and scarcely fired a shot during the whole day. In the evening the Charon frigate of forty-four guns was set on fire by a hot ball from the French battery on the left, and entirely consumed. Her guns and stores had been taken out. By the report of a deserter, our shells, which were thrown with the utmost degree of precision, did much mischief in the course of the day.[86]

Next night the second parallel was opened 300 yards in advance of the first, and fifty-two pieces commenced firing. It was at this moment that Cornwallis received Clinton's letter of September 30, informing him that his start was delayed. Thereupon it was suggested to Cornwallis that he should carry the Yorktown garrison over to Gloucester and attempt to cut his way out, as Washington feared he might do. According to Tarleton this was a feasible operation. He wrote:

The army had, exclusive of the navy, many boats and much small craft, which, properly manned, could transport twelve hundred infantry at a trip, and with the assistance of the navy, above two thousand. No difficulties occur, therefore, to impede a great part of the troops withdrawing in the night, embarking, crossing the river, and destroying the boats after the passage. Gloucester was not besieged; Brigadier de Choisy only blockaded that post with the Duke de Lauzun's legion (three hundred and fifty men) seven hundred marines and twelve hundred militia . . .[87]

This was Cornwallis's last chance of escape, yet for some unknown reason he did not take it, and that day (October 11) he wrote to Clinton: "We have lost about seventy men, and many of our works are considerably damaged; with such works on disadvantageous ground against so powerful an attack we cannot hope to make a very long resistance."[88]

On the 12th and 13th the bombardment continued, and as a direct approach was held up by Redoubts No. 9 and No. 10—on the extreme British left—the allied command decided to carry them by assault. This was done on the night of the 14th, No. 9 being stormed by the French and No. 10 by the Americans. This operation sealed the doom of Cornwallis; yet, ironically, it was on this day that Clinton wrote to him suggesting various courses of action, and ending by saying: "I expect we shall certainly sail in a day or two."[89]

The next day Cornwallis, fully realizing that his position was now untenable but not wishing to surrender without some show of fight, ordered a detachment of four hundred men to storm two American batteries, which they gallantly did, but at no great profit. Finally, on the 16th—a week too late—he decided to abandon Yorktown and carry such troops as he could over to Gloucester. Embarkation began at 11 P.M., but when part of the army had been carried over, a sudden storm scattered the boats and put a stop to the evacuation. "Thus," writes Tarleton, "expired the last hope of the British army."[90]

On the 17th—the anniversary of Burgoyne's surrender at Saratoga —at 10 o'clock in the morning, under cover of a white flag, a drummer in red mounted the parapet on the left of the Yorktown works and beat a "parley." As Johnston writes, he was indeed a momentous figure. "He seemed publicly to confess the end of British domination in America, and proclaim the success of the 'rebel' Revolution."[91] The cannon ceased to fire, and a little while later the following note from Cornwallis was handed to Washington:

I propose a cessation of hostilities for twenty-four hours, and that two officers may be appointed by each side, to meet at Mr. Moore's house, to settle terms for the surrender of the posts of York and Gloucester.[92]

Later came a longer letter requesting that, so long as they undertook
not to fight again against the allies, the British should be sent to Britain
and the Germans to Germany.[93] Remembering, however, the trouble
that had arisen out of the capitulation of Saratoga, Washington would
not agree to this, stating that all officers and men were to be surrendered
as prisoners of war.[94] These terms [95] were accepted, whereupon the un-
named chaplain wrote in his diary—"Hallelujah!" [96]

The number surrendered was 7,157 soldiers, 840 seamen, and 80 camp
followers—in all, 8,077.[97] During the siege the British lost 156 killed
and 326 wounded, and the allies 75 killed and 199 wounded, two-thirds
of these casualties being sustained by the French. For the Americans it
was an exceedingly cheap victory.

When, on the 19th, Cornwallis's men marched out to pile their arms,
they did so to the appropriate tune of "The World Turned Upside
Down." Henry Lee (Light-Horse Harry), who was present, says of the
march past: "Universal silence was observed amidst the vast concourse,
and the utmost decency prevailed, exhibiting in demeanour an awful
sense of the vicissitudes of human life, mingled with commiseration for
the unhappy." [98]

On the 20th, Cornwallis sent to Clinton his final dispatch,[99] and
Washington asked de Grasse to move to the relief of Charleston. This
de Grasse refused to do, as he had to return to the West Indies.[100] Four
days later, Colonel Tilghman—Washington's aide—galloped into Philadelphia to announce the news of the victory. Meanwhile Clinton, who
at length had set out on the 19th, arrived off Cape Charles and Cape
Henry—five days too late. There was nothing he could do but return to
New York.

Thus was concluded the crowning campaign of the war. Though the
conflict was not brought to its official end until November 3, 1783,
when the Treaty of Paris was signed, to all intents and purposes land
operations ceased. At sea the war was continued in spite of the fact that
by the Battle of the Saints, fought and won by Rodney over de Grasse
on April 12, 1782, Great Britain regained her supremacy of the seas.
Thus did Rodney atone, at least in part, for his blundering during the
previous summer.

An American victory was—in the long run—inevitable. A new idea
had taken root in the wilderness and backwoods of America: the essential worth of freedom to man and to his society. And when a new idea
comes into opposition and then into conflict with an old idea, sooner or

later a physical clash is inevitable. Around this fact revolve all politics.

The strength of the Americans did not lie in money or credit, but, as Stedman says, because "they learned to stand in need only of a few things, to be contented with the small allowance that nature requires; to suffer, as well as to act. Their councils, animated by liberty, under the most distressing circumstances, took a grand and high-spirited course, and they were finally triumphant." [101] Of the weakness of their adversaries he writes: "On the whole, the British government did not proceed on any grand system that might control particular circumstances and events; but studied to prolong their own authority by temporary expedients. They courted their adversaries at home, by a share of power and profit; and the public enemies of the state, by partial concessions." [102] In brief, on one side stood self-sacrifice and on the other self-interest.

This self-interest, by divorcing the British government from reality, imbued its ministers with a fatal contempt not only of the Americans, but also of strategical principles. This is well illustrated by the following extract of a letter written by Sir Guy Carleton to Burgoyne on November 12, 1777—one month after his surrender at Saratoga:

This unfortunate event, it is to be hoped, will in future prevent ministers from pretending to direct operations of war, in a country at three thousand miles distance, of which they have so little knowledge as not to be able to distinguish between good, bad or interested advice, or to give positive orders in matters, which from their nature are ever upon the change; so that the experience or propriety of a measure at one moment may be totally inexpedient or improper in the next.[103]

Such are a few contemporary readings into the cause of this disaster. Other causes are the support Germaine gave Cornwallis against Clinton, the difficulties of communications between all three; [104] the separation of naval command from military; [105] and above all, loss of command of the sea, which became all but inevitable once Spain had entered the war. It is interesting to note that, whereas in January, 1781, Great Britain had 32 sail of the line in the West Indies and 8 in North American waters to the French and Spanish 21 and 7 respectively, in October, that year, Great Britain had only 28 beyond the Atlantic to the French and Spanish 45.[106]

The leadership displayed in the war was on the whole of a high order. Howe, Burgoyne, Clinton, Cornwallis, Tarleton, Rawdon, and Simcoe on the one side, and Washington, Greene, Arnold, Morgan,

Sumter, and Henry Lee on the other, were all skillful leaders of men. Washington was more a strategist than a tactician, and though his surprise moves at Trenton and Princeton were audacious and his march to Yorktown a remarkable undertaking, I am of opinion that his finest qualities were more clearly revealed at Valley Forge during the years 1778–1781.

Equal to him as a tactician was Nathanael Greene, a resolute leader of great common sense, and a skillful commander of guerrillas. But in my opinion, also in Fortescue's, as a fighting general Benedict Arnold easily tops the American list. Of him, that British historian says: "To boundless energy and enterprise he united quick insight into a situation, sound strategic instinct, audacity of movement, wealth of resource, a swift and unerring eye in action, great personal daring, and true magic of leadership." [107]

Finally, let us turn to the results of the war as a whole.

Though the surrender of Yorktown was the greatest disaster in British history up to the summer of 1940, it was far more than a military event. It brought a world epoch to a conclusion and in doing so, it liberated a new idea. When, on December 6, 1777, Louis XVI wrote "approved" on Vergennes' proposals for an American alliance, he signed his death warrant with his own hand. And when Spain entered the war, to all intents and purposes she renounced her colonial empire.

It was not in France but in America that the French Revolution sprang to life. It was from America that the French soldiers brought home with them the seeds of liberty, equality, and fraternity. Summing up his impressions of that war, the youthful Saint-Simon exclaimed:

I felt that the American Revolution marked the beginning of a new political era; that this revolution would necessarily set moving an important progress in general civilization, and that it would, before long, occasion great changes in the social order then existing in Europe.[108]

And Mathieu Dumas wrote:

We listened with avidity to "Doctor Cooper," who, while applauding our enthusiasm for liberty said to us: "Take care, take care, young men, that the triumph of the cause on this virgin soil does not influence overmuch your hopes; you will carry away with you the germ of these generous sentiments, but if you attempt to fecund them on your native soil, after so many centuries of corruption, you will have to surmount many more obstacles; it cost us much blood to conquer liberty; but you will shed torrents before you establish it in your old Europe.[109]

REFERENCES

[1] *The Writings of George Washington*, Ford, vol. VIII, p. 345.

[2] *Ibid.*, vol. IX, pp. 106–107. For other similar remarks see Letters to Jefferson, June 8, to Rochambeau, June 13, and to Lafayette, November 15, in vol. IX, pp. 274, 280, and 405.

[3] See *ibid.*, vol. IX, p. 91.

[4] *Ibid.*, vol. IX, p. 117.

[5] *Ibid.*, vol. IX, p. 93.

[6] *The Campaign in Virginia 1781, Clinton-Cornwallis Controversy*, Benjamin Franklin Stevens, vol. I, p. 448. On the same day he wrote to General Phillips that should the report that Arbuthnot was to be recalled prove untrue, "I shall probably retire and leave him to Lord Cornwallis's management" (vol. I, p. 452).

[7] *Ibid.*, vol. I, p. 334.

[8] *Ibid.*, vol. I, pp. 417–418.

[9] *Ibid.*, vol. I, p. 406.

[10] *Ibid.*, vol. I, p. 459.

[11] *Ibid.*, vol. I, pp. 465–469.

[12] *Ibid.*, vol. I, pp. 431–432.

[13] *The History of the Origin, Progress and Termination of the American War*, C. Stedman, vol. II, p. 383 (1794).

[14] Ford, vol. II, pp. 136, 141–143.

[15] *Clinton-Cornwallis Controversy*, vol. I, pp. 437–439.

[16] *Ibid.*, vol. I, pp. 398–399.

[17] *Ibid.*, vol. I, pp. 425, 426, and 429.

[18] See above references 12 and 15.

[19] *An Answer to that Part of the Narrative of Lieutenant-General Sir Henry Clinton K. B., etc.*, Earl Cornwallis, pp. 63, 175, 176 (1783).

[20] *Clinton-Cornwallis Controversy*, vol. I, p. 475.

[21] *Ibid.*, vol. I, p. 480.

[22] *Ibid.*, vol. I, pp. 493, 494, 497.

[23] *Life of General Greene*, F. V. Greene, vol. III, p. 556.

[24] *The Yorktown Campaign and The Surrender of Cornwallis, 1781*, Henry P. Johnston, p. 37.

[25] *Clinton-Cornwallis Controversy*, vol. I, p. 488.

[26] See Stedman, vol. II, pp. 387–389.

[27] *Clinton-Cornwallis Controversy*, vol. II, pp. 20–21. (See also Clinton's letters dated June 15 and 18, pp. 24–25 and 26–28.)

[28] *Ibid.*, vol. II, p. 37.

[29] For this interesting action, see *A History of the Campaign of 1780 and 1781 in the Southern Provinces of North America*, Lieutenant-Colonel Tarleton, pp. 354–357 (1787). Also: *Original and Authentic Journal, etc.*, R. Lamb, p. 373; Stedman, vol. II, p. 394, and Johnston's *Yorktown Campaign*, pp. 61–68.

[30] See Tarleton, pp. 358–359.

[31] *Clinton-Cornwallis Controversy*, vol. II, pp. 51–53.

[32] *Ibid.*, pp. 57, 58.

[33] *Ibid.*, pp. 63, 64.

[34] *Ibid.*, p. 68.

[35] *Ibid.*, pp. 74–75.

[36] *Ibid.*, p. 100.

[37] *Ibid.*, p. 108.

[38] "Journal of the Siege of York in Virginia, by a Chaplain of the American Army," *Collection of the Massachusetts Historical Society,* vol. IX (1804), pp. 103–104. Count de Revel says that Gloucester consisted of four houses (*Journal Particulier,* p. 171).

[39] *A History of The British Army,* Hon. J. W. Fortescue, vol. III, pp. 396–397.

[40] Ford, vol. IX, pp. 251–254.

[41] *With Americans of Past and Present Days,* J. J. Jusserand, pp. 62–63.

[42] Ford, vol. IX, pp. 265–266.

[43] *Ibid.,* vol. IX, pp. 259–262.

[44] Stedman, vol. II, pp. 392–393.

[45] Ford, vol. IX, pp. 282–284. In his *Memoires militaires historiques et politiques de Rochambeau,* vol. II, p. 277. Rochambeau states that after the Wethersfield meeting he privately informed de Grasse "that an enterprise in the Chesapeake Bay against Lord Cornwallis would be the most practicable."

[46] *The Diaries of George Washington,* John C. Fitzpatrick, p. 20.

[47] *Ibid.,* pp. 248–249. (See also Ford, vol. IX, pp. 332–333.)

[48] *Ibid.,* pp. 253–254.

[49] *Ibid.,* p. 254. (See also Ford, vol. IX, pp. 334–336.)

[50] *Ibid.,* p. 255.

[51] Ford, vol. IX, pp. 336–340.

[52] The French did not all cross until September 26.

[53] Lieutenant-Colonel Jonathan Trumbull writes in his diary, August 21: ". . . By these manoeuvres and the correspondent march of the Troops, our own army no less than the Enemy are completely deceived. No movement perhaps was ever attended with more conjectures, or such as were more curious than this. Some were indeed laughable enow'; but not one, I believe, penetrated the real design." (*Massachusetts Historical Society Proceedings,* vol. XIV, p. 332.)

[54] Ford, vol. IX, p. 352.

[55] See Fitzpatrick, p. 257.

[56] Ford, vol. IX, pp. 358–359.

[57] Fitzpatrick, p. 258. "No person is more interested than I am in the arrival of M. de Grasse in these seas." (*Memoires de Rochambeau,* vol. I, p. 276.)

[58] See *Letters and Papers of Charles, Lord Barham,* vol. I, pp. 121–124.

[59] A list of the British ships is given in *The Royal Navy,* Wm. Laird Clowes, vol. III, p. 497.

[60] Stedman, vol. II, p. 400. See also Gordon's *History,* vol. IV, p. 182 (1788).

[61] *Letters written by Sir Samuel Hood,* p. 28. See also *The Private Papers of John, Earl of Sandwich,* vol. IV, p. 186.

[62] *Signals and Instructions, 1776–1794,* Julian S. Corbett, p. 54.

[63] *The Sandwich Papers,* vol. IV, pp. 181–182.

[64] Clowes, vol. III, p. 498.

[65] Hood's *Letters,* pp. 29–30.

[66] *The Influence of Sea Power upon History, 1660–1783,* Captain A. T. Mahan, p. 391.

[67] Both Rodney and Hood disliked Graves.

[68] *Signals and Instructions,* pp. 54–56.

[69] *Clinton-Cornwallis Controversy,* vol. II, p. 142.

[70] *Ibid.,* vol. II, p. 149.

[71] *Ibid.,* vol. II, p. 148.

[72] *Ibid.,* vol. II, pp. 152–153.

[73] See Tarleton, pp. 368–370, and Stedman, vol. II, pp. 407–408.

[74] *Clinton-Cornwallis Controversy,* vol. II, pp. 157–158.

[75] *Ibid.*, vol. II, p. 160.

[76] *Ibid.*, vol. II, pp. 163 and 172.

[77] Fitzpatrick, p. 260.

[78] Ford, vol. II, pp. 367–368.

[79] Continentals—5,645; Militia—3,200, and French—7,800. A full description of the opposing armies is to be found in Johnston's *The Yorktown Campaign*, pp. 109–119.

[80] *Massachusetts Historical Society*, vol. IX (1st Series), p. 104.

[81] For defenses of Yorktown and Gloucester, see Tarleton, pp. 371–372 and 361–362.

[82] See Tarleton, p. 374.

[83] Ford, vol. IX, p. 272.

[84] *Ibid.*, vol. IX, p. 375.

[85] *The History of the Rise, Progress and Establishment of the Independence of the United States of America*, William Gordon, vol. IV, p. 191 (1788).

[86] Ford, vol. IX, p. 381.

[87] Tarleton, p. 380.

[88] *Clinton-Cornwallis Controversy*, vol. II, p. 177.

[89] *Ibid.*, vol. II, p. 186.

[90] Tarleton, p. 388.

[91] *Johnston's Yorktown Campaign*, p. 151. This incident is mentioned by Washington in his *Diary*, see Fitzpatrick, p. 268.

[92] *Clinton-Cornwallis Controversy*, vol. II, p. 189.

[93] *Ibid.*, vol. II, p. 192.

[94] *Ibid.*, vol. II, p. 193.

[95] For articles of capitulations see *ibid.*, vol. II, pp. 199–203.

[96] *Massachusetts Historical Society*, vol. IX (1st Series), p. 107.

[97] *The Revolutionary War*, Francis Vinton Greene, pp. 275–276. Fortescue, (vol. III, p. 401) says 6,630, including 2,000 sick and 2,500 were Germans; Tarleton says—7,427.

[98] *Memoirs of the War in the Southern Department of the United States*, Henry Lee, vol. II, p. 343 (1812).

[99] *Clinton-Cornwallis Controversy*, vol. II, p. 205.

[100] Ford, vol. IX, pp. 389, 391.

[101] Stedman, vol. II, p. 449.

[102] *Ibid.*, vol. II, pp. 447–448.

[103] *A State of the Expedition from Canada*, etc., Lieut.-General Burgoyne, Appendix, p. XXVII (1780).

[104] See Cornwallis, *An Answer to that Part*, etc., p. XV.

[105] See Rodney's opinion in Hood's *Letters*, p. 47.

[106] *The Sandwich Papers*, vol. IV, p. 125.

[107] Fortescue, vol. III, p. 410.

[108] *Œuvres de Saint-Simon*, vol. I, p. 12 (1865–1878).

[109] *Souvenirs du Lieutenant-General Comte Mathieu Dumas*, vol. I, p. 108 (1839). In his *Memoirs* the Chevalier de Pontgibaud, aide-de-camp to Lafayette, wrote: "When we think of the false notions of government and philanthropy which these youths acquired in America, and propagated in France with so much enthusiasm, and such deplorable success—for this mania of imitation powerfully aided the French Revolution though it was not the sole cause of it,—we are bound to confess that it would have been better, both for themselves and us, if these young philosophers in red-heeled shoes had stayed at home . . ." (Quoted by Trevelyan, *George the Third and Charles Fox*, vol. II, pp. 401–402.)

1783–1812

SYNOPSIS OF BACKGROUND EVENTS

THOUGH the Treaty of Paris terminated the War of Independence, it in no way eradicated the war's causes. Rather did it accentuate them, because the trade restrictions which precipitated that conflict and the Navigation Acts upon which these restrictions were founded remained potent elements in British foreign policy. Consequently, the very factors that had brought on the war corrupted the peace which followed it, until to gain full independence—commercial as well as political—the new-born Republic of the West was forced into yet another war with its parent, a war which by some historians has aptly been called—"The Second War of Independence." "To have shrunk from resistance," wrote Madison, ". . . would have acknowledged that, on the element which forms three-fourths of the globe which we inhabit, and where all independent nations have equal and common rights, the American people were not an independent people, but colonists and vassals. With such an alternative war was chosen."

From 1783 onwards, and more particularly between the years 1807 and 1812, the commercial policy of Great Britain continued to be describable by the one word "monopoly"; its purpose to keep the British Isles the world hub of imports and exports, towards which all foreign ships would be attracted like filings to a magnet. This policy was maintained not merely to pile up wealth by depriving other nations of their share. British agriculture was already beginning to prove inadequate to meet the food requirements of the people, and consequently in order to be able to pay for her necessary imports it was essential that Great Britain maintain her export trade. In brief, the time had passed when this trade represented the surplus abundance of the nation: henceforth it represented the overdraft of its agricultural deficiencies.

Important though these considerations were to Britain, they were already running counter to the spirit of the age, a spirit which was daily demanding more and more liberty and less and less servitude between nations as well as within them. As early as 1780—that is, during the recent war—Catherine of Russia had created the League of Armed Neutrality, an association of nations whose object it was to safeguard its members against the British blockade system. After the war ended, as Captain Mahan writes: "The difficulty of the problem was increased by the fact that the governments of the world generally were awaking to the disproportionate advantages Great Britain had been reaping from them for more than a century, during which they had listlessly acquiesced in her aggressive absorption of the carriage of the seas. . . . 'It is manifest,' wrote Coxe in 1794, 'that a prodigious and almost universal revolution in the views of nations has taken place with regard to the carrying trade.' "

An important factor in this revolution was that, owing to their abundance of timber, the Americans could build ships at a lower cost than the English, and because of their intercourse with the West Indies and Southern Europe, were fast becoming trade rivals to the British themselves.

Nevertheless, in this rivalry there was for Great Britain a saving clause: the political disunity of the United States and the military and naval weakness arising out of it. For instance, whereas in 1785 Massachusetts forbade "import or export in any vessel belonging in whole or in part to British subjects," the following year Pennsylvania "repealed laws imposing extra charges on British ships, and admitted all nations on equal terms with her sister states." "The ministry in England," wrote Adams, "build all their hopes and schemes upon the supposition of such divisions in America as will for ever prevent a combination of the States, either in prohibition or in retaliatory duties." In 1787, Washington wrote: "At present, under our existing form of confederation, it would be idle to think of making commercial regulations on our part. One state passes a prohibitory law respecting one article; another state opens wide the avenue for its admission. One assembly makes a system, another assembly unmakes it." This disunity led direct to military and naval weakness. Consequently, during the administration of John Adams and Jefferson (1797–1801 and 1801–1809) and that of Madison up to the outbreak of war in 1812, American foreign policy was deprived of that essential persuasive—fighting force.

This rivalry—weak on the one side and selfish on the other—came to a peak over the West Indies trade. By 1789, the year the new Constitution came into being under the leadership of Washington and the year which also witnessed the outbreak of the French Revolution, that trade was carried almost wholly in American bottoms. That year was one of the great turning points in world history, for during it the yeast of the American Revolution began to raise the political dough of Europe. The inevitable result was a clash between the two most powerful European nations—France and Great Britain—war being declared between them in 1793. Continental power challenged oceanic, and at once America was brought face to face with reality. In June, Great Britain, having declared food a contraband of war, seized American ships carrying provisions bound for France. Then, on November 6, the British government directed the seizure of "all ships laden with goods and produce of any colony belonging to France, or carrying provisions or other supplies for the use of any such colony." This meant that neutrals were forbidden to trade with any of the French colonies.

Such was the First Order in Council which was based on the so-called "Rule of 1756." By that Rule, made by Great Britain, a neutral was forbidden to prosecute in time of war a trade which had been closed to him in time of peace. In other words, it was the reinforcement of the Navigation Act, which had precipitated the War of Independence. Yet, in spite of this Order in Council, the mercantile prosperity of America rose by leaps and bounds, a fact that may be judged from the following figures: in 1791 the U.S.A. possessed 363,110 tons of shipping; in 1800—669,921 tons, and in 1810—1,000,000.

This conflict of interests continued until 1805, when all hope of a French invasion of England was frustrated on October 21 by Nelson's victory at Trafalgar. Thereupon Napoleon turned eastwards, and at Austerlitz—fought and won on December 2—made himself master of the Empire. Thus, deprived of her European markets, and needing to make good their loss, Great Britain set about increasing her trade with the Baltic, the Indies, and America. This turn of affairs brought into relief the rivalry between the British and American shipowners. The former found an effective advocate in James Stephens, who, in a pamphlet entitled *War in Disguise: or The Frauds of the Neutral Flags*, argued that the Americans, "by prosecuting the carrying trade between colonies belonging to belligerent powers and the mother countries," were guilty of unfriendly acts, and had committed breaches of neutrality, and consequently should be punished. So it came about that, when during the winter of 1805–1806 British pressure grew more and more severe, Jefferson approved the Non-Importation Act. This act provided that after November 15, 1806, it would be unlawful to import certain goods of British manufacture into the United States. Later, the date was extended to December, 1807. Then, on May 16, the British government issued an Order in Council which declared that a commercial blockade of the coast from the river Elbe to Brest was to be established. This Order and the Non-Importation Act brought the United States into the arena of the commercial war then raging between Great Britain and France.

Soon this economic war—which was the real struggle between Great Britain and France—assumed a still more acute form. After decisively defeating Prussia at Jena on October 14, 1806, Napoleon, in his Berlin Decree of November 21, declared the British Isles to be in a state of blockade. This meant that all merchandise shipped from America to England was liable to confiscation.

In retaliation, on January 7 the following year, the British government issued an Order in Council prohibiting to neutral shipping the coasting trade of France and her allies. Then, on June 14, came the defeat of Russia at Friedland. On November 11 another Order in Council prohibited trade with such ports as were barred to British shipping, unless neutral ships first called at a British port and paid duty on their cargoes. Finally, on December 17 came Napoleon's Milan Decree, by which any neutral ship which had come from or was bound to a British port, or had paid duty to the British government, would be confiscated. What these various orders and decrees meant to America was clear:

(1) No American ship could visit a French port unless her master had first paid tribute to Great Britain.

(2) Should an American ship do so, or even visit a British port, she rendered herself liable to confiscation by the French.

To make matters worse, for some time now British warships had made use of American waters in order to intercept American vessels bound to or from American ports. Further still, they had pursued French ships into these waters in order to sink or capture them. Not content with such piratical activities, they seized not only cargoes but men who had deserted from the British service, even if since their desertion they had become American citizens. This highhanded action, more than any other, roused the fury of liberty-loving Americans. In 1807 it all but precipitated a war, when, on June 22, the British warship *Leopard* of 50 guns fired on the American frigate *Chesapeake*. Twenty-one of her crew were killed and wounded, and four were seized as alleged deserters.

The feeling roused in America by these arbitrary acts may be judged from the following quotations. Jefferson declared that "the English being equally tyrannical at sea as" Bonaparte "is on land and that tyranny bearing on us in every point of either honor or interest, I say 'Down with England' "; and, in May, the following year, John Quincy Adams wrote in the New York *Evening Post:* "The Orders in Council if submitted to, would have degraded us to the condition of colonists." That they did not was due to the fact that, on December 22, 1807, the Senate had passed an Embargo Bill, which, though modified by the House of Representatives, provided for the stoppage of all American export and foreign navigation with Europe.

To Great Britain this Act proved catastrophic: at the very moment when Alexander of Russia had become party to Napoleon's Continental System, which closed European ports to her, she found herself deprived of cotton, tobacco, and other raw materials, which formed a considerable part of her commerce with the Continent. The results to America herself were also far-reaching, for the act greatly increased her internal commerce, especially on the Great Lakes. In addition to this, by fostering home manufacture in the states north of Maryland it accentuated the increasing differences between the North and the South.

As the quarrel deepened, Napoleon invaded Spain in order to strengthen his blockade; and when in May, 1805, the Spaniards rebelled, Great Britain sent troops to the Peninsula, not so much to liberate her new allies, as to open a market for her goods.

The next development occurred on March 4, 1809, when the Non-Intercourse Act, prohibiting trade with Great Britain and France only, was substituted for the Embargo Act. A little later George Canning informed the British minister in Washington that the government was willing to withdraw their Orders in Council, provided the United States would abrogate their interdiction and agree to intercourse between the two countries. Madison—who had succeeded Jefferson in March—agreed to this on April 19, only to learn that the British government had issued a new Order in Council declaring the whole area from the river

Ems to Spain as well as the French and northern Italian ports in the Mediterranean under blockade. This cynical action immediately resulted in the revival of the restrictions on trade with Great Britain. Then, in 1810 Congress enacted the Macon Act which provided that should one of the belligerents remove its restrictions on neutral trade before March 3, 1811, and the other belligerent not do so, the United States would revive nonintercourse against the recalcitrant Power. Seeing his chance of forcing America into war with Great Britain, on August 5, 1810, Napoleon accepted the Macon Act, and as of November 1 revoked the Decrees of Berlin and Milan so far as they affected America. Thereupon, on November 2, Madison issued a proclamation revoking all restrictions on French commerce, simultaneously announcing that unless Great Britain within three months repealed her Orders in Council the Non-Intercourse Act would be revived against her. This threat was carried out on March 2, 1811, at a moment when commercial and industrial conditions in Great Britain were critical. In the United States the temper of the people was by now thoroughly aroused, for the tempest had fanned the rising spirit of nationalism. In May an American frigate fired on a British warship; in November a considerable victory was won over the northwest Indians at Tippecanoe, which limited British intrigue among the savages south of the Great Lakes. James Monroe, who had become secretary of state during the preceding April, day in and day out urged an appeal to arms. So vehement were his words that in Great Britain the question was at length asked: Is the maintenance of the Orders in Council worth a war with America? This question was answered on June 16, 1812, when Lord Castlereagh announced that these Orders would be suspended on the 23d of that month. But by the time the announcement of this revocation was received in America, the fatal step had been taken. On June 1, Madison, after enumerating in Congress the international wrongs perpetrated by Great Britain, recommended for deliberation the question of peace or war. Three days later the House of Representatives by seventy-nine votes to forty-nine, decided: "that a state of war existed between the United States and Great Britain." On the 17th the bill was carried in the Senate by nineteen yeas to thirteen nays; whereupon it was signed by Madison, war being proclaimed on the following day—that is five days before the repeal of the British Orders in Council.

CHAPTER IV

THE BATTLES OF LAKE ERIE AND LAKE CHAMPLAIN
1813 AND 1814

T O all but the Expansionists, the War of 1812, as it is generally called, was as unwanted as an illegitimate child. Great Britain was still deeply involved in the Peninsula War; Percival—her premier— had but recently been assassinated; her king had once again become insane; and, on June 24, at the head of 450,000 men Napoleon had crossed the Niemen on his way to Moscow.

As for the United States, she was virtually without an army or a navy, because Jefferson and Madison had neglected both. The policy of Jefferson, which had been continued by Madison, hinged on the conviction he had expressed in his inaugural address of 1801: that the Government of the United States was the only one "where every man would meet invasions of the public order as his own personal concern," and that "a well-disciplined militia was (its) best reliance for the first moments of war, till regulars may relieve them." [1] As war approached, Congress voted men by tens of thousands, yet provided neither for enlistment nor maintenance. The whole idea of war was exceedingly unpopular, especially in the New England states. [2] When war was declared, the flags in Boston harbor were flown at half-mast. Toward the end, delegates from the New England states met at Hartford to meditate secession from the Union. However, throughout the war, those states did not fail to turn it to their profit. Whereas in 1810 the deposits in the Massachusetts banks were $2,671,619 and the specie held was $1,561,034, in 1814 these figures stood at $8,875,589 and $6,393,718 respectively. [3]

The strategy of the war, since the contending nations were separated by the Atlantic Ocean, necessarily depended on maritime considerations. The first fact to be noted is the disproportion in naval strengths. Great Britain had a hundred pennants afloat, whereas the American Navy consisted of but four frigates and eight sloops of war. Yet the American deficiency was in part made good both by superior facilities in shipbuilding, and superior construction. Secondly, bearing this disparity in mind, it is obvious that it was totally impossible for the United States even to attempt to blockade Great Britain. All they could do was to set on foot a *guerre de course,* which, though it led to the destruction of 1,650 British ships, proved far less effective than the British blockade, which, before the war ended, virtually brought American navigation to a standstill. Of the numerous duels that took place at sea, such as those between the *Constitution* and the *Guerrière,* the *Wasp* and the *Frolic,* and the *Chesapeake* and the *Shannon,*[4] I do not intend to write. Although they were gallant and exciting episodes, they were in fact of minor importance.

For the United States effectively to attack Great Britain on the seas was not possible, therefore they were compelled by circumstances to seek a decision by attacking Canada, with whom they had no quarrel.

Outside the fact that Canada had to be protected by Great Britain, she was at this particular moment especially valuable to her foster mother, because the recent closing of the Baltic to British shipping had forced the British government to obtain its timber from that colony.[5] Her conquest was strenuously advocated by Monroe. On June 13 he wrote: "In case of war, it might be necessary to invade Canada; not as an object of the war, but as a means to bringing it to a satisfactory conclusion."[6] Nor was he alone in this contention, which ever since Arnold's audacious raid had been a topic of conversation. For instance, in March, John C. Calhoun, then a member of Congress, had said: "So far from being unprepared, Sir, I believe that in four weeks from the time a declaration of war is heard on our frontier, the whole of Upper Canada and a part of Lower Canada will be in our power."[7]

These views were stimulated by the fact that Canada was virtually defenseless. To man the fortresses of Quebec and Kingston and to hold a frontier of some 1,700 miles in length, but four regular regiments— the 8th, 41st, 49th, and 100th Foot—had been allotted. They numbered in all with artillery, engineers, etc., about 4,450 men,[8] supported by some 2,000 militia in the Lower Province and perhaps an equal number in the Upper. Consequently, there was much to be said for American optimism, had Congress been strategically minded. Not only were there some 8,000 regular or semiregular troops at its disposal, but also, on paper at least, a formidable militia,[9] as well as 2,753 pieces of heavy ordnance, 611,339 cannon shot, 513,939 pounds of gunpowder, and 475,555 stands of arms.[10] In 1810 the total inhabitants of the states numbered 7,250,000, including one and a quarter million slaves, whereas it has been estimated that in Canada, in 1811, the population numbered 77,000 in the Upper Province, 335,000 in the Lower, and 65,000 in Nova Scotia. Yet, as we shall see, this vast superiority in material and personnel was largely discounted by the fact that Congress was blind to the most elementary requirements of strategy, which hinged on two factors—the theater of war and its native inhabitants.

Though by now the Indians had lost all power to stay the advance of the white man, nevertheless, because of the natural difficulties of the theater of war, they were, when co-operating with one side against the other, still sufficiently powerful to turn the scales. Wayne's campaign of 1794 had dealt them a severe blow and so had Harrison's of 1811. It was only natural that, when the War of 1812 was declared, their inclination was towards the British. And once again a great leader had arisen among them—namely the Shawnee brave Tecumseh, who in intelligence and astuteness was the equal of Pontiac and Joseph Brant.

The theater of war was limited to a narrow strip of country, or rather of waterways, ranging from Quebec to Lake Superior. Hence, though the main operations were to be fought on land and not at sea, nevertheless, they assumed a naval character, particularly since at this date water communication completely outclassed movements by road, tract, or trail. To show what this meant strategically, it is only necessary to quote Sir George Prevost, Governor-General of Canada: "The command of the lakes enables the enemy to perform in two days what it takes the troops from Kingston sixteen to twenty days of severe marching. Their men arrive fresh; ours fatigued, and with exhausted equipment. The distance from Kingston to the Niagara frontier exceeds two hundred and fifty miles, and part of the way is impracticable for supplies." [12] The Duke of Wellington held the same opinion.[13]

This long water frontier stretched from Michilimackinac and Sault St. Marie in the west, past Detroit, Kingston, and Niagara in the center to Montreal and Quebec in the east, and covered two provinces—Upper and Lower Canada—which were separated by the Ottawa river.

Strategically it may be divided into five military zones; Lake Huron, Lake Erie, the Niagara Peninsula, Lake Ontario, and Lake Champlain, the last-named linking New York to the St. Lawrence. Of this frontier Channing writes:

An attack anywhere along this line, except at its far western end, implicated every part of the line to the westward of the point where the attack was made. The Niagara Peninsula marked a transferring point of food and supplies from one lake to the other: the occupation of it was vital to Upper Canada. The permanent conquest of any part of the St. Lawrence by the Americans would necessitate the abandonment of all Canada above that point. Evidently, from a military point of view, a quick and fierce stroke at Montreal, or the river between that city and Quebec, was the thing to do . . .[14]

Such a stroke had several factors to recommend it. In the first place, it would sever Canada from British support, and so largely nullify the advantage Great Britain possessed through her command of the Atlantic. In the second place, it was strategically simple because the rich and populous provinces of New England as well as the City of New York were linked to Montreal by the route of the Hudson, Lake George, and Lake Champlain, and to Kingston by the Hudson, the Mohawk River, and Lake Oneida. Strategy demanded that the offensive should proceed along this historic line. Nevertheless, political considerations turned attention in the opposite direction. The Administration could not afford to risk Michilimackinac, Chicago (Fort Dearborn), and Detroit, because their loss would precipitate the Indians into the lap of the British, which in turn would mean massacre and inevitable political reaction. As recently as 1808, Lieutenant-Governor Gore of Upper Canada had written to the Governor-General, Sir James Craig: "If we could destroy the American posts at Detroit and Michilimackinac, many Indians would declare for us . . . if not for us, they will surely be against us." [15]

Congress saw the military situation from an identical point of view. In war it is circumstances—reality—which decide whether politics or strategy shall have precedence, and in this conflict politics won. The war sentiment was in the Northwest and not in the Northeast, for the people of the Northwest firmly believed that, because of the real and supposed intrigues of the British among the Indians, there could be no security until Canada was conquered. Therefore, it was impossible for Congress to give first place to strategical considerations. This is clearly to be learnt from a letter written by Jefferson as early as August 17, 1812, in which he says:

It would probably have been best, if it had been practicable in time, to have concentrated a force which could have seized on Montreal, and thus at one stroke, have secured the upper Province, and cut off the sap that nourished Indian hostilities. But this could not be attempted, without sacrificing the Western and N. W. Frontier, threatened with an inundation of savages under the influence of the British establishment near Detroit. Another reason for the expedition of Hull was that the unanimity and ardor of Kentucky and Ohio, promised the requisite force at once for that service, whilst it was too distant from the other points to be assailed.[16]

Hence it came about that the American offensive was launched in the wrong direction, or rather in two wrong directions—toward Detroit and Niagara. The first was to be carried out by Brigadier William Hull, then fifty-nine years old, and the second by General Henry Dearborn, three years his senior. Opposed to them was Major-General Isaac Brock, lieutenant-governor and military commander of Upper Canada, a man of vision, who, had he lived, might well have brought this war to a victorious termination for his side.

On June 26, 1812, learning of the American declaration of war and clearly seeing what strategy demanded, Brock ordered Captain Charles Roberts, then in command of St. Joseph's Island, Sault St. Marie, to capture the American post of Michilimackinac. No sooner was this accomplished than, as Brock had foreseen, the Indians of the Northwest abandoned the American cause and flocked to the British. Thus this small action completely upset the political foundations Congress was building on.

Hull did not learn of the fall of Michilimackinac until August 3, although Brock received the news on July 29. Meanwhile, on June 30, Hull had collected some two thousand men on the Maumee River, and not yet having heard of the declaration of war, sent a schooner to Detroit, which fell into British hands. His official papers, which were discovered on board, revealed to Brock—then at York (Toronto)—the strength of his army. Next, on July 12, Hull crossed the Detroit river to the Canada side, where he received orders from John Armstrong, Secretary of War, to capture Fort Malden.

On hearing of this invasion, Brock at once dispatched Colonel Henry Proctor to take command of that post, from where he cut Hull's land communications with the Maumee River. Then, on August 6, Tecumseh and his Indians successfully ambushed some two hundred of the enemy, whereupon two days later Hull retired to Fort Detroit. Five days later still Brock arrived at Malden, and on the 15th, Proctor lay siege to Detroit. On the following day Hull capitulated to him. Thereupon, leaving Proctor in charge of the fort, Brock set out for Fort George on the Niagara River in order to confront Dearborn.

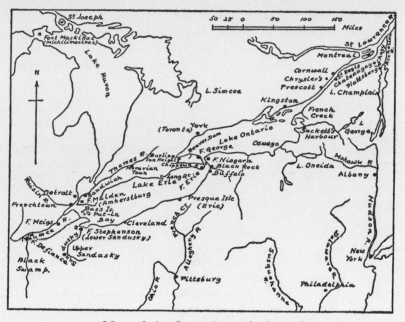

9. Map of the Campaigns of 1812–1814

This disaster, following the fall of Michilimackinac, electrified all Canada. The Americans began to see that in war strategy should take precedence over politics. A few weeks later Madison wrote: "The command of the Lakes by a superior force on the water ought to have been a fundamental part in the national policy from the moment the peace (of 1783) took place." [17] This is true.

Brock's success at Detroit not only rallied the Indians by thousands to his cause, but also enabled him to concentrate his efforts in the Niagara region, while the existing British naval superiority on Lake Erie and Lake Ontario kept open his communications from Kingston to Niagara and from Niagara to Malden and thence by Detroit to Michilimackinac.

Meanwhile, though Dearborn was too slow to take advantage of Brock's absence from Fort George, two men appeared on the scene who were destined to modify the situation in favor of the Americans. The first was Captain Isaac Chauncey, who was sent from New York to take over the naval command on Lakes Erie and Ontario, and the second was his subordinate, Lieutenant Jesse D. Elliott, whom he ordered to Buffalo on September 14. On October 8, Elliott raided Fort Erie capturing two British brigs—the *Detroit* and the *Caledonia*.

This loss of two ships, small though they were, was little short of a disaster, because it tilted the command of Lake Erie away from the British. This was realized by Brock, who on reporting it to Prevost informed him:

This event is particularly unfortunate and may reduce us to incalculable distress. The enemy is making every exertion to gain a naval superiority on both lakes; which if accomplished, I do not see how we can retain the country. More vessels are fitting for war on the other side of Squaw Island, which I should have attempted to destroy but for your Excellency's repeated instructions to forbear. Now such a force is collected for their protection as will render every operation against them very hazardous.[18]

Elliott's success at once raised the morale in Dearborn's command and led on October 13 to an attack on Queenston Heights by General Stephen Van Rensselaer. Brock, hearing the firing, galloped up from Fort George, took over command, drove his enemy back and then unfortunately was killed.[19] Later, General Sheaffe, who succeeded him, carried the position, taking 1,000 prisoners, among whom was Colonel Winfield Scott.[20]

Meanwhile General William H. Harrison—victor of the Tippecanoe —succeeded Hull at Sandusky. Early in January he moved out and seized French Town on the Raisin River; whereupon Proctor moved against him, and defeated his lieutenant, General Winchester. Capturing Winchester and some 500 of his men, Proctor speedily retired because his prisoners outnumbered the white men he could detail to guard them. He set out again on April 23, with 400 men of the 41st Foot and 1,200 Indians under Tecumseh, and laid siege to Fort Meigs, but finally abandoned it. On July 20, he advanced again, this time against the American post of Stephenson (Sandusky), from which in turn he was forced to withdraw.

While these unprofitable movements were being made in the West, a new plan of campaign was taking form in the East. Armstrong instructed Dearborn to move 4,000 of his troops from Lake Champlain to Sackets Harbor and 3,000 to Buffalo. Directly navigation reopened, he was to embark the former and take York, the capital of Upper Canada, after which, in co-operation with the Buffalo force, Forts George and Erie were to be reduced. Though, on the 27th, York capitulated on terms, it was plundered and burnt, apparently as a reprisal for alleged Indian excesses. This done, Dearborn sailed for the mouth of the Niagara River and landed his men at Four Mile Creek. Reinforced there by his Buffalo troops, which brought his total strength up to some 6,000 all told, on May 27 he attacked Fort George—the British headquarters on the Niagara front—then held by Brigadier-General John Vincent and 2,500 soldiers, mostly militiamen. Vincent, not trusting his men to put up a fight, fell back to Burlington Heights, which were occupied on the 29th. The net result was that the entire line of the Niagara passed into American hands. Dearborn, hoping to destroy Vincent's force before it could be reinforced by Proctor, pressed on to Stoney Creek where, on June 8, Vincent suddenly attacked him. Although the assault he had planned was spoilt by his men cheering and firing prematurely,[21] he succeeded in taking 100 prisoners including two Generals. Thereupon the Americans fell back ten miles to Forty Mile Creek. In spite of faulty execution, the small battle of Stoney Creek proved to be the turning point in this campaign; for though it gave the Canadians new heart, it seriously depressed their enemy.

Having been reinforced, Vincent advanced from his position, pushing out outposts along the Fort George and Beaver Dam roads. The first was under Major de Haren at St. Catherine's and the second under Lieutenant FitzGibbon at a building known as de Cou's House. It consisted of 50 men of the 49th Foot—all Irish [22]—and a party of Indians under one of the sons of Joseph Brant. This post the American decided to dislodge, entrusting the enterprise to Colonel Boerstler and 600 men.

Unfortunately for Boerstler, this project came to the ears of a young woman, a Mrs. Laura Secord,[23] who, setting out early on the 23d, walked twenty miles to FitzGibbon's post and told him of what was impending. As a result, when Boerstler advanced on de Cou's House during the morning of the 24th, he fell into an ambush and was compelled to surrender.[24]

Shortly before this campaign was opened by the Americans, the British Admiralty, waking up to the obvious fact that the defense of Canada hinged on the naval command of the lakes, sent out Captain Sir James Yeo, who had just turned thirty, to take over the small fleet at Kingston. He had hardly arrived when, on May 22, Prevost raided Sackets Harbor, Chauncey then being engaged against Fort George.

Thus the naval phase of the war opened, and, although two indecisive actions between Yeo and Chauncey were fought on Lake Ontario, it was on Lake Erie that the first decision was gained.

In January, Chauncey had sent a young naval officer, Captain Oliver Hazard Perry, to take over command on Lake Erie. There, on May 27, he was engaged in the operations against Fort George. Then he moved his naval base from Black Rock to Presque Isle, where he established himself on June 12. At the same time, Captain Robert H. Barclay was sent by Admiral Sir John Warren—then commander in chief on the American station—to assist General Prevost. On his arrival, Prevost placed him in command of the small British fleet. Establishing himself at Malden, Barclay sailed on July 20 to Presque Isle to blockade Perry. He maintained the blockade until August 2, when, for some reason not exactly known, he sailed away.[25] Perry then hastened to bring his ships from their anchorage over the bar, which ran across the mouth of the harbor. This was a formidable task, because all his vessels had to be unloaded, and by means of scows or "camels" raised some two feet.[26] By the 4th this work was completed, and Barclay, having by then returned, found that he had been outwitted. Thereupon he sailed to Malden where his new ship, the *Detroit*, had just been launched. Thus, and to his credit, Perry was left in control of the lake. On the 10th he was reinforced by Commander Elliott and 102 men, and two days later he sailed westwards to carry stores and provisions to Sandusky, then, as we have seen, attacked by Proctor. On September 6th, Perry established his headquarters at Put-in-Bay in the Bass Islands.

While the two opposing squadrons faced each other, Proctor's position grew daily worse. Not only did Perry straddle his water communications with Malden, but that fort itself—his base—was so badly provisioned that its retention would become impossible unless Barclay could keep open its line of supply with Long Point. On this question Barclay writes:

So perfectly destitute of provisions was the post, that there was not a day's flour in store, and the crews of the squadron under my command were on half allowance of many things, and when that was done there was no more. Such were the motives which induced Major-general Proctor . . . to concur in the necessity of a battle being risked . . .[27]

The shortage was partly due to Prevost's lack of prevision, but mainly to the improvidence of Proctor's Indians, concerning whom, an eyewitness—Major John Richardson—writes:

The quantity of provisions already consumed had been enormous; for independently of the wanton destruction of cattle by the Indians, who often shot or stabbed them merely to possess themselves of the horns, in which they secured their powder, leaving the carcasses to putrify in the sun, ten thousand rations were daily issued to the warriors and their families; the latter apparently increasing in numbers, as our means of supplying them became more contracted.[28]

Barclay did not want to fight, because he knew that his squadron was inferior to Perry's. Though James enumerates his difficulties and deficiences, such as that "round shot cost one shilling a pound for the carriage from Quebec"; and anchors were worth "their weight in silver" and that his crews were mainly made up of "Canadian peasants and soldiers . . . sorry substitutes for British seamen." [29] his real inferiority lay in the fire power of his ships. This may be gauged from the following two tables: [30]

BARCLAY'S SQUADRON

Vessel	Tons	Crew	Broadside in 16s	Long Guns	Caliber	Short Guns	Caliber
Detroit	490	150	126	2	24	1	24
				1	18	1	18
				6	12		
				8	9		
Queen Charlotte	400	126	181	3	12	14	24
Lady Prevost	230	86	74	3	9	10	12
Hunter	80	45	28	2	6	2	12
				4	4		
				2	2		
Little Belt	90	18	21	1	9		
				2	6		
Chippewa	70	15	9	1	9		
	1,360	440	439	35		28	

PERRY'S SQUADRON

Vessel	Tons	Crew	Broadside in 16s	Long Guns	Caliber	Short Guns	Caliber
Lawrence	480	136	300	2	12	18	32
Niagara	480	155	300	2	12	18	32
Caledonia	180	53	80	2	24	1	32
Ariel	112	36	48	4	12		
Somers	94	30	56	1	24	1	32
				1	32		
Scorpion	86	35	56	1	24		
Porcupine	83	25	32	1	32		
Tigress	96	27	32	1	32		
Trippe	60	35	24	1	24		
	1,671	532	928	16		38	

As Theodore Roosevelt writes: "The important fact was that though we had nine guns less, yet, at a broadside, they threw half as much metal again as those of our antagonists. With such odds in our favor it would have been a disgrace to have been beaten." [31]

Such were the unfavorable conditions under which, on September 9, Barclay put out from Fort Malden, "fully expecting to meet the enemy next morning, as they had been seen among the islands," so he writes in his report. At sunrise next day, Perry informs us, while his squadron was at anchor, he saw his enemy approaching and at once got under way "and stood for them." Barclay bore up hoping to bring Perry to action among the islands. This intention was frustrated, when at 10 A.M. the wind hauled to the southeast, bringing the Americans to windward. Thereupon Barclay decided to await attack in the following order: the schooner *Chippewa* in the van, then the *Detroit* (his flagship), *Hunter*, *Queen Charlotte*, *Lady Prevost*, and *Little Belt*.

The night before, at a conference, Perry had announced which of his ships was to fight which of Barclay's. He also produced a large blue battle flag which bore in white letters the inscription "DONT GIVE UP THE SHIP," informing his officers that "When this flag shall be hoisted to the main-royal masthead, it shall be your signal for going into action." Finally he said to them: "Gentlemen, remember your instructions. Nelson has expressed my idea in the words, 'If you lay your enemy close alongside, you cannot be out of your place.' Good night." [32] Now, seeing his enemy's disposition, he arranged his squadron in the following order of battle:

The *Lawrence* (his flagship) moved forward, flanked on her port side by the schooners *Scorpion* and *Ariel*. To starboard of the *Lawrence* stood the *Caledonia*. The object of these four vessels was to engage the *Chippewa*, *Detroit*, and *Hunter*. Following the *Caledonia* came the *Niagara*, under Captain Elliott, with orders to fight the *Queen Charlotte*, and astern of her the *Somers*, *Porcupine*, and *Tigress*, which were to engage the *Lady Prevost* and *Little Belt*.

At 11.45 A.M. the *Detroit* opened fire on the *Lawrence*, which replied to her ten minutes later. "From the heights over-hanging the lake, and nearly opposite to the islands," writes Richardson, the garrison of Malden "watched the battle until the ships were lost to sight in the smoke." [33] Then, according to Perry:

Finding their fire very destructive, owing to their long guns, and its being mostly directed at the Lawrence, I made sail, and directed the other vessels to follow, for the purpose of closing with the enemy. Every brace and bow-line being shot away, she became unmanageable, notwithstanding the great exertions of the sailing-master. In this situation she sustained the action upwards of two hours, within canister-distance, until every gun was rendered useless, and the greater part of her crew either killed or wounded.[34]

Meanwhile, on the British side, Captain Finnis of the *Queen Charlotte* was killed. With him, Barclay informs us, fell his "greatest support." Her command was taken over by Lieutenant Irvine, "but his experience was much too limited to supply the place of such an officer as Captain Finnis, hence she proved of far less assistance than I expected." [35] Barclay himself was now badly wounded.

At 2.30 P.M. the *Lawrence* dropped astern of the *Detroit,* more than half her ship's company lying dead or wounded on her deck. With only one gun left she was a beaten ship. So was the *Detroit,* who was in as parlous a condition. Close to her lay the *Queen Charlotte,* while the *Hunter* was astern of her and the *Lady Prevost* had lost her rudder. The battle was anyone's who could bring into action an undamaged ship. Fortunately for the Americans, this was the position Perry now found himself in; for thus far during the fight Elliott's ship—the *Niagara*—had lagged behind and was virtually untouched. Then, as the wind freshened, she bore up. Perry, taking to an open boat, rowed over to her; whereupon the *Lawrence,* then under the command of Lieutenant Yarnall, struck her colors. Once on board the *Niagara,* Perry took over command. Elliott, boarding the boat Perry had come in, rowed through a shower of balls and brought up the smaller ships to support Perry. Next, the helm of the *Niagara* was put up, and accompanied by the *Ariel, Scorpion,* and *Caledonia,* she bore down ahead of the *Detroit.* Then, writes Barclay, the *Detroit* being "now a perfect wreck," the enemy bore up, and "supported by his small vessels, passed within pistol-shot, and took a raking position on our bow; nor could I prevent it, as the unfortunate situation of the *Queen Charlotte* prevented us from wearing." [36]

Coming steadily on, the *Niagara* stood between the *Chippewa* and *Lady Prevost* on one side, and the *Detroit, Queen Charlotte,* and *Hunter* on the other, pouring in her broadsides as she did so. No sooner had the smoke cleared than the *Queen Charlotte* struck. The *Little Belt* and *Chippewa,* attempting to escape to leeward, were shortly after brought to by the *Scorpion* and *Trippe.* The end was inevitable and the *Detroit,* now completely unmanageable and raked by the American ships ahead and astern, struck her colors. Meanwhile the *Lawrence* had rehoisted hers, and, reboarding her, Perry received the surrender of Barclay and his officers on her deck. Then he wrote two brief notes, the first to General Harrison, which read: "We have met the enemy, and they are ours; two ships, two brigs, one schooner and one sloop"; [37] and the second to the Hon. W. Jones, Secretary of the Navy: "It has pleased the Almighty to give to the arms of the United States, a signal victory over their enemies on this lake. The British squadron, consisting of two ships, two brigs, one schooner and one sloop, have this moment surrendered to the force under my command, after a short conflict." [38]

The casualties in this battle were as follows: British, 41 killed and 94 wounded; American, 27 killed and 96 wounded, of whom 21 were killed and 61 wounded on board the *Lawrence*.

"The effect of this victory upon the whole country," writes Lossing, "was electric and amazingly inspiriting . . . Illuminations, bonfires, salvoes of artillery, public dinners . . . were the visible indications of popular satisfaction in every city, village and hamlet . . ." [39] until a veritable legend was created. Though it is true, as Adams writes, that "More than any other battle of the time, the victory on Lake Erie was won by the courage and obstinacy of a single man," [40] it is also true that, as Roosevelt says: "In short our victory was due to our heavy metal." [41]

Strategically, it changed the whole complexion of the war. First, it sounded the death-knell of the British possession of Detroit and Fort Malden, as well as of Proctor's campaign on the Sandusky. Secondly, it shook to its foundations the allegiance of the Indians to the British cause. Thirdly, it opened the road to Canada; for no sooner did Prevost, on the 22d, receive the news of the disaster than he ordered Proctor to retire to the Thames. This Proctor did, destroying Forts Malden and Detroit on his way. Thereupon General Harrison occupied their ruins, and then setting out in pursuit, on October 5 caught up with Proctor and routed his numerically inferior and now demoralized force at Moravian Town.[42] In this engagement, Tecumseh, then in his forty-fourth year, was killed. The victory his, Harrison retired to Detroit.

Meanwhile, in the East, General James Wilkinson had replaced General Dearborn. On October 24, acting under the instructions of Armstrong, reinforced by 1,300 of Harrison's men and supported by Chauncey's squadron, he advanced by water on Montreal, while General Wade Hampton moved on that same city from Lake Champlain. The arrangement was that the two forces should unite at St. Regis before operating against their common goal.

Hampton set out on October 21, but close by Chateaugay he was so roughly handled by a small force of Canadians that he fell back to Plattsburg. Meanwhile, Wilkinson delayed his advance until November 1, when he descended the St. Lawrence to French Creek, and, on the 9th, reached the head of the Long Sault Rapids, at the foot of which lay St. Regis. He was followed up by some 900 men of the 49th and 89th Foot under Colonel Morrison, accompanied by a gunboat flotilla, apparently in order to clear their rear. On November 10, Wilkinson landed 2,000 men under General Brown on the Canadian shore, not far from Cornwall. The next day he set ashore another detachment of 1,800 under General Boyd, who attacked Morrison at Chrysler's Farm and was repulsed. Boyd counterattacked but was finally routed. Thus the American invasion of Canada ended in a fiasco, made doubly disgraceful by the fact that militia under M'Clure, who held Fort George, deserted in such numbers that he was compelled to evacuate that stronghold. But before he retired, he burnt Newark, close by, driving 400 women and children "from their houses into the snows of a Canadian winter."

This fort was at once occupied by the British under Colonel J. Murray. A few days later Lieutenant-General Gordon Drummond, arriving from England, took over the command of Upper Canada from General de Rottenburg, who a year back had succeeded Vincent. Immediately on his arrival Murray set before him a plan to retake Fort Niagara, which he approved, and, on December 19, Fort Niagara was surprised and occupied. On the same day Major-General Phineas Riall moved on Fort Lewiston (south of Fort Niagara), which was abandoned. Then, on the 29th, he advanced on Black Rock, carried it, and drove the Americans out of Buffalo. "Black Rock was burned, and every remaining settlement on the river was destroyed. The whole of the frontier, in fact, was laid in ashes as reprisal for the burning of Newark." [43] Then Drummond went into winter quarters.

Though the battle of Lake Erie opened the doorway into Canada, the reconquest of the Niagara peninsula closed it. In March, 1814, Armstrong decided that it could only be reopened by a direct attack on Kingston and Montreal; but unfortunately General Brown—who was to operate against Kingston—misread his instructions and bungled the whole affair. Next, Drummond, balked by Prevost from attacking

Sackets Harbor, turned against Oswego, and, on May 3, stormed that fort and then abandoned it. As a result, Brown was ordered to advance against York, while General Izard from Plattsburg on Lake Champlain carried out a diversion against Montreal.

On the night of July 2, Brown crossed the Niagara River, whereupon the British under General Riall abandoned Fort Erie and fell back to the Chippewa River. There on the 5th a small battle was fought which resulted in Riall withdrawing to Burlington Heights. Then, when Chauncey and his squadron failed to support Brown, Brown withdrew to the Chippewa. Riall, having meanwhile been reinforced, next advanced, and, on the 25th, his advanced guard occupied a hill one mile northwest of the Niagara Falls. There the Battle of Lundy's Lane was fought, the best-contested fight of the whole war, some 2,800 men on each side struggling and clinching for over three hours. The British losses were 878 killed and wounded and the American 860, to which must be added 117 prisoners. Honors rested with the British, for the Americans fell back to the Chippewa, and, on the 26th, retired to Fort Erie.

Drummond then advanced and lay siege to Fort Erie on August 3, whereupon Armstrong, on the 12th, most foolishly ordered General Izard and 4,000 men from Plattsburg to Sackets Harbor in order to co-operate with Brown. On September 21, Drummond abandoned the siege. Following a series of unimportant moves Izard blew up Fort Erie on November 5 and withdrew altogether from British territory.

While Drummond and Brown were literally wasting each other's time and their respective resources around Niagara, the complete change in the European situation was making itself felt in America. In October, 1813, Napoleon had been decisively defeated at Leipzig; on March 31, 1814, Paris had been occupied by British and Russian troops, and, on May 11, the French Emperor had abdicated his throne. Though this downfall was hailed with great joy by the Federalists, it set free the British troops in Spain which were then sent in large numbers across the Atlantic.

The situation the Americans now found themselves in was, therefore, a peculiarly anxious one. For two years they had overlooked the fact that the historic front door to Canada was to be found on Lake Champlain and not at Detroit or Niagara. Had this doorway been forced when Great Britain was involved in Spain, the probabilities were that Canada would have fallen. Their situation was made still more precarious by General Izard's orders to move from Plattsburg to Sackets Harbor with 4,000 men. It is astonishing to find that in his order of August 12th, Armstrong had written to Izard: "It is very distinctly my opinion that it has become good policy on our part to carry the war as far to the westward as possible, particularly while we have an ascendancy on the Lakes." [44] Izard and his men set out on the 29th, leaving General Alexander Macomb at Plattsburg in command of 3,300 men, of whom only 1,500 were effectives. [45]

For the British this line of advance was not only the most practical one for an offensive operation, but also administratively the soundest, because vast quantities of food stocks were pouring into Canada along this route. On this question Izard reported to Armstrong on July 31:

From the St. Lawrence to the ocean, an open disregard prevails for the laws prohibiting intercourse with the enemy. The road to St. Regis is covered with droves of cattle, and the river with rafts, destined for the enemy. The revenue officers see these things, but acknowledge their inability to put a stop to such outrageous proceedings. On the eastern side of Lake Champlain the high roads are found insufficient for the supplies of cattle which are pouring into Canada. Like herds of buffaloes they press through the forest, making paths for themselves . . . Were it not for these supplies the British forces in Canada would soon be suffering from famine, or their government be subjected to enormous expense for their maintenance. [46]

This is corroborated by Prevost, who on August 27 acknowledged that two-thirds of his army in Canada were eating beef drawn from the states of Vermont and New York. At this date his army lay cantoned between the Richelieu River and the St. Lawrence and consisted of the following troops:

(1) Major-General Robinson's Brigade; 3/27th, 39th, 76th, and 88th Foot, with artillery, 2,888 rank and file.
(2) Major-General Brisbane's Brigade; 2/8th, 13th, 49th Foot, and De Meuron's Canadian Chasseurs, 4,048 rank and file.
(3) Major-General Power's Brigade; 3rd, 5th, 2/27th, and 58th Foot, 3,801 rank and file.
(4) Major-General Kempt's Reserve; 9th, 37th, 57th, and 81st Foot, 3,549 rank and file.
(5) Major-General de Watteville's Line of Communications Troops, 16th and 17th Foot, 1,483 rank and file.

In all, including officers but not counting Canadian militia, there were about 16,000 troops. Therefore it was twice as strong as Burgoyne's expedition of 1777. Yet there was this difference; then, the command of Lake Champlain was assured, now it had to be won, if only to keep open the army's line of communication with Canada.

While this army was being assembled, Macomb was fortifying Plattsburg, a town of some seventy houses built on both sides of the Saranac River, which was bridged. He built three redoubts between its right bank and Lake Champlain, namely, Forts Brown, Moreau, and Scott, in order to protect the peninsula he had occupied from attack from the west.

On August 31, Prevost set out at the head of his formidable army and, on September 4, reached Chazy. The next day he met with some slight opposition. On the 6th, although he had lost no more than two hundred men killed and wounded, instead of carrying his enemy's position, which undoubtedly he could have done, he halted, and from the 7th to the 11th employed his time in preparations for battering the forts. Meanwhile the greater part of the British squadron under Captain Pring had advanced to Isle la Motte (north of Plattsburg), where on the 2d it was joined by the remainder of the flotilla under Captain George Downie, who took over its command. On the American side, Captain Thomas Macdonough brought his squadron into Plattsburg Bay, and anchored it about a mile from the shore.

Prevost now decided on a joint land and sea attack, but whether he intended the navy to help the army or *vice versa* is not clear. All we know is that he and Downie agreed that, when the squadron was seen rounding Cumberland Head—which lies on the eastern flank of the bay and faces Plattsburg—Major-General Robinson was to ford the Saranac and storm the forts.

Though the British army of invasion was in every respect the most formidable which had hitherto been seen in North America, like a cherry, it hung on a slender stalk—naval power. Could the command of Lake Champlain be gained and held, nothing short of a miracle could save the Americans. If not, then, in spite of numerical superiority and discipline, its failure was preordained, for the maintenance of its line of communications was vital to its success. Everything depended on the opposing fleets.

Both squadrons were unready; both were manned by amateur crews, though it would seem that in this respect the British were at a disadvantage, if James's statement is not an exaggeration. "The seamen," he writes, "were men of inferior quality, and character; and who, as it is termed, *volunteered,* or rather, were forced from their respective ships; where they had been in disgrace. Some of them, indeed, had been liberated from irons, for the very purpose of proceeding to the lakes! None of the marines joined earlier than 9th of September; and a part of the seamen, only the night before the action. Of course, time did not admit of the men becoming acquainted with their officers, or with each other. Captain Downie himself was acquainted with no officer on board his ship but his first-lieutenant and the latter with none of the other officers!" [47] Otherwise the two fleets were of far more equal power than those which had faced and fought each other on Lake Erie, as the following tables make clear: [48]

DOWNIE'S SQUADRON

Vessel	Tons	Crew	Broadside in Lbs.	Long Guns	Caliber	Short Guns	Caliber
Confidence	1200	325	468	31	24	6	32
Linnet	350	125	96	16	12		
Chubb	112	50	90	1	6	10	18
Finch	110	50	84	4	6	7	18
				3	24	8	32
12 Gunboats	630	387	436	5	18	1	18
	2,402	937	1,174	60		32	

MACDONOUGH'S SQUADRON

Vessel	Tons	Crew	Broadside in Lbs.	Long Guns	Caliber	Short Guns	Caliber
Saratoga	734	240	414	8	24	6	42
						12	32
Eagle	500	150	264	8	18	12	32
Ticonderoga	350	112	148	4	18	5	32
				8	12		
Preble	80	30	36	7	9		
10 Gunboats	580	350	300	6	24	6	18
				4	12		
	2,244	882	1,162	45		41	

Henry Adams points out that "in one respect Downie held a decisive superiority"—namely, "He had no less than sixty long-range pieces, while Macdonough had but forty-five," and that they threw "at least eleven hundred pounds" to his "seven hundred." [49] This undoubted advantage I think may be discounted, when the unpreparedness of his flagship—the *Confidence*—is taken into consideration. She was launched on August 25,[50] and the carpenters were still working on her during the morning she went into action: "In fact, the hammering and drilling continued until two hours before the ship came under fire, when the last gang shoved off, leaving her still unfinished." [51]

But in one respect at least the Americans had a decided advantage, and this was in their leader—Macdonough. Born in 1783,[52] he had seen service in the Tripolitan War and had commanded the naval forces on Lake Champlain since the spring of 1813. He was not only a man of courage, but of foresight, and it was this latter quality which above all others won him his battle. As Theodore Roosevelt says, he took into consideration the prevailing wind and currents of the lake. Judging that at that season Downie would not risk waiting outside the bay until the wind favored him, Macdonough anchored his squadron one mile from its western shore, out of effective gun-range should the British occupy Plattsburg. Then, besides preparing to spring his ships—that is, swing them round when at anchor—he arranged the necessary cables in such a manner that they would not be shot away during the engagement. "This timely precaution," writes Cooper, "gained him the victory." [53]

Though undoubtedly Macdonough was an abler seaman than Downie, it is difficult to criticize the actions of the British commander, because he was rushed into battle by Prevost with quite unnecessary haste. Instead of assaulting Plattsburg and carrying the American position before calling on Downie's squadron, Prevost insisted on a combined attack. Had Plattsburg been occupied first, Macdonough would most certainly have had to weigh anchor, which would have allowed Downie to attack him at advantage.

A little before dawn on September 11, with the wind blowing from the northeast, the British squadron weighed anchor and stood out for Plattsburg Bay. Then the prearranged signal for the attack was given— a salvo of blank—and at 7 A.M. the enemy came into full view. Half an hour later the ships hove to, and Downie in a boat, reconnoitered the American squadron. From north to south Macdonough's order of battle ran—*Eagle, Saratoga, Ticonderoga, Preble,* with the gunboats inshore of these ships. Downie decided that the *Confidence* should engage the *Saratoga* by anchoring across her bows, while the *Linnet* supported by the *Chubb* engaged the *Eagle,* and the *Finch* accompanied by the gunboats attacked the enemy's rear. Then his squadron once again stood up the lake, the *Finch* leading followed by the *Confidence, Linnet,* and *Chubb*. On rounding Cumberland Head, Downie was astonished to find that the land attack had not yet begun. At 8 A.M. the gunboats opened fire, and a few minutes later the first broadside of the *Confidence* struck the *Saratoga* with terrible effect. Then the wind failed, and the *Confidence,* having by now had two anchors shot away, was obliged to anchor at about five hundred yards from the American line. No sooner had she done so than a shot from the *Sarotoga* struck one of her long-guns, which was thrown off its carriage and hurled against Captain Downie, killing him instantly. Lieutenant Robertson took command.

Meanwhile the *Linnet* closely engaged the *Eagle,* driving her out of the line; but a short time after, the *Chubb,* losing her bowsprit and main boom as well as many of her cables, became unmanageable. Instead of anchoring she drifted through the American line to strike her colors. Simultaneously the *Finch*—not overwell-handled—failed to reach her position. Crippled by a broadside from the *Ticonderoga* she drifted helplessly out of the fight and later on went ashore off Crab Island. The result of this mishap was that the *Ticonderoga* was unattacked, except by the British gunboats, four of which, under the command of Lieutenant Bell, fought gallantly. "Had they driven off the *Ticonderoga,*" writes Roosevelt, "they would have won the day for their side, and they pushed up till they were not a boat-hook's length distant, to try to carry her by boarding; but every attempt was repulsed and they were forced to draw off, some of them so crippled by the slaughter they had suffered that they could hardly man the oars." [54] Victory might have been theirs had the remaining gunboats supported them. Instead, manned by militia, they took flight soon after the action opened. Thus the *Ticonderoga* was able to maintain her station to the end, but the *Preble* was forced from her anchors and ran ashore off Plattsburg.

The fight now became a struggle between the *Saratoga* and the *Eagle* on the one side and the *Confidence* and *Linnet* on the other. Then, "at half-past 10 o'clock the *Eagle,* not being able to bring her guns to bear," cut her cable, and anchored "in a more eligible situation," between the *Saratoga* and the *Ticonderoga,* where, though annoying the *Confidence* and *Linnet,* she left the *Saratoga* exposed to a galling fire. Then, continues Macdonough in his report of September 13, "Our guns on the starboard side [of the *Confidence*] being nearly all dismounted, or not manageable, a stern-anchor was let go, the bower-cable cut, and the ship winched with a fresh broadside on the enemy's ship . . ." [55] The *Con-*

fidence then attempted to carry out the same evolution; but, because her stern anchor cable had been shot away, all that happened was that she turned at right angles to the American line, when she was so raked that she struck her colors at 10.33 A.M.[56] "The whole attention of the enemy's force," writes Pring, "then became directed towards the *Linnet*. The shattered and disabled state of the masts, sails, rigging, and yards, precluded the most distant hope of being able to effect an escape by cutting the cable"; consequently to prevent a useless waste of life, at 10.45 A.M. Pring ordered her colors to be struck, and the battle ended in a total American victory.

In this fight, the British losses were 54 killed and 116 wounded to the Americans' 52 killed and 58 wounded.[57] The *Saratoga* had 55 round shot in her hull and the *Confidence* 105.

Meanwhile, what of the land attack? When Downie's signal was given, the British land batteries opened up, and under their fire General Robinson advanced. But through a mistake on the part of his guide he missed the ford across the Saranac, and when countermarching was ordered to withdraw. This is what Prevost himself says:

Scarcely had his majesty's troops forced a passage across the Saranac, and ascended the height on which stand the enemy's works, than I had the extreme mortification to hear the shout of victory from the enemy's works, in consequence of the British flag being lowered on board the "Confidence" and "Linnet," and to see our gun-boats seeking their safety in flight. This unlooked-for event, depriving me of the co-operation of the fleet, without which the further prosecution of the service was become impracticable, I did not hesitate to arrest the course of the troops advancing to the attack, because the most complete success would have been unavailing, and the possession of the enemy's works offered no advantage, to compensate for the loss we must have sustained in acquiring possession of them.[58]

Thus ignominiously ended the war in Lower Canada.

Writing on this engagement between eight small ships of war, Captain Mahan says: "The battle of Lake Champlain; more nearly than any other incident of the War of 1812, merits the epithet 'decisive.' " This is true, because the joy it created in America was only equaled by the consternation it aroused in England. There, Lord Liverpool offered the command in Canada to the Duke of Wellington, who replied: "That which appears to me to be wanting is not a General or general officers or troops, but a naval superiority on the lakes . . . The question is whether we shall acquire this naval superiority. If we can't, I shall do but little good in America, and I shall go there only to prove the truth of Prevost's defence." Then a few days later he added: "Does it not occur to you that by appointing me to go to America at this moment, you give ground for belief all over Europe that your affairs there are in a much worse situation than they really are?" [60]

As the natural advantages possessed by the Americans on the Lakes, especially in shipbuilding, were so great, peace was now inevitable. Yet before I conclude this chapter I will bring the land operations to their ultimate end; because two events took place that had a profound influence upon the aftermath of the war. The first was the burning of Washington, and the second Andrew Jackson's victory at New Orleans.

The first arose out of a diversion [61] in favor of Prevost's advance on New York, its object being to draw American forces away from the Hudson and toward the Chesapeake. Its military leader was Major-General Robert Ross, who sailed from the Gironde with three regiments to Bermuda and was there joined by Admiral Cochrane. Having organized a force some 4,500 strong, early in August Ross and Cochrane proceeded to Chesapeake Bay, where they joined Admiral Cockburn, then on blockading duty. Having chased an American gunboat flotilla, commanded by Captain Joshua Barney, up the Patuxent River, the troops were landed and a decision taken to march on Washington and burn the public buildings there in retaliation for the destruction of York and Newark.[62] Advancing on Bladensburg, the English troops engaged in a skirmish with the American militia on August 24. After the first few shots the Americans bolted and the British entered Washington that evening. The next day, all public buildings were burnt, though private dwellings were respected. Ross and Cochrane retired on the 26th. It was a foolish act, as reprisals so often are.

Next, an attack—really a naval booty-hunt—was made on Baltimore. It proved unsuccessful and during the course of it Ross was killed. In October, the expedition sailed for Jamaica, arriving there on November 1. After reorganizing, it continued on to New Orleans, north of which General Andrew Jackson was winding up his campaign against the Creek and Choctaw Indians, who had been stirred up by the British.

As Fortescue informs us, it was on naval advice that New Orleans was selected as the next objective, "due chiefly to the desire for prize money," which he says, "had for nearly two centuries been the motive for all amphibious operations recommended by the Navy." [63] Jackson had arrived there on December 2, and was assembling a force of some 6,000 strong, including the formidable militias of Kentucky and Tennessee. Six days later Admiral Cochrane anchored off Ship Island in Mississippi Sound, bringing with him some 8,000 to 9,000 soldiers under the command of General Sir Edward Pakenham—the Duke of Wellington's brother-in-law. Seven days later, a landing was effected in rear of New Orleans, and after a series of movements and minor attacks, early in January, 1815, Pakenham decided to launch a frontal attack on Jackson's fortified position.

Early on the 8th the assault was made under a "cloud of rockets," which "continued to fall in showers during the whole attack." [64] It was met by a terrific and accurate rifle fire, which mowed the troops down by hundreds.[65] Pakenham was killed and his next two senior officers dangerously wounded. Then a second assault was made, which, writes Latour, "was received with the same rolling fire of musketry and artillery, till, having advanced without much order very near our lines, it at last broke again, and retired in the utmost confusion." [66] The battle then concluded with a truce to bury the dead.

Over 2,000 British fell, and the American losses, though variously given, did not exceed sixty to seventy. This indeed was the most disastrous attack on the American continent since Abercromby's headlong assault at Ticonderoga in 1758.

From New Orleans, unmolested by their enemy, the expedition sailed to Mobile, where, after the capture of Fort Bowyer, they received news that peace had been made.

By no means was it a sudden conclusion. Within eight days of the war's declaration, Monroe had directed Jonathan Russell, then in charge of American affairs in London, to discuss its termination with the British government, whereas almost simultaneously that government directed Admiral Sir John Warren—then on the American station—to open negotiations at Washington.[67] So rooted became the idea of the war's illegitimacy that, as already mentioned, in December, 1814, delegates from the New England states met at Hartford to hint at secession from the Union. Nevertheless, Macdonough's victory in Plattsburg Bay was the strategical turning point from war to peace, not so much because the British were defeated, but because this defeat, as previously stated, led the government in London to turn to their greatest strategical authority—the Duke of Wellington—who in thinly veiled words proclaimed the war to be strategically absurd.

On August 8, 1814, negotiations were opened at Ghent, where a peace of stalemate, rather than of settlement, was agreed to. It was a peace which settled nothing of importance, such as questions of blockade, impressment and frontiers, but was confined solely to drawing-room gentilities; the contracting parties agreeing that they "would use their best endeavours to promote the entire abolition of the slave trade," and would not again in war use Indians against each other. The treaty was signed on December 24, and ratified by the United States on February 17, 1815—nine days before Napoleon stood out from Porte Ferrajo on his return to France and Waterloo.

Far more important than the Treaty of Ghent were the lessons and influences of this war. Its leadership and strategy had with few exceptions been contemptible, owing largely to the war's democratic character, as Fortescue infers when he writes:

In truth war, an ugly thing at the best of times, is rarely so inhuman as when waged by amateurs. It is difficult enough to keep disciplined men in hand when flushed by victory or discouraged by defeat; but with un-disciplined men and untrained leaders the task is impossible. . . . But democracies, whether American or British, have short memories and no love for the lessons of history. The only quality that never fails them is conceit, and the only teacher that can prevail with them is disaster.[69]

During this war Canada passed from youth to maturity, because she was fighting for freedom, for hearth, and for home. It was indeed a national struggle, which ended by reconciling, so far as it was possible, the English and French within her frontiers.

For Great Britain, as Lucas points out: "The same spirit which had inspired and carried to success the American War of Independence was now enlisted on the side of Great Britain, and the successful defence of Canada by regiments from Great Britain and Canadian colonists com-binded, meant that a new British Empire was coming into being *pari passu* with the growth of a young nation within its limits. The war of 1812 determined that North America should not exclusively belong to the American Republic, that Great Britain should keep her place on the continent, but that she should keep it through this new community al-ready on the high-road to legislative independence."[70]

For the United States the first great result of the war was this: it clearly showed that, although America is separated by three thousand miles of sea from Europe, when oceanic power dominates an European war, the chances are that America will be involved in it. Secondly, this war concluded the War of Independence by finally breaking the domination, economic as well as political, of Great Britain over America. From now onward, with her back to the East, America could face the West and address herself to her internal growth. Finally, as Albert Gallatin wrote:

The war has been productive of evil and of good, but I think the good preponderates. Independent of the loss of lives, and of the property of individuals, the war has laid the foundations of permanent taxes and military establishments, which the Republicans had deemed unfavorable to the happiness and free institutions of the country. But under any former system we were becoming too selfish, too much attached exclusively to the acquisition of wealth, above all, too much confined in our political feelings to local and state objects. The war has renewed and reinstated the national feelings and character which the Revolution had given and which were daily lessening. The people have now more general objects of attachment, with which their pride and political opinions are connected. They are more Americans; they feel and act more as a nation; and I hope that the permanency of the Union is thereby better secured.[71]

REFERENCES

[1] Quoted from *Sea Power in Its Relation to the War of 1812*, Captain A. T. Mahan, vol. II, p. 213 (1905).

[2] See *Life and Times of Major-General Sir Isaac Brock*, D. R. Reed, p. 193, and *The Annual Register*, 1812, p. 201.

[3] See *Niles' Weekly Register*, vol. VII, p. 195. While in Boston flour sold for $12.00 the barrel, in Baltimore and Richmond it stood at $6.50 and $4.50. "Probably," writes Henry Adams, "New England lent to the British government during the war more money than she lent to her own. The total amount subscribed in New England to the United States loans were less than three millions" (*History of the United States of America*, vol. VII, p. 389).

[4] For a list of them see *Warden Refuted; being a Defence of the British Navy*, William James, p. 13 (1819).

[5] "The exports from Quebec only, amounted during the last year to near six millions of dollars, in ship-timber, and provisions for support of her fleets and armies." Quoted by William F. Coffin, *1812; the War and Its Moral*, p. 22 (Montreal, 1864).

[6] *The Writings of James Monroe*, edited by S. M. Hamilton, vol. V, p. 207.

[7] Quoted by Mahan, vol. I, pp. 303-304. See also *Annals of Congress*, 11th Congress, Pt. I, p. 580; *Jefferson's Writings*, collected and edited by P. L. Ford, vol. VIII, p. 450.

[8] *A Full and Correct Account of the Military Occurrences of the Late War between Great Britain and the United States of America*, William James, vol. I, p. 49 (1818).

[9] The following is a statement compiled from War Department returns made in 1805 to 1810 (*American State Papers, Military Affairs*, vol. I, p. 298) and the census of 1810:

Section of Country	White Males between 16 and 45	Enrolled Militia
New England	274,463	140,538
Middle States	382,698	231,484
Southern States and D. C.	294,879	223,462
The West	167,859	99,251
	1,119,899	694,735

See *A History of the United States,* Edward Channing, vol. IV, p. 457.

[10] *American State Papers, Military Affairs,* vol. I, pp. 300, 303, 307, and 317. (Further state equipment is included in these pages.)

[11] President Madison in his speech on March 4, 1813, said: "Our nation is, in numbers, more than half that of the British Isles." (*The Annual Meeting,* 1813, p. 395.)

[12] *Report on Canadian Archives,* 1896, Lower Canada, p. 36.

[13] See *Wellington's Dispatches,* Gurwood, vol. II, p. 525 (1838).

[14] Channing, vol. IV, p. 462.

[15] *Report on Canadian Archives,* 1893, Lower Canada, p. 3.

[16] *The Writings of James Madison,* edited by Gaillard Hunt, vol. VII, p. 211.

[17] *Letters and Other Writings,* James Madison, vol. II, p. 547. (Madison to Dearborn, October 7, 1812.)

[18] *Life and Correspondence of Sir Isaac Brock,* Ferdinand Brock Tupper, p. 315 (1847).

[19] A graphic account of this battle is to be found in the *Life of Sir John Beverley Robinson.*

[20] That evening, when dining with General Sheaffe, Scott was called out of the room and saved from assassination at the hands of two Indians—Jacob Norton and Brant the younger—by the general's A.D.C.—Colonel Coffin. See *The Campaign of General Scott in the Valley of Mexico,* Edward B. Mansfield, p. 47, and *Life of Joseph Brant, Thayendanega,* William L. Stone, vol. II, p. 214.

[21] See *Documentary History of the Campaign on the Niagara Frontier in 1812,* edited by Captain E. Cruikshank, Part II, p. 15.

[22] *Ibid.,* Part I, 1813, p. 154.

[23] For an account of this really heroic exploit, see *A Veteran of 1812, the Life of James FitzGibbon,* Mary Agnes FitzGibbon (1894).

[24] See *Documentary History, Cruikshank,* Part II, 1813, pp. 120–121.

[25] When questioned at his court-martial on this point, his answer was: "I blockaded as closely as I could, until I one morning saw the whole of the enemy's force over the bar, and in a most formidable state of preparation," which explains nothing. J. Fenimore Cooper in his *History of the Navy of the United States of America* (vol. II, p. 450) says that it was reported that he lost command of the Lake by accepting an invitation to dinner.

[26] An account of this operation is given in Cooper, vol. II, p. 451.

[27] "Captain Barclay's Report to Sir James Yeo, September 12, 1813." See James's *Naval Occurrences,* Appendix 54, p. LXXXIII (1817).

[28] *Richardson's War of 1812,* Edited by Alexander Clark Casselman, p. 190 (Toronto, 1902).

[29] James's *Naval Occurrences,* pp. 285–287. On account of defective matches and tubes, many of his guns had to be fired by pistols (p. 289). As regards crews the proportion of Canadian boatmen to soldiers and militiamen was 9 to 13 (*The His-*

tory of Canada, William Kingsford, vol. VIII, p. 310). In the American ships it was much the same (see *The Naval War of 1812,* Theodore Roosevelt, pp. 278–279). Perry employed some Negroes and Barclay some Indians, also after the engagement the Americans discovered a large bear on board the *Detroit* "which was found in the enjoyment of lapping the blood from her decks" (*Historical Sketch of the Second War between the United States of America and Great Britain,* Charles J. Ingersoll, p. 156).

[30] *Richardson's War of 1812,* p. 193. Roosevelt's *Naval War of 1812* (pp. 260–261) gives very similar tables.

[31] Roosevelt's *Naval War of 1812,* p. 272. See also Henry Adams, vol. VII, p. 121 (1891).

[32] *The Pictorial Field-Book of the War of 1812,* Benson J. Lossing, p. 519.

[33] *Richardson's War of 1812,* pp. 191–192.

[34] "Perry's Report," James's *Naval Occurrences,* p. XC.

[35] "Barclay's Report," *ibid.,* p. LXXXIV.

[36] *Ibid.,* p. LXXXV.

[37] Lossing, p. 530.

[38] James's *Naval Occurrences,* p. LXXXIX.

[39] Lossing, pp. 533–534.

[40] Adams, vol. VII, p. 126.

[41] Roosevelt's *Naval War of 1812,* p. 274.

[42] For an interesting account of this battle, see *Richardson's War of 1812,* chap. XI, pp. 204–242.

[43] *A History of the British Army,* The Hon. J. W. Fortescue, vol. IX, p. 345. This mutual destruction of private property was a disgraceful feature of this war, though in recent years—1914–1940—it has become the leading characteristic of air-barbarians. Fortescue's condemnation of it is worth quoting. He writes: "Under generals so helpless, nerveless and shiftless as Dearborn, Wilkinson, Hampton and M'Clure the American militiaman, with all the material in him to make a grand fighting man, became too often a skulking marauder, while more competent officers were paralysed because the troops entrusted to them were a mere rabble. The officers, when they did not fall to the same level as their men, found vent for their feelings in the exchange of recrimination; the men indemnified themselves for the discomfort of service by plunder and wanton destruction of property. Reprisals followed as a natural consequence, and the unfortunate settlers blamed the Indians, the British and their own generals, for what was really the fault of the American Government or, more truly, of the ignorant democracy which inspired its action" (p. 349).

[44] *Izard's Correspondence,* p. 69. Quoted by Adams, vol. VIII, p. 100.

[45] Niles, vol. VII, p. 60.

[46] *Izard's Correspondence,* p. 57.

[47] James's *Naval Occurrences,* pp. 405–406.

[48] See Roosevelt's *Naval War of 1812,* pp. 376–381. Adams (vol. VIII, p. 106) calculates the broadsides at 1,864 lbs. for the British ship and 2,033 for the American.

[49] Adams, vol. VIII, p. 106.

[50] James's *Naval Occurrences,* p. 404.

[51] Mahan, vol. II, p. 373.

[52] Adams, vol. VIII, p. 106. Roosevelt (p. 387) says that at the time of the battle he was 28 years old.

[53] Cooper, vol. II, p. 500.

[54] Roosevelt's *Naval War of 1812,* p. 392.

[55] "Macdonough's Report," James's *Naval Occurrences*, Appendix 92, p. CLXIII.

[56] See "Pring's Report," *ibid.*, Appendix 90, p. CLVIII.

[57] *Ibid.*, Appendix 90, p. CLXII, and Appendix 92, p. CLXV.

[58] Quoted from Kingsford, vol. VIII, pp. 539–540.

[59] Mahan, vol. II, p. 381.

[60] *Wellington's Supplementary Despatches*, vol. IX, pp. 425, 435.

[61] Simultaneously another diversion was carried out by Sir John Cope Sherbrooke, Governor of Nova Scotia, against the mainland between the New Brunswick frontier and the Penobscot River.

[62] For a long letter, written by John Strachan of York, dated January 30, 1815, and addressed to Thomas Jefferson explaining this, see Coffin, pp. 273–285. For Cochrane's views, see *American State Papers, Foreign Relations*, vol. III, p. 694.

[63] Fortescue, vol. X, pp. 150–151.

[64] *Historical Memoir of the War in West Florida and Louisiana in 1814–15*, Major A. Lecarrière Latour, p. 154 (1816). The rockets were those invented by Major-General Sir W. Congreve in 1804, and first used at the bombardment of Boulogne in 1806.

[65] See *The Campaign of the British Army at Washington and New Orleans, 1814–1815*, Rev. G. R. Gleig, Chaplain to the Forces, p. 178 (1879); also Latour, p. 155.

[66] Latour, p. 155. For descriptions of the field after the battle, see Gleig, p. 182.

[67] See *American State Papers, Foreign Relations*, vol. III, pp. 585, 586, 590, and 595.

[68] In *The Annual Register*, 1814, (p. 176) we read: "The unhappy war with the United States of America, an epithet it peculiarly deserves, as having no great object on either side, the attainment of which can in the least compensate its evils."

[69] Fortescue, vol. IX, p. 349.

[70] *The Canadian War of 1812*, C. P. Lucas, pp. 259–260.

[71] *The Writings of Albert Gallatin*, edited by Henry Adams, vol. I, p. 700.

1783–1824

SYNOPSIS OF BACKGROUND EVENTS

I N de Tocqueville's *Democracy in America,* first published in 1835, we read: "It is not to be imagined that the impulse of the Anglo-Saxon race can be arrested. Their continual progress towards the Rocky Mountains has the solemnity of a providential event. Tyrannical government and consequent hostilities may retard this impulse, but cannot prevent it from ultimately fulfilling the destinies for which that race is reserved. No power on earth can close upon the emigrants the fertile wilderness, which offers resources to all industry, and a refuge from all want . . . Thus, in the midst of the uncertain future, one event is sure. At a period which may be said to be near, the Anglo-Americans alone will cover the immense space contained between the Polar Region and the Tropic, extending from the coast of the Atlantic to the shores of the Pacific Ocean." The story of how this expansion took form and the conflicts it engendered will carry us from this point to the end of this book.

Though its beginnings date back to the days of the Tudors, it was not until 1763 that a new form of imperial expansion began to take root. Then, as to all intents and purposes the French disappeared from North America, the field was left to the English. Twenty years later this imperialism became the inheritance of the Americans, because, as Frederic L. Paxson writes in his *History of the American Frontier, 1763–1893,* the Treaty of Paris "left in American hands the future of American life."

The severance of America from England left the Indian problem in the hands of the newborn republic, and with it the question of the ownership of the unoccupied lands. Large tracts of Tory property were confiscated, and a vast and little-known region, stretching westward of the old colonial frontier, was claimed by the bordering states. These claims led to internal friction, because though the frontier population urged its free disposal the states concerned saw in the territory a valuable asset and a source of revenue. The result was that "The colonial idea that had been strongest in the proprietaries spread over all the States, and carried the social clash of the colonial period over into the Union." It brought about a division between East and West—the inhabitants of the one remaining the exploiters of trade while those of the other became the graspers of land.

The first great wave of expansion immediately followed the Revolutionary War, for not only did many soldiers of the Continental Army desire to move westward, but also hundreds of small farmers whose barren acres were covered with mortgages.

This expansion, in its turn, led to a renewal of the clash with the Indians, which had begun in 1774, when Lord Dunmore, Governor of Virginia, defeated Cornstalk and his Shawnee braves on the field of Point Pleasant, at the mouth of the Great Kanawha. This war, with few intervals, was continued throughout the Revolution, and now every new settlement west of the Ohio River was an encroachment on Indian lands. In 1790, General Joseph Harmar was sent to the Maumee villages, only to be surprised and repulsed. Then followed Arthur St. Clair with no greater success, for on a branch of the Wabash he was ambushed by Little Turtle and Tecumseh, a Shawnee warrior.

To retrieve the situation, Washington commissioned General Anthony Wayne to raise an army. He began recruiting near Pittsburg during the summer of 1792, but not until he had disciplined his men did he, in the spring of the following year, set out down the Ohio. Then, instead of seeking a fight, he marched to the scene of St. Clair's defeat and built Fort Recovery. The next year he took the field, advanced to the Maumee and annoyed the English by building Fort Defiance. Some forty miles below it, where a tornado had left a natural breastwork of tree trunks, on August 20, 1794, he decisively defeated Little Turtle in the battle of Fallen Timbers, after which whisky and syphilis accomplished the rest.

This battle was followed by fifteen years of peace. Then, in 1809, Tecumseh repudiated the treaties Wayne had made with the Indians. However, there was no actual fighting until 1811, when, in September, Harrison marched up the Wabash River. Early on the morning of November 7, the Indians attempted to rush his camp south of Tippecanoe Creek, but were defeated. This victory—though a somewhat doubtful one—did for the Wabash country what Fallen Timbers had done for the Maumee: "it broke the rising tide of Indian consciousness" as well as the prestige of Tecumseh. Further south, on March 27, 1814, Andrew Jackson decisively defeated the "Redsticks" or hostile Creek warriors at Horseshoe Bend on the Tallapoosa River. After this victory, except for occasional forays and murderings, the Indian menace passes into legend and storybook and the age of Fenimore Cooper opens.

The second great wave of expansion followed the "long embargo," which ruined trade between the years 1807–1812. The third came in the footsteps of the War of 1812, to be accentuated by the slump that followed it. Then streams of broken people moved West, until between the years 1816–1820 the western highways were choked with emigrants.

During these three waves of expansion nine new states came into being and were added to the Union—namely, Vermont (1791), Kentucky (1792), Tennessee (1796), Ohio (1803), Louisiana (1812), Indiana (1816), Mississippi (1817), Illinois (1818), and Alabama (1819). When added to the thirteen states of 1783, they raised the total to twenty-two, eleven being free and eleven slave.

When, in 1819, Missouri asked to be admitted, the free-soil members of Congress were determined that slavery should be prohibited in that region, whereas those of the slave-holding states took the opposite point of view. The difference was settled by the Missouri Compromise, by which it was agreed that slavery should be recognized in Missouri, while all other territory in the Louisiana Purchase lying north of parallel 36° 30′ should be free. As part of this Compromise and in order to balance this extraordinary politico-economic arrangement, in 1821 Maine was admitted into the Union as a Free State, making twelve of each.

It was in these new states (excepting Vermont and Maine) rather than in the old that Americans both rapidly and truly became American. The clue to this enigma is given to us by Paxson when he informs us that "In nearly every case the unit working on the frontier was a young married couple." It was a society of young people which moved West, settled, and bred, and whose children when grown up moved further west still. Therefore these expansions acquired the character of a constantly moving wave of youth, which, unrestrained by the voice of age, broke away from tradition and became violently independent. These pioneers formed a society in which equality passed from theory into fact. Life was as hard for the rich as for the poor: a life of plowing, sowing, and reaping for the men and of bearing, nursing, and tending for the women.

The Frontier did more than change the English into Americans. As it pushed constantly westward the colonial conception of empire was lost, the idea of colonies separated from the motherland giving way to the idea of an amalgamation between the two, until spiritually the West swallowed up all that the Revolution had left of the earlier conception.

The establishment of a contiguous and homogeneous empire was vastly assisted by improvements in communication. In 1787, John Fitch had invented a steamboat, and in 1807 Robert Fulton's *Clermont* was plying up and down the Hudson. Two years later, Nicholas J. Roosevelt in a stern paddle-wheel ship steamed from Pittsburg to New Orleans, and in 1817, *Walk in the Water* was carrying passengers and cargoes on Lake Erie. In 1825 the Erie Canal was opened, and in 1827 a charter was granted to Maryland and Pennsylvania for the first American railroad—the Baltimore-Ohio.

As the future lay west of the Mississippi, it was largely in that vast tract of country that the new Americans were born. There friction with the Spanish was constant, and to understand it it is necessary to enter a little into the history of that region.

In 1763, Louis XV had ceded to Spain the ill-defined Province of Louisiana, which included the whole of the western half of the basin of the Mississippi from the coastline of the Gulf of Mexico to the sources of the Missouri River. Then, on October 1, 1800, by the treaty of San Ildefonso Spain retroceded this province to France, and on April 30, 1803, Napoleon sold it to the United States for 60,000,000 francs— $11,250,000. Boundary disputes between the Spaniards and Americans followed until 1819, when the United States agreed to abandon all claims to Texas, and on payment of $4,500,000 to receive as a *quid pro quo* East and West Florida, the western boundary of Louisiana in the extreme south being fixed along the Sabine River and not on the Rio Grande del Norte (Rio Bravo) as had previously been claimed.

Meanwhile Mexico was in a state of dissolution. With a few short breaks this was to continue until Porfirio Diaz established his dictatorship in 1876.

Since the days of Cortés and his followers the country had been largely bastardized, and the half-caste race resulting had not yet had time to form those traditions so necessary to nationhood. Trade was fettered by restrictions; smuggling was reduced to a system; the manufacture of all articles that could be provided by Spain was forbidden. The rearing of silkworms and the cultivation of the olive and the vine were prohibited, as was the growing of hemp, flax, indigo, and coffee. It was the English system of colonization by trade and navigation act run mad, with both place and power falling to the lot of governors and bureaucrats loaned from Spain—still a characteristic of the British system in India. Thus the country was systematically prepared for revolution.

The first outbreak occurred in 1810, following Napoleon's overthrow of the Spanish monarchy in 1808, when a decree of the Council of the Indies transferred the Spanish American Dominions to his brother Joseph, whom he had made King of Spain. Its leader was a priest, Don Miguel Hidalgo Castilla of Dolores, who had attempted to ameliorate the lot of his flock by the cultivation of silk and the vine. Proscribed by Vanegas, the viceroy, in September, 1810, Hidalgo sacked Guana-juato, marched on the capital, and beat the royalists at Las Cruces. He followed up this victory by a series of minor operations, and then, in January, 1811, at the head of 60,000 foot, 20,000 horse, and 100 cannon, was defeated by General Calleja and 6,000 men at the Bridge of Calderon near Guadalajara. Later on he was shot.

The challenge was then taken up by José Maria Morelos, who in February, 1812, repulsed Calleja at Cuatla, was there besieged and eventually cut his way out. Again minor operations followed until in April, 1813, he took Acapulco and then appearing before Valladolid was routed. In January he made his final stand at Puruaran, was betrayed and shot on December 22, 1815. Though his followers continued the struggle, the revolution died out in January, 1817.

A hectic peace followed until the tidings of the constitutional revolution in Spain were received in 1820. Then Vicente Guerrero reraised the standard of revolt and defeated Augustin de Iturbide, who forthwith joined the rebels and took over command of the revolutionary army. On February 24, 1821, he felt strong enough to announce the famous Plan of Iguala, proclaiming the independence of Mexico. In September he entered the capital to be proclaimed emperor. Surrounded by flatterers and traitors, he soon abused his newly won power, whereupon Antonio Lopez de Santa Anna, who had gained a captaincy in 1811, "pronounced" for a republic. This precipitated yet another revolution, which forced Iturbide's abdication in 1823. Retiring to Italy, Iturbide shortly after returned to Mexico and was shot.

The Centralists' faction collapsed with his fall. The Federalists chose Guadalupe Victoria as first President of the Mexican Republic, and in

1824 a Federal Constitution was adopted. Coincidentally with these many upheavals, revolution swept over the Spanish South American Colonies—Colombia, Chili, Peru, and Buenos Aires—and on May 4, 1822, President Monroe signed a Bill, recognizing their independence as well as that of Mexico. Then, fearing that some European Power might attempt to take possession of one or more of these newborn republics, on December 2, 1823, he announced in his Annual Message to Congress three principles which since have become known as the Monroe Doctrine. These principles were:

(1) The United States will "not interfere in the internal concerns" of any European Power.

(2) But if any European Power should attempt to extend its political system to any part of North or South America "for the purpose of oppressing" the nations or "controlling in any other manner their destiny," the United States will interfere.

(3) That (with reference to the Russian territory of Alaska) no further portion of the American continents will be "considered as subjects for future colonisation by any European Powers." (In 1824 the boundary between Alaska and Oregon was fixed on latitude 54° 40′.)

Thus came into existence a new form of expansion—expansion by reservation—the whole of the New World being excluded from European land hunger and placed in cold storage for the eventual economic exploitation of the United States. As the nineteenth century closed and the twentieth took its course, this exploitation approached nearer and nearer to that financial dictatorship so fondly dreamed of by Columbus when he exclaimed: "Gold is a wonderful thing. Whoever owns it is lord of all he wants. With gold it is even possible to open for souls a way into paradise."

CHAPTER V

THE BATTLES OF SAN JACINTO,
CONTRERAS–CHURUBUSCO, AND CHAPULTEPEC
1836 AND 1847

FROM 1783 onward it was inevitable that, once the Indian menace
was overcome, sooner or later the expansion westward would reach
the Spanish border, giving rise to a new war problem. This certainty
became apparent to many when the purchase of Louisiana was made, an
event that almost led to a severance of the Union, because the Federalists
were bitterly opposed to any acquisition of territory by the South.
Though this clash was delayed for a generation, expansion in the end
proved a stronger force than politics. However, for years it was restricted to filibuster raiding which culminated in James Long's feeble
attempt in 1819.

Barely had this excitement subsided, when a more reasonable person
appeared—namely, Moses Austin of Connecticut who, in 1819, was
granted permission by the Mexican government to establish an American colony within the Spanish border. As he died shortly after, his son
Stephen F. Austin carried out his project by planting the first Anglo-
American Settlement at San Felipe de Austin in 1821. Soon he was
followed by other *"empresarios"* (contractors), each contracting to
bring from two to three hundred families with them, until a spate of
pilgrims flooded Texas, which, under the Constitution of 1824, was
linked to the State of Coahuila. So rapidly did wave follow wave that
in 1825 the British diplomatic representative in Mexico warned his
government that the Mexicans were suffering "by an absurd mixture of
negligence, and weakness, the whole disputed territory . . . to be

quickly taken possession by the very men, whose claim to it, they are resisting here." [1]

During the following year Hayden Edwards, an *empresario,* looking upon the Mexicans east of the Rio Grande as intruders, seized the town of Nacogdoches and proclaimed a new republic, which he called "Fredonia." Though it lasted but a few days, his "rebellion" caused a tremendous stir in the American press, for "In sharpest black and white the ardent Americans of 1827 pictured their kinsmen defeated in Mexico as apostles of democracy crushed by an alien civilization." [2]

This typically American reaction, which instinctively favors the underdog, was followed by an equally typical American proposal—that the difficulty could be settled by a financial transaction. Consequently an envoy, Mr. Poinsett, was sent to the Mexican government with an offer to buy out the territories between the Sabine and Rio Grande for $1,000,000, or between the Sabine and Colorado for half that sum. Though this checkbook settlement was refused, in 1829, during the first year of Andrew Jackson's Presidency, it was once again pressed. At the same time Spain attempted to reconquer Mexico, a fiasco that enormously enhanced the power of the Mexican Santa Anna. Now a general, Santa Anna pocketed the government, forced it to abolish the Federal Constitution of 1824 and substitute for it a centralized system, which meant military rule. On top of this, further emigration into Texas was prohibited in 1830. This restriction brought onto the scene Texas's man of delivery—Sam Houston.

Of Scotch-Irish stock, Houston was born at Timber Ridge Church in Rockbridge county, Virginia, on March 2, 1793.[3] In the War of 1812 he served under Jackson and became his intimate friend. In 1827 he was made Governor of Tennessee. Two years later he married but soon separated from his wife. Accused of all manner of crimes, he refused to defend himself, saying: "If my character cannot stand the shock, let me lose it. The storm will soon sweep by and time will be my vindicator." [4] He then retired into Arkansas to live with the Cherokee Chief Oolooteka, who years before had adopted him as his son, and soon became known amongst his braves as "Big Drunk." [5] In 1830 he suddenly appeared in Washington to seek a government contract for furnishing Indian supplies. Several discussions took place between him and Jackson, which led, two years later, to his leaving for Texas with a plan in his head to annex that province to the United States.

The moment was certainly propitious. Mexico was once again in a state of chaos, and Texas was by now largely occupied by Americans who firmly believed, and with some logic, that the earth belongs to him who tills it. Like their ancestors in 1765, they were determined to pay no more customs duties to a government that could not enforce their collection.

By the date Houston arrived, the first clash had already taken place. In 1831 a settler—William Barrett Travis—was seized and arrested, whereupon 150 men, headed by John Austin (not to be confused with Stephen Austin) demanded his release. As the Mexican government refused to free him, on June 26, 1832, Henry Smith, district commissioner at Brazoria, with 112 Texans launched a night attack on the Mexican garrison of Velasco and seized two cannon. In October, a Convention of Texans assembled at San Felipe de Austin and demanded a return to the Constitution of 1824, as well as the separation of Texas from Coahuila.

Nothing much happened until April 1, 1833, when Santa Anna became president. A second Convention assembled and demanded the right to trial by jury and the privilege of *Habeas Corpus.* This memorial was taken to the capital by Stephen Austin who was at once seized and imprisoned for many months. On his return in 1835, a Committee of Safety was organized under his chairmanship. On September 19, he issued a circular in which he expressed himself as follows: "WAR is our only resource. There is no other remedy. We must defend our rights, ourselves, and our country, by force of arms." [6] Santa Anna counterattacked with a decree ordering all Texans to disarm. The settlement of Gonzales—64 miles east of San Antonio de Bexar—refused to surrender its weapons and called for help. Thus was precipitated the Lexington of Texas. Up and down the valleys of the Colorado and Brazos the call to arms was heard. On October 2, 160 Texans attacked the Mexicans threatening Gonzales, and routed them at the cost of one man wounded and one enemy killed. The gauntlet thus thrown down was picked up by General Cos, who the day before had occupied Goliad and was now about to move on San Antonio de Bexar.

At once the excitement of war swept over the scattered settlements. "Like our fathers of the Revolution," cried the colonists, "we have sworn to live free or die—like our fathers of 1776, we have pledged to each other our lives, fortunes, and sacred honors—and have vowed to drive every Mexican soldier beyond the Rio Grande, or whiten the plains with our bones." [7] The post of Goliad was occupied on the 8th;

leaden water pipes and clock weights were molded into bullets, and on the 11th the Western Army was organized under the command of Stephen Austin. Two days later he set out for Bexar, in the vicinity of which his subordinate, James Bowie,[8] and a detachment of 92 men fought and won the Battle of the Concepcion on the 28th, at the cost of one man killed and none wounded. Then, on November 13, a provisional government was formed with Henry Smith as governor and Houston as general, with his headquarters at Washington on the Brazos.

Meanwhile Bexar was being besieged by General Burleston. After many skirmishes and much street fighting, Cos surrendered on terms, on December 11, nineteen cannon and several hundred stands of arms falling into Texan hands. Thus the first campaign was brought to a successful ending, while Santa Anna was assembling a large force at San Luis Potosi.

Success, it would appear, turned the heads of the provisional government. Without considering the difficulties, Governor Smith and his Council decided to reduce Matamoras, ordering Colonel Francis W. Johnson, then commanding at Bexar, and Dr. Grant to carry out this enterprise. As a result, only seventy-five men were left to hold the town.

Meanwhile Santa Anna had passed through Saltillo at the head of 8,000 men, a powerful train of artillery, an immense mass of baggage and innumerable women, and was now heading for the Rio Grande. His second-in-command was General Vicente Filisola, and his confidential adviser Colonel Almonte. On February 12 they reached the Rio Grande. There a halt was called and the whole countryside wasted. Every outrage was allowed in order to induce the troops to remain with the colors. When the army set out again on the 16th, Santa Anna sent the following order to his advanced guard commander: "The foreigners who are making war on the Mexican nation in violation of every rule of law, are entitled to no consideration whatever, and in consequence no quarter is to be given them, of which order you will give notice to your troops."[9] As Santa Anna neared Bexar on the 23d, William Barrett Travis, then holding that town with 185 men,[10] at once sent an express to San Felipe urgently calling for relief, and next withdrew to the Alamo, a strongly built Franciscan mission house. There on March 1, he was invested by some 4,000 Mexicans.

On this same day the Texas provisional government met at Washington and issued a declaration of independence, and while it was still in session Travis's dispatch arrived. On the 4th, Houston was unanimously appointed commander in chief over all forces in the field. On the 7th, with three or four companions he rode to Gonzales to take command of a small force of militia, and attempt the relief of the

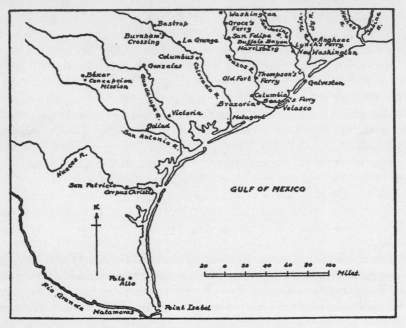

10.   Map of the San Jacinto Campaign, 1838

Alamo. However, at Gonzales he learnt that the Alamo had been attacked on the 6th, and after a desperate room-to-room fight its garrison killed to a man. "Thermopylae," said a Texan orator, "Thermopylae had its messenger of defeat, the Alamo had none." [11] Nevertheless, this heroic defense of the old mission house was not in vain, because the time spent by Santa Anna in taking it was of incalculable value to the Texans.

At the date of this calamity, the number of the volunteers in Texas was between 400 and 500 men. The bulk of them were under Colonel James W. Fannin at Goliad, from which place Colonel Johnson and Dr. Grant had advanced to San Patricio on the Nueces River. There, at about the time the Alamo was attacked, their small party was cut up,

Johnson and one other alone escaping. This disaster, coupled with the fate of Travis, decided Houston to fall back from Gonzales to the Colorado. Setting fire to the town and ordering Fannin to abandon Goliad and retire to Victoria, he set out on the 14th with such haste that the whole countryside took panic, men, women, and children flying frantically toward the United States border, many of the volunteers joining them.[12]

On receiving Houston's order to fall back, Fannin foolishly delayed for five days—that is until the 19th—in spite of the fact that the order had contained these words: "The immediate advance of the enemy may be confidently expected as well as a rise of water. Prompt movements are therefore highly important." [13] When he finally did retire, he encumbered his small column with a heavily laden ox train. About midday, five miles from the Coleta River, he was overtaken by General Urrea's cavalry and compelled to form laager. All that day the fight continued,[14] but on Sunday the 20th, after most of his animals had been killed, he surrendered on terms.

From the battlefield Fannin and his men were sent back to Goliad, where they were joined by other batches of prisoners—in all numbering about five hundred—and placed under the guard of two hundred Mexicans commanded by Lieutenant Colonel Portilla. Early on the morning of the 27th, by express orders received from Santa Anna, about 350 of these unfortunates were marched out on the prairie, shot in cold blood, and their bodies burned. Fannin was the last to be killed.[15]

This succession of disasters, entirely due to lack of military instinct on the part of the Texans, convinced Santa Anna that the war was as good as won and that he could now safely return to Mexico and enjoy his triumph. Filisola, becoming alarmed, persuaded him to postpone his return to the capital. At this time, while Houston with some six hundred followers was at Burnham's Crossing on the Colorado, Santa Anna's own forces were distributed as follows: General Gaona was at Bastrop; Ramirez y Sesma was approaching San Felipe, Urrea was at Goliad, and he himself was at Bexar, nearly one hundred miles distant from any one of these three detachments.

At Bexar, Santa Anna remained until the 24th, when Sesma reported that he was in touch with 1,200 Texans and that he could not cross the Colorado as it was in flood and all boats had been removed. Thereupon Santa Anna ordered Gaona and Urrea to march on San Felipe and Sesma to remain where he was until reinforced. The last of these instructions was needless, because Houston, learning of Fannin's surrender, for some reason not explained, abandoned his camp on the Colorado and withdrew to the Brazos, reaching San Felipe on the 28th. From there he marched up the river to Groce's Ferry, where he remained until April 12.

Santa Anna arrived at the Colorado on April 5, and found General Sesma in the process of crossing. Ordering Filisola to remain there until he had gathered in the rear of his scattered forces, Santa Anna pushed on with the van to San Felipe, arriving there on the 7th. The Brazos was in flood and all boats had been removed by Houston, whom he learned had gone upstream. Not waiting for Filisola and having lost touch with Gaona, he turned downstream with a hundred men, apparently to look for boats. Setting out from San Felipe on the 9th, he reached Old Fort (Thompson's Ferry) on the 11th. Discovering two or three boats, he sent back orders to Sesma to join him. When Sesma came up on the 14th, Santa Anna crossed the river at the head of 750 men and on the following day occupied Harrisburg. Finding it in flames, he decided to move on Lynch Ferry, which lies some fifteen miles east of Harrisburg, on the San Jacinto River. On the 16th he learned that his enemy was retreating by way of Lynch Ferry to the Trinity River, but for some inexplicable reason, instead of waiting at the Ferry, he moved on the 18th to the hamlet of New Washington.

Meanwhile Houston, at Groce's Ferry, was daily being pressed by his men to advance on Santa Anna. It was a difficult position for Houston. He realized how undisciplined his men were, believed his enemy to be stronger than he actually was, and knew that should he himself be defeated the war would be lost.[16] On the 16th he set out eastward, telling no one what he intended to do. Some twenty miles east of the Brazos the van of his column struck the fork road to Nacogdoches and Harrisburg, whereupon a "loud and joyous shout" went up as the leading men swung to the right—that is toward the second of these villages.[17]

On the 18th, Houston reached Buffalo Bayou, opposite Harrisburg, where he learned that Santa Anna had passed through during the morning on his way to New Washington. In consequence he found that instead of retiring he was actually pursuing his enemy—that is to say, he was on his tail.

Next day he sent out a scout—Erastus Smith (Deaf Smith)—who had the good fortune to capture one of Santa Anna's officers bearing a dispatch to Filisola giving full information of the Mexican movements. Thereupon he sent the following message to Colonel H. Raguet at Nacogdoches:

This morning [the 19th] we are in preparation to meet Santa Anna. It is the only chance of saving Texas. From time to time I have looked for reinforcements, in vain. The Convention adjourning to Harrisburg struck panic throughout the country. Texas could have started at least 4,000 men; we only have about 700 to march with, besides the camp guard. We go to conquer. It is wisdom growing out of necessity to meet and fight the enemy now. Every consideration enforces it. No previous occasion would justify it. The troops are in fine spirits, and now is the time for action.[18]

Then he moved south, crossing the Buffalo Bayou, halted, and as dusk fell moved off again eastward to encamp his men by "a border of timber" half a mile from Lynch Ferry. It was the very spot on the map that Andrew Jackson had some time before placed his finger on, saying to James Buchanan, the future President: "Here is the place. If Sam Houston is worth one bawbee, he will make a stand here, and give them a fight." [19]

Early on the 20th, as Santa Anna was about to march back to Lynch Ferry, which he should never have left, a scout galloped up to him and reported that Houston was close on his rear. An extraordinary scene of confusion ensued. In a frenzy of rage Santa Anna mounted his horse and drove his terrified troops down a narrow lane, throwing them into utter disorder. At length, reaching the open prairie, he formed them into column of attack; but as no enemy was in sight he halted, then moved forward again toward Lynch Ferry.

About two o'clock, the Texan scouts discovered his advance. Houston in his report writes:

Disposition was immediately made of our forces, and preparation for his reception. He took a position with his infantry, and artillery in the centre, occupying an island of timber, his cavalry covering the left flank. The artillery, consisting of one double fortified medium brass twelve-pounder, then opened on our encampment. The infantry in column advanced with the design of charging our lines, but were repulsed by a discharge of grape and canister from our artillery . . .[20]

Santa Anna then withdrew his troops about three-quarters of a mile from the Texan camp and set them to work entrenching. A little before sunset, Colonel Sherman and eighty-five mounted Texans who had been sent out to reconnoiter, had "a sharp recounter" with the Mexican cavalry.

At daybreak the next morning, Santa Anna had a breastwork of pack-saddles, baggage, and sacks of hard bread thrown up on his left, with an opening in the middle for his one and only cannon. At 9 o'clock, General Cos arrived with 400 reinforcements, which brought his total strength—according to Houston—up to 1,400 men—that is, nearly double his own. As they were dog-tired—so it seems—Santa Anna decided not to fight that day. Anyhow, as evening approached, "Most of his soldiers were sleeping; some few were eating; while others were scattered in the wood procuring boughs wherewith to construct a shelter for the night. The cavalry men were riding bare-back to and fro as they watered their horses, and an indifferent watch was kept by the drowsy piquets. His excellency, fatigued with his morning ride and excitement, slumbered in his tent. His staff, too, was fast asleep." [21]

Meanwhile, at about noon, Houston had held a council of war. The question put was: "Should they attack the enemy in his position, or await his attack on theirs?" Two of the six officers present voted for the first of these alternatives and four for the second. The council was dismissed, Houston expressing no opinion. Instead he sent out Deaf Smith to destroy Vince's Bridge,[22] which lay some eight miles away, in order to prevent additional reinforcements reaching his enemy, and also to cut his line of retreat should he be forced to fall back. Houston had made up his mind, saying to Smith before he set out: "Make the best of your way to Vince's Bridge; cut it down, and burn it up, and come back like eagles, or you will be too late for the day." [23]

At half-past three o'clock, Houston suddenly ordered his army, 783 strong, to parade. Under cover of the islands of timber the following order of battle was formed: In the center, Colonel Burleson and the 1st Regiment of Texas Volunteers; on the left, Colonel Sherman and the 2nd Regiment, and on the right, the artillery and four companies of regular infantry, commanded by Lieutenant Colonel Millard, on whose right were posted the cavalry, 61 troopers in all under Colonel Mirabeau Bonaparte Lamor.

At about four o'clock all was ready. The Texans in double file moved silently through the timber and debouched onto the open prairie, the cavalry trotting out toward the enemy's left in order to distract his attention. Then, "just as the first charge was starting, a horseman, flecked with foam from his panting charger . . . dashed along the lines . . . as Houston had arranged that he should do, calling out clearly that all might hear, this death knell to hope of possible escape: 'I have cut down Vince's Bridge! Now fight for your lives, and remember the Alamo!' " [24] In answer came the terrific yell of "Remember the Alamo!" which struck terror into the hearts of the Mexicans; [25] then a rattling volley, followed by a wild charge. Houston wrote:

The conflict in the breastwork lasted but a few moments; many of the troops encountered hand to hand, and not having the advantage of bayonets on our side, our riflemen used their pieces as war clubs, breaking many of them off at the breach. The rout commenced at half-past four, and the pursuit by the main army continued until twilight.[26]

"Such slaughter on our side, and such almost miraculous preservation on the other," wrote Captain Tarlton, a participant, "have never been heard of since the invention of gunpowder." [27] It was no exaggeration, for Houston reported 630 Mexicans killed, 208 wounded, and 730 prisoners, against his own loss of two killed and twenty-three wounded. Though Rives considers [28] the number of killed exaggerated, as Santa Anna had not more than 1,150 men, nevertheless for the Mexicans this defeat was annihilating, because, at the highest reckoning, not more than forty of them escaped.

The next morning, when the prisoners were paraded, it was found that Santa Anna was neither among them nor the dead and wounded. Houston remarked: "You will find the Hero of Tampico, if you find him at all, making his retreat on all fours, and he will be dressed as bad at least as a common soldier." [29] This proved a true prediction, because a few hours later and eight miles from the battlefield, El Presidente was discovered "clad in a blue cotton jacket and linen trowsers, with a leather cap and red worsted slippers," crawling away through the grass towards the Brazos.[30]

Learning of the disaster on the 28th, Filisola rapidly withdrew to the Rio Grande. On May 5, Santa Anna put his signature to the Treaty of Velasco, by which the independence of Texas was recognized and its western frontier fixed on the Rio Grande. On the 26th this treaty was ratified by Filisola, and, on March 3, 1837—the last day of his Presidency—Andrew Jackson signed the resolution of Congress acknowledging the independence of Texas.

Small, sharp, and short though the battle of San Jacinto was, few in the history of America have been more decisive in their results. By

adding over a quarter of a million squares miles to the territories inhabited by Americans, it not only led to the Mexican War, but so complicated the internal politics of the Union that it was also, indirectly,
one of the causes of the Civil War of 1861–1865. Much history then
was to be built upon the shoulders of Sam Houston—a man, as Jackson
declared, "who was made by the Almighty, and not by a tailor." [31] On
September 1 he was elected president of the newborn republic and was
inaugurated on October 22.

To all who could see through the thickening mists of factional
politics, it was evident that Texas could not long endure as an independent republic. Like the satellite she was, and situated as she was
within the attractive orbit of the United States, it was inevitable that
one day she would amalgamate with that greater power. That this did
not at once happen was due to the rising political differences between
the Northern and Southern states; for the former were fully awake
to the fact that annexation would mean ten to twenty new proslave
votes in Congress. Therefore, during the years following the victory of
San Jacinto, this question largely monopolized politics.

Briefly, the events of these years were as follows: In December,
1838, Mirabeau Bonaparte Lamor succeeded Houston as president,
and Houston, after a series of mad adventures, was re-elected in 1841.
Then, in March, 1842, came a Mexican raid into Texas, to be followed
on Christmas Day by a counterraid into Mexico. These filibustering
expeditions made Houston's position a perplexing one. It was in no way
eased when Commodore Jones laid siege to unsuspecting Monterrey.[32]
This act greatly increased the tension not only between Americans and
Mexicans, but also between Northerners and Southerners, the slave
question being so violently agitated that the threat to annex Texas
caused John Quincy Adams to declare that should annexation be agreed
to, it would justify the dissolution of the Union.

Also, England was interested in the slave trade. In 1840, Palmerston
"turned the flank" of the United States by recognizing the independence
of Texas upon condition that her government agree to mutual right
of search by warships of both powers in suppressing the slave traffic. This
condition was accepted in 1842, and was immediately interpreted by the
United States in the most sinister light. When Houston, in order to
bring pressure on Congress to agree to annexation, turned to England,
representatives and senators became convinced that England was aiming at the maintenance of Texan independence in order to establish a

rival to the United States. The upshot was that when in 1844, Calhoun—whose bugbear was Great Britain—became Secretary of State, a battle royal was fought between him and Almonte, then Mexican minister at Washington.

The question of annexation became now still more acute. First, it was agreed to by the House of Representatives; next, it was rejected by the Senate, and then at length, on March 1, 1845, it was adopted by both Houses, just three days before James K. Polk succeeded John Tyler as president. Thereupon Almonte demanded his passports and left for Mexico. Lastly, on July 4, Texas accepted the invitation to enter the Union. At once the cry which the fate of the Alamo had inspired on the banks of the San Jacinto River, after nine years of echoing through the corridors and cabinets of diplomacy, again burst forth savagely upon the American world. War was to decide what words could not—the greeds, envies, and loyalties of men.

The war that was now to be waged was not to lead, as many thought, to the end of Mexico, but instead to the extermination of slavery within the United States. It was in fact the first round in a far greater struggle—namely, that of 1861–1865. It was opened by Polk, who, shortly after the annexation of Texas, sent John Slidell to Mexico to win over the short-lived government of Herrera, which appeared to desire peace. Polk's dream, however, carried him far beyond Texas. In imagination he soared over the mountains and California to the Pacific Ocean—the Ultima Thule of his dream. He saw that in that vast region there was no government; that it was the land of American adventurers, a place "where all the wandering English and American vagabonds found a refuge in which they could not be disturbed by any Mexican authorities"—and his desire was to possess it. He believed that by divine right the English race was destined to expel the Spanish. Then, on December 30, 1845, the Herrera government gave way to that of Paredes, who immediately began to prepare for a Texan war. Slidell asked for his passports and returned to Washington.

Finding it impossible to effect a peace with Paredes, the United States government took the somewhat risky course of turning to Santa Anna, who, since May, 1845, had sought refuge in Havana. The intention was to place him once again in the presidential chair. So he was smuggled back into Mexico, and Paredes was deposed.[33]

Having amidst frantic popular rejoicing re-entered Mexico, Santa Anna at once raised an army some 20,000 strong at San Luis Potosi.

It was the typical Mexican army, which it is well to note, because its character goes far to explain how a minute American army gained the remarkable victories soon to be described.

First, as regards its officers. Their advancement depended not on merit, but on political trickery. Writing in 1846, the British minister in Mexico said: "The officers . . . are, as a Corps, the worst perhaps to be found in any part of the world. They are totally ignorant of their duty . . . and their personal courage, I fear, is of a very negative character." [34] In 1838 there were 160 generals in an army of 30,000 men—that is, one to every 200 private soldiers! The men were mainly Indians and half-breeds, who were hunted off the fields and frequently caught by lassoing. "From the hands of the recruiting sergeant," writes Mayer, "the conscript passes into those of the drill sergeant. The chief duty of this personage is to teach him to march, counter-march, and to handle an unserviceable weapon. From the drill sergeant, he succeeds to the company officer and here, perhaps, he encounters the worst foe of his ultimate efficiency." [35] Battles, when fought, were nearly always mob fights ending in a cavalry charge; and not infrequently were won by bribery. The artillery seldom hit anything, and when fighting took place in the cities it was generally restricted to street assassinations and rooftop shootings, as in the days of Cortés.

Polk's first move was to order General Zachary Taylor—"Old Rough and Ready," as his men called him—and his troops into Texas. They camped in the vicinity of Corpus Christi until April 24, 1846, when at length a skirmish on the left bank of the Rio Grande detonated the war. On May 8 a battle was fought at Palo Alto, after which Avista, the Mexican general, retired to Resaca de la Palma, where, on the following day, he was routed. Thereupon Taylor occupied Matamoras and made the Rio Grande the actual frontier between the United States and Mexico.

Next, he fixed on Monterrey as his objective, and took it on September 24. At this point Santa Anna, who by now had broken all promises he had made to Polk, appeared on the scene. On February 23–24, he was defeated by Taylor on the field of Buena Vista in a battle in which Colonel Jefferson Davis, the future president of the Confederacy, greatly distinguished himself. In spite of being routed, Santa Anna proclaimed his defeat a victory, and then with the utmost speed withdrew the shattered fragments of his army to San Luis Potosi.

As Polk had realized all along, Taylor's campaign was at best nothing more than a diversion. Consequently, on October 17 he consulted Mr. Diamond, late United States consul at Vera Cruz, who assured him that "it was perfectly practicable to land a military force at Sacrificios, about four miles from Vera Cruz and out of reach of the guns of the castle [San Juan Ulua]." [36] This decided Polk to land a force there and strike at the Mexican capital. The man he somewhat reluctantly selected for this enterprise was General Winfield Scott.[37]

Scott, as we have seen, had fought through the War of 1812, and was now sixty years old. Though not a general of the first order, he was an educated and thorough soldier, possessed of a shrewd eye for men. He was inordinately vain, and his men called him appropriately enough "Old Fuss and Feathers." His presence was magnificent, and in 1839 it left an indelible impression on the mind of a young cadet— Ulysses S. Grant—who said of him: "With his commanding figure, his quite colossal size and showy uniform, I thought him the finest specimen of manhood my eyes had ever beheld, and the most to be envied. I could never resemble him in appearance, but I believe I did have a presentiment for a moment that some day I should occupy his place on review—although I had no intention then of remaining in the army." [38]

A week before Taylor's victory at Buena Vista, Scott had arrived at Lobos Island, south of Tampico and 125 miles north of Vera Cruz. There he assembled his army, eventually to number 12,000 officers and men, and organized it in four divisions as follows:

1st Division, General William J. Worth, consisting of the 4th, 5th, 6th, and 8th Regiments of regular infantry, two regiments of artillery serving as infantry, and two batteries of field artillery. It was divided into two brigades—Garland's and Clarke's.

2nd Division, General David E. Twiggs, consisting of the Rifle Regiment, 1st, 3rd, and 7th regular infantry, two regiments of artillery serving as infantry, and one battery of field artillery. It also was divided into two brigades—Smith's and Riley's.

3rd Division, General Gideon J. Pillow, consisting of two brigades: the first under Cadwalader—Voltigeurs, 11th, and 14th Regiments (newly raised), and Magruder's battery—the second under Pierce, comprising the newly raised 9th, 12th, and 15th Regiments.

4th Division, General John A. Quitman, of two brigades, the first consisting of New York and South Carolina Volunteers Regiments under Shields, and the second of Marines and Pennsylvanian Volunteers under Watson.

On March 7, Scott embarked his army in 160 transports, and two days later he landed it, without the loss of a man, on the open beach, three miles south of Vera Cruz. At once he invested that fortified city by land and sea, and after he had poured some half million pounds of shot and shell onto it,[39] causing several thousand casualties, its commander, General Landero, capitulated on the 26th.

Dreading a delay on that fever-stricken coast, on April 6, Scott issued orders for an advance. Two days later, following much the same road as that trodden by Cortés in 1519, the army set out for the city of Mexico "on one of the most famous marches in history," as McMaster says.[40] On the 18th they forced the fortified pass of Cerro Gordo, and pushed on to Jalapa, where, in order to collect supplies, a halt was called until May 15. Then an advance was made to Puebla, which was occupied without serious resistance. There the army rested for nearly three months, not only to collect reinforcements, but also because politics had intervened.

When Scott's expedition was first mooted, Calhoun had taken alarm, so in order to prevent a defection among his Democratic followers, Polk had decided to limit his demands to those indicated by Calhoun. Mexico was to cede all territory east of the Rio Grande as well as New Mexico and Upper and Lower California. To bring this about, Polk selected as his plenipotentiary Nicholas P. Trist, who arrived at Puebla shortly after Scott had occupied the town. Trist met with an exceedingly chilly reception, being as Scott described him, a man who, had he but "an ambulatory guillotine . . . would be the personification of Danton, Marat, and St. Just, all in one."[41]

Eventually, negotiations were opened with Santa Anna, who was far too astute not to turn them to his advantage. He demanded a subsidy of a million dollars, of which ten thousand were to be paid as an advance on royalties in order to enable him to quell such opposition as he might meet with. Falling into the trap, Scott and Trist sent him the douceur. Once this was in his pocket, he said that in order to get the government to accept the treaty, it was imperative that a display of force should be made by advancing further inland and so threatening the capital. Then, with the American army thundering outside the city walls, he (Santa Anna) would be able to defy his domestic enemies and open its gates to his deeply respected foe.

This extraordinary compact, which permitted of an incalculable number of double-crossings, was apparently accepted as workable. On August 7, once again the army set out to meet its accommodating enemy,

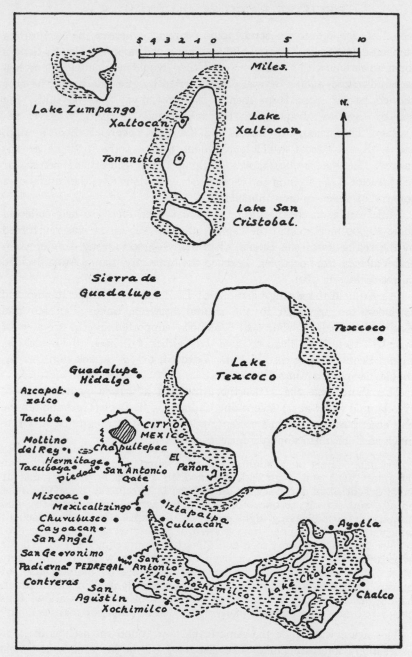

II. Map of the Valley of Mexico, 1847

who was reputed to be some 30,000 strong, whereas the Americans numbered 10,738 well-trained and well-equipped rank and file. As Scott's communications with his base—Vera Cruz—would automatically lengthen as he advanced, and as he was daily worried by guerrilla bands, he now decided to cut loose from them, "to throw away," as he said, "the scabbard and to advance with the naked blade in hand." [42] Rives remarks: "The memory of Cortés and his ships never left Scott's mind, and with a boldness which subsequent events fully justified he advanced, like the *conquistadores,* without the possibility of retreat or reinforcement, to attempt the capture of a populous city, the capital of a country of seven million inhabitants."

Santa Anna, in the meantime, had not been idle. He had collected some 20,000 men around the capital, and on August 11 was reinforced by the remnants of the Buena Vista army—4,000 strong—under General Valencia, who occupied Texcoco the same day. Santa Anna decided on the following plan:

(1) To hold the strong positions of El Peñon and Mexicaltzingo and so block the approach to the capital between Lakes Texcoco and Xochimilco-Chalco; while (2) Valencia, supported by the cavalry of Juan Alvarez, held Texcoco, and (a) either fell back to Guadalupe, should Scott advance east of Lake Texcoco, or (b) attack him in rear, should he move against El Peñon.

This same day—the 11th—the American advanced guard occupied Ayotla, and Scott at once sent out Captain R. E. Lee to reconnoiter the El Peñon position. When Lee reported back on its strength, Scott wrote much as Cortés had done three centuries earlier:

The city stands on a slight swell of ground, near the center of an irregular basin, and is girdled with a ditch . . .—a navigable canal of great breadth and depth—very difficult to bridge in the presence of an enemy, and serving at once for drainage, custom-house purposes, and military defense; leaving eight entrances or gates over arches, each of which we found defended by a system of strong works, that seemed to require nothing but some men and guns to be impregnable. . . . All the approaches near the city, are over elevated causeways, cut in many places (to oppose us), and flanked on both sides by ditches, also, of unusual dimensions. The numerous cross-roads flanked in like manner, having bridges at the intersections, recently broken. The meadows thus chequered, are, moreover, in many spots under water, or marshy . . .[43]

The strategical tangle the Americans now found themselves in is an exceedingly interesting one. The discovery of the loose end—the most profitable line of advance—was the beginning of the problem. The question was:

(1) Whether to move by the highroad which ran to the north of Lake Chalco, which in turn meant the forcing of the strong positions of El Peñon or of Mexicaltzingo; a frontal attack with Valencia hovering on the right flank and rear, or

(2) to move east of Lake Texcoco by way of Guadalupe-Hidalgo, which meant not only crossing thirty miles of country destitute of wood and water,[44] but also the abandonment of the line of communications to Puebla, or

(3) to avoid both these lines of approach and move south of Lake Chalco on San Augustin. This line was not strongly fortified, but the road was so bad that Santa Anna had not taken an advance along it into his reckonings.[45] Neither at first did Scott; because, since Santa Anna held the hub of the strategical wheel, all he need do in order to block this approach was to move his troops from El Peñon, etc., to San Antonio.

Though favoring an advance on Mexicaltzingo, covered by a demonstration against El Peñon, Scott decided nothing until the 14th, when General Worth, having reconnoitered the San Augustin road,[46] reported it passable for artillery and wagons. Thereupon, Scott made up his mind, and, on the evening of the 15th, he ordered for the morrow an advance along the southern track. The move was easily executed, Twiggs's division occupying San Augustin on the 18th. Santa Anna then moved strong forces to the fortified positions of San Antonio and Churubusco, and brought in Valencia from Texcoco,[47] ordering him to form up *en potence* on the right flank by occupying the line Cayoacan-Tacubaya. But that general, who as Santa Anna's political rival was eager to add to his own reputation, set aside this order and pushed on to San Angel. As Justin H. Smith writes: "Notes worthy of the most finished and effusive pirates were then exchanged; and in the end Santa Anna, who longed to remove his insubordinate general but dared not, authorized him to do as he pleased and assume, of course, the attendant responsibility."[48] Next, to make things worse, on the 19th, Valencia, with bands playing, advanced well to the south of San Angel to a small hill facing the hacienda of Padierna—known to the natives as the Pelon Cuauhtitla—and thus was completely separated from the Mexican main forces.[49]

Knowing nothing of these movements, Scott, at San Augustin, found

himself in a difficult tactical situation. A mile north of that spot stood
the fortified hacienda of San Antonio, and two miles north of it the
fortified convent and bridge of Churubusco; to the immediate west lay
the Pedregal, a vast field of all but impassable volcanic rock, crossed

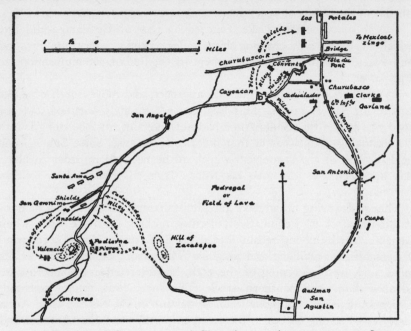

12. Battles of Contreras and Churubusco, August 19–20, 1847

by one track, which ran from San Augustin to the San Angel road.
In order to avoid a frontal attack on the San Antonio position, Scott
sent out Captain Lee with an escort to reconnoiter this track. Lee advanced as far as the hill of Zacatepec, where he became engaged
with an enemy patrol. On his return, he reported that, were the track
improved it would be practicable for guns, so Scott, deciding to outflank San Antonio, issued orders for Pillow's and Twiggs's divisions to
advance along it the next day. The former was to open the road, while
the latter protected the working parties.

Early on the 19th, Pillow set out, and shortly came into contact with
the enemy. Twiggs moved forward and on gaining the summit of
Zacatepec was compelled to halt by the Mexican artillery fire. There-

upon Pillow sent back to Scott suggesting that, when Twiggs advanced and opened the battle, he should send a brigade by a mule track Pillow had discovered leading in the direction of San Geronimo, in order to outflank the enemy's position. Undoubtedly, this was the correct thing to do, because frontally Valencia's position was a strong one, a deep ravine lying between it and the direct line of the American attack. Besides, the hill which commanded Padierna was now entrenched, with artillery planted along the Padierna parapet, behind which Valencia had massed his infantry—alleged to number 7,000 men—with cavalry on their flanks. Strangely enough, though he had thrown out a line of skirmishers on the far side of the ravine—that is to his front—he did not post a single picket on the summit of the hill immediately in the rear of him, although it overlooked his camp.[50]

When Twiggs advanced, Valencia's skirmishers fell back. Thereupon Magruder's battery and a rocket battery were brought forward, but as the guns were too light, little resulted from their fire.

As soon as Twiggs was engaged, Pillow, realizing that his frontal attack was unlikely to succeed, ordered Riley's brigade—not yet engaged—to attempt to gain San Geronimo by the mule track and "operate on the flank and rear of the enemy."[51] When Twiggs reached the ravine, Valencia's guns unmasked; whereupon Smith, who was in the van of the attack, drew his troops under shelter. Pillow ordered forward Cadwalader's brigade to support Riley, and a little later sent Morgan's regiment of Pierce's brigade to follow him.

Scott, arriving with his advanced headquarters at Zacatepec at about 3.30 P.M., was surprised to find so severe an action in progress. He thereupon ordered Shields's brigade to that spot. Meanwhile Santa Anna, hearing the cannonade around Padierna, moved forward some 12,000 men from San Antonio, Churubusco, and the City of Mexico to San Angel. This force was seen by Scott from Zacatepec.

On reaching the San Angel road in the vicinity of San Geronimo, Riley collected his troops and occupied that village. Passing through it, he moved on to the high ground lying to its southwest. There, after gaining contact with a party of enemy cavalry, he halted, but on hearing that Santa Anna had occupied the ground north of San Geronimo, he fell back to that village. A little later on, he was joined by Cadwalader and Morgan.

While these movements were taking place, Smith's brigade was withdrawn from the Padierna front and dispatched to San Geronimo.

Valencia, now faced only by two regiments of Pierce's brigade and the batteries, instead of attacking, sent a messenger to Santa Anna proclaiming a great victory. A little before sunset Smith arrived at San Geronimo, and believing himself to be the senior officer on the spot, though Cadwalader ranked him, assumed command of all forces assembled there. Meanwhile, Shields and his brigade, having reached Zacatepec, were sent on to follow Smith.

As night set in the dispositions of the opposing forces was as follows: Valencia was still holding his entrenched camp faced by Pierce, who by now had occupied the hacienda of Padierna. Smith's, Cadwalader's and Riley's brigades were at San Geronimo. Santa Anna held the high ground north of that village, and Shields was still toiling through the Pedregal towards it.

At 11 P.M. Captain Lee, making his way over the Pedregal, a task of quite exceptional difficulty, arrived at Scott's headquarters at San Augustin, bringing with him from San Geronimo Smith's plan for the 20th. It was to move forward at 3 A.M. and fall on Valencia's rear. To assist in this assault, he asked that Pierce should be instructed to make "a powerful diversion" on Valencia's immediate front. Scott agreed, and once again the weary Lee set off over the Pedregal to warn Pierce.

While these preparations were in hand, Santa Anna, not placing much reliance on Valencia's "glorious victory," and realizing the desperate situation his lieutenant was now in, sent him an order to spike his guns, destroy his supplies, and fall back into the mountains to the west of his camp. On receiving Valencia's refusal to obey, the Mexican commander in chief, leaving an outpost on the ridge, withdrew his forces from San Angel.

Smith, unaware of this retreat, posted Shields's brigade—which arrived about midnight—to watch him. At 3 A.M., as a noisy musketry fire was heard in the direction of Padierna, the three brigades, with Riley's leading, set out in pitch darkness through a sea of mud toward the hill overlooking Valencia's camp. So bad was the road that it was not until daylight was breaking that the rear of the advance cleared the village. By that time Riley's men had reached a small ravine, running behind their enemy's position. Here two columns of assault were formed. A moment later it became apparent that the enemy had discovered the approach.

At once Riley threw out a line of skirmishers. Then came the command, "Men forward." "And we did forward," writes a participant,

". . . The crack of a hundred rifles startled the Mexicans from their astonishment," but "before they could turn their pieces on us, we were on them." [52] "His whole force [Riley's]," writes Ripley, "soon became hotly engaged with the enemy, who served two guns upon it with rapidity and received the shock with a noisy, rolling discharge of musketry. The aim was, however, inaccurate . . . The advance was not retarded one instant, for the American troops, having delivered their fire, rushed down with loud shouts in a vigorous charge, and entered the intrenchments almost as a body." [53] During this wild rush, Cadwalader's brigade came up in support, as Smith's—now commanded by Major Dimick—moved toward the left flank and fell upon the Mexicans who were breaking away along the San Angel road.

Within a few minutes of the launching of the assault, the rout was complete. "All was now confusion in the camp; infantry, horse, artillery, mules, women, laborers in a mob . . . like a bag turned upside down, the camp was empty of all the Mexicans who could get away. Again General Smith drew out his watch. 'It has taken just seventeen minutes,' he remarked." [54]

While Pierce scrambled after their rear, the mob of fugitives on the San Angel road were caught in flank by Shields and driven into the Pedregal. How and when Valencia fled is not known, but he got away.

Thus,[55] [writes General Scott], was the great victory of Contreras achieved; one road to the capital opened; seven hundred of the enemy killed; eight hundred and thirteen prisoners, including, among eighty-eight officers, four generals; besides many colors and standards; twenty-two pieces of brass ordnance; . . . thousands of small arms and accoutrements; and immense quantity of shot, shells, powder, and cartridges; seven hundred pack mules, many horses, etc.—all in our hands.[56]

The American losses were insignificant; some sixty killed and wounded.

Directly order had been restored, Twiggs and Pillow arrived on the field, and the pursuit was taken up toward Cayoacan. At that village orders were received to halt, and a little later Scott came up and established his headquarters there.

Thus ended this extraordinary battle, which, conceived as a secondary operation, turned into a decisive attack. It was a victory gained by the initiative of subordinate commanders working to no concerted plan, with the higher command not on the stage but in the gallery. Now, though the object had been gained—the San Antonio defenses turned and a road opened to the city by way of Cayoacan—the real battle, so far as fighting is concerned, was about to begin. It was to end in a self-imposed strategical defeat.

During the night of the 19th–20th, while Smith, in command of the bulk of Pillow's and Twigg's divisions, lay at San Geronimo, Scott, viewing his position with anxiety, had ordered Worth to leave one of his brigades at San Augustin and march with the rest of his division and Quitman's remaining brigade to the support of Smith. Then, early on the 20th, hearing of Smith's success, he countermanded their march, ordering Quitman to remain with the trains at San Augustin, while Worth moved against San Antonio. Worth set out at 11 A.M., and soon after found that General Bravo, who was in command there, was in full retreat on Churubusco. There Santa Anna had determined to make a stand. His position, had it not been for the fact that it was already turned by Pillow's and Twigg's divisions at Cayoacan, would have been a formidable one. It ran along the Rio de Churubusco, a canalized stream running west to east and emptying into Lake Xochimilco. To the south, where the stream was crossed by the San Antonio causeway, lay the scattered village of Churubusco. On the western border of the village stood the strongly defended Convent of San Mateo, garrisoned by 3,000 men under General Rincon. The road bridge over the stream was defended by a solidly constructed *tête du pont*.

When Scott arrived at Cayoacan, he learned that Bravo had abandoned San Antonio. Knowing nothing of the defenses of Churubusco and taking no steps to have them reconnoitered, instead of forcing their evacuation by a powerful flanking movement from the west, he decided to brush their garrison aside and so open the direct road for his trains from San Augustin to the capital. To this end, he ordered Pillow with Cadwalader's brigade to swing right-handed from Cayoacan down the road leading to San Antonio, so that they might co-operate with Worth's division, now advancing from the south. Twiggs was to keep straight on and clear the convent. A little later, he ordered Pierce's brigade, followed by Shields's, to move north and then east in order to come in on the causeway in rear of Santa Anna's defenses. Thus, as Ripley says, a totally unnecessary battle was initiated.[57]

Worth, meanwhile, in full pursuit of Bravo, had cut his retreating column in half. Then pushing on toward Churubusco, he formed his line of attack as follows: Clarke's brigade on the right of the causeway, with Garland's on its right, the 6th Infantry Regiment moving straight up the causeway on the *tête du pont*.

As the 6th Infantry entered the village it was met by so heavy a fire that it was forced to fall back. Meanwhile Cadwalader's brigade had come up on its left, and Twiggs—ignorant of Worth's operations—had launched his men into a dense growth of corn against the convent, which "was one sheet of flame and smoke." [58] Then he brought up Riley's brigade on the left of his line in order to work to the rear of the convent, but with no result.

As these maneuvers were taking place, Worth sent Garland's brigade well east of the causeway to overlap the eastern side of the village, and ordered Clarke's to keep straight on with Cadwalader's on its left. Both these brigades were at once held up by cross fire from the bridge and the convent.

Meanwhile Pierce's and Shields's brigade crossed the Churubusco stream and were moving toward the causeway when the Mexican reserves in rear of the village formed front toward them and opened a devastating fire. Regiment after regiment was sent forward by Pierce and Shields, only to be hurled back in disorder. "The advance was checked for a while," writes Ripley, "but those unhurt struggled on, and, finally, the Mexican line wavered, broke, and fled, a disordered multitude, down the road to the city . . ." [59] This sudden break was caused not so much by the vigor of the attackers as by a success gained to the south of them.

There, Worth's and Pillow's men had pushed slowly forward and toward the enemy's left. After more than two hours' fighting, the Mexican left gave way "and fled through the cornfields to their rear toward the city." This rout enabled Worth's right to get behind the *tête du pont*. His troops facing it then rushed "through the wet ditches, waist-deep, over the parapets and into the work . . . A few shots were delivered, a few bayonets crossed," whereupon the Mexicans holding it broke and fled northward. "The fall of the *tête du pont*," writes Ripley, "ensured the rout of the troops engaged with Shields's and Pierce's. These were then brought up to the causeway."

The *tête du pont* cleared, Pillow swung his men westward to face the northern flank of the convent. At this point Rincon raised the white flag and surrendered with 1,200 men.

The resistance of the Mexicans was now completely broken, but Scott, instead of pressing the pursuit, called a halt at the hacienda of

Portales, though he allowed Captain Philip Kearny and his dragoons to follow up the fugitives to the Garita (Gate) of San Antonio.

The casualties of this severely fought battle are variously given. For the two days' fighting Scott's amounted to 1,056; the Mexicans' are unknown, though Ripley suggests 7,000. That night Worth's division and Shields's brigade remained at the hacienda of Portales and the village of Churubusco, Twiggs's at Cayoacan and San Angel. Pillow's fell back to San Antonio and Scott returned to his headquarters at San Augustin. ". . . no preparations were made," writes Ripley, "for renewing the advance and entering the city on the following morning." [61]

Why was this? The answer is that Scott still trusted Santa Anna—in accordance with his Puebla agreement—to surrender the capital to him. Santa Anna then played his last card. Realizing that, in order to pull his army together, a prolonged truce was indispensable, and also that Scott had suffered heavily and could not be reinforced, he persuaded the British legation to visit his enemy's camp and ask for an armistice pending the settlement of peace negotiations.[62] This the secretary of the legation and the consul general did, with the result that Scott once again was trapped.[63]

Scott's mistake was that, as his desire to end the war without further slaughter was sincere, he attributed similar sentiments to Santa Anna. Though Bankhead, the British minister in Mexico, shared his views,[64] the fact remains the Mexican president was so totally amoral that the chances were that his sole intention was to play for time in the hope that either a miracle or some astute trickery might save him.

Scott should have seen through this consummate rascal—a double-crosser of double-crossers. Even if he considered that his army was not sufficiently strong to risk another battle, before agreeing to an armistice he should have demanded certain military guarantees, including the evacuation of Chapultepec, as he was urged to do by Worth and Pillow.[65] The armistice was signed and published on August 24, and peace negotiations were opened. It was almost at once discovered that Santa Anna's main interest lay in strengthening the fortifications of the capital and its approaches. On September 6, Scott demanded that the terms of the armistice be adhered to, and when by noon the following day no satisfactory reply was received, he declared his intentions to resume offensive operations.

The position of the Americans was now distinctly worse than it had been before the armistice was signed. Furthermore, Scott had ordered no reconnaissances, and was almost completely in the dark as regards the Mexican defenses. Then, on the night of the 6th–7th, he was informed that cannon were being cast and bored in the old foundry of Molino del Rey (The King's Mill). The following day, having examined that position from the roof of the Bishop's Palace near Tacubaya—his headquarters—he decided to have the machinery broken up, and ordered General Worth and his division to carry out this task that night.

On reconnoitering Molino del Rey, Worth discovered that it was more formidable than Scott supposed. It consisted of a row of strongly built stone houses some three hundred yards long, running from north to south. These had been fortified and were held by General Leon, while four hundred yards west of their northern extremity General Perez occupied the Casa Mata, a stone building surrounded by a bastioned fieldwork.

Worth, having reported to Scott that the position was far stronger than he had at first supposed, suggested that a full-dress attack should be mounted to include Chapultepec as well. This Scott refused to consider, because he was of opinion that the best line of attack on the capital was from the south and not from the west. He agreed, however, to substitute a dawn for a night attack, and strengthened Worth's division by attaching to it Cadwalader's brigade.

At 3 A.M. on the 8th, after a far too brief artillery preparation,[66] Worth advanced to be met by a devastating fire from the *azoteas* of Molino del Rey as well as the outworks of Casa Mata. His men, writes Ripley, fell "almost by platoons and companies in an incredibly short space of time." [67] To make matters worse, many of the wounded were massacred by the Mexicans.[68] Then both sides were reinforced, Santa Anna sending back the five battalions he had the night before withdrawn, and Scott supporting Worth with Pillow's division. At length the garrison of Molino del Rey was forced to fall back on Chapultepec. When, at about 7 A.M., the Casa Mata was also evacuated, it was found that all it contained were a few old cannon molds.

Once again Worth urged General Scott to allow him to press on and carry Chapultepec.[69] Scott refused, and instead ordered the attackers to retire to Tacubaya, which they reached at about noon. Thus ended "the hardest contested battle of the whole war" and beyond doubt the least necessary. The casualties were heavy—116 killed, 653 wounded, and 18 missing out of 3,447 men engaged [70]—and the results were negligible.[71]

Santa Anna at once proclaimed the retreat a victory.[72] Worse still, as Justin Smith points out, the American generals blamed each other, the discord between them reaching down to the rank and file. Nevertheless, "Scott faced the situation with unshaken fortitude, but those who knew him intimately saw that he felt anxious." [73]

There was every reason for his anxiety. His army now had been reduced to slightly less than 8,000 effectives, and another attack could not be mounted for several days, during which the enemy could still further strengthen his defenses. Santa Anna took full advantage of the delay, working hard on the fortifications which covered the Garita Nino Perdido and the Garita de San Antonio. He believed that the objective of Scott's attack on the 8th had been the hill of Chapultepec, and as he had failed to take it, his next attack would be delivered against the southern front of the capital.

On the 10th these works were reconnoitered by Pillow and again on the following morning, when it was discovered that the area between the two gates had been flooded. That day Scott held a conference of his general officers at the Hermitage (on the Nino Perdido causeway) to decide on a plan of attack and whether its objective should be Chapultepec or the defenses of San Antonio.

On each of these fronts there were two lines of approach, on the first the causeway known as the Calzada de San Cosmé and the Calzada de la Veronica running to the gates of San Cosmé and Belén; and on the second the causeways of Nino Perdido and San Antonio. To move along the first it was necessary to carry Chapultepec, whereas the advance up the second was restricted by the flooded fields. Though Quitman, Pillow and Captain Lee favored an attack against the southern front, Scott, supported by Twiggs, favored an attack against the western, and finally decided on it. Apparently he was of opinion that, once Chapultepec was stormed, the enemy's resistance would cave in.[74] His plan was: under cover of a feint attack with Twiggs's division on the Garita of San Antonio, to bombard Chapultepec heavily and then carry it by assault. To prepare for this, he ordered forward Worth's division at Tacubaya after nightfall. Meanwhile, leaving General Bravo in command at Chapultepec, Santa Anna concentrated the bulk of his army about the San Antonio position.

The hill of Chapultepec consists of a volcanic ridge of rock some six hundred yards long, rising out of the plain to a height of 195 feet. Its summit had been leveled to form a platform for a palace, built in 1783 for the viceroy Matias de Galvez. In 1833 it was converted into a military college. The hill itself was surrounded by a wall 1,600 yards long and some fifteen feet high; the palace was also walled. To the west of the hill and within the enclosure was a cypress grove standing in marshy soil. On this flank the ascent of the hill, though rugged, was practical for infantry. On the northern and eastern sides it was precipitous, but on the south a zigzag road led to the summit from the plain below. Though Santa Anna had left General Bravo 2,000 men to hold this position, by the night of Sunday the 12th so many had deserted that but 1,200 were left, some 370 of whom were posted in the grove.

At 7 A.M. on the 12th the American bombardment opened and was continued all day, Twiggs's division meanwhile demonstrating before the Garita of San Antonio. That evening Scott summoned Pillow, Quitman, and Worth to his headquarters to receive their final instructions. It was agreed that at dawn the following morning the bombardment should once again open and continue until 8 A.M. Then, when the guns ceased fire, Quitman was to advance along the Tacubaya Road against the southern front, while Pillow, who had already occupied Molino del Rey without any opposition, was to move through the cypress grove and assault the western front. Worth was ordered to hold his division in readiness to support Pillow, and Twiggs was instructed to send one of his brigades to support Quitman, the other to continue the demonstration.

At 5.30 A.M. the next morning the bombardment was resumed. For two hours shot and shell were poured on the palace and its defenses, followed by half an hour's grape and canister fire directed into the grove. Then, at 8 o'clock, Pillow launched his attack in three detachments. The first, on the left, consisted of two regiments under Colonel Trousdale, who moved north of the enclosure wall to prevent reinforcements reaching General Bravo. The second, in the center, consisted of a battalion of Voltigeurs under Colonel Andrews, followed by two regiments of infantry. They crossed the meadows east of Molino del Rey and entered the grove, where they met a heavy fire. "The moral and physical effect of the Mexican shot, crashing and tearing as it did through the foliage, was such as in some cases to render the men averse to leave the shelter of the trees." [75] Nevertheless, the grove was at length occupied. The third detachment, on the right, a battalion of Voltigeurs, under Lieutenant Colonel Johnston, moved close along and outside the southern wall of the enclosure, and driving the enemy out of redan B, it passed through a gap in the wall. Capturing redoubt C and entrenchment D it gained the angle in the zigzag road. At this point Johnston's left linked up with Andrew's right. Next, the breastwork at E was captured. The wall of the palace platform and the buildings above it appeared through the

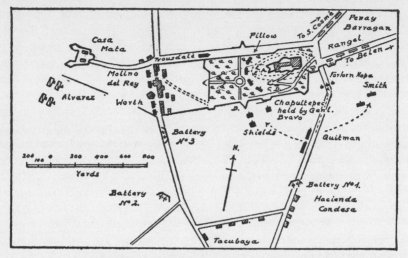

13. Battle of Chapultepec, September 13, 1847

smoke, "a sheet of flame" pouring from the parapets and *azoteas*. The assaulting parties were now called up, when it was discovered that the detachments detailed to carry forward the scaling ladders "had thrown them down in the grove, and for the most part engaged in the combat." [76] At once parties were sent back to carry these forward.

Meanwhile, from the south Quitman's main attack was pressing up the Tacubaya causeway, preceded by a forlorn hope of 120 stormers and 40 pioneers, whose objective was the gateway battery, which when captured would sever the main line of retirement from Chapultepec to the capital by way of the Belén Gate. To support this advance, Smith's brigade moved across the fields to its right to turn the battery from the east. In spite of this outflanking movement, when the forlorn hope got to within two hundred yards of its objective, it was forced to take cover and then fall back to prevent annihilation. Seeing that this attack could not be pushed further, Quitman moved Shields's brigade off the causeway and to the left. In spite of heavy fire, it got in rear of redan B, and then, by breaking a gap through the wall of the enclosure, it gained contact with Johnston's right.

At this juncture Worth's scaling ladders came up. Ripley describes the final assault as follows:

When they were brought up, parties from different corps, running quickly forward over the rugged though short space between the crest of the hill, and the ditch, leaped in, and at once planted their ladders . . . Lieutenant Selden first mounted to scale the walls. From Azoteas and windows the Mexican redoubled their musketry fire . . . struck down Selden, and with him several soldiers who had been the first to follow his example; but the assailants in the ditch clustered thick round the ladders already planted and constantly being raised. Many fell wounded or dead, yet their places were immediately taken; and, finally, Captain Howard, of the Voltigeurs, gained the parapet unhurt . . . a crowd of gallant officers and men followed after. Long ladders were brought up and laid across the ditch, and, with a shout of victory, the great body of the troops rushed over, under fire from the buildings inside of the castle, and the priest-cap [western works of the palace platform—A] was gained.[77]

Soon the whole southern front of the palace was won. Then fire was opened from the platform on the enemy's batteries still contesting Quitman's advance up the Tacubaya causeway. Simultaneously the whole palace was occupied, quarter being rarely given and many of the enemy, regardless of the height, jumping down the eastern side of the rock, "while the Americans pelted them from the parapets." In the midst of this melee General Bravo was taken prisoner, when the Mexican flag was torn down and the battle ended.

Immediately the rock was in American hands, the pursuit was taken up, not by Scott, who had not considered it in his plan, but independently by Worth and Quitman, the first pushing north along the Calzada de la Veronica while the second turned east on the Calzada de Belén. Scott then hurried forward Clarke's and Cadwalader's brigades to support the former and Pierce's the latter. After severe fighting Worth's van came up against the San Cosmé Garita at 5 P.M. This advance was materially assisted by Lieutenant U. S. Grant, who had a mountain howitzer dragged up the belfry of the Church of San Cosmé to open fire on the gate. At length, at 6 P.M., it was carried. Meanwhile Quitman's leading troops slowly gained ground on the Belén causeway, until within storming distance of the garita. They then rushed it through a withering fire, its garrison falling back on the citadel a little to the east of it.

It was to this gate that Santa Anna had retired after the fall of Chapultepec, and, at the time Quitman was approaching it, hearing of Worth's advance, he galloped over to the San Cosmé gate, but on nearing it learnt that the Belén gate had fallen. Thereupon he hurried back to the citadel where he was met by Quitman's advancing troops. About 5 P.M. he received an urgent message from San Cosmé, so he galloped back, arriving just in time to witness its capitulation. Then he returned to the citadel.

There he summoned a council of war, which decided on a withdrawal. This began at 1 A.M. on the 14th, the remnants of the now utterly demoralized army retiring to Guadalupe Hidalgo. Early that morning, when Scott and his staff occupied the palace of the government, firing began from the windows and roofs of the adjoining houses, and a guerrilla war broke out throughout the city. Thereupon the streets were swept by grape and canister, no quarter being offered the rabble of deserters, convicts, and leperos. It was a salutary and severe lesson. Captain Hitchcock informs us: "Our people in a single day killed more Mexicans in the streets than fell during the entire three weeks of one of their domestic wars." [79] Within thirty-six hours order was restored, and the campaign to all intents and purposes was brought to a successful end.[80]

The losses suffered by Scott's army between the 12th and 14th were not light, for they numbered in all 862 officers and men, of whom 130 were killed, 703 wounded, and 29 missing. For the entire campaign the total American casualties amounted to 2,703,[81] or nearly 25 per cent of the army when it marched from Puebla. What the total Mexican losses were is unknown, but they included 3,730 prisoners, of whom 13 were generals (3 had been presidents of the Republic), 20 standards, 75 field pieces, 57 wall pieces, and 20,000 stands of arms.

The capital lost, Santa Anna was planning a *coup* against Scott's depot at Puebla when he was forced to resign the Presidency, which devolved on Don Manuel de la Peña y Peña. A provisional government was established and negotiations of peace were opened between Peña y Peña and Mr. Trist. They took an unexpected course, as most things seem to do in Mexico. Polk, thinking that Trist would be too merciful to the enemy,[82] ordered him home. Trist, setting this order aside, nevertheless made use of it to terrify Peña y Peña into coming to terms. His three main demands were:

(1) The Rio Grande to be the boundary of Mexico in the east.

(2) Upper California and New Mexico to be surrendered to the U.S.A.

(3) In compensation for them $15,000,000 to be paid to Mexico.

Trist named the day when, unless these points were accepted, negotiations would be broken off. Scott, now working hand in glove with Trist, let Peña y Peña know that, should this happen, he would be compelled to march on the seat of the provisional government at Queretaro. Peña y Peña yielded and peace was signed at Guadalupe Hidalgo on February 2, 1848, and ratified by Congress on March 10 following. By terms of the peace, the future states of New Mexico, Arizona, California, Nevada, Utah, and part of Colorado were added to the United States, and the annexation of Texas confirmed.[83]

Thus ended this remarkable war, which, Ripley says, in its "astonishing success silences cavil or complaint concerning the conduct of the troops or the execution of the attack." [84] Nothing like it had been seen since the days of Cortés; for when Scott moved forward from Puebla he was as completely cut off from retreat as the great Spaniard when he scuttled his ships. Mexico had to be conquered or his army perish in the attempt, because a severe setback would have given his enemy something they could not give themselves—namely, an object to contest. Justin H. Smith says: "Mexico was defeated because she did not fight; and she did not fight because she had nothing to fight for." [85]

As for the Americans, expansion was in their bones. Once the Pacific Ocean was reached, finding no more worlds to conquer, they set about to conquer themselves. A few months before the crafty Trist and the fearful Peña y Peña set seals and signatures to the Treaty of Guadalupe Hidalgo, Daniel Webster prophetically declared at Springfield, Massachusetts: "Peace may soon come. I hope to hear it before the dawn of another morning. But I cannot conceal from myself that peace may bring with it a crisis more dangerous than war." [86]

REFERENCES

[1] Quoted from *History of the American Frontier*, 1763–1893, Frederic L. Paxson, pp. 306–307.

[2] *Texas and the Mexican War*, Nathaniel W. Stephenson, p. 17.

[3] A brief account of his early activities is to be found in *History of the Pacific States of North America*, Hubert Howe Bancroft, vol. XI, pp. 239–243.

[4] *Life of Sam Houston*, Anon., p. 47.

[5] *Life of General Houston*, Henry Bruce, p. 160.

[6] *Texas: The Rise, Progress and Prospects of the Republic of Texas*, William Kennedy, vol. II, p. 104 (1841).

[7] "Address of the General Council of the People of Texas," San Felipe de Austin, October 23, 1835. Quoted by Kennedy, vol. II, p. 113.

[8] Brother of Razin P. Bowie of "bowie knife" fame.

[9] *Memorias para la Historia de la Guerra de Tejas,* Vicente Filisola, vol. II, p. 245 (Filisola was an Italian).

[10] Anon., *Life,* p. 88.

[11] Quoted by George Lockhart Rives, *The United States and Mexico, 1821–1848,* vol. I, p. 330.

[12] See "Reminiscences of Mrs. Dilue Harris," *Quarterly of the Texas State Historical Association,* vol. IV, pp. 163–164.

[13] *History of Texas from its First Settlement in 1685 to its Annexation to the United States in 1846,* Henderson Yoakum, vol. II, p. 472.

[14] For a description of the Battle of the Coleto, see Kennedy, vol. II, pp. 204–209.

[15] In mitigation of this atrocious act it should be remembered that it was a recognized custom in Mexico to shoot insurgent prisoners. (See Bancroft's *History of Mexico,* vol. IV, pp. 226, 230.) In turn, insurgents submitted their prisoners to the same fate (*ibid.,* p. 249).

[16] See Yoakum, vol. II, p. 485. Bancroft writes: "The impatience of the troops at the Fabian policy of General Houston was so great that the expression of it bordered on mutiny, and it is an undeniable fact that while they were in camp on the Brazos several meetings were openly held at which the question was discussed of appointing another leader" (vol. XI, p. 251).

[17] See Rives, vol. I, p. 346.

[18] Quoted from Kennedy, vol. II, p. 221.

[19] Anon., *Life,* p. 114.

[20] See Kennedy, vol. II, p. 223.

[21] Bancroft, vol. XI, p. 257.

[22] See Houston's Report, Kennedy, vol. II, p. 224.

[23] Anon., *Life,* p. 126.

[24] *The Winning of the Far West,* Robert McNutt McElroy, p. 27. (See also Anon., *Life,* p. 128.)

[25] Writes Captain Calder: "I am by no means certain that our shot was more effective in creating confusion and panic in the ranks of the enemy than this tremendous yell, preceded, as it had been, by almost perfect silence, and a steady advance under their fire." (Bancroft, vol. XI, p. 261.)

[26] Houston's Report, Kennedy, vol. II, p. 225.

[27] Kennedy, vol. II, p. 228.

[28] Rives, vol. I, p. 350. Bancroft (vol. XI, p. 263) accepts Houston's figures. Most of the Mexican losses took place at Vince's Bridge, where, according to an eyewitness, "there were an infinite number of dead, piled upon the other, till they might have served as a bridge." (Rives, vol. I, p. 350.) Anon., *Life* (p. 143) says that only seven Mexicans were known to have escaped.

[29] Anon., *Life,* p. 144.

[30] Bancroft, vol. XI, p. 264.

[31] Anon., *Life,* p. 76.

[32] Both the eventual American occupation of California and the settlement of the Oregon dispute with England lie outside the argument of this chapter; nevertheless it should be borne in mind that both fall directly within the orbit of expansion, and that both California and Oregon added vast territories, together another quarter of a million square miles, to the United States.

[33] For a personal description of Santa Anna see *Mexico, Aztec, Spanish and Republican,* Brants Mayer, vol. I, p. 432. He lost a legion in 1838 (see *The War in Mexico,* Justin H. Smith, vol. I, p. 49).

[34] Quoted by Justin H. Smith, vol. I, pp. 9–10.

[35] Mayer, vol. II, p. 119.

[36] *The Diary of James K. Polk,* edited by Milo Milton Quaife, vol. II, pp. 195–196.

[37] *Ibid.,* vol. II, p. 243.

[38] *Personal Memoirs of U. S. Grant,* vol. I, p. 41.

[39] See Young's *History of Mexico,* p. 470.

[40] *A History of the People of the United States, from the Revolution to the Civil War,* John Bach McMaster, vol. VII, p. 507.

[41] Quoted from McElroy, p. 260.

[42] *Memoirs of Lieutenant-General Scott,* written by himself, p. 460.

[43] Scott's Report of September 18, 1847. Quoted by McElroy, p. 270.

[44] See remarks of Major General George H. Gordon in *Papers of The Military Historical Society of Massachusetts,* vol. XIII, p. 566.

[45] See Mayer, vol. I, pp. 385–386.

[46] See Lieutenant Colonel Duncan's Report, *The War in Mexico,* R. S. Ripley (Staff Officer to General Pillow), vol. II, Appendix 2, p. 648.

[47] According to Rives (vol. II, p. 462), Santa Anna seems to have wished Valencia to follow the Americans towards San Augustin; but instead he marched by way of Guadalupe and Mexico City to San Angel, where he arrived on the 16th.

[48] Justin H. Smith, vol. II, p. 102.

[49] If Santa Anna had a plan, which seems doubtful, it was to fall back on the city and meet his enemy under its walls.

[50] See Ripley, vol. II, p. 219.

[51] *Ibid.,* vol. II, p. 220.

[52] *Life and Military Services of General Scott,* D. Mansfield, p. 421.

[53] Ripley, vol. II, pp. 242–243.

[54] Justin H. Smith, vol. II, p. 109.

[55] The Americans mistook the hacienda of Padierna for that of Contreras, close by; hence this name. More correctly the Mexicans called this battle after Padierna.

[56] "Scott's Report of August 28, 1847," quoted from McElroy, p. 280.

[57] Ripley, vol. II, pp. 311–312. (See also Rives, vol. II, pp. 488–489.)

[58] *Ibid.,* vol. II, p. 261.

[59] *Ibid.,* vol. II, p. 265.

[60] These are Rives's figures (vol. II, p. 487).

[61] Ripley, vol. II, p. 284.

[62] See Rives, vol. II, pp. 494–499.

[63] For Scott's views, see "Report of August 28, 1847," quoted by McElroy, p. 288.

[64] See Rives, vol. II, p. 518.

[65] Ripley writes: "Worth . . . desired that its surrender should be made a *sine qua non* in the negotiation of an armistice . . . Pillow was opposed to the whole negotiations on account of the danger of Mexican treachery . . ." (vol. II, p. 321).

[66] Rives (vol. II, p. 33) says, twenty rounds.

[67] Ripley, vol. II, p. 372.

[68] Major General George H. Gordon, speaking in 1883, says: "Again were the wounded murdered in cold blood and such atrocities perpetrated that I remember them with horror through the long years that have passed since that attack . . ." (*Papers of the Military Historical Society of Massachusetts,* vol. XIII, p. 610).

[69] U. S. Grant, who was present, says: "Had this victory been followed up promptly, no doubt Americans and Mexicans would have gone over the defences of Chapultepec so near together that the place would have fallen into their hands without further loss" (*Personal Memoirs,* vol. I, p. 152).

[70] These are Rives's figures (vol. II, p. 536). Justin Smith (vol. II, p. 147) gives, 124 killed and 582 wounded. The Mexicans appear to have had from 9,000 to 10,000 men present, and to have lost up to 2,000 in killed and wounded and 739 captured.

[71] See Ripley, vol. II, p. 383.

[72] See Rives, vol. II, p. 536.

[73] Justin Smith, vol. II, p. 147.

[74] See Rives, vol. II, p. 542.

[75] Ripley, vol. II, pp. 417–418.

[76] *Ibid.,* vol. II, p. 420.

[77] *Ibid.,* vol. II, pp. 421–422.

[78] *Personal Memoirs of U. S. Grant,* vol. I, pp. 157–158.

[79] *Fifty Years in Camp and Field,* Ethan Allen 'Hitchcock, p. 307.

[80] A few minor guerrilla operations followed the occupation of the capital, but none was of importance or had a chance of reversing the decision gained on September 14.

[81] 383 killed, 2,245 wounded, and 85 missing.

[82] Polk wanted to annex Lower California as well as Upper California, and many Americans, more especially in South Carolina, wanted to absorb the whole of Mexico.

[83] In 1853 the Gadsden Purchase established the southern boundary of the United States as it is today. Alaska was bought from Russia in 1867.

[84] Ripley, vol. II, p. 447.

[85] Justin Smith, vol. II, p. 312.

[86] *Writings and Speeches of Daniel Webster,* vol. XIII, p. 361 (National edition). On September 29, 1847.

1783–1861

SYNOPSIS OF BACKGROUND EVENTS

D URING this mighty territorial expansion westward a less conspicuous yet equally fateful phenomenon was in process of development. It was the industrial differentiation between the Northern and Southern states, which commercially grouped them into two separated peoples, as definitely as the Holy Roman Empire had been divided at the opening of the seventeenth century.

The primal factor in the dissensions which were now to arise between these two groups, and which were to be settled by the greatest civil war since the Thirty Years' War was fought, was the political impotence of the Constitution under which the states were governed. It was an instrument devised to control a congerie of extensive parishes, and therefore was totally inadequate to sustain the solidarity of a rapidly growing empire, consisting in the greater part of all but uninhabited virgin land. Consequently it is necessary to understand what this Constitution entailed.

It originated out of the breakdown of the Confederation, the Articles of which were agreed upon in 1777. As that association of states was no more than "a firm league of friendship," each state followed its own path, for Congress had "no power to levy a tax of any kind, to regulate trade with foreign countries or between the States, or compel obedience to its own ordinances." The outcome was that, ten years later, a Convention assembled at Philadelphia, under the chairmanship of George Washington, to consider the formulation of a Federal Constitution. Its master mind was Alexander Hamilton, who proposed a legislature of two houses, a Senate and an Assembly; the one to have sole power of declaring war, and the other, to coin money, regulate trade, levy taxes, duties, imposts and excises, to pay the debts of the United States, and to provide for the common defense of the nation.

Once the new Constitution was framed, it was presented to Congress, where, by July, 1788, eleven states having adopted it, it was decided that New York should be the seat of government and that the Senate and House should meet on the first Wednesday in March, 1789.

This momentous change coincided with the outbreak of the French Revolution, which, by keeping European nations fully occupied, for twenty years left the Americans free to consider their domestic affairs. During this interval of upheaval and war, these were increasingly influenced by the economic revolutions which simultaneously took place in the Southern and Northern states. In the South, Eli Whitney's invention of the cotton gin completely revolutionized the cotton trade. The result was the political supremacy of the cotton planter in the South, and an ever-increasing political divergence from the North. Though in the Southern states trade was vastly simplified, in the Northern it had become diversified because of the increasing commerce enjoyed during the period of the twenty years' war in Europe, which, as we have seen, brought prosperity to New England and the commercial states, and then, due to the "long embargo," industrialization.

The clash between the agricultural revolution in the South and the economic revolution in the North begot economic differentiation. In the North, overspeculation was followed by slumps; in the South, the planting of cotton, year after year, stripped the fertility of the soil. In the North tariffs were essential to protect the young industries from being swamped by European competitors; in the South which had to dispose of an ever-increasing cotton crop, they were a disadvantage. Thus differentiation rapidly led to a demand for separation, the crisis coming to a head over the question of tariffs.

By 1824, when John Quincy Adams was elected president, the movement for protection was gaining steadily. During that year Henry Clay urged his "American System" upon his countrymen. Pointing out "the paradox of bankruptcy" which had engulfed his own state, "in a land of opportunity and plenty," he asked: Why this distress? And answered that question by asserting that "during almost the whole existence of this government, we have shaped our industry, our navigation, and our commerce, in reference to the extraordinary war in Europe, and to foreign markets, which no longer exist." The peace in Europe, he pointed out, had been followed by a cessation of imports of food from the United States; therefore as Europe would now grow her own food, and as the American surplus would be required for the American people, who in numbers were doubling every twenty-five years, it was hopeless to look to Europe for a remedy for American depression. The sole cure was to build up the home market, in order to render the country independent of European fluctuations, and so establish an economic system parallel to the political system of Monroe. In other words—to place the United States on a self-sufficient footing.

From the Southern point of view, however, the snag in this argument was that cotton was not grown in Europe, and that, whether in wartime or during peace, Europe must buy cotton.

Nevertheless, in spite of opposition in the West and the South, Clay's System was adopted and protection as a policy was fastened on the U.S.A. Then, three years later, a new tariff bill passed the House, to be tabled in the Senate by the casting vote of Calhoun, the vice-president. Yet, in January, 1828, it was passed unexpectedly by both Houses of Congress and was accepted by Adams. In the South it became known as the "Tariff of Abominations," the ships in Charleston harbor flying their flags at half-mast.

The quarrel now took upon itself a constitutional complexion, because Calhoun once again stepped into the breach, and in his memorandum, since known as the "South Carolina Exposition," he asserted that the Tariff Act of 1828 was unconstitutional, and that under such circumstances a state might refuse to obey an act of Congress.

This same year, 1828, Georgia addressed a long memorial to the anti-tariff states; in 1829, Mississippi advised resistance, and Virginia resolved that the tariff ought to be repealed. Then, in 1832, Congress removed the duties on a long list of imports, but instead of allaying the storm, this only rendered it more violent. At once South Carolina called a state convention, at which the Tariff Act of 1828 and the 1832 Amendment were declared null and void. At length in March, the following year, a compromise was agreed upon, and the first phase of the struggle for state rights was terminated.

Having thus changed from an economic into a political question, it was not long before the quarrel developed moral aspects as well, and became concerned with the rights and wrongs of slavery. Though in the North slavery was unpopular, its extinction there had been due to the fact that it was unprofitable. In the South it was only less unpopular, and it would undoubtedly by now have also become extinct there, but for the firmly rooted belief that none but Negroes could cultivate cotton.

As a moral issue, the dispute acquired a religious significance, state rights becoming wrapped up in a politico-mysticism which, defying definition, could be argued over for ever without any hope of a final conclusion being reached.

In 1829 a Negro, named David Walker, published a pamphlet entitled *Walker's Appeal,* in which he lauded the bravery of the blacks over the whites and urged the former to revolt. A rising of slaves in Virginia, known as "Nat Turner's Insurrection," was attributed to this pamphlet as well as to the *Liberator,* a Boston newspaper edited by William Lloyd Garrison, whose followers were known as the Abolitionists. In the South demands were made that they should be suppressed; yet, though their meetings were broken up and Negro schools sacked, their antislave literature continued to pour into the Southern states. Then, in 1835, a kind of Boston Tea Party was held, the mob breaking into Charleston post office and destroying sacks of antislavery tracts which had come from New York. Thus the quarrel deepened, until for a time it was distracted by the insurrection in Texas, the Texan problem, and the Mexican War, which, as we have seen, added hundreds of thousands of square miles to the United States. This accretion of land, as well as the discovery, in 1848, of gold in California once again accentuated the differences between the North and South.

The finding of gold caused violent social disturbances throughout the recently acquired territory. "Labourers left their fields, tradesmen their shops. Seamen deserted their ships in every harbour; soldiers defiantly left their barracks. Neither threats nor punishment could hold men to their legal engagements." Then, as Congress had not provided a government for California, the people proceeded to establish one of their own. In September, 1849, a convention assembled at Monterey and, having drawn up a Free-State Constitution, made formal application for the admission of California into the Union. This was violently opposed by the South, because it would upset the balance of power between the Free and the Slave states in the Senate; nevertheless, after a series of tremendous debates in which Clay, Calhoun, Webster, Seward, and Jefferson Davis took part, in 1850 a compromise was agreed to. It settled nothing, because in the new territories the problem of slavery remained in solution, and one day these territories would become states. So it came about that, though economically and demographically the South stood still, the North continued to expand, for the opening up of the West, like the opening of a sluice gate, gave freedom to the latter to flood into the yet undeveloped lands, whereas the stagnation of the former rendered the Constitution as lifeless and brittle as fleshless bones.

Meanwhile, changes beyond legal arguments were pushing the contending parties further and further apart. Yearly, scores of thousands of immigrants were pouring into the United States, caring little about politics and much about the gaining of wealth. Railways were advancing daily, mile by mile; more than 6,000 miles were constructed between 1840 and 1850, and the Morse telegraph was adopted in 1844. Yet the South did not grow, rather did her states shrink, for many of their citizens migrated to the North and West.

It was not the actual existence of slavery that antagonized the North, but its possible extension to the new regions. Therefore, so long as these remained unsettled, the quarrel continued, to reach its climax during the Presidency of James Buchanan (March 4, 1857–March 3, 1861) which were years of trade depression. In 1858, a comparatively unknown man, by name Abraham Lincoln, appeared upon the scene. In his contest with Stephen A. Douglas for the Senatorial seat of Illinois, he flashed no little common sense on the burning question, and won the ears of the whole country by proclaiming: "A house divided against itself cannot stand. I believe this government cannot endure half slave and half free. I do not expect the house to fall, but I expect it will cease to be divided. It will become all one thing or all the other."

Next, in May, 1858, the Free state of Minnesota entered the Union, to be followed in 1859 by the Free state of Oregon, when the balance between Free and slaving holding states was destroyed. Compromise was now at an end, and the inevitable clash was hastened when, on October 17, one John Brown at the head of some twenty followers seized the arsenal at Harper's Ferry in Virginia, in order to set on foot a servile insurrection. This blew the quarrel into white heat, for though he was speedily dealt with and hanged, his purpose was massacre; therefore, Union or no Union, antislavery must be fought to the death.

Thus matters stood, when, on November 6, 1860, the Presidential elections were again held. There were four candidates, Bell, Breckinridge, Douglas, and Lincoln. Lincoln was elected practically on the votes of the eighteen Free states of the Union, receiving no electoral votes in the South. "The verdict thus expressed gave notice to the South that its dream of slavery extension was over, and that thereafter the North held the political balance of power."

Forthwith, on December 20, South Carolina passed an ordinance of secession; Georgia, Alabama, Mississippi, Florida, Louisiana, and Texas followed suit. Their militias were called out and the federal forts, arsenals, and customhouses in the Southern states were occupied. Thus some 1,000 guns and 115,000 stands of arms were seized. Meanwhile Buchanan tried in vain to steer a middle course. On January 5, 1861, a caucus of cotton-state senators in Washington drew up a revolutionary program and called a convention to assemble at Montgomery, Alabama, to organize a confederacy of seceding states. A few days before this decisive step was taken, Major Robert Anderson, the federal commander of the Charleston Forts, removed his garrison from Fort Moultrie to Fort Sumter. When General Winfield Scott sent 200 men to reinforce him, on January 9 the ship carrying them—*Star of the West*—was fired upon by the Confederate battery at Charleston Harbor and forced to withdraw.

On February 4 the Secession delegates met at Montgomery and formed a provisional government, known as the Confederate States of America, with Jefferson Davis as its president. And exactly a month later, Lincoln, then fifty-one years of age, addressed an earnest appeal to the South, concluding it by saying: "In your hands, my dissatisfied fellow-countrymen, and not in mine, is the momentous issue of civil war. You can have no conflict without being yourselves the aggressors."

CHAPTER VI

THE SEVEN DAYS' BATTLE
1862

W HAT were the strategical problems that faced the contending parties? In themselves they were exceedingly simple: to re-establish the Union the North must conquer the South, and to maintain the Confederacy and all that it stood for, the South must resist invasion. On the one side the problem was offensive, on the other defensive. To conquer the North was out of the question; therefore the Southern problem resolved itself into inducing Europe to intervene and in tiring the North out, and so compelling the Union to abandon the contest. As it was uncertain what Europe would do, the second half of the problem was the more important; consequently, of equal importance was the question: how long could the Southern resources stand the strain?

As the South depended on the industries of both the North and Europe, on April 19, 1861, Lincoln proclaimed a blockade of the Southern ports. Simultaneously he called for the enrollment of 75,000 volunteers, in spite of the fact that the federal commander in chief, Lieutenant General Winfield Scott, considered that "300,000 men under an able general might carry the business through in two or three years." [1] Lincoln, however, did not see, as Scott did, the vital relationship between economic pressure and land attack, nor how the first should be made the basis of action of the second. Consequently he failed to appreciate the value of Scott's project, which was a threefold one: (1) To capture New Orleans by a joint naval and military expedition and seal up all the Southern ports; and (2) to form two large armies, (*a*) one to move down the Mississippi and so cut the Western Confederate states off from the Eastern, while (*b*) the other threatened Richmond and contained the Confederate forces in Virginia.[2]

Of the ports and harbors between Cape Charles and the Mississippi there were only nine with railroads running into the interior—namely,

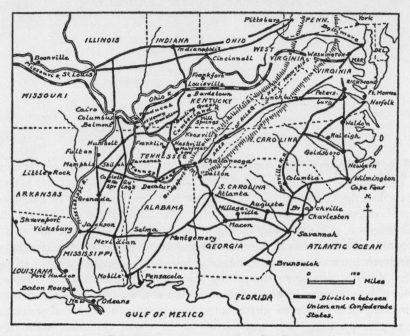

14. Strategical Map of the Confederacy

Newbern, Beaufort, Charleston, Wilmington, Savannah, Brunswick, Pensacola, Mobile, and New Orleans. By the end of April, 1862, all, except Mobile, Charleston, and Wilmington, were closed, thanks largely to Scott's prevision in holding fast to Fort Monroe; for under the protection of its guns was assembled every expedition to attack the Southern coast. Although Scott was derided and ridiculed, the fact remains that had these three remaining ports been occupied in 1862, the war would most definitely have been shortened. For instance, on the outbreak of the war there were less than 200,000 muskets in the Confederate arsenals, which were equipped with no machinery "above the grade of a foot-lathe." One hundred thousand were required yearly for replacements alone, and more than 400,000 were imported during 1862–1863. "Colonel William Lamb, who was in command at Fort Fisher from July, 1862, until its fall, says that there were at least one hundred vessels engaged running in and out of Wilmington. One ship ran to Nassau with almost the regularity of a mail packet." [3]

Turning now to land attack. As the defensive was by force of policy and circumstances thrust upon the South, Jefferson Davis should have at once recognized that the strategic frontier of the Confederacy did not coincide with the political. Whereas the latter ran from the Potomac to the Ohio, and thence to Columbus on the Mississippi and westward along the Missouri, the former ran from the Potomac along the Alleghany mountains to Chattanooga, thence along the Tennessee River to about Savannah, across to the Mississippi at Fulton, and from there to Little Rock on the Arkansas River. Had he recognized this, and had he realized that the states of Kentucky, Tennessee, and Missouri were no more than advanced positions, or tactical outworks, to the main strategic line of defense, then his strategy would have taken concrete form. He would have at once seen that the key to it was the area Chattanooga-Atlanta, because the two main lateral railroads in the Confederacy ran through these towns and linked the entire strategical area up with the supply ports of Memphis, Vicksburg, New Orleans, Mobile, Pensacola, Savannah, Charleston, Wilmington, and Richmond. Should Chattanooga-Atlanta be lost, then, from a supply point of view, to all intents and purposes the Confederacy would be reduced to the Carolinas and Virginia. [4]

Had Davis understood this strategy he would also have seen that the Alleghany mountains cut the main theater of the war, which lay between the Mississippi and the Atlantic, into two subtheaters, political and strategical. In the political theater the security of the two capital cities and their governments was the predominant factor; whereas the strategical theater was largely determined by the great river lines of approach—namely, the Mississippi, Tennessee, Cumberland, and Ohio. Then he would also have seen that, as the most certain means of winning the war was to wear the North out—that is, to prolong the war indefinitely—the most suitable grand tactics were to base the main forces on Chattanooga and carry out a defensive-offensive campaign in Tennessee, while a covering force operated in Virginia. Such a campaign, if pushed with vigor, would not only have protected the great supply states of Mississippi, Alabama, and Georgia, but would have kept open the vital crossings into Missouri, Arkansas, and Louisiana, and have stretched out a helping hand to Kentucky. It may be said that had these grand tactics been decided upon, the Federals would have occupied Virginia, from where they would have pushed south through the Carolinas.

This is unlikely, even had Virginia been overrun. Not only would the Confederate operations in Tennessee have drawn the bulk of the Federal forces westward, but the topographical conditions in the East would have proved as difficult to overcome as they were in 1775–1783. What did General Nathanael Greene do in North Carolina in 1781? He avoided pitched battles, and instead relied upon rapidity of maneuver to strike at weakness and the British lines of communication. Had the Federals penetrated into North Carolina, they would have had to rely on the Danville railway, and every mile of advance would have laid that line open to more certain attack; therefore its protection would eventually have crippled their field army. Further, in order to protect this central line of supply, they would have been compelled to have advanced on an enormously extended front; therefore their progress would have been excessively slow, especially as the country they advanced through was hostile.

On the Federal side, after the failure to adopt Scott's plan, strategy was vague, bottomless, and upside down. Though at intervals Lincoln was a strategical visionary—that is, a man who could see what should be done without possessing an idea of how to do it—from the opening of the war he fell victim to a series of second-rate generals urged blindly on by a first-rate democracy. Quite early in the struggle he hankered after carrying the war into East Tennessee, not only because this would bring relief to the loyal population in that area, but because such an advance would threaten Chattanooga. Yet nothing much came of this essentially sound idea, because from the opening of the struggle and for three years onward his attention was riveted on the political theater of the war, which included his enemy's capital. It was Howe and Philadelphia over again.

Into the hands of Lincoln and Davis was thrust the destiny of a divided people. Lincoln was the son of the soil, Davis, the product of the study. One had breathed into his soul the freedom of Nature, and could best express his inner feeling through parables. The other had breathed the air of the cloister, and his soul had grown stiff as the parchment it had fed upon. Lincoln was very human, Davis artificial, autocratic, and forever standing on the pedestal of his own conceit, a man of little humor, who could dictate, but who could not argue or listen, and who could not tolerate either assistance or opposition. Relying upon European intervention to scuttle the war, he had no foreign policy outside establishing Cotton as King. Early in the war the Hon. James Mason, Confederate commissioner in Europe, stated that all cotton in that continent would be exhausted by February, 1862, "and that . . . intervention would [then] be inevitable";[5] yet before the end of 1861 Europe was learning to do without cotton. Davis, however, could not believe that he was wrong; he staked the fortunes of his government and his people on this commodity and lost. On the other hand, Lincoln pinned his faith on what he believed to be the common right of humanity. In spite of division he saw one people, and in spite of climate and occupation, one nation. To him the Union was older than any state, for it was the Union which had created the states *as* states. He saw that whatever happened the nation could not permanently remain divided. His supreme difficulty was to maintain the unity of the North so that he might enforce unity upon the South; whereas Jefferson Davis's ship of state was wrecked on the fundamental principle of his policy that each individual state had the right to control its own destiny, a policy which was incapable of establishing united effort.

From the military point of view both men were incapable, Lincoln even more so than Davis. This was not to be wondered at, because the two causes, political ideas, and ways of living produced two very different and intricate military problems.

The Confederacy being immense in size, badly roaded and preeminently agricultural, its soldiers naturally took to guerrilla warfare, as their forefathers had done during the War of Independence. In order to conquer such a people, operations had to be methodical; for individual valor and initiative are best overcome by discipline and solidarity. Unfortunately for the Federals they sought to establish these conditions on the conventional European pattern. They copied instead of creating, and at the outbreak of the war, possessing the army headquarters and the bulk of the small regular establishment, they expanded it not only bodily, but spiritually in the form they found it. In short, the South, though less military, was more soldierlike, free from shibboleths, and the Confederate soldier could adapt himself to changing events,[6] whereas the Federal sought to overcome difficulties by textbook rules.

This individualism was also largely stimulated by the change in firearms that had taken place during the previous twenty years. In the Napoleonic Wars the flintlock musket, which possessed an effective range of less than a hundred yards, was considerably outranged by cannon firing grape or canister; consequently the gun was the superior weapon. But, by 1861, the musket had given way to the muzzle-loading percussion-capped rifle,[7] a weapon with an effective range of 500 yards, a range outclassing that of case and canister fired either by smooth-bore or rifled guns. Therefore the whole of fire tactics underwent a profound change; the gun having to fall back in rear of the infantry and becoming a support weapon, while the infantry fire fight opened at 400 yards' range, instead of from 50 to 100. The result of this long-range fire-fighting was that the bayonet assault died out; individual good shooting became more effective than volley firing, and for full effectiveness it demanded initiative and loose order. Therefore the percussion-cap rifle well fitted the character of Confederate tactics and the character of the Southern soldier.

In short, the Federal soldier was semiregular and the Confederate semiguerrilla. The one strove after discipline, the other unleashed initiative. In battle the Confederate fought like a berserker, but out of battle he ceased to be a soldier.[8] For instance, Robert Stiles, a Southerner, tells us that on his way to Gettysburg he rode up to a house, asked for a drink of water, rested there, chatted, wrote a letter, and after wasting an hour or two, rejoined his unit.[9] In the Confederate Army straggling was an inalienable right, a fact which jeopardized success time and again.

Such, in brief, was the background of this war. It opened at 4.30 A.M. on April 12, 1861, when the Confederates at Charleston bombarded Fort Sumter, which surrendered at noon on the 14th.

When those guns opened fire, Colonel Robert E. Lee was still in the United States Army. On April 20 he resigned his commission, and three days later was entrusted with the defense of Virginia, which had seceded but had not yet joined the Confederacy. This was an event of the greatest importance for the South, as Lee's position not only as a soldier but also as a citizen was outstanding. Son of General Henry Lee (Light Horse Harry), he was born at Stratford, Virginia, on January 19, 1807, and, in 1831, by marrying Mary Randolph Custis, great-granddaughter of Martha Custis, the wife of George Washington, he became the representative of the family which more than any other had founded American liberty.[10]

His first act was to send Colonel Thomas J. Jackson, soon to become famous as "Stonewall" Jackson, to seize Harper's Ferry. Then, on May 10, Lee was appointed commander in chief of the forces of the Confederacy, and held that appointment until June 8, when Jefferson Davis assumed direct control, Lee becoming his nominal chief of staff. Lee's first problem was to secure Northern Virginia. He accomplished this by sending General Joseph E. Johnston and 11,000 men to Harper's Ferry, while General P. G. T. Beauregard held Manassas Junction with 22,000. This was too much for the people and the press in Washington, whose eagerness to attack and whose slogan "On to Richmond" forced the hands of Lincoln and General Scott. On July 18, General Irvin McDowell, having concentrated some 36,000 partially trained men at Centerville, advanced to Bull Run, close by Manassas Junction, and on the 21st was defeated, his men taking panic and breaking back to Washington.

Though this battle led to no strategical results, its influence on the grand strategy of the war was profound. First, it imbued the Southern politicians with an exaggerated idea of the prowess of their soldiers, and so led them to underestimate the fighting capacity of their enemy; secondly, it so terrified Lincoln and his government that, from then onward until 1864, the defense of Washington colored every Federal operation east of the Alleghanies.

The day after this battle Lincoln summoned to Washington Major General George B. McClellan, then commanding the Army of the West in the Department of Ohio. On the 27th, McClellan, under General Scott, assumed control of the 50,000 troops in and about the capital, and soon replaced Scott as general in chief.

Born on December 3, 1826, he had served in Mexico, was selected as one of the Military Commission sent out to the Crimean War, and, in 1857, retired from the army to become chief engineer of the Illinois Central Railroad. He was a man of great energy and gifted with marked powers of organization as well as charm. He soon won over the routed troops, whom he formed into the Army of the Potomac, raising their numbers to nearly 150,000 by October 27. On August 4 he set before the government an elaborate appreciation of the war,[11] which demanded an army 273,000 strong. A little later on, finding that so great a force could not be raised, he modified his ideas and began to consider an advance on Manassas or wherever the Confederates might be. But in December he was taken ill, which meant that the operation he had in mind had to be postponed until the early spring.

Though McClellan could win over his soldiers, he utterly failed to win over the politicians, mainly because he never condescended to take them into his confidence. Yet the fault was not altogether his, for as John C. Ropes writes: "Few men at the head of affairs during a great war have ever given such evidence of an entire unfitness to have any general direction over military men as Mr. Lincoln and Mr. Stanton [his Secretary of War]." [12]

Behind the politicians stood the public, who, having forgotten Bull Run, were once again clamoring for an advance. Had McClellan possessed more *nous* he would have propitiated them by taking Norfolk [13] or by reducing one or more of the Confederate batteries on the Potomac. Instead, he drew too heavily on their faith, when a little understanding and above all action would have drawn them to him.

While he was ill, Lincoln, apparently glad to be rid of him, took the extraordinary course of consulting his subordinate commanders, Franklin and McDowell. To the latter he said: "If something was not soon done, the bottom would be out of the whole affair; and if General McClellan did not want to use the army, he would like to *borrow* it, provided he could see how it could be made to do something." [14] When McClellan returned to duty on January 27, Lincoln, without consulting him, attempted to terminate what he held to be an unwarranted delay by an order "for a general movement of the land and navy forces of the United States against insurgent forces"—certainly one of the most extraordinary orders in the history of war. [15]

Of course nothing happened. Then, on February 3, McClellan proposed to abandon the overland advance on Richmond because of the impassable condition of the roads, [16] and to substitute for it a movement by water to Urbana on the lower Rappahannock, or should that spot be not found suitable, then to Mob Jack Bay or Fort Monroe. [17]

At once the president and his Secretary of War took fright, because such an operation would remove the army from before Washington while the Confederates still held Manassas Junction. At length, however, it was provisionally agreed to, when, on March 8, Lincoln issued another of his personal orders, by which he directed that "no change of the base of operations of the Army of the Potomac" was to "be made without leaving in and about Washington such a force as in the opinion of the General-in-Chief and the Corps Commanders shall leave said city entirely secure." [18]

No objection was raised to this; but, apparently, in order to persuade

McClellan to abandon his scheme he was forbidden to transport his army to Urbana.[19]

Two events now occurred, which in McClellan's mind rendered the Urbana scheme futile. The first was the memorable fight in Hampton Roads on the 9th between the Federal *Monitor* and the Confederate *Virginia,* usually called by her former name, *Merrimac*—the first of the ironclad engagements. Though neither ship was seriously damaged, the *Monitor* proved that she could match her rival and so protect the transports which were to carry the Army of the Potomac to Fort Monroe. The second was Johnston's evacuation that same day of Manassas Junction and the Potomac batteries, and retreat to the Rapidan. Four days later, McClellan summoned his four corps commanders —McDowell (First Corps), Sumner (Second Corps), Heintzelman (Third Corps), and Keyes (Fourth Corps)—to a council of war, at which it was decided that the landing of the army could best be undertaken at Old Point Comfort or Fort Monroe and that to protect Washington a force of 40,000 men would be sufficient.[20] These decisions were accepted by the president, and the embarkation of the troops was at once put in hand, the first convoy sailing on the 17th. Nevertheless, neither Lincoln nor Stanton troubled to ascertain what troops were to be left in Washington, and when McClellan suggested that one of his ablest officers—General Franklin—should be placed in command of its garrison, Lincoln appointed General Wadsworth, a volunteer officer of no experience. When McClellan objected, Stanton replied: "that Wadsworth had been selected because it was necessary, for political reasons, to conciliate the agricultural interests of New York, and that it was useless to discuss the matter, because it would in no event be changed." [21]

Nothing further seems to have been done until April 1; when, on the point of sailing for Fort Monroe, McClellan wrote to Stanton that "there would be left for the garrison and the front of Washington, under General Wadsworth, some 18,000, inclusive of the batteries under instructions," [22] or less than half the number decided upon on the 13th and agreed to by the president. However, as Swinton points out, besides this garrison there were in the neighborhood of the capital the following troops: At Warrenton, 7,780; at Manassas, 10,859; in the Shenandoah Valley, 35,467, and on the lower Potomac, 1,350; in all, therefore, 73,456 officers and men.[23]

Though clearly McClellan must have known that he was contravening the president's order of March 8, Washington was in no danger; for no sooner had McClellan set out than Johnston was ordered to carry his army from the Rapidan to Richmond, where he was placed in command of the Confederate forces in the Peninsula and at Norfolk, which were under Generals Magruder and Huger.[24] When the Federals landed, Lee, who on March 13 had been entrusted by Jefferson Davis with the conduct of the war,[25] recommended that Johnston's army should be sent south to reinforce Magruder. This Davis agreed to, whereupon Magruder and 13,000 men [26] took up an entrenched position along the Warwick River.

Such was the Confederate position when, having landed his Second, Third, and Fourth Corps, McClellan pushed forward the last, which at once came into contact with Magruder. He next intended to direct McDowell's First Corps on Gloucester as soon as it arrived from Alexandria, in order to turn the strong Confederate works at Yorktown. But on the 6th he was informed by Stanton that, because of the defenseless state in which Washington had been left, the president had decided to retain this corps in its neighborhood. This McClellan stigmatized as "the most infamous thing that history has recorded . . . The idea of depriving a general of 35,000 troops when actually under fire." [27]

The occupation of Gloucester would have opened the York River to the fleet, which then could have turned the Yorktown defenses. Since this was now impossible, McClellan set to work to besiege the town. On May 3, Johnston carried his army back to Williamsburg, where two days later a bloody engagement was fought. On the 10th the Confederates destroyed the *Merrimac* and evacuated Norfolk. This important event opened the James River to the Federal warships, which now could sail to within seven miles of Richmond. On the 16th McClellan established his headquarters at White House on the Pamunkey River—twenty miles east of the Confederate capital.

Though events proved that the establishment of the Federal base at White House was unfortunate, barely sixty miles to the north of it lay McDowell's corps, which had now been moved to Fredericksburg, where it was awaiting the arrival of Shields's division before marching south on Richmond. The White House was, therefore, well secured against a flanking attack and McClellan was well placed for a combined advance of all his four corps on his enemy's capital.

Meanwhile, the Confederate situation had worsened. "Stragglers," wrote Johnston to Lee on May 9, "cover the country and Richmond is no doubt filled with the 'absent without leave' . . . The men are full of spirit when near the enemy, but at other times, to avoid restraint, leave their regiments in crowds. To enable us to gather the whole army for battle would require a notice of several days." [28] So desperate was the situation in the capital that preparations were made to remove all military papers,[29] and even Jefferson Davis in a letter to Johnston spoke of the "drooping cause of our country." [30]

This letter was written on May 10, the day Norfolk was lost, yet ten days before this Johnston had written to Lee:

We are engaged in a species of warfare at which we can never win.
It is plain that General McClellan will adhere to the system adopted by him last summer, and depend for success upon artillery and engineering. We can compete with him in neither.
We must therefore change our course, take the offensive, collect all the troops we have in the East and cross the Potomac with them, while Beauregard, with all we have in the West, invades Ohio.
Our troops have always wished for the offensive, and so does the country . . . We can have no success whilst McClellan is allowed, as he is by our defensive, to choose his mode of warfare.[31]

When McClellan left for Fort Monroe, Lincoln, instead of placing the forces in and around the capital under a single command, divided that subtheater of war into three departments, each under an independent general—McDowell, Frémont, and Banks. The first was responsible for the defenses of Washington, the second and third were posted in the Shenandoah Valley. Similarly, on the Confederate side, the defense of Richmond was also perturbing Jefferson Davis, who with General Lee realized that the main threat to the capital lay in the almost certain move south of McDowell's corps. Their obvious move was, therefore, to play on Lincoln's fears, and an opportunity to do so arose on April 28, when Jackson, who was facing Banks in the Valley, suggested that he should attack him.[32] To this Lee agreed, because he considered that such a blow would result in McDowell being ordered north—that is away from McClellan and Richmond. Thereupon Jackson, setting out down the Valley, threw Lincoln and Stanton into such a panic that, on May 24, McDowell was ordered to lay "aside for the present the movement on Richmond" and "to put 20,000 men in motion at once for the Shenandoah moving in the line or in advance of the line of the Manassas Gap railroad." [33] Simultaneously McClellan was notified of this change.[34]

At the time McDowell received this order, he was eight miles south of Fredericksburg, waiting to make his own move on Richmond until General Fitz-John Porter, at the head of a selected force, 12,000 strong, had cleared its front by driving the Confederates out of Hanover Junction. There a sharp encounter took place on the 27th, when the right of the Army of the Potomac established itself within fifteen miles of McDowell's van.

This second withholding of McDowell—in circumstances far less justifiable than the first—threw McClellan's admirable combined operation completely out of gear. What Lincoln could not see was that the most certain protection of Washington lay in an immediate advance on Richmond, and not in falling into the trap set by the wily Jackson in the Valley. As Ropes writes: ". . . this concentration of 150,000 men in the immediate vicinity of Richmond would have compelled its speddy evacuation, is certainly very probable. It was, at any rate, obviously the true course for the Federal authorities to take. That this course was not taken was due entirely to the action of President Lincoln, who, contrary to the urgent remonstrances of the generals charged with the conduct of operations against Richmond, broke up deliberately one of the most promising combinations for the defeat of the Confederates and the capture of their capital that fortune was ever likely to afford to the Federal cause." [35]

The recall of McDowell left the Army of the Potomac divided,[36] for between the 20th and 24th the Fourth Corps, followed by the Third, had crossed the Chickahominy, while the Second, Fifth, and Sixth Corps [37] took position on the north side of that river. The latter were respectively commanded by Sumner, Porter, and Franklin.

Though this distribution had been decided on in order to gain contact with McDowell, McClellan made no change in it when he was withdrawn. Consequently his army remained divided by a treacherous river, which, though of no size, was a formidable military obstacle because of the boggy lands bordering it.[38] Halting his forward movement, McClellan set to work bridging the Chickahominy, while Johnston in Richmond, realizing the faulty situation McClellan was now in, entrusted General Longstreet with the task of overwhelming Keyes and Heintzelman. The result was the muddled and bloody battle of Fair Oaks or Seven Pines, fought on the 31st and continued throughout June 1. At about seven o'clock that evening, Johnston was severely wounded. He was succeeded by General Gustavus W. Smith, who by order of the president handed the army over to General Lee on the following day.[39]

Though this battle was indecisive, there can be little doubt that, on the 2d, McClellan should have launched a vigorous counteroffensive.

Had he done so, the probabilities are he would have routed his disorganized enemy. Instead, he returned to his bridge building, which, because of the rainy weather, occupied his army for the next three weeks. Changes he certainly did make in his distribution, for he withdrew all troops except the Fifth Corps—Fitz-John Porter's—from the north to the south of the Chickahominy, and set about constructing elaborate fieldworks from Golding's Farm to White Oak Swamp and also immediately to the east of Beaver Dam Creek, while the approaches from the south side were "strongly defended by intrenchments." [40] During this period and in response to urgent demands for reinforcements, McCall's division, 9,500 strong, was sent to him and added to Porter's corps, as were 11,000 troops from Baltimore and Fort Monroe. On June 20, the strength of his army was 105,445 officers and men. [41]

Once the bridges were finished, there can be no possible doubt that McClellan should forthwith have assumed the offensive, if only because Jackson was still in the Valley and might at any moment descend on his communications with White House, which since the withdrawal of McDowell were largely uncovered. Certainly he realized this possibility, [42] which was all but confirmed by a hostile cavalry raid on his communications on June 11; because, as we know, he took the precaution to send by water a quantity of his stores from White House to Harrison's Landing on the James River, [43] besides having the ground between the railway and White Oak Swamp and the roads leading to the James reconnoitered. [44]

Meanwhile Lee's position was a difficult one, for not only was the army badly demoralized by its failure at Fair Oaks, but his own reputation was not high. In August and September, 1861, he had failed in West Virginia. Since then, and until his summons to Richmond on March 13, he had been lost to sight among the coast defenses of Georgia, South Carolina, and Florida. Therefore he was virtually unknown to his army, and, as his military secretary—General Long—said, "lacked its confidence." [45]

Seeing that Richmond must be held at all costs, his first action was a wise one—namely, to secure it from the south by a line of works extending from "Chaffin's Bluff, on the James River . . . to a point on the Chickahominy a little above New Bridge, and then continued up that stream to Meadow Bridge." [46] Simultaneously he set out to reorganize his army, which consisted of six divisions—Longstreet's, Huger's, D. H. Hill's, Magruder's, Whiting's, and A. P. Hill's.

Once this work was in hand, on June 5 he reconnoitered the Federal position On the evening of that day he wrote to the president suggesting that, if Jackson could be reinforced, he might be able to "cross Maryland into Penn." Then he said: "I am preparing a line that I can hold with part of our forces in front, while with the rest I will endeavour to make a diversion to bring McClellan out." [47] It would seem that here we first touch upon the origin of the Seven Days' Battle; because three days later and after another reconnaissance he wrote to Jackson:

Should there be nothing requiring your attention in the Valley, so as to prevent your leaving it in a few days, and you can make arrangements to deceive the enemy and impress him with the idea of your presence, please let me know that you may unite at the decisive moment with the army around Richmond. Make your arrangements accordingly, but should an opportunity occur of striking the enemy a successful blow, do not let it escape you.[48]

Next, on the 11th, Lee wrote to him again, informing him that he was sending him six regiments under Brigadier General Lawton and eight under Brigadier General Whiting to assist in crushing "the forces opposed to you." Then, he added, guard the passes and "move rapidly to Ashland by rail or otherwise . . . and sweep down between the Chickahominy and Pamunky, cutting up the enemy's communications, etc., while this army attacks General McClellan's in front." [49]

Simultaneously, in order to discover the exact situation of McClellan's right flank, Lee sent out General J. E. B. Stuart and his 1,200 cavalry to reconnoiter towards the York River railroad.[50] By the 13th, Stuart had discovered that McClellan's entrenchments did not extend beyond Beaver Dam, and that there was no indication that McClellan intended to change his base. "But the most valuable and important information obtained by General Stuart was the fact that the enemy had neglected to fortify the ridge between the head waters of the Beaver Dam . . . and an affluent of the Pamunkey," [51] for it was along this ridge that Lee hoped to strike at McClellan's communications.

The value of this information was largely nullified by sending out so powerful a force under so impulsive a leader as Stuart. Instead of returning after he had fulfilled his mission, he set out to ride round McClellan's entire army, and by attacking its trains and rear services he opened McClellan's eyes to the danger he was in.[52]

Having circled McClellan, Stuart was back in Richmond on the 15th. Lee, receiving his report, wrote on the following day to Jackson suggesting a meeting.[53] Then, accompanied by Colonel Long, he rode out to reconnoiter the Federal position north of the Chickahominy.[54] Having made up his mind to bring Jackson down on McClellan's right, he mentioned this to Longstreet on his return. Meanwhile Jackson, having received Lee's letter of the 15th, moved his 18,500 men down the Virginia Central Railroad and arrived at Frederick's Hall ahead of them on Sunday the 22d. There he remained attending religious meetings until the Sabbath was over; [55] and, at one o'clock on Monday morning, he rode the fifty-two miles to Lee's headquarters, arriving at 3 P.M. "Had he kept on the freight train to Richmond," writes General Alexander, "he would have arrived early Sunday morning. His brigades on the march also kept Sunday in camp. It was usually the general's custom to keep account of Sundays spent in fighting or marching, and to make up for each by a week-day rest, and sermons, at the earliest opportunity." [56]

This waste of precious military time, as we shall see, was the initial cause that wrecked Lee's plan.

On his arrival, Lee at once assembled a conference, which Jackson, Longstreet and the two Hills attended. To them he outlined his plan. The general idea was that, while Huger and Magruder held the entrenched lines east of Richmond and south of the Chickahominy, Jackson was to outflank McClellan's position north of that river, and by turning his right and falling on his rear and severing his line of communications, compel him to retire. Then Longstreet and the two Hills would advance on Beaver Dam Creek and assail his retiring front.[57]

As is obvious, the success of this maneuver depended on the careful timing of the advance by Longstreet and the two Hills with Jackson's attack. Equally obvious was it at the time that, should McClellan either before or after the action withdraw to the south of the Chickahominy, break down the bridges over it and then move on Richmond, the bulk of Lee's army would be completely outmaneuvered. But, knowing how cautious McClellan was, Lee was convinced that he would not seize such an opportunity, which in any case would necessitate the moving of his base to James River, but would instead retire down the Peninsula to Fort Monroe.[58]

According to Freeman, Lee's total effective strength was about 67,000 men and Jackson's 18,500, making a grand total of 85,500 of all arms. His order of battle was as follows:

Defensive Force: Magruder's division, 12,000 men, and Huger's, 9,000.

Attacking Force: Jackson's division, 18,500 men, covered by Stuart's cavalry division, 1,800 sabers.

Pursuit Force: Longstreet's division, on the right, 9,000 men; A. P. Hill's division, in the center, 14,000, and D. H. Hill's division on the left, 9,000.

River James Defense Force: Holmes's division, 6,500 men, and Wise's command, 1,500.

Reserve Artillery: General Pendleton, 23 batteries—3,000 men.

Cavalry South of the Chickahominy: 1,200 men.[59]

To return to McClellan. Without counting the 10,000 men still at Fort Monroe, he had under his command 117,000 officers and men present for duty, of whom 105,500 were effectives. Therefore he outnumbered his opponent by 20,000 in all.

On the 23d a rumor was picked up by his Secret Service Corps, or bureau of detectives, that a formidable combination was being planned against him. On the following day, he learned from a deserter that Jackson was marching from Gordonsville to Frederick's Hall in order to fall upon his rear on the 28th.[60] Nevertheless, he ordered a forward movement of his picket line on the 25th. A sharp engagement, known as the Skirmish of Orchard or Oak Grove, followed. This advance was to be preparatory to a general move on Richmond on the 26th. But on returning to his headquarters that evening, he found that further rumors of Jackson's advance had been received; whereupon, accepting without question a report that Beauregard had joined Lee, he telegraphed Stanton that he was faced by 200,000 Confederates.[61]

Though both Lee and McClellan respectively believed themselves to be outnumbered by two to one, the difference between their generalship is measured by the fact that, whereas the former decided to attack, the latter determined to retire. True, McClellan's communications were but weakly protected by Porter's 30,000 men, now the sole Federal force north of the Chickahominy; nevertheless, to attack them decisively Lee could not rely on Jackson alone, and this must have been clear to McClellan. Therefore, to overthrow the Federal right wing Lee would have to strip his own right wing, and so risk its being overthrown by the Federal forces south of the Chickahominy.

As we have seen, Lee did strip his right, leaving with it Magruder and Huger in command of some 21,000 men to face over three times their number. And having accepted this risk, largely because he had accurately measured McClellan's worth, he now depended for success upon Jackson.

If Jackson struck Porter before he could be reinforced, then, as General Alexander writes, "the game was Lee's for a great success—the greatest ever so fairly offered to any Confederate general." [62] Most unfortunately

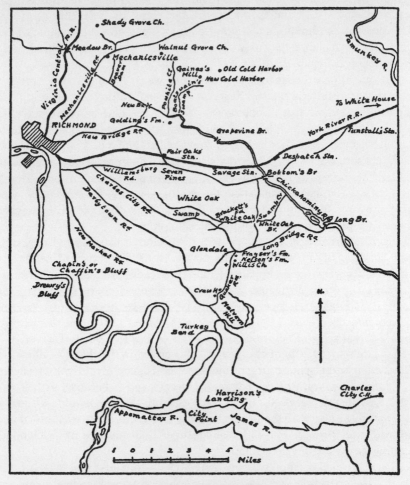

15. Map of the Seven Days' Battle, June 24—July 1, 1862

for Lee and the entire South, Jackson failed him. Not only did Jackson's men, as we have seen, spend Sunday in praying instead of marching, but they made so poor an advance on Monday that by Tuesday morning they had arrived no further than Beaver Dam Station, about eighteen miles from Ashland, where Jackson "was expected to camp that night, and about 25 miles from the Virginia Central R. R., near the Stark Church, whence order No. 75 required Jackson to march at 3 A.M. Thursday, June 26" [63]—ten miles from his goal. Instead, he crossed that railroad at 9 A.M.,[64] and then marched but eight miles further on, to go into bivouac at Hundley's Corner at about 5 P.M.; and this in spite of the fact that at that time he was within two miles of Porter's rear and could hear heavy firing in the distance.[65]

Meanwhile Lee waited. Noon came and went. At about two o'clock a report was received that the Federals were evacuating certain gun positions. Thereupon Lee, Longstreet, and D. H. Hill went forward to verify this report. Then of a sudden heavy firing was heard to the north, and it was supposed that at length Jackson had arrived. However, it was not Jackson, but A. P. Hill's division; for that general having decided to wait no longer, had, without orders, advanced. Thereupon the Federals fell back through Mechanicsville to an all but impregnable position they had prepared behind Beaver Dam Creek. This position Hill attacked fiercely, and was repulsed with great slaughter.

As this premature attack caused the Federals opposing Longstreet and D. H. Hill to withdraw, the divisions of these two officers were ordered forward. Hill launched Ripley's brigade "in a direct charge on perhaps the very strongest point of the whole Federal position." So writes General Alexander, and adds: "A more hopeless charge was never entered upon . . . There they were killed until their bodies lay, as a Federal account described it, 'as thick as flies in a bowl of sugar.' " [66] Thus Lee's first battle of the Seven Days ended in "a ghastly failure." [67] That evening he sent an urgent message to Huger: "Hold your trenches to-night at the point of the bayonet if necessary," [68] because, as his plan had now been disclosed, he feared that McClellan would withdraw Porter to the south of the Chickahominy, and from there with his united army break through Magruder and Huger and advance on Richmond, cutting Lee off from the capital.[69]

That McClellan should have done this is obvious; but as Swinton says: "the operation overlooked by its boldness the methodical genius of the Union commander." [70] Instead, having received a report from his Secret Service Corps that Lee now headed 180,000 men,[71] he decided to withdraw to the James, and establish there a new base from which to reopen offensive operations.[72] To cover this retirement, he should either have withdrawn Porter's command to the south side of the

Chickahominy, or have reinforced it. He did neither, but instead, at day-break on the 27th, knowing now that Jackson had joined Lee, he ordered Porter to withdraw to a prepared position along Boatswain's Swamp in the neighborhood of Gaines's Mill. This retirement was successfully carried out.

While Porter was consolidating his new position, Lee rode over to Walnut Grove Church, which lies east of Mechanicsville, and there met A. P. Hill and Jackson, the latter making no apologies for halting at Hundley's Corner. Expecting that the battle would be fought on Powhite Creek, which flows immediately west of Boatswain's Swamp, Lee planned that, while A. P. Hill, supported by Longstreet on his right, assaulted Powhite Creek, Jackson and D. H. Hill were to advance against Porter's rear. In short, A. P. Hill and Longstreet were to sweep the Federals into the arms of D. H. Hill and Jackson. As usual Lee's instructions were verbal.

At 2 P.M. the battle opened with a furious assult by A. P. Hill, who anticipated that Jackson's whole army would simultaneously be on the move. As Hill was repulsed, Lee ordered Longstreet to come up on his right. Assault after assault followed, only to be shattered. Though Lee kept on sending messengers to Jackson, urging him to hurry forward, once again, as Long informs us, he had lost his way and "being obliged to countermarch in order to gain the right road, caused a delay of several hours in the operations of General Lee and materially affected his plan of attack." [73]

It did more than this; it ruined it. At 4 P.M. Porter, who valiantly had been holding his own, was reinforced by Slocum's division of Franklin's corps, some 9,000 strong. Toward evening, Jackson at length having come into line, Lee ordered a general assault all along the front. Porter's center was broken and 22 guns and 2,800 prisoners—including 1,200 wounded—were taken. Thus Lee won the battle of Gaines's Mill at the cost of some 8,000 men killed and wounded, while his adversary, now further reinforced by two brigades of Sumner's corps, fell back in good order. "Briefly it may be said of this battle," writes Alexander, "that it seems to have been left in the hands of the division commanders until it was nearly lost. Only at the last moment was the hand of the general in command revealed. But had Jackson's march that morning been pushed with the fierce swiftness natural to him on such occasions, and had he, during A. P. Hill's attack, thrown his whole force upon McClellan's right, a comparatively easy victory would have resulted." [74]

That night, while Porter was withdrawing in good order to south of the Chickahominy, the Federal corps commanders were informed of McClellan's intention to fall back on Harrison's Landing on the James

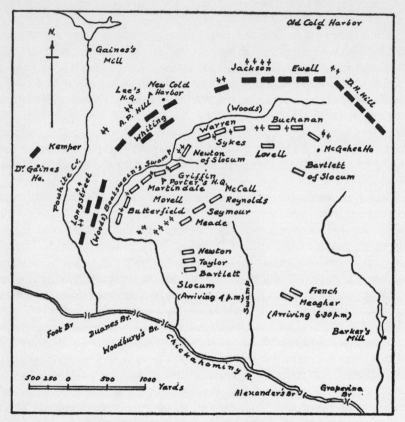

16. Battle of Gaines's Mill, June 26, 1862

River,[75] whereupon the bridges over the Chickahominy were destroyed.[76]

Lee's misuse of his cavalry, more than the burning of these bridges, delayed his advance. Instead of sending Stuart to work round McClellan's right, he ordered him to co-operate with Ewell's division "in a wholly useless expedition against the York River railway, from which Jackson had already cut the Federal army. Thus," as Sir Frederick Maurice writes, "he deprived himself of his eyes." [77]. Not until the 30th did he order Stuart to recross the Chickahominy. Consequently, he arrived too late for the final battle of the Seven Days. The result was that Lee was unable to determine whether McClellan was withdrawing to Fort Monroe or to the James River.[78]

Meanwhile, McClellan's army lay between the Chickahominy and White Oak Swamp, busy throwing two bridges over White Oak Swamp Creek. The first was finished in the morning, whereupon the Fourth Corps, under Keyes, crossed to take up a position four miles to the south, at which it could block the Charles City, New Market, and Quaker roads. The reserve artillery then crossed, followed, early on the morning of the 29th, by a herd of 2,500 slaughter cattle and the trains of the army—3,600 wagons and 700 ambulances. The whole was safely across White Oak Swamp by afternoon.

The same day McClellan reported events to Stanton in one of the most extraordinary dispatches ever penned. It ended with these words: "If I save this army now, I tell you plainly that I owe no thanks to you or to any other persons in Washington. You have done your best to sacrifice this army." [79]

Not until a little after sunrise on the 29th did Lee learn that McClellan was falling back on the James. His spirits at once rose; for "What fairer opportunity could any soldier ask than to attack his adversary in retreat and while changing base?" [80] Forthwith he issued the following orders, which he had every reason to assume would result in his enemy's annihilation; but as usual they were verbal.

While Ewell was to remain at Bottom's Bridge and come under the orders of Jackson, and Stuart was to watch the lower crossings of the Chickahominy, Jackson was to rebuild Grapevine Bridge and with all speed directly press the enemy's rear. Simultaneously Magruder, advancing down the Williamsburg Road and Huger down the Charles City Road, were to attack his right flank, whereas Longstreet and A. P. Hill were to cross the Chickahominy at New Bridge, pass in rear of Magruder and Huger, gain the Darbytown Road and block the head of the Federal retreat to the James.[81] Much again depended on Jackson, for with D. H. Hill and Ewell, his command, numbering 25,000 all told, was by far the strongest of these columns.

Having issued these orders, Lee first rode over to Magruder and then to Huger, with whom he remained. From that time on he lost all grip of the pursuit, because, as during the last two days, his subordinate commanders utterly failed to co-operate with each other or to communicate with him. The result was a complete muddle.

To begin with, Magruder, mistakenly thinking that Huger had been ordered to take the Williamsburg Road and support him, and believing also that he was opposed in strength, called upon Lee for reinforcements. Lee responded by sending the two rear brigades of Huger's division, but authorized Huger to recall them should it develop that Magruder did not actually need them. In this case Huger was to move his whole division forward.[82] Huger decided that Magruder did not need the two brigades, and recalled them. Waiting for their return, he advanced no more than six miles that day.

Meanwhile Magruder waited for Huger on his right and for Jackson on his left. When Huger failed to appear, he got into touch with Jackson through General D. R. Jones, who commanded one of his brigades. From him he learned that Jackson could not help him, as he had "other important duty to perform." [83] Thereupon Magruder attacked the Federal rearguard opposing him, and drove it back on Savage Station, which lay in the direct path of Jackson's advance.

When, late that evening, Lee heard of this, he wrote as follows to Magruder: "I learn from Major Taylor that you are under the impression that General Jackson has been ordered not to support you. On the contrary, he has been directed to do so and to push the pursuit vigorously." [84]

Why had not Jackson complied with this order, and what was the "other important duty" he had to perform? Several reasons have been advanced; but, in my opinion, the true and obvious one is that the 29th was a Sunday, and as General Alexander writes, "Jackson gave it strict observance. The greater part of his troops remained in camp all day and until after midnight Sunday night. Then they made a start at, or before 2.30 A.M." [85]

The general result of these misunderstandings, coupled with Jackson's devotions, was that McClellan was able to slip the bulk of his retiring army over the swamp on the 28th and 29th, while Longstreet and Hill, who advanced thirteen miles to Atlee's Farm, were left in the air, with General T. H. H. Holmes and 6,000 men, who had come down the New Market Road on their right flank.

That night Lee issued his orders for the following day

1. Holmes to advance down the New Market road and take a strong defensive position at New Market Heights near the junction of his route and the Long Bridge road.

2. Magruder to return from Savage Station, enter the Darbytown road by the shortest byway, advance down it, and take position as a general reserve.

3. Longstreet and A. P. Hill to continue down the Darbytown road to the Long Bridge road and to prepare to attack the Federals when they were located.

4. Huger to march down the Charles City road, and to open with his artillery when he established contact with the enemy.

5. Jackson, with Whiting and D. H. Hill, to march to White Oak Swamp bridge, cross there, and attack the enemy in rear.

6. Stuart's previous orders to stand still—to move to the main army and to co-operate as circumstances permitted.[86]

The opening of Huger's guns was to be the signal for the general advance.

Early the next morning Lee rode over to Savage Station, where he met Jackson, who had joined Magruder at 3.30 A.M. There Robert Stiles relates: "The two Generals greeted each other warmly . . . They stood facing each other . . . Jackson began talking in a jerky, impetuous voice, meanwhile drawing a diagram on the ground with the toe of his right boot. He traced two sides of a triangle with promptness and decision; then starting at the end of the second line, began to draw a third projected toward the first. This third line he traced slowly and with hesitation, alternately looking up at Lee's face and down at the diagram, meanwhile talking earnestly; and when at last the third line crossed the first and the triangle was complete, he raised his foot and stamped it down with emphasis saying 'We've got him,' then signalled for his horse." [87]

Lee next sought out Magruder, and, having explained to him his orders, rode on and joined Longstreet, the head of whose column was approaching the junction with Long Bridge Road. About noon, the enemy was reported on the Willis Church Road, whereupon Longstreet's division was formed into line of battle, soon to begin skirmishing with the pickets of Heintzelman's corps. Next, at 2.30 P.M., gunfire was heard in the direction of Huger's division, which all supposed was the signal to launch the battle. Though at three o'clock it ceased, Longstreet's leading brigade had by then become engaged with the Federal infantry.

Simultaneously Lee received a report from Holmes—then moving down the New Market Road—that enemy columns could be seen withdrawing southwards over Malvern Hill. Were this true, it meant that McClellan had all but escaped the trap set for him; therefore to verify it, Lee galloped down the Long Bridge Road to the New Market junction, and on arriving there found this information to be correct.

While Lee was away, Longstreet instructed Magruder to march to the support of Holmes, but on Lee's return he was ordered back to reinforce Longstreet, for Huger's and Jackson's attacks were still hanging fire. It then became obvious to Lee that, were Longstreet and A. P. Hill to wait much longer, the enemy would escape, so at 5 P.M. he ordered them forward through the woods and clearings about Glendale and Frayser's Farm. (It was from this farm that the action was named. It is also called the battle of Nelson's Farm—another close-by settlement.)

The attack was a somewhat disjointed affair. Longstreet's leading brigade rushed the woods and clearings so impetuously that it outran those in support. As a result, though McCall's division which was holding the center of the Federal line was driven back, Hooker's and Kearney's divisions of Heintzelman's corps, which flanked it, stood firm. These divisions assisted by Sedgwick's division and other troops—set free by Huger's and Jackson's inactivity—prevented Longstreet and Hill from reaching the Quaker Road along which the Federal trains were moving to Malvern Hill. In short, this attack accomplished little or nothing beyond the capture of fourteen guns and several hundred prisoners.

Meanwhile Huger, in accordance with his orders, had set out down the Charles City Road, but with extreme caution, as he was fearful that until Jackson's attack developed his left flank might be turned. Finding the road obstructed by felled timber,[88] he set to work to clear it and soon found himself opposed by detachments of Slocum's and Sedgwick's men. It was then that his guns opened, not as a signal of attack, but in order to clear the way. Instead of attempting to flank the road by extending through the woods, he continued along it, his enemy felling the trees as fast as his men could remove them. In all he advanced no more than two miles by nightfall, but for some reason, sent no single message to Lee, nor received one from him.

Meanwhile Jackson, with Ewell's division in support, spent so much time in collecting discarded Federal rifles and equipment that he did not cover the seven miles to White Oak Swamp Creek until noon, when he found the bridge broken and a Federal battery—one of Franklin's— in action on its southern side.

We now come to one of the strangest incidents in the whole of this war. On the 22nd and 29th the probabilities are that Jackson's fanatical regard for the Sabbath was accountable for his inaction. But this reason cannot hold good for the 30th, which was a Monday, unless he was canceling out some previously violated Sabbath. Yet, once again, Jackson remained immobile.

Though the bridge was broken, the creek averaged no more than from ten to fifteen feet in width, and above the bridge were four fords—Chapman's, Jourdain's, Fisher's, and Brackett's—and below it, Carter's. Colonel Mumford without difficulty got the 2d Virginian Cavalry over the creek, and General Hampton also crossed it and on returning to Jackson asked his permission to build a bridge for infantry. This request was granted, and the bridge was built in "a few minutes." Then, wrote Hampton:

On my return to our side of the swamp, I found General Jackson seated on a fallen pine alongside of the road that led down to the ford, and seating myself by him, I reported the completion of the bridge and the exposed position of the enemy. He drew his cap down over his eyes which were closed, and after listening to me for some minutes, he rose without speaking, and the next morning we found Franklin with the rest of the Federal troops concentrated on Malvern Hill . . . I believe that if Franklin, who opposed us at White Oak, could have been defeated, the Federal army would have been destroyed.[89]

Dabney, who was with Jackson at the time, credits this lethargy to "sleeplessness" and "the wear of gigantic cares." He writes: "after dropping asleep from excessive fatigue, with his supper between his teeth, he [Jackson] said, 'Now, gentlemen, let us at once to bed, and rise with the dawn, and see if to-morrow we cannot *do something!*' Yet he found time, amidst the fatigues of this day, to write to Mrs. Jackson, with a heart full of piety and of yearning for domestic happiness."[90]

During the evening and night of this day, the Federal forces, which had maintained themselves at Frayser's Farm, fell back in good order to Malvern Hill. This skillful withdrawal was, however, in no way due to McClellan's personal leadership; for, on the 29th, having issued orders to his corps commanders, he left the battle in their hands and retired to Malvern Hill in order to lay out its defenses. Well may Ropes write: "If his army had been beaten on that day, McClellan would have been cashiered, and justly. That the Federal corps-commanders,—although cordially and efficiently co-operating with each other,—acted on this day without a head, is evidenced by the fact that, at night, Franklin's (as he says himself) 'took the responsibility of moving' his 'command to the James River.' "[91]

Thus ended the battle of Frayser's Farm or Glendale, which, in the opinion of Freeman, "was one of the great lost opportunities in Confederate military history." [92] Alexander says:

I have often thought that in his [Lee's] retrospect of the war no one day of the whole four years would seem to him more unfortunate than June 30, 1862. It was, undoubtedly, the opportunity of his life, for the Confederacy was then in its prime, with more men available than ever before or after. And at no other period would the moral or the physical effect of a victory have been so great as upon this occasion.[93]

Early on the morning of July 1, Magruder's division arrived at Frayser's Farm and at once relieved Longstreet's and Hill's exhausted troops. Soon after, contact was established with Jackson, who at length had crossed White Oak Swamp Creek. Lee then issued his orders for the continuation of the pursuit.

Jackson was to move down the Willis Church Road [94] and Magruder along the Quaker Road,[95] while Mahone's and Ransome's brigades of Huger's division were to follow Jackson; Armistead's and Wright's divisions were to advance along a track leading south from the Charles City Road across the Long Bridge Road to Malvern Hill. Longstreet's and A. P. Hill's divisions were to remain in reserve and Holmes to halt for the time being on the New Market Road. Lee, as usual, left the execution of his orders to his divisional commanders.[96]

Meanwhile McClellan had united his entire army on Malvern Hill, a position of great natural strength, which had been carefully reconnoitered by Fitz-John Porter. It was a plateau a mile and a half long from north to south and about three-quarters of a mile wide, flanked on the south by Turkey Island Creek, and also by the fire of the Federal gunboats in the James River, and on the northeast and east by a stream called Western Run. It was, Lee says, surrounded by country "broken and thickly wooded, and was traversed nearly throughout by a swamp, passable at but few places and difficult at those." [97]

According to McClellan his general distribution was as follows:

Porter's corps held the left of the line (Syke's division on the left, Morell's on the right) . . . Couch's division was placed on the right of Porter; next came Kearney and Hooker; next Sedgwick and Richardson; next Smith and Slocum; then the remainder of Keyes's corps, extending by a backward curve nearly to the river. The Pennsylvania reserve corps was held in reserve, and stationed behind Porter's and Couch's position. One brigade of Porter's was thrown to the left on the low ground to protect that flank from any movement direct from the Richmond road.[98]

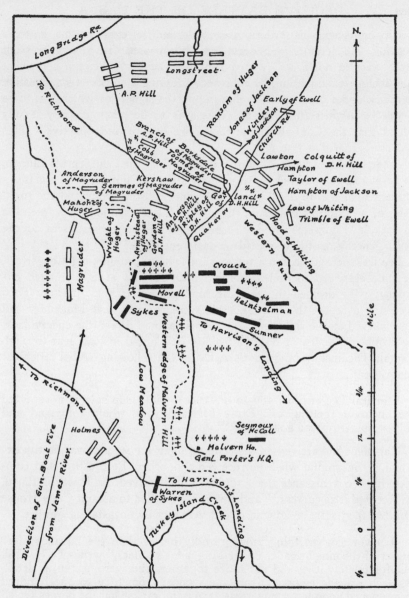

17. Battle of Malvern Hill, July 1, 1862

Having issued his orders, Lee rode out to examine his enemy's position. He found the Federal artillery massed "in a long crescent from west to northeast" with infantry in support. After a somewhat perfunctory examination, he returned, adopting Longstreet's suggestion to attack under cover of a bombardment, the signal for which was to be a yell by Armistead's brigade. This was to be given directly it was found that the Confederate artillery fire had proved effective.[99] This order was issued at 1.30 P.M.

After some delay a feeble fire was opened by the Confederate cannon, to be at once smothered by the enemy's massed gunfire. ". . . this inefficient artillery service," writes Alexander, "so discouraged the prospects of an assault that before three o'clock Lee abandoned his intention to assault. Longstreet was informed, but no notice was sent to the other generals, as there seemed no apparent need."[100]

Lee now determined on a turning movement. Summoning Longstreet, he rode eastward to find a suitable position, and after a hurried examination he decided to seize the high ground in that quarter. Then receiving a report that the Federals were retiring, that Magruder had now arrived on the right and that Armistead had driven the enemy back, he dropped the idea of outflanking McClellan and instead sent through Captain Dickinson (Magruder's A.D.C.) the following verbal order for Magruder:

"General Lee expects you to advance rapidly. He says it is reported the enemy is getting off. Press forward your whole command and follow up Armistead's success."[101]

Magruder had arrived on the right at about 4 P.M., and was hastily examining the ground when he received this order. Before he could complete his reconnaissance the 1.30 P.M. order arrived. As it was untimed, he accepted it as current,[102] and forthwith decided to assault Crew House Hill. At 4.45 P.M. he advanced and was met by devastating gunfire.

"I never saw anything more grandly heroic than the advance after sunset of the nine brigades under Magruder's orders," writes D. H. Hill. "Unfortunately, they did not move together, and were beaten in detail. As each brigade emerged from the woods, from fifty to one hundred guns opened upon it, tearing great gaps in its ranks; but the heroes reeled on and were shot down by the reserves at the guns, which a few squads reached. Most of them had an open field half a mile wide to cross, under the fire of field-artillery in front, and the fire of the heavy ordnance of the gun-boats in their rear. It was not war—it was murder."[103]

Then D. H. Hill, hearing a shout on his right followed by musket fire, and supposing it to be the signal for the attack, which he did not know had been canceled, ordered his division to advance. It was met by blasts of canister. Magruder called for support from Longstreet; D. H. Hill appealed to Jackson. Thus more and more men were poured into the inferno until night put a stop to the carnage.[104]

Lee had failed. Riding through the bivouacs of his shattered army he found Magruder.

" 'General Magruder,' he asked, 'why did you attack?'

"Magruder answered unhesitatingly: 'In obedience to your orders twice repeated.'

"Lee said nothing in reply, for there was nothing to say." [105]

That night Stuart returned from the Chickahominy.

Instead of counterattacking Lee on the 2d, as Porter, Hunt and Sumner urged, McClellan decided to continue his retreat to Harrison's Landing. In pouring rain he finally changed his base from the Pamunkey to the James. Meanwhile Lee sent Stuart and his cavalry in pursuit and ordered Jackson, Longstreet, and A. P. Hill to move south, while the rest of the army remained at Malvern Hill, except Holmes, who was ordered back to Drewry's Bluff.

On the 2d, only a two-mile march was made. On the 3d, Lee received a message from Stuart informing him that he had reached Harrison's Landing and had discovered that an extensive plateau, called Evelington Heights, which dominated it, had been left unoccupied. This dispatch sent, Stuart, more noted for his dash than his brains, put the finishing touch to the many follies committed during this campaign. Instead of avoiding these heights, so as not to draw McClellan's attention to their nakedness, he sent forward onto the Heights his one and only howitzer, then "nearly out of ammunition" with some cavalry, and opened fire on the enemy's camp below. The result was that McClellan at once occupied the Heights in strength.

On the 3d, Longstreet missed his road and Jackson covered only three miles. On the 4th, Lee rode forward to find his army in line of battle ready to regain Evelington Heights, but a rapid reconnaissance made him realize that they were now too strongly held to warrant an attack. On the 7th he published an order thanking his army, and two days later he took the army back to Richmond.

The price paid in the seven days following June 25 was for both sides a heavy one. Lee's army lost in killed and wounded 19,739, and McClellan's 9,796, to which must be added 6,053 men missing.[106]

Thus ended probably the most interesting and instructive campaign of this conflict. It was certainly one of its most important, because, in spite of numerous blunders, the Army of Northern Virginia, under the guidance of Lee, saved Richmond. Had Richmond fallen into Federal hands, the whole course of the war would have been changed.

That McClellan could have occupied Richmond is all but a certainty, in spite of the withdrawal of McDowell. That Lee could have routed the Army of the Potomac had Jackson of the Seven Days lived up to his recently gained reputation is also, so far as hypothesis allows, all but a certainty. Why both men failed to achieve their desired ends is a question which hinges on their generalship, for Federal and Confederate fought with equal valor. McClellan, though an able staff officer, was a fainthearted commander; Lee, though an audacious commander, was an indifferent staff officer. This stricture on Lee I will reinforce by quoting the opinions of two Confederate generals. D. H. Hill writes:

Throughout this campaign we attacked just when and where the enemy wished us to attack. This was owing to our ignorance of the country and lack of reconnaissance of the successive battle-fields.[107]

And General Richard Taylor says:

Indeed it may be confidently asserted that from Cold Harbour to Malvern Hill inclusive, there was nothing but a series of blunders, one after another, and all huge. The Confederate commanders knew no more about the topography of the country than they did about Central Africa.[108]

Though Lee mentions this "ignorance of the country" in his report,[109] and throughout the campaign made use of a map which might have been drawn by a child of ten,[110] he never seems to have realized that it was his duty to overcome this ignorance by establishing a well-organized intelligence department and mapping service. Nevertheless, in spite of his shortcomings and mistakes, his audacity saved Richmond. Because it prevented the fall of the capital the Battle of the Seven Days, though tactically a bungle, will always be considered as one of the great decisive strategical victories of this war.

REFERENCES

[1] *Leading American Soldiers,* R. M. Johnston, p. 130.
[2] See *Papers of the Military Historical Society of Massachusetts,* vol. XIII, p. 396, and *Campaigns of the Army of the Potomac,* William Swinton, pp. 41-42.

³ *Military Historical Society of Massachusetts,* vol. XIII, pp. 405–406. So late as April 23, 1862, we find General Lee suggesting to Brigadier General French at Wilmington that "you might arm the regiment at Wilmington by placing pikes in the hands of the men at the heavy batteries and giving their muskets, as far as they will go, to the unarmed regiment, and make up deficiency by arming some of the center companies with pikes, the flanking companies having the rifles" (*The War of the Rebellion: A Compilation of the Official Records of the Union and Confederate Armies,* vol. IX, p. 463—cited as *W.R.* See also *ibid.,* vol. IX, p. 719).

⁴ According to the census of 1850, Texas possessed four times as many cattle and horses as all the other Southern states combined.

⁵ *An Aide-de-Camp of Lee, Papers of Colonel Charles Marshall,* edited by Major-General Sir Frederick Maurice, pp. 10 and 19.

⁶ For a description of the Southern soldier see *Southern Historical Society Papers,* vol. XIII, p. 261.

⁷ The percussion cap was invented by the Rev. Alexander John Forsyth in 1805, but was not accepted for military arms until some thirty years later. Various rifles were used during this war, the more important being the Minié, invented by Captain Minié, a Frenchman, and used in the Crimean War. Its weight was 10½ lbs., length 3 ft. 3 in., its barrel four-grooved, its bore .702 in., and it was sighted from 100 to 1,000 yards. The form of its bullet was cylindro-conoidal with a hemispherical iron cap fixed in its base.

⁸ Lieutenant-General Richard Taylor writes: "They could always be relied on when a battle was imminent; but when no fighting was to be done they had best be at home attending to their families and interests" (*Destruction and Reconstruction,* p. 28, English edition).

⁹ *Four Years under Marse Robert,* Robert Stiles, p. 20.

¹⁰ For my own estimate of his character and personality, see my *Grant and Lee: A Study in Personality and Generalship,* chap. III.

¹¹ See *W.R.,* vol. V, pp. 6–8.

¹² *Military Historical Society of Massachusetts,* vol. I, p. 77. For stringent criticism of Stanton, see also *The Story of the Civil War,* John Codman Ropes, Vol. I, p. 225, and *Personal Memoirs,* U. S. Grant, Vol. II, pp. 104–105.

¹³ General Webb says, "The capture of Norfolk would have changed everything" (*The Peninsula: McClellan's Campaign of 1862,* p. 31), which we shall see is only too true. Writing to Mr. Stanton on April 24, 1862, Gideon Welles says: ". . . but the capture of Norfolk would, in my opinion, next after New Orleans, be the most decisive blow that could be struck for the suppression of the rebellion" (*ibid.,* pp. 170–171).

¹⁴ Swinton, p. 80.

¹⁵ See *W.R.,* vol. V, p. 41. February 22 was Washington's birthday.

¹⁶ *Ibid.,* vol. V, p. 45.

¹⁷ *Ibid.,* vol. V, p. 42.

¹⁸ *Ibid.,* vol. V, p. 50.

¹⁹ See *McClellan's Own Story,* by George B. McClellan, pp. 227–228.

²⁰ *W.R.,* vol. V, pp. 55–56.

²¹ *McClellan's Own Story,* p. 226. Simultaneously, when McClellan was absent from Washington, Lincoln took the opportunity of issuing an order relieving him from the command of all the armies, and restricting him to the control of the Army of the Potomac (*W.R.,* vol. V, p. 54). McClellan first learnt of this through the newspapers. (*McClellan's Own Story,* pp. 220, 224–225.)

²² *W.R.,* vol. V, p. 61.

²³ Swinton, p. 92.

[24] *W.R.*, vol. XVIII, p. 846.

[25] *Ibid.*, vol. V, p. 1099.

[26] *Narrative of Military Operations, Directed, during the Late War between the States*, by Joseph E. Johnston, p. 111.

[27] *McClellan's Own Story*, p. 308. See also p. 310.

[28] *W.R.*, vol. XIV, p. 503.

[29] *Ibid.*, vol. XIV, p. 504.

[30] *Ibid.*, vol. XIV, p. 508.

[31] *Ibid.*, vol. XIV, p. 477.

[32] *Ibid.*, vol. XVIII, p. 870.

[33] *Ibid.*, vol. XVIII, p. 219.

[34] *Ibid.*, vol. XII, p. 30.

[35] *The Story of the Civil War*, vol. II, pp. 132–133.

[36] White House was selected as a base with a view to McDowell's co-operation, and troops were moved north of the Chickahominy in order to protect its forward communications.

[37] The Fifth and Sixth "Provisional" Corps were organized on May 15 (see Webb, p. 84).

[38] See Swinton, p. 130.

[39] *W.R.*, vol. XIV, p. 568.

[40] *Ibid.*, vol. XIII, p. 490.

[41] *Ibid.*, vol. XIV, p. 238.

[42] *Ibid.*, vol. XII, p. 53.

[43] *Ibid.*, vol. XIII, p. 191.

[44] *Battles and Leaders of the Civil War*, vol. II, p. 431.

[45] *Memoirs of Robert E. Lee*, by A. L. Long, p. 163.

[46] *Ibid.*, p. 164. His A.D.C., Colonel Charles Marshall, tells us that for doing so Lee was abused by the press for dawdling (*Papers of Colonel Charles Marshall*, p. 79).

[47] *Lee's Dispatches*, edited by Douglas Southall Freeman, pp. 6–7.

[48] *W.R.*, vol. XVIII, p. 908. On June 6, Jackson had written Johnston hinting that his command might be wanted at Richmond. So, apparently, the same idea had also occurred to him.

[49] *Ibid.*, vol. XIV, p. 589, and vol. XVIII, p. 910. See also *Destruction and Reconstruction*, p. 102.

[50] "You are desired to make a secret movement to the rear of the enemy" (*W.R.*, vol. XIV, p. 590).

[51] *Papers of Colonel Charles Marshall*, p. 82.

[52] *Military Memoirs of a Confederate*, E. P. Alexander, p. 114. A recent writer, Captain John W. Thomason, in his *Jeb Stuart*, pp. 154–155, holds a similar though less outspoken opinion.

[53] *W.R.*, vol. XIV, p. 602, and vol. XVIII, p. 913.

[54] Long, p. 168.

[55] See D. H. Hill in *Battles and Leaders*, vol. II, p. 349.

[56] Alexander, p. 115. In my opinion, Jackson was from the religious point of view unbalanced . . . "Therefore Jackson not only refrained from writing letters on Sunday: he would not read a letter on Sunday; he even timed the sending of his own letters so that they should not encumber the mails on Sunday" (*Memoirs of Stonewall Jackson*, by Mary Anna Jackson, p. 75). "Had I fought the battle on Sunday instead of on Monday I fear our cause would have suffered" (*ibid.*, p. 249). Yet there was nothing of the New Testament about him, rather of the Old: He

said, "No quarter to the violators of our homes and firesides" (*ibid.*, p. 310). And again, when someone deplored the necessity of destroying so many brave men, "No; shoot them all; *I* do not wish them to be brave" (*Life and Campaigns of Lieut.-Gen. Thomas J. Jackson*, by Prof. R. L. Dabney, p. 397).

[57] *W.R.*, vol. XIII, pp. 490, 498.

[58] *Ibid.*, vol. XIII, pp. 493-494, Lee's report. Also see *General Lee of the Confederate Army*, by Fitzhugh Lee, p. 162 (English edition).

[59] *R. E. Lee, a Biography*, Douglas Southall Freeman, vol. II, pp. 116-117.

[60] *W.R.*, vol. XII, p. 49.

[61] *Ibid.*, vol. XII, p. 51.

[62] Alexander, p. 112.

[63] *Ibid.*, p. 115. See also *Lee's Dispatches*, pp. 15-16.

[64] *W.R.*, vol. XIV, p. 620.

[65] Longstreet writes: "Jackson came up, marched by the fight without giving attention, and went into camp at Hundley's Corner (p. 124). Page informs us that, on June 26, Jackson's guide lost his way on account of the new roads cut by the Federals. His name was Lincoln Sydnor" (*General Lee Man and Soldier*, by Thomas Nelson Page, p. 304).

[66] Alexander, pp. 119, 121.

[67] Freeman, vol. II, p. 135.

[68] *W.R.*, vol. XIV, p. 617.

[69] Magruder, in his report to Lee, dated August 12, 1862, says: "Had McClellan massed his whole force in column and advanced it against any point in our line of battle, . . . though the head of his column would have suffered greatly, its momentum would have insured him success, and the occupation of our works about Richmond, and consequently of the city, might have been his reward." (*W.R.*, vol. XIII, p. 686.)

[70] Swinton, p. 147.

[71] *W.R.*, vol. XII, p. 269.

[72] See *McClellan's Own Story*, p. 412, and pp. 422-423.

[73] Long, p. 172.

[74] Alexander, p. 132.

[75] *W.R.*, vol. XII, p. 60.

[76] These bridges were, the Foot Bridge, Duane's Bridge, Woodbury Infantry Bridge, Woodbury and Alexander's Bridge, and Sumner's Upper (or Grapevine) Bridge. The Railroad Bridges and Bottom's Bridge were burnt on the morning of the 29th (see *W.R.*, vol. XII, p. 118, and vol. XIII, pp. 192 and 200).

[77] *Robert E. Lee the Soldier*, by Major-General Sir Frederick Maurice, p. 115.

[78] *W.R.*, vol. XIII, p. 494.

[79] *McClellan's Own Story*, pp. 424-425.

[80] Freeman, vol. II, p. 166.

[81] For these various movements see *W.R.*, vol. XIII, p. 607, 517, 687, 494, 662, 679. Also Alexander, pp. 134-135.

[82] *W.R.*, vol. XIII, p. 789.

[83] *Ibid.*, vol. XIII, p. 675. Incorrectly dated June 28.

[84] *Ibid.*, vol. XIII, p. 687.

[85] Alexander, p. 136. Henderson's account of Jackson's delay (*Stonewall Jackson and the American Civil War*, vol. II, pp. 56-58) is so misleading as to be almost fictitious. For other accounts, see *The Life and Campaigns of Major General J. E. B. Stuart*, by Major H. B. McClellan, pp. 80-81; *Longstreet*, p. 150; *Destruction and Reconstruction*, p. 113; *Battles and Leaders*, vol. II, pp. 402-403, 389, and 381, by

210 DECISIVE BATTLES OF THE U. S. A.

Longstreet, D. H. Hill, and Franklin respectively; *Papers of the Southern Historical Society*, vol. XXV, p. 211; *The Army of Northern Virginia in 1862*, William Allan, p. 121, and Alexander, pp. 146–153.

[86] Freeman, vol. II, pp. 177–178.
[87] Robert Stiles, pp. 98–99.
[88] *W.R.*, vol. XIII, p. 789.
[89] Alexander, pp. 150–151. See also *Battles and Leaders*, vol. II, p. 381, and *Papers of Colonel Charles Marshall*, pp. 110–112.
[90] Dabney, p. 467.
[91] Ropes, vol. II, p. 199.
[92] Freeman, vol. II, p. 199.
[93] Alexander, p. 155.
[94] *W.R.*, vol. XIII, pp. 495, 557.
[95] *Ibid.*, vol. XIII, p. 667. The Quaker Road was the same as the Willis Church Road, but apparently Lee thought they were two separate roads.
[96] Webb, p. 161.
[97] *W.R.*, vol. XIII, p. 496.
[98] *McClellan's Own Story*, p. 434.
[99] *W.R.*, vol. XIII, p. 677.
[100] Alexander, pp. 160–161. See also Freeman, vol. II, p. 209. The mix-up of the Confederate units on the plan shows this confusion clearly.
[101] *W.R.*, vol. XIII, pp. 677–678.
[102] *Ibid.*, vol. XIII, p. 669.
[103] *Battles and Leaders*, vol. II, p. 394.
[104] For the chaos which reigned, see *Military Historical Society of Massachusetts*, vol. I, pp. 266–267.
[105] Freeman, vol. II, p. 218.
[106] *Numbers and Losses in the Civil War in America*, 1861–65, by Thomas L. Livermore, p. 86.
[107] *Battles and Leaders*, vol. II, p. 395.
[108] *Destruction and Reconstruction*, pp. 107–108. Jefferson Davis writes: ". . . we had no maps of the country, in which we were operating; our generals were ignorant of the roads, and their guides knew little more than the way from their homes to Richmond . . ." (*History of the Confederacy*, vol. II, p. 142).
[109] *W.R.*, vol. XIII, pp. 496–497.
[110] See Freeman, vol. II, facing p. 138.

1862

SYNOPSIS OF BACKGROUND EVENTS

ON the day the Battle of Mechanicsville was fought, June 26, Lincoln placed Frémont, Banks, and McDowell under the command of Major General John Pope, ordering Pope to cover Washington, secure the Valley, and by operating against Charlottesville draw the Confederate forces away from McClellan. Then, on July 11, he appointed Major General H. W. Halleck commander in chief of all the armies of the United States, and summoned him to Washington.

From Harrison's Landing, McClellan appealed to Halleck: "Here directly in front of this army, is the heart of the Rebellion . . . It is here on the banks of the James, that the fate of the Union should be decided." However, he so exaggerated Lee's strength that it was thought impossible sufficiently to reinforce him, and on August 3 he was ordered to withdraw his army north.

Meanwhile Lee, foreseeing that McClellan would not move, and learning of Pope's advance on Charlottesville, sent Jackson to Gordonsville. North of here, at Cedar Mountain, he fought a successful action with Banks on August 9, and then retired across the Rapidan. Four days later, hearing rumors of McClellan's embarkation, Lee at once decided to move north. Leaving only two brigades for the defense of Richmond, he ordered his army on Gordonsville. From there, on August 15, he decided to turn Pope's right flank by interposing his army between the Rapidan and Washington. Fortunately for Pope, Lee's orders fell into his hands, and realizing the danger of his position around Gordonsville, he withdrew to the Rappahannock.

At once Lee followed him up. After endeavoring to turn his right, he decided on a move of exceptional audacity—to hold Pope and his 70,000 men with from 25,000 to 30,000, before McClellan could complete

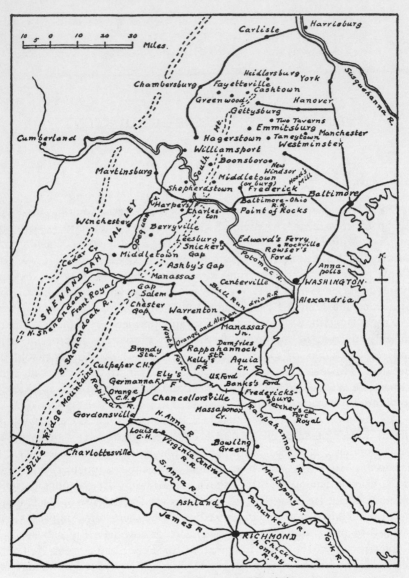

18. Map of Eastern Virginia

his withdrawal and support Pope in full. Jackson, accompanied by part of Stuart's cavalry—some 24,000 all told—was to advance by a circuitous route through Thoroughfare Gap and fall upon Pope's base—Manassas Junction. Though the danger of so widely separating the two forces was great, it was not unwarranted; for Lee's idea was to compel Pope to fall back, instead of risking battle, and then to threaten Washington by carrying his army into the Valley. From now onward the key to Lee's strategy is to be sought in the name of the army he commanded—namely, "Northern Virginia," for that area became his strategic goal.

On the 25th, Jackson set out from Jefferson, marching to Salem by way of Amissville. Then, on the 26th, he marched through Thoroughfare Gap, and, reaching Bristoe Station, he sent Stuart forward to Manassas Junction. Pope thought Jackson was bound for the Valley, but on hearing of Stuart's successful raid, he abandoned the line of the Rappahannock and ordered a concentration on Manassas Junction.

By this retirement the first of Lee's two aims was gained. To carry out the second—an advance into the Valley—all that was necessary was to order Jackson to move with all possible speed by way of Aldie and Snicker's Gap on Berryville, while with the rest of the army he himself marched via Ashby's Gap to that same place. Holding Front Royal and the Gaps north of it, he could have advanced on Harper's Ferry, and from there, by threatening Washington, could have compelled the withdrawal of the Federal forces for the defense of that city.

Remembering that the policy of the South was defensive, and that in its application it demanded an offensive strategy and defensive tactics, and further still, considering that Lee was a past master in offensive strategical movements, it is astonishing to find him committing once again the same error he fell into during the Seven Days—that of abandoning the strategical offensive and assuming a tactical offensive. Instead of moving on Ashby's Gap, he advanced through Thoroughfare Gap (which, except for an error on the part of Pope's subordinates, he would have found occupied by Union forces), and uniting with Jackson west of the Bull Run Mountains, on the 29th and 30th he handsomely—but not decisively—defeated Pope at the Second Battle of Manassas or Bull Run. Pope, who fell back on Centerville on the 31st, was left there in peace—there was no pursuit. This campaign, though successful, was tactically unremunerative, for out of an effective total of 45,527 men, between August 27 and September 2, Lee lost 9,197—that is 20 per cent.

On the 31st, not considering it profitable to attack Pope in position, Lee decided to turn his right flank. To prepare for this he ordered his army to move north of Centerville and advance on Fairfax Court House. (An assault on the fortifications of Washington was out of the question, because Lee's army was so badly supplied that it was impossible for it to remain for more than a few days in any one place.) The arrival of McClellan's army forced him to abandon this turning movement, as he was by now vastly outnumbered.

He was loath to fall back on the Rappahannock until winter prevented a Federal advance south and as his army was so badly found, he was compelled to look for a well-stocked area. He could find one either in the Shenandoah Valley or in Maryland and Pennsylvania. An advance across the Potomac, though risky, was nevertheless strategically sound, so long as he avoided battle. Maryland was enemy country, and was well stocked. Also, many of its inhabitants sympathized with the South. Lee could supply himself there, possibly gather in recruits, and certainly draw his enemy farther away from Richmond.

On September 3 he wrote to Jefferson Davis, pointing out that "The present seems to be the most propitious time since the commencement of the war for the Confederate Army to enter Maryland"; but that the army "is not properly equipped for an invasion . . . is feeble in transportation . . . the men . . . in thousands of instances are destitute of shoes."

On the 4th, without waiting for a reply, he issued his orders for an advance. The next day, in a letter to Davis, he asked for a bridge to be built over the Rappahannock, so that, in the event of having to fall back, he could take up a position about Warrenton and threaten any advance on Richmond. Between the 4th and 7th his army crossed the Potomac in the vicinity of Leesburg, not without a great deal of straggling. On the following day—the 8th—he wrote to Davis as follows: "The present position of affairs, in my opinion, places it in the power of the Government of the Confederate States to propose with propriety to that of the United States the recognition of our independence." His recent startling successes seem to have upset his balance: to him the Union appeared virtually down and out, and as for the Northern soldiers— "those people," as he called them—they were beneath contempt. He appears to have overlooked two obvious and important points: that the invasion of Maryland would rouse the North, and that his past successes

were due not to lack of courage on the part of the Federal soldiers, but
to lack of leadership in the Federal generals.

He crossed the Potomac east of the Blue Ridge, because he considered
that this would threaten Washington and Baltimore. At Frederick City
he was surprised to learn that the Federal garrisons at Harper's Ferry
and Martinsburg had not been withdrawn. On the 9th he detached Jackson and McLaws to round them up. This was an astonishing move, for
though his eventual line of retirement would almost certainly be the
Valley, and these places lay on that line, he had no intention of holding
them once they were captured; therefore there was nothing to prevent
their reoccupation after he had passed north. The truth would appear to
be that, though McClellan had now replaced Pope in command, Lee
held his enemy in such utter contempt that he saw no danger in sending
half his army in one direction, while he proceeded with the remaining
half in the other. This in face of an army which outnumbered his own
by nearly two to one! Of this risky dispersion of force General Longstreet writes: "The great mistake of the campaign was the division of
Lee's army. If General Lee had kept his forces together, he would not
have suffered defeat . . . The next year on our way to Gettysburg,
there was the same situation of affairs at Harper's Ferry, but we let
it alone."

To make matters worse, on the 13th a copy of Lee's order No. 191
was found in an abandoned Confederate camp and sent to McClellan.
That general finding himself in possession of his enemy's order of battle,
should have made a night march on the Gaps in the South Mountains,
have stormed them and dealt with the halves of his enemy's army in
detail. Instead, he delayed his advance until the 14th, when Lee, learning
that his plans had been disclosed, hurriedly turned about his column
at Hagerstown and marched towards the Gaps to support their weak
garrisons. But on the afternoon of that day, as Turner's Gap was stormed
by the Federals, Lee was forced to retire. At first he decided to cross
the Potomac at Shepherdstown Ford; then, a few hours later he determined to concentrate his divided army at Sharpsburg and there accept battle.

The reason for this was, I think, Lee's excessive contempt for his
enemy. Furthermore, his personal pride could not stomach the idea that
such an enemy could drive him out of Maryland, although he knew that
there was nothing to prevent him from being attacked on the 16th—

that is, before Jackson could rejoin him, since Harper's Ferry did not fall until the 15th.

The battle of Sharpsburg, or Antietam, was fought on the 17th, a totally unnecessary battle, and a very costly one; for though the Federal assaults were repulsed, Lee lost 13,724 men.

That this battle was fought to vindicate personal pride, its sequel would appear to show. When, on the evening of the 17th, Longstreet, D. H. Hill, J. B. Hood, and S. D. Lee recounted their losses and urged Lee to retire, his reply was: "Gentlemen, we will not cross the Potomac to-night . . . If McClellan wants to fight in the morning I will give him battle again. Go!" Again, on September 25, writing to the president, he said: "In a military point of view, the best move, in my opinion, the army could make would be to advance upon Hagerstown and endeavour to defeat the enemy at that point. I would not hesitate to make it even with our diminished numbers, did the army exhibit its former temper." That it did not is not surprising, seeing that it had lost 25 per cent of its strength at Sharpsburg.

On the night of the 18th he crossed the Potomac and withdrew to Winchester. Obviously McClellan should have followed him hot-footed, but obsessed by the idea of Lee's numerical superiority, he did not cross the Potomac until October 26, and then at the head of 110,000 men. On November 7 he moved to the neighborhood of Warrenton, where he handed his command over to General Ambrose E. Burnside.

Leaving Jackson's corps at Winchester, on November 2, Lee with Longstreet's corps moved to Front Royal, and thence to Culpeper Court House. On the 10th he pointed out to the Secretary of War that, as he was too weak to attack, he would be compelled to rely on maneuver. In truth, his army was not sufficiently well equipped to do either, for a little later on he deplored the fact that he had between 2,000 and 3,000 barefooted men and then added: "I am informed that there is a large number of shoes now in Richmond in the hands of extortioners, who hold them at an extravagant price."

Burnside's plan was to base himself on Aquia Creek, and from Fredericksburg march directly upon Richmond. Lincoln, when giving this plan his blessing, ominously added that he thought it might succeed if Burnside moved rapidly, "otherwise not." This remark was made on November 14, yet, on the 24th, Burnside was still waiting for pontoons, and it was not until December 11 that his army began to cross the Rappahannock.

Such a delay was more than enough for Lee to fathom his adversary's plan; so, on November 18, he ordered Longstreet from Culpeper's Court House to Fredericksburg. The next day he wrote to Jackson stating that he did not anticipate "making a determined stand north of the North Anna," to which Jackson agreed, but the Richmond government objected. In spite of this objection it was not until the 26th that he ordered Jackson to join him. Jackson arrived on the 30th, five days after Burnside's pontoons had arrived, and four days after the Aquia Creek-Falmouth railway was completed. Thus, by the end of November the two armies faced each other on the Rappahannock, Burnside's numbering 122,000 and Lee's 78,500.

Under cover of a powerful artillery assembled on Stafford Heights, Burnside's plan was to cross the river a little below Fredericksburg, with Sumner's corps on his right, Hooker's in the center, and Franklin's on his left, and to advance on Lee, whose position—a formidable one— ran from Hamilton Crossing, a little north of Massaponax Creek, on the right, to Taylor's Hill, immediately opposite Falmouth, on the left. This position was to all intents and purposes impregnable, and to make matters worse Burnside selected Lee's left flank—his strongest—as the goal of his decisive attack.

On the 12th the Federal deployment on the right bank of the Rappahannock was ended. According to Heros von Borcke (a German officer serving on Stuart's staff), Jackson and Stuart were of opinion that the best plan was "to make a sudden general attack upon the enemy under cover of the fog"; but Lee wisely decided against an offensive, "preferring to fight behind his entrenchments and to inflict a severe blow upon the enemy without the risk of fearful loss of life."

The following morning the attack was launched. "A military panorama," writes von Borcke, "the grandeur of which I have never seen equalled. On they came in beautiful order, as if on parade, a moving forest of steel, their bayonets glistening in the bright sunlight." At the sight of it Jackson turned to von Borcke and exclaimed: "Major, my men have sometimes failed *to take* a position, but *to defend* one never. I am glad the Yankees are coming." Every assault was shattered, Burnside losing 12,653 men to Lee's 5,309.

Burnside's repulse was complete, and Lee still had in hand two-thirds of his force intact. Walter H. Taylor in his *Four Years with General Lee* says: "It was certainly the most easily won of all the great battles of the war." "It was very cold and very clear," writes Robert

Stiles, "and the aurora-borealis of the night of December 13th, 1862, surpassed in splendour any like exhibition I ever saw." For Lee to have attacked on that night was probably impossible; but when on the following morning Burnside's army remained inactive and still on the right bank of the Rappahannock with its back to the river, an opportunity was offered to the Confederate commander which seldom occurs in war. It is true that the guns on Stafford Heights covered the Federal forces; nevertheless in the early morning mist of the 14th it would have been possible for Lee to have advanced so close to his enemy as to have rendered their protective fire as dangerous to friend as to foe. "Had Lee, on the morning of the 14th," writes Captain C. C. Chesney (an English eyewitness), "thrown his whole force frankly against the Northern Army, reduced as the latter was in numbers, and much more in morale by the severe repulse, it is scarcely to be doubted that a mighty advantage would have been obtained . . . It is possible, indeed, that the scenes of Leipsic or the Beresina might have been repeated on the Rappahannock, and the greater part of the Federal corps have been captured or destroyed . . ."

But on the evening of the 13th no preparations for a counteroffensive were made. "Our commander-in-chief," says von Borcke, "adhering to his earliest idea, still objected to a forward movement, for which, in my judgment, the golden moment had now passed, had he inclined to favour it." Further, he writes: "Not one of our generals was aware of the magnitude of the victory we had gained, of the injury we had inflicted upon the enemy, and of the degree of demoralization in the hostile army; everybody regarded the work as but half done, and expected a renewal of the attack the following morning."

When morning dawned, and no renewal of the battle was attempted, Jackson proposed a night attack. In order to avoid the confusion and mistakes so common in such operations, he recommended, says Colonel Fremantle (an English officer) "that we should all strip ourselves perfectly naked." The time of year was midwinter!

When, on the 15th, Burnside recrossed the river and returned to his encampments at Falmouth, Lee was "extremely chagrined that the Federals should have succeeded in so cleverly making their escape." Thus Lee in this campaign, like McClellan at Antietam, missed a wonderful opportunity to annihilate his enemy.

CHAPTER VII

THE BATTLE OF GETTYSBURG, 1863

THE first day of the New Year—1863—"marks," as Livermore says, "an era in the history of the United States of America, second only to the 4th of July, 1776"; [1] for on that day President Lincoln issued his final Proclamation of Emancipation, freeing the slaves in the rebellious states. Though this announcement could not take full effect until the war was won, its influence on the remainder of its course was prodigious. First, at one blow it shattered all possibility of compromise: the war had now to be fought to a finish. Secondly, its influence on Europe was decisive, because it turned the tide of sympathy, particularly in England, from the South to the North, and in consequence undercut Jefferson Davis's hope of European intervention.

The next event, not so propitious, occurred on January 25, when Major General Joseph Hooker was appointed to replace Burnside in command of the Army of the Potomac. This, like the appointment of General Wadsworth, was a foolish selection and a purely political one.[2] Nevertheless, Hooker had his good points. He was a skillful organizer and trainer of men. He infused vitality through his staff and administrative services; placed the cavalry under able leaders; instituted a system of furloughs, which stopped desertion, and substituted seven corps for the four grand divisions into which the army was divided.

All this was to the good. In spite of the humiliating defeat which awaited him, the disciplinary seeds he sowed were destined to sprout into a tactical crop, which, as we shall see, was harvested by Grant during the last lap of the war. The same cannot be said of Lee, who, in spite of his vastly superior generalship, was a poor administrator and altogether too kindhearted to excel as a disciplinarian. His men were shockingly clothed, poorly housed, and badly fed. On January 26 he wrote to Seddon, Secretary of War: ". . . As far as I can learn, we have now about one week's supply, four days' fresh beef, and four days' salt meat, of the reduced ration [¼ lb.]. After that is exhausted, I know not whence further supplies can be drawn . . ." [3]

It was not that supplies were lacking,[4] but that the Confederate railroads were in so shocking a condition that food, etc., could not be transported from place to place.[5] If Lee was not altogether responsible for this, his consistent politeness and subservience to the government certainly did not help things. Further, he seems to have taken little interest in disciplining and training his men.[6]

Thus the winter of 1862–1863 passed, the Army of the Potomac improving, while the Army of Northern Virginia, facing its enemy, stood still, its right resting on Port Royal and its left extending to near-by United States Ford.

At this time Joseph E. Johnston was operating against Grant on the Mississippi and Beauregard against Buell in East Tennessee. As they were hard pressed, Lee suggested to Seddon on April 9: "Should Hooker's army assume the defensive, the readiest method of relieving the pressure upon General Johnston and General Beauregard would be for this army to cross into Maryland." [7] This was his stock strategical move. Next, on the 19th, he wrote to President Davis: "I do not think General Hooker will venture to uncover Washington City by transferring his army to James River . . . My only anxiety arises from the present immobility of the army, owing to the condition of our horses and the scarcity of forage and provisions. I think it all-important that we should assume the aggressive by the 1st of May . . . If we could be placed in a condition to make a vigorous advance at that time, I think the Valley [Shenandoah] could be swept of Milroy, and the army opposite thrown north of the Potomac . . ." [8] Finally, on the 23d, he wrote to Jackson: "I think that, if a real attempt is made to cross the river, it will be above Fredericksburg." [9]

This was a shrewd appreciation of approaching events, for, on April 11, Hooker had communicated his plan of attack to President Lincoln. It was to turn Lee's left and, by placing the Army of the Potomac between the Confederate forces and Richmond, cut them off from their base. The forward move began on April 27 and led to the Battle of Chancellorsville, fought between May 1 and 4. The battle ended in

Hooker's ignominious withdrawal across the Rappahannock on the 5th. He lost in all 16,800 men to Lee's 13,100. Yet to Lee this was a barren victory. He is reported to have said:

At Chancellorsville we gained another victory; our people were wild with delight. I, on the contrary, was more depressed than after Fredericksburg; our loss was severe, and again we had gained not an inch of ground, and the enemy could not be pursued.[10]

Nevertheless, to the world at large, this victory was so daring and so unexpected that it not only endowed Lee with world fame; but imbued him and his men with a feeling of invincibility which was unjustified; for though they had pulverized Hooker, in that pulverization the Army of the Potomac remained unbeaten and intact. Rightly does Bigelow end his great history on Chancellorsville with these words:

The interval of two months between the battles of Chancellorsville and Gettysburg was for the South—notwithstanding the irreparable loss it sustained in the death of Jackson—the brightest period of the Civil War. But its brightness was that of a false and treacherous light. The over-confidence born of the victory of Chancellorsville carried the Army of Northern Virginia against the impregnable front of the Federal lines of Gettysburg; and it was the victory of Gettysburg that sustained the Army of the Potomac in its desperate wrestling in the Wilderness, and in gaining the point of vantage from which it finally started on the arduous, decisive and fateful race to Appomattox.[11]

Far distant on the Mississippi, Grant was approaching Vicksburg, while Rosecrans at Murfreesborough, in co-operation with Burnside, was preparing to advance against Bragg in East Tennessee. Something had to be done to disrupt these moves.

Beauregard suggested an offensive campaign in Tennessee and Kentucky.[12] So did Longstreet, whose idea was to defeat Rosecrans, and then by marching on the Ohio compel the Union government to call Grant north.[13] Early in May he placed this plan before Lee; but Lee, who throughout the war never failed to take into consideration the security of Virginia,[14] set it aside, answering that equal if not better results could be obtained by a direct invasion of the North. Longstreet reluctantly agreed, so long as "the campaign should be one of defensive tactics."[15] Next, on June 8, Lee wrote to Seddon stating that nothing could be gained by waiting on the defensive,[16] and two days later he wrote to President Davis:

While making the most we can of the means of resistance we possess
. . . it is nevertheless the part of wisdom to carefully measure and
husband our strength, and not to expect from it more than in the ordinary
course of affairs it is capable of accomplishing. We should not, therefore,
conceal from ourselves that our resources in men are constantly diminish-
ing, and the disproportion in this respect between us and our enemies, if
they continue united in their efforts to subjugate us, is steadily aug-
menting . . .

It seems to me that the most efficient mode of accomplishing this
object, now within our reach, is to give all the encouragement we can,
consistently with truth to the rising peace party of the North . . .

Should the belief that peace will bring back the Union become general,
the war would no longer be supported, and that after all, is what we are
interested in bringing about.[17]

Lee was mistaken on two points and so was Jefferson Davis. Though
there was a strong peace party in the North, they did not realize, first,
that Lincoln's Emancipation Proclamation had settled once and for
all the question of foreign intervention, and second, that to invade the
North would consolidate the Federals instead of dividing them.

Having decided on an offensive, they were at once faced with the
question of "Where?" This was answered not by strategic, but by
economic needs. As I have already pointed out, Lee was one of the
worst quartermasters in history, for, normally, his army was half-
clothed and half-fed. On May 21 he had written to the president: "The
desertion of the North Carolina troops from this army is becoming so
serious an evil that, unless it can be promptly arrested I fear the
troops from that State will become greatly reduced." [18, 19]

As Lee could not subsist his troops in Virginia,[20] and as he could
"obtain all necessary supplies in Pennsylvania," [21] supplies decided the
question. As Freeman writes: "Of all the arguments that weighed with
him, the most decisive single one was that he could no longer feed
his army on the Rappahannock. He had to invade the North for provisions, regardless of all else." [22] In other words, the forthcoming
campaign was to be a food hunt.

While these points were being considered and discussed, Lee re-
organized the infantry of his army into three corps of three divisions
each:

First Corps, Longstreet; Divisional Commanders—McLaws, Pickett,
and Hood.

Second Corps, Ewell;[23] Divisional Commanders—Early, Johnson,
and Rhodes.

Third Corps, A. P. Hill; Divisional Commanders—Anderson, Heth, and Pender.

The field artillery was grouped into fifteen battalions of four batteries each, besides which there were six batteries of horse artillery. Stuart's cavalry was left as it was, but his troopers were for the most part remounted.

In preparation for the campaign, Longstreet's corps had already set out on June 3 from Fredericksburg for Culpeper, where Stuart then was. On the 4th and 5th it was followed by Ewell's and Hill's corps. Though this was a risky flank movement, Lee held Hooker and his army in such contempt that he saw nothing rash in it. As Heth says: "General Lee believed that the Army of Northern Virginia . . . could accomplish anything." [24]

While Lee was concentrating around Culpeper, Hooker informed Lincoln that he suspected the enemy to be planning a movement similar to the one carried out during the previous year on Manassas Junction.[25] Lincoln replied on the same day, warning him not to cross the Rappahannock should Lee be moving north. "In one word," he wrote, "I would not take any risk of being entangled upon the river, like an ox jumped half over a fence and liable to be torn by dogs front and rear, without a fair chance to gore one way or kick the other." [26] Thereupon Hooker ordered Sedgwick to bridge the Rappahannock at Franklin's Crossing and ascertain what the enemy was doing. This led to a clash between the Federal and Confederate cavalry at Brandy Station; whereupon, on the 10th, Hooker informed Lincoln that he thought it probable that Lee intended to raid Maryland.[27] He asked the president: Should this be found to be the case, "will it not provoke the true interest of the cause for me to march to Richmond at once?" To which came the reply:

I think Lee's army, and not Richmond, is your sure objective point. If he comes towards the Upper Potomac, follow on his flank and on his inside track, shorten your lines, while he lengthens his. Fight him, too, when opportunity offers. If he stays where he is, fret him and fret him.[28]

This was sound advice, for Hooker had a grand opportunity to strike at his enemy in detail; yet it would seem that, after his recent experiences at Chancellorsville, he had no stomach for a fight.

Whereas on the 3d, Lee's three corps faced him along the Rappahannock from Port Royal to Fredericksburg, on the 9th Hill alone held that position. The next day, Ewell, covered by Jenkins's cavalry brigade, set out for the Valley with orders to clear Berryville, mask Winchester, cross the Potomac, move through Maryland, and carry the war into Pennsylvania.

At this time General Schenck, whose headquarters were in Baltimore, was in command of the Federal forces in the Valley. These were distributed as follows: 5,500 at Winchester and 1,500 at Berryville—both under Milroy; 1,300 at Martinsburg and 5,300 at Harper's Ferry. When Ewell advanced, the garrison of Berryville fell back on Winchester, where Milroy was routed early on the 15th, while attempting to escape. After losing half his force he finally got off with the remainder to Harper's Ferry.

Meanwhile Longstreet, Hill, and Stuart, with a total of 47,000 men, continued to face Hooker's 85,000. But Hooker, instead of seizing the passes over the Blue Ridge with the object of cutting Lee's army in half, deliberately moved away from his enemy; for, on the 13th, he ordered the First, Third, Fifth, and Eleventh Corps as well as the cavalry to fall back on Manassas Junction, and the Second, Sixth, and Twelfth Corps to withdraw to Dumfries and there await orders.[29] Reporting this fatuous move to the President, he received the following common-sense reply:

So far as we can make out here, the enemy have Milroy surrounded at Winchester and Tyler at Martinsburg. If they could hold out a few days, could you help them? If the head of Lee's army is at Martinsburg and the tail of it on the Plank Road between Fredericksburg and Chancellorsville, the animal must be very slim somewhere. Could you not break him?[30]

Placed as he was, Hooker obviously could not do so. The upshot was that no sooner had he abandoned the Rappahannock than Hill moved up to Culpeper Court House, while Longstreet set out for Ashby's and Snicker's Gaps with the bulk of Stuart's cavalry covering his front and right flank, Hampton's and Jones's brigades following Hill. Lee's army was now stretched out from Hagerstown to Culpeper, a distance of seventy-five miles; yet Hooker did nothing. On the 16th, Halleck informed him that Schenck could not for long hold out at Harper's Ferry, whereupon Hooker replied that he would march to its relief.

The next day Longstreet reached the Blue Ridge, and on the 19th he occupied Ashby's and Snicker's Gaps, Hill crossing the Ridge at Chester Gap and pushing on in rear of him. This advance, which should have been made with the greatest speed possible, was considerably slowed down by lack of supplies. This may be gathered from the following dispatches. On the 19th, Lee wrote to Davis: "The difficulty of procuring supplies retards and renders more uncertain our future movements"; [31] and, on the 22d, the following message was sent to Ewell: "It will depend upon the quantity of supplies obtained . . . whether the rest of the army can follow." [32]

Ewell, acting upon Lee's instructions of the 22d, began to move on to the Susquehanna, reaching Carlisle on the 27th. Next, on the 24th, Longstreet and Hill again set out, occupying Chambersburg and Fayetteville respectively on the 27th. In General Order No. 73 of that date, Lee exhorted his men "to abstain, with most scrupulous care, from unnecessary or wanton injury to private property," and to behave themselves like Christian soldiers.[33]

By now the advance had carried the Army of Northern Virginia so far from the Rappahannock that Lee began to grow nervous about his line of retreat, as well as the safety of Richmond. Therefore, on the 23d and again on the 25th he asked Davis to push forward behind him a reserve army under General Beauregard.[34] It was now far too late in the campaign for such a suggestion to be met.[35] So, on the 25th, unsupported by any reserve force in rear with the bands playing *Dixie* amidst the "intense enthusiasm" [36] of his men, Lee crossed the Potomac on his most fateful adventure. Perhaps it was then that a Northern woman cried out: "Look at Pharaoh's army going to the Red Sea." [37]

I must now go back ten days in the history of this campaign, in order to trace the blunder which as much as any other wrecked Lee at Gettysburg.

Stuart, it will be remembered, had set out north with Longstreet. At the time he had with him three cavalry brigades—Fitz Lee's, W. H. F. Lee's, and Robertson's, while Hampton's and Jones's followed Hill; later on Hampton's and Robertson's swapped round. Perhaps because Stuart, as Long says, loved "the éclat of a bold raid," [38] Lee was much attached to him; anyhow, according to Taylor, his confidence in him was "unlimited." [39] Nevertheless, as early as the 15th, we find Lee complaining to Longstreet that he could obtain no information from Stuart,[40] and this complaint was repeated again on the 17th.[41] On the 22d, as we have seen, he ordered Ewell to move, and immediately after informed Marshall that his intention was "to leave some cavalry at Snicker's and Ashby's Gaps to watch the army of General Hooker, and to take the main body of the cavalry with General Stuart to accompany the enemy into Pennsylvania." [42] Thereupon he sent Stuart the following message:

I judge the efforts of the enemy were to arrest our progress and ascertain our whereabouts. Perhaps he is satisfied. Do you know where he is and what he is doing? I fear he will steal a march on us, and get across the Potomac before we are aware. If you find that he is moving northward, and that two brigades can guard the Blue Ridge and take care of your rear, you can move with the other three into Maryland, and take position on General Ewell's right, place yourself in communication with him, guard his flank, keep him informed of the enemy's movements, and collect all the supplies you can for the use of the army. [43]

Except for the last thirteen words, these orders were excellent.

This message having been dispatched, Lee informed Ewell that Stuart had been ordered to cross the Potomac and place himself on his right. [44]

Lee's letter to Stuart was forwarded through Longstreet, who, when posting it on, suggested to Stuart "that he was to pass to the enemy's rear, if he thinks he may get through." [45] This apparently perturbed Lee, for at 5 P.M. on the 23d he sent Stuart the following message:

If General Hooker's army remains inactive, you can leave two brigades to watch him, and withdraw with the three others, but should he not appear to be moving northward, I think you had better withdraw this side of the mountain tomorrow night, cross at Shepherdstown the next day, and move over to Frederickstown.

You will, however, be able to judge whether you can pass around their army without hindrance, doing them all the damage you can, and cross the river east of the mountains. In either case, after crossing the river, you must move on and feel the right of Ewell's troops, collecting information, provisions, etc. [46]

These suggestions—Lee seldom gave directions—are so badly worded that it is difficult to make sense of them. Stuart, thruster and *beau sabreur* that he was, interpreted them as a sanction for another White House raid, and having warned Robertson and Jones to hold the gaps south of the Potomac, [47] he set out on the 24th, not as the right flank guard of the Army of Northern Virginia, but instead on a glorified foray. As Marshall says: ". . . two armies invaded Pennsylvania in

1863, instead of one. One of these armies had little cavalry, the other had nothing but cavalry. One was commanded by General Lee, the other by General Stuart." [48] He bumped into Hancock, swung round him, crossed the Potomac at Rowser's Ford—less than twenty miles above Washington—on the 27th, and captured a wagon train near Rockville. This greatly delayed his march, which was further slowed down by paroling prisoners and damaging the Baltimore and Ohio Railroad at Hood's Mill. [49] So slowly did he progress, because of the booty collected, that not until the afternoon of July 2 did he rejoin Lee, exhausted and too late to be of any service. [50]

To return now to General Hooker. On the 22d, Schenck's command was placed under his orders, and on the 24th he wrote to Washington: "Ewell, I conclude, is over the river, and is now up the country, I suppose, for purposes of plunder. If the enemy should conclude not to throw any additional force over the river, I desire to make Washington secure, and, with all the force I can muster, strike for his line of retreat in the direction of Richmond." [51] On the 24th, hearing that yet another corps had crossed the Potomac, he decided to cross himself, and did so at Edward's Ferry on the 26th and 27th. Reynolds he sent forward to seize the passes over the South Mountains, while Sickles and Howard moved on Middleton. Simultaneously he asked [52] Halleck's permission to abandon Maryland Heights (Harper's Ferry). His request refused, he asked to be relieved of his command. [53]

His resignation was accepted, and General George G. Meade was directed to relieve him. Meade took over on the 28th, at which time he received the following instructions:

Your army is free to act as you may deem proper under the circumstances as they arise. You will, however, keep in view the important fact that the Army of the Potomac is the covering army of Washington as well as the army of operation against the invading forces of the rebels. You will, therefore, manoeuvre and fight in such a manner as to cover the capital and also Baltimore . . . [54]

Not often has a general been placed in so difficult a position. Meade's army was not vastly stronger than his enemy's, it was already in movement, and his adversary was acclaimed to be the greatest general of his age.

Knowing that Lee must scatter to subsist, Meade decided to advance and if possible destroy him in detail. [55] Therefore, on the 29th, he put his army in motion, and by that evening his left was at Emmitsburg and his right at New Windsor, with Buford's cavalry at Fairfield and Kilpatrick's near Hanover. Ewell was then at Carlisle; Longstreet at Chambersburg, and Hill between Fayetteville and Cashtown. The respective orders of battle were as follows:

Army of Northern Virginia

First Corps (21,400) Longstreet. Divisions—McLaws, Pickett, and Hood. Guns—84.
Second Corps (22,200) Ewell. Divisions—Early, Johnson, and Rodes. Guns—84.
Third Corps (22,000) Hill. Divisions—Anderson, Heth, and Pender. Guns—80.
Cavalry (10,000) Stuart. Brigades—Hampton, Robertson, Jones, Fitz Lee, Jenkins, and W. H. F. Lee. Guns—24.

In all, 75,000 officers and men and 272 guns.

Army of the Potomac

First Corps (11,900) Reynolds. Divisions—Wadsworth, Robinson, and Doubleday. Guns—23.
Second Corps (12,200) Hancock. Divisions—Caldwell, Gibbon, and Hays. Guns—24.
Third Corps (11,300) Sickles. Divisions—Birney and Humphreys. Guns—30.
Fifth Corps (12,200) Sykes. Divisions—Barnes, Ayres, and Crawford. Guns—26.
Sixth Corps (13,800) Sedgwick. Divisions—Wright, Howe, and Newton. Guns—48.
Eleventh Corps (10,300) Howard. Divisions—Barlow, Steinwehr, and Schurz. Guns—26.
Twelfth Corps (10,500) Slocum. Divisions—Ruger, Geary, and Indep. Guns—20.
Cavalry (13,900) Pleasanton. Divisions—Buford, Gregg, and Kilpatrick. Guns—50.
Provost Guard and Artillery Reserve (5,200). Guns—110.

In all, 101,300 officers and men and 357 guns.

The day Meade took over his command, Lee was preparing to advance on Harrisburg. That night, as he says in his report, dated July 31, 1863, "information was received from a scout that the Federal Army, having crossed the Potomac, was advancing northward, and that the head of the column had reached the South Mountain." [56] Longstreet informs us that the scout's name was Harrison, and that he sent him under care of Colonel Fairfax to general headquarters, where

Lee declined to see him.[57] This, seemingly, is incorrect. According to Freeman, Lee turned to Fairfax and said: "I do not know what to do. I cannot hear from General Stuart, the eyes of the army. What do you think of Harrison? I have no confidence in any scout, but General Longstreet thinks a good deal of Harrison." [58]

"Lee heard Harrison through without a tremor," writes Freeman, "but he was profoundly concerned by the intelligence the spy brought. Hooker on the north side of the Potomac, close to his rear, and not a cavalry man at hand [59] to ascertain whither he was moving! There could hardly have been worse news."

As soon as Harrison had finished, Lee sent an order to Ewell to abandon his advance on Harrisburg and fall back on Cashtown or Gettysburg, while Hill was directed to recross the mountains and move on Cashtown, Longstreet following the next day. Simultaneously he ordered Robertson and Jones, still guarding the passes of the Blue Ridge, to rejoin the army,[60] for Imboden, who might have supplied men for reconnaissance, was a two days' ride away. As Freeman writes: "So completely was Lee stripped of cavalry that the foraging actually had to be done by men mounted on horses from the artillery, or the wagon train." [61]

The truth was that, unknown to Lee, Stuart had been separated from the Army of Northern Virginia by Meade's unexpectedly rapid advance. As Lee's columns were moving on Cashtown, Meade pushed on. On the 30th, Meade placed Reynolds in charge of Sickles's and Howard's corps in addition to his own. Reynolds, a born fighter, advanced, and Buford's cavalry entered Gettysburg during the forenoon, just in time to meet Pettigrew's brigade of Hill's corps.

That evening Meade ordered Sickles's corps to march to Emmitsburg; Hancock's to Taneytown; Sykes's to Hanover; Slocum's to Two Taverns, Reynolds's and Howard's to Gettysburg, and Sedgwick's to Manchester, with the cavalry out on either flank. At the same time he issued the following memorandum:

It is no longer his [Meade's] intention to assume the offensive until the enemy's movements or position renders such an operation certain of success. If the enemy assume the offensive, and attack, it is his intention, after holding them in check sufficiently long, to withdraw the trains and other *impedimenta;* to withdraw the army from its present position, and form a line of battle with the left resting in the neighbourhood of Middleburg, and the right at Manchester, the general direction being that of Pipe Creek.[62]

This memorandum shows nervousness on the part of its writer. However, though Meade little suspected it, his great adversary was more nervous than he.

Meanwhile the Confederate columns were moving toward Cashtown and Gettysburg. From Gettysburg, their distances were as follows:

First Corps, Chambersburg and Greenwood: 24 and 16 miles.

Second Corps, and Jenkins's cavalry, Heidlersburg and Green Village: 10 and 23 miles.

Third Corps, Greenwood and Cashtown: 16 and 8 miles.

Stuart's cavalry, Robertson's, and Imboden's were beyond reach.[63]

In this campaign the matter of communications made it almost certain that any great battle would be fought at Gettysburg. Here twelve roads converged, making it an easy spot to move on and to strike from. Moreover, it was defensively a strong position. West of the town ran Willoughby's Run between two low ridges, the one nearest to Gettysburg being called Seminary Ridge; and to the south of the town ran yet another ridge. The northern extremities of this ridge were called Cemetery Hill and Culp's Hill, and the southern, Little Round Top and Round Top.

Early on July 1, Heth's division of Hill's corps, with Pender's in support, occupied the ridge west of Willoughby's Run. There they were amused by Buford's cavalry until about 10 A.M., when Reynolds came up with Wadsworth's division, which formed behind Seminary Ridge and to the north of the Chambersburg Pike road. Advancing, it came into contact with Davis's brigade of Heth's division and was driven back. Immediately after, Reynolds was killed and succeeded by General Doubleday, who soon was outflanked. At 11 A.M. a lull occurred during which Howard came up. As he ranked Doubleday, he took over command. Observing that enemy forces—Rodes' division of Ewell's corps—were pouring in from the north against Doubleday's right, he brought up the remainder of Reynolds's corps to meet them. At 1 P.M. Howard's corps arrived and Schurz's and Barlow's divisions were sent north of the town, where they soon became engaged with Early's division of Ewell's corps.

The night of the 30th, Lee had spent at Greenwood. There to his consternation he learnt from Hill that, when Pettigrew's brigade had that day gone from Cashtown to Gettysburg to procure shoes, it had been fired upon by Federal cavalry. Early the next morning he set out with Longstreet, when riding ahead of the troops they heard the distant rumble of gunfire. Whereupon Lee, growing impatient, pressed on to Cashtown, where he met General Anderson of Hill's corps.[64]

From Cashtown, Lee galloped toward Gettysburg, and on arriving

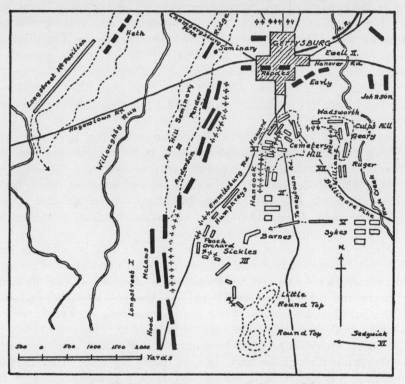

19. Battle of Gettysburg, July 2, 1863

there was anxious not to bring on a general engagement until his troops were up. He learnt that Hill's men were disorganized and that prisoners captured from the First and Eleventh Federal Corps had stated that the whole of Meade's army was moving on Gettysburg. Unable to push Hill forward, he sent discretionary orders to Ewell to take Cemetery Hill, so long as his action did not commit the whole army to battle.[65] The result was that nothing happened.

Then Longstreet came up and joined him. Together they closely examined the Federal positions as well as Cemetery Hill, which they at once saw was an excellent defensive locality. "'I said,'" writes Longstreet, "'We could not call the enemy to position better suited to our plans. All that we have to do is to file around his left and secure good ground between him and his capital.' This, when said, was thought to be the opinion of my commander as much as my own. I was not a little surprised, therefore, at his impatience, as, striking the air with his closed hand, he said, 'If he is there to-morrow I will attack him.'" To which Longstreet answered "'If he is there to-morrow it will be because he wants you to attack,'" and queried "'If that height has become the objective, why not take it at once? We have forty thousand men, less the casualties of the day; he cannot have more than twenty thousand.'" [66]

At this point Long came up and reported to Lee that the enemy was holding Cemetery Hill in force, and that, in his opinion an attack on it would be hazardous.[67] Whereupon Lee rode over to see Ewell.

Meanwhile Rodes had attacked Doubleday and had been driven back. Next, at about 3 P.M., Early drove in Schurz, whereupon Barlow put up a fine fight. Lastly Doubleday was again attacked, this time by Hill, and was forced to retire.

Meade, at Taneytown, hearing that Reynolds had been killed, sent Hancock forward to take command of Reynolds's and Howard's corps, in addition to his own and Sickles's, then at Emmitsburg. At the same time he instructed him, should he find the position at Gettysburg better suited to a defensive battle than Pipe Creek, to let him know, whereupon all troops would be ordered forward to occupy it.

Hancock arrived at 3.30 P.M. Finding units of Reynolds's and Howard's corps retiring through the town, he gave orders for a line of battle to be formed on Cemetery Hill, which was already partially occupied by Howard. Next, having with Warren reconnoitered the ground and come to the conclusion that it was to be preferred to Pipe Creek, he ordered Wadsworth's division to hold Culp's Hill and the rest of Reynolds's corps to take up position on its left linking with the left of Howard's corps. At 4 P.M. when Williams's and Geary's divisions of Slocum's corps arrived, Williams's division was placed on Wadsworth's right, and Geary's on the high ground immediately north of Little Round Top. Hancock then sent a messenger to Meade informing him that the position was a very strong one, in spite of the fact that it might easily be turned. At about 6 P.M. Slocum himself came up and Hancock transferred the command to him and returned to Taneytown.

By about midnight the positions of the remaining corps of the Army of the Potomac were as follows: Sickles's, two miles to the east, Hancock's three miles to the south, Sykes's six miles to the east, and Sedgwick's still from twelve to fifteen miles to the southeast of Gettysburg.

At about the time Slocum took over from Hancock, Lee found Ewell and with him Early and Rodes. The next day's operations were then discussed. Turning to Ewell, Lee said: "Can't you, with your corps, attack on this flank tomorrow?" Whereupon Early—not Ewell—contended that an assault would be a most costly and doubtful issue. Instead, he suggested that the attack should be made on the Round Tops, which if occupied would dominate the entire field. On Ewell and Rodes agreeing, Lee asked whether it would not then be best to draw Ewell's corps "around towards our right." To this Early could not agree. He suggested that Longstreet's corps deliver this attack on the right. Once Longstreet had engaged the enemy, he pointed out, the Second Corps would be well placed to follow up his success by advancing against and destroying the enemy's right.

Though not altogether convinced, Lee tentatively accepted this proposal on the assumption that the attack by Longstreet was to be made as early as possible the next morning.[68]

Lee then returned to Seminary Ridge, and was overjoyed to learn that Stuart had arrived at Carlisle. He immediately ordered him to hasten his march on Gettysburg. This done, he turned over in his mind the portentous question of whether to attack or withdraw. The answer is given in his report, and it reads as follows:

It had not been intended to deliver a general battle so far from our base unless attacked, but coming unexpectedly upon the whole Federal army, to withdraw through the mountains with our excessive trains would have been difficult and dangerous. At the same time we were unable to await an attack, as the country was unfavorable for collecting supplies in the presence of the enemy, who could restrain our foraging parties by holding the mountain passes with local and other troops. A battle had, therefore, become in a measure unavoidable, and the success already gained gave hope of a favorable issue.[69]

What does this mean? That General Subsistence and not General Lee decided that an attack had to be made.

This being so, the next question was: Where should the attack be launched? General Alexander, who was Longstreet's chief of artillery, suggested that they attack the salient formed by Culp's Hill and

Cemetery Hill, which position "offered the only hopeful point of attack upon the enemy's entire line." [70] But as Ewell did not favor it for the main assault, Lee set it aside and instead determined to attack Meade's left. This meant that Longstreet would have to carry out the action.

Longstreet had already objected to any form of attack, particularly until his 3d Division—Pickett's—had rejoined him. Nevertheless, according to Captain Chesney, "the will of the younger and more ardent spirits of the conclave prevailed." [71] However the fact remains that no specific orders were given to Longstreet to attack or even to prepare to do so. This is beyond doubt. [72] Longstreet says: "When I left General Lee, about seven o'clock in the evening, he had formed no plans beyond that of seizing Culp's Hill as his point from which to engage, nor given any orders for the next day . . ." [73] The whole situation may be summed up in Lee's own words as recorded by Long: "Gentlemen, we will attack the enemy in the morning as early as practicable" [74]—a somewhat pious wish. Thus closed July 1.

Meade was up and about very early on the 2d, for at 3 A.M. he met General Howard at the Cemetery Gate and rode with him round his position. Five hours later, except for two brigades, the whole of the Fifth, Twelfth, First, Eleventh, Second, and Third Corps formed a continuous line from the Baltimore Pike near Rock Creek along Culp's Hill and Cemetery Ridge to Little Round Top. The Sixth Corps, still twelve miles to the southeast, was approaching. Meade, therefore, was fully prepared to meet an attack on his three-mile front so long as Culp's Hill and the Round Tops held firm.

About the same time that Meade met Howard, Longstreet met Lee, [75] and once again he urged him to turn Meade's left instead of attacking him. [76] Though Lee could not agree to this, he havered and sent Colonel Venable of his staff to Ewell "to see whether, after viewing the position in his front by daylight, he could not attack from his flank, but the work of thousands of men during the night made the hills too strong to assault . . ." Lee then rode over to Ewell; but "not wishing to drive [him] into battle when he did not want to go, . . . saw nothing could be done, so at eleven o'clock gave a positive order to Longstreet to move to his right and attack." [77] According to Alexander, "Anderson's division of Hill's corps was directed to extend Hill's line upon Seminary Ridge to the right, while Longstreet with Hood's and McLaws's divisions should make a flank march to the right and pass beyond the enemy's flank, which seemed to extend along the

Emmitsburg Road. Forming them at right angles to this road, the attack was to sweep down the enemy's line from their left, being taken up successively by the brigades of Anderson's division as they were reached. Ewell's corps holding the extreme left, was to attack the enemy's right on hearing Longstreet's guns. Longstreet was directed, in his march, to avoid exposing it to the view of a Federal signal station on Little Round Top Mountain." [78]

Once again the eventual fiasco was sown by verbal orders.[79] First, a delay of thirty minutes occurred for Law's brigade of Hood's division to come up.[80] Then a dispute arose over how McLaws's division was to deploy.[81] Meanwhile Lee sent a staff officer out to reconnoiter the approach to Meade's left. On his return the officer was instructed "to lead the troops of the First Corps and conduct them by a route concealed from view of the enemy." [82] Whereupon Longstreet set out accompanied by Lee for "a mile or more." Why, knowing that Longstreet's heart was not in this attack, did Lee not remain with him? The answer is that once he had issued his orders he invariably resigned himself to fate; in fact the battle passed out of his hands. This is borne out by Colonel Fremantle who writes: "What I remarked especially was, that during the whole time the firing continued, he [Lee] only sent one message, and only received one report. It is evidently his system to arrange the plan thoroughly with the three corps commanders, and then leave to them the duty of modifying and carrying it out to the best of their abilities." [83]

Had he only remained with Longstreet, he would have learned that further on the road became exposed to the view of the Federals, and that another had to be sought, which necessitated a countermarch. This "delayed the opening of the battle nearly two hours." [84] Thus it was not until 3.30 P.M. that the Confederate guns opened fire.

Meanwhile on the enemy's side one of those unpredictable incidents had occurred upon which the fate of a battle so often depends.

As we have seen, during the evening of the 1st, Hancock had placed Geary's division immediately to the north of Little Round Top. That position Geary held until the morning of the 2d, when he was relieved by part of Sickles's corps. Sickles, not liking his position, sent back to Meade asking for permission to advance it. Without waiting for a reply, he moved his line forward to the Peach Orchard on the Emmitsburg Road. This necessitated the abandonment of the high ground, and in consequence uncovered the Federal flank.

Later Meade rode over to see Sickles, and at once disapproved of the change; but as at that moment Longstreet began to advance, no alteration could be made. Meade, seeing the supreme danger Sickles now faced, at once sent for the Fifth Corps and Caldwell's division of the Second, leaving Warren to look after the Round Top situation. Warren, finding Little Round Top unoccupied except for a signal station, sent back to Meade for immediate assistance, which arrived only in the nick of time.[85] Had Little Round Top been occupied by Longstreet, not only would Sickles's corps have been taken in reverse, but the left flank of Meade's army would have been turned and enfiladed.

Hood's division of Longstreet's corps advanced at 4 P.M. Hood had appealed several times to be allowed to move to the right in order to overlap Round Top, instead of making a direct attack, as Lee had ordered. Longstreet however would not agree to this,[86] so that of his four brigades, Law's alone moved on Round Top and Little Round Top. There it was met by Vincent's brigade of Sykes's corps, which had just been led into position by Warren. When Vincent was driven back, Warren brought up Weed's brigade and saved the hill.

Meanwhile Hood's remaining brigades—Benning's, Anderson's, and Robertson's—moved directly on the Round Tops, while Kershaw's brigade on McLaws's right, followed by Semmes's brigade, moved against Peach Orchard and drove Sickles's men back. The fighting now became mixed and disunited. Longstreet says that he was left alone to fight the Army of the Potomac single-handed, the Second and Third Corps remaining idle,[87] which was largely true. The upshot was that though the Federals lost Peach Orchard, they held the Round Tops, the battle ending with the appearance of Sedgwick's corps, which threw back Longstreet's final assault. After this last abortive attempt on the part of the Confederates, Longstreet held such ground as he had gained on the right and withdrew his left to the Peach Orchard, while Hill's troops fell back to Seminary Ridge.

Ewell's attack, though far less costly, was equally muddled. Not until 6 P.M. did he order Johnson's division forward against Culp's Hill, and it was eight o'clock before he attacked. Simultaneously Early advanced two brigades against Cemetery Hill, actually penetrating the Federal position, but, unsupported, they were driven back.

Thus ended the second day of this battle—a day of gallant fighting and of muddled generalship. As General Alexander writes: "Few battle-fields can furnish examples of worse tactics"; [88] and General Taylor exclaims: "The whole affair was disjointed. There was an utter absence of accord in the movements of the several commands . . ." [89] The truth is, though Lee could conceive a battle, his system of command or rather lack of a system of command, rendered any form of combined direction impossible.

That night Meade assembled a council of war at which Butterfield, his chief of staff, put the question: "Should the army attack or wait the attack of the enemy?" The second alternative was agreed upon. General John Gibbon gives us the following interesting particulars: As the council broke up, Meade said to him, "If Lee attacks to-morrow, it will be in *your front*." And when Gibbon asked him why, he replied: "Because he has made attacks on both our flanks and failed, and if he concludes to try it again it will be on our center." [90]

At about the same time Lee, still confident of victory, decided to renew the battle on the 3d. In his report he says:

The result of this day's operations induced the belief that, with proper concert of action, and with the increased support that the positions gained on the right would enable the artillery to render the assaulting columns, we should ultimately succeed, and it was accordingly determined to continue the attack. The general plan was unchanged. Longstreet, reinforced by Pickett's three brigades which arrived near the battle-field during the afternoon of the 2nd, was ordered to attack the next morning, and General Ewell was directed to assail the enemy's right at the same time. [91]

This plan decided upon, once again verbal orders were sent out, and though "Longstreet received no orders during the night, and the troops required for his attack could not be gotten into position before noon," Ewell, under the impression that Longstreet would attack at daylight, ordered Johnson to attack Culp's Hill at that vague hour. As he was on the point of doing so, he was himself attacked; held his own, counterattacked, and was repulsed, losing 1,873 in killed and wounded.

During this premature opening of the battle of the 3d, Lee rode over and saw Longstreet and gave him his orders.

His plan [writes Longstreet] was to assault the enemy left centre by a column to be composed of McLaws's and Hood's divisions reinforced by Pickett's brigades. I thought that it would not do; that the point had been fully tested the day before, by more men, when all were fresh; that the enemy was there looking for us . . . that thirty thousand men was the minimum of force necessary for the work . . . that the column

would have to march a mile under concentrated battery fire, and a
thousand yards under long-range musketry; that the conditions were
different from those in the days of Napoleon, when field batteries had
a range of six hundred yards and musketry about sixty yards.[92]

Lee, however, persisted in his intention, and selected as the objective of the assault "a small grove of unbrella-shaped chestnut oaks,
known locally as Ziegler's Grove." [93]

Alexander then informs us:

Longstreet pointed out to Lee the enemy's position on the Round Tops
and the danger of withdrawing Hood and McLaws from our right,
which would be necessary if they were to take part in the attack upon
the enemy's left centre. Lee recognized the necessity and substituted six
brigades from Hill's Corps [Heth's division and two of Pender's
brigades under Trimble] . . .

Longstreet further objected that the enemy's artillery on the "high
rocky hills" would enfilade the lines assaulting the left centre. Col. Long,
of Lee's staff, in his *Memoirs of Lee* [p. 288], writes:

"This objection was answered by Col. Long who said that the guns on
Round Top could be suppressed by our own batteries [they could not].
This point being settled, the attack was ordered and Longstreet was
directed to carry it out."

[Longstreet, in his *Manassas to Appomattox* pp. 386–387, describing
the same conversation, gives further detail as follows]:

I asked the strength of the column. He (Lee) stated, 15,000. Opinion
was then expressed that the 15,000 men who could make successful
assault over that field had never been arrayed for battle; but he was
impatient of listening and tired of talking, and nothing was left but to
proceed.[94]

Meanwhile Meade's troops were distributed as follows:

. . . Slocum at Culp's Hill, Howard at Cemetery Hill, Hancock and
Newton, now commanding the I Corps, along Cemetery Ridge, Sykes
and Sedgwick at the Round Tops . . . Birney, with Sickles's corps was
in reserve behind Hancock and Sykes . . . Six batteries were on
Cemetery Hill behind Howard's corps; five behind the right and centre,
and ten directly in front of the left of Hancock's corps; and two of
long-range rifles on Little Round Top. The point of attack was held by
Hancock's corps, which was drawn up on a line beginning near the
Emanuel Trostle house on the Emmitsburg road about half a mile
from the outskirts of Gettysburg, and extending south about five hundred
yards along Hays's front, the southern half along a stone wall which
then ran westward one hundred yards and then south again, along
Gibbon's front, forming the "bloody angle." There the wall was lower,
and surmounted by a country post and rail fence for about one hundred

yards to a point directly in front of the clump of trees to which Longstreet's attack was directed; south of this the stone wall was replaced by
an ordinary rail fence, which had been thrown down to form the revet-
ment of a shelter trench, which afforded cover against direct fire to
troops lying down.[95]

Against the left center of this formidable distribution, Lee's column
of assault of ten brigades, deployed in the following order:

Pettigrew	Pickett

Brockenbrough	Davis	McGowan	Archer	Garnett	Kemper

Trimble

Lane	Scales

Armistead

Wilcox (of Anderson's)

In all, 47 regiments totaling 15,000 officers and men. Alexander says:
"Both flanks were in the air and the left without any support in the
rear. It was sure to crumble away rapidly under fire." [96]

To prepare the advance, 172 guns were brought into line immediately
in front, Longstreet's 83 pieces being commanded by General E. P.
Alexander. No attempt was made to concentrate their fire or to enfilade the Federal position.[97]

"Between 10 and 11 A.M.," writes General Henry J. Hunt, Meade's
chief of artillery, ". . . a magnificent display greeted my eyes. Our
whole front for two miles was covered by batteries already in line
or going into position . . . Never before had such a sight been witnessed on this continent, and rarely, if ever, abroad. What did it
mean?" Assuming the most probable answer to be an assault on the
center, he continues: "It was of the first importance to subject the
enemy's infantry, from the first moment of their advance, to such a
cross-fire of our artillery as would break their formation, check their
impulse, and drive them back, or at least bring them to our lines in
such a condition as to make them an easy prey. There was neither time
nor necessity for reporting this to General Meade, and beginning on the
right, I instructed the chiefs of artillery and battery commanders to
withhold their fire for fifteen or twenty minutes after the cannonade
commenced, then to concentrate their fire with all possible accuracy on
those batteries which were most destructive to us—but slowly, so that
when the enemy's ammunition was exhausted, we should have sufficient left to meet the assault." [98]

A little after noon, when the artillery deployment was nearly completed, Alexander received the following note from Longstreet:

Colonel: If the artillery fire does not have the effect to drive off the enemy or greatly demoralize him, so as to make our effort pretty certain, I would prefer that you should not advise Pickett to make the charge. I shall rely a great deal upon your judgment to determine the matter, and shall expect you to let Gen. Pickett know when the moment offers.[99]

This was an extraordinary responsibility to delegate to a subordinate. At 1 P.M. the bombardment opened, when Hunt writes:

. . . the scene was indescribably grand. All the batteries were soon covered with smoke, through which the flashes were incessant, whilst the air seemed filled with shells, whose sharp explosions, with the hurtling of their fragments, formed a running accompaniment to the deep roar of the guns . . . Most of the enemy's projectiles passed overhead . . . and his fire instead of being concentrated on the point of attack, as it ought to have been, and as I expected it would be, was scattered over the whole field . . . Our fire was deliberate but on inspecting the chests I found that the ammunition was running low, and hastened to General Meade, to advise its immediate cessation and preparation for the assault which would certainly follow.[100]

Though to Alexander "it seemed madness to order a column in the middle of a hot July day to undertake an advance of three-fourths of a mile over open ground," he felt that something had to be done. Therefore at 1.25 P.M. he sent the following note to Pickett:

General: If you are to advance at all, you must come at once or we will not be able to support you as we ought. But the enemy's fire has not slackened materially and there are still 18 guns firing from the cemetery.

Hardly had this note been sent than the Federal fire began to slacken. Then, noticing that some of the enemy's guns were limbering up, at 1.40 P.M. he sent Pickett yet another note, which read:

For God's sake come quick. The 18 guns have gone.[101] Come quick or my ammunition will not let me support you properly.

When Alexander's first note was handed to Pickett, it found him with Longstreet. "He read it and handed it to Longstreet. Longstreet read and stood silent. Pickett said, 'General, shall I advance?' Longstreet knew that it must be done, but was unwilling to speak the words. He turned in his saddle and looked away. Pickett saluted and said, 'I am going to move forward, sir,' and galloped off."

At about 1.50 P.M. Longstreet joined Alexander, and on learning that the gun ammunition was running short, he said sharply: "Go and stop Pickett where he is and replenish your ammunition." To which Alexander replied: "We can't do that, sir. The train has but little. It would take an hour to distribute it, and meanwhile the enemy would improve the time."

Then Longstreet exclaimed with great emotion: "I do not want to make this charge. I do not see how it can succeed. I would not make it now but that Gen. Lee has ordered it and is expecting it." [102]

Meanwhile the assaulting columns moved forward down the slope, and as they did so the Confederate batteries opened fire over their heads. The Federal guns did not attempt to silence their fire, but instead poured their shot and shell on the advancing infantry.[103]

Of the charge itself I will quote two Confederate writers—Fitzhugh Lee and A. L. Long. The first writes:

To the left of Pickett the four brigades under Pettigrew and the two under Trimble charged . . . They made their assault in front of Hays's and Gibbon's division, Second [Federal] Corps, in the vicinity of Ziegler's Grove . . .
"They moved up splendidly," wrote a Northern officer, "deploying as they crossed the long sloping interval. The front of the column was nearly up the slope and within a few yards of the Second Corps's front and its batteries, when suddenly a terrific fire from every available gun on Cemetery Ridge burst upon them. Their graceful lines underwent an instantaneous transformation in a dense cloud of smoke and dust; arms, heads, blankets, guns, and knapsacks were tossed in the air, and the moan from the battlefield was heard amid the storm of battle." Sheets of missiles flew through what seemed a moving mass of smoke, human valor was powerless, and the death-dealing guns were everywhere throwing blazing projectiles in their very faces. No troops could advance and live.[104]

As these troops were thrown back in disorder, and as Wilcox "perceiving that the attack had grown hopeless, failed to advance . . . the consequence was that Pickett was left entirely unsupported." Then Long continues the story:

Yet the gallant Virginians marched steadily forward, through the storm of shot and shell that burst upon their devoted ranks, with a gallantry that has never been surpassed. As they approached the ridge their lines were torn by incessant volleys of musketry as by a deadly hail. Yet with unfaltering courage the brave fellows broke into the double-quick, and with an irresistible charge burst into the Federal lines and drove everything before them toward the crest of Cemetery Hill, leaping the breastworks and planting their standards on the captured guns with shouts of victory.

The success which General Lee had hoped and expected was gained, but it was a dearly-bought and short-lived one. His plan had gone astray through the failure of the supporting columns . . . The victory which seemed within the grasp of the Confederate army was lost as soon as won. On every side the enemy closed in on Pickett's brigades, concentrating on them the fire of every gun in that part of their lines. It was impossible to long withstand this terrific fusillade. The band of heroes broke and fell back, leaving the greater part of their number dead or wounded upon the field or captive in the hands of their foes.[105]

Much has been written on this famous assault, and many writers, notably Colonel Walter H. Taylor [106]—Lee's adjutant general—considers that had Pickett been supported by Hood and McLaws the Federals would have been routed. Though, personally, I doubt this, the question arises whether Hood and McLaws had been ordered to support Pickett in the first place. Colonel C. S. Venables, on Lee's staff, answers "yes" . . . "for I heard him [Lee] give the orders when arranging the fight; and called his attention to it long afterwards, when there was a discussion about it. He said, 'I know it! I know it!' " [107] Longstreet says—"no," and in a letter to Taylor, written on February 2, 1877, he writes: "In reply to your inquiry for a statement in regard to the supposed orders of General Lee in reference to the battle of the third day, I have only to say that General Lee gave no orders for placing the divisions of McLaws and Hood in the column of attack on that day." [108] But it is impossible to say who is right, because all orders were issued verbally. Considering that General Alexander, Longstreet's chief gunner, did not even know the objective of the attack, it is quite understandable that no one in particular knew whether Hood and McLaws were to take part in the assault or not. Anyhow, as Fitz Lee says: ". . . one half of Hill's, and the whole of Ewell's stood like fixed stars in the heaven as their comrades marched into the 'jaws of death.' " [109]

The burden of this mistake and the many others that characterized this battle must rest on the shoulders of Lee, who throughout its course failed to grasp events or impose his will on either his subordinates or his enemy. Nevertheless, once the final disaster was accomplished, he rose above it, as he always did, nobly accepting all responsibility, as noted by Colonel Fremantle, who was present at the time.[110]

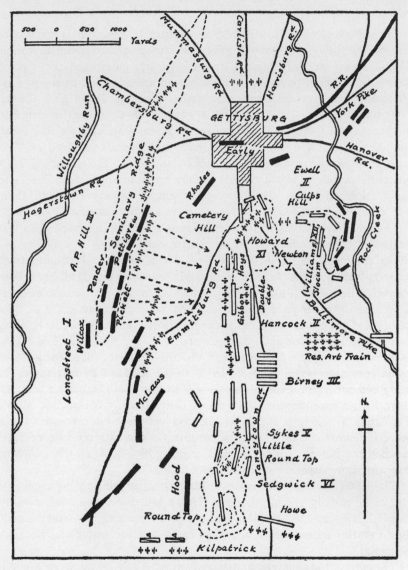

20. Battle of Gettysburg, July 3, 1863

Once Pickett was thrown back, as Fremantle says: "It is difficult to exaggerate the critical state of affairs as they appeared about this time. If the enemy or their general had shown any enterprise, there is no saying what might have happened." [111] And according to Fitzhugh Lee, Pleasanton rode up to Meade and said: "General, I will give you an hour and a half to show yourself a great general; order the army to advance while I take the cavalry, get in Lee's rear, and we will finish the campaign in a week." [112] But Meade would not move and so "lost here an opportunity as great as McClellan lost at Sharpsburg." Thus writes Alexander, and then adds: "Our ammunition was so low, and our diminished forces were, at the moment, so widely dispersed along our unwisely extended line, that an advance by a single fresh corps . . . could have cut us in two." [113] Meade's failure to attack then was probably the worst blunder of the entire campaign.

On the next day, the opportunity for a successful counterattack passed, because "the very windows of heaven seemed to have been opened. The rain fell in blinding sheets; the meadows were soon overflowed, and fences gave way before the raging streams" [114] . . . "the best standing points were ankle-deep in mud, and the roads halfway to the knee, puddling and getting worse . . ." [115] This day Lee issued *in writing* his orders for retreat.[116] On the following day, encumbered by an enormous wagon train loaded with the spoils of Pennsylvania, the army set out southward, but so slowly that it was not until 2 A.M. on the 6th that Ewell cleared the field of Gettysburg.[117] Meanwhile Meade did little or nothing, and when he did set out, his advance was a mere follow-up and in no sense a pursuit. On the 13th the Confederates reached the Potomac, Ewell's corps crossing by 8 A.M. on the following day and Longstreet's and Hill's by 1 P.M.

Thus ended one of the greatest filibustering expeditions in history. It cost the Federals 17,684 officers and men killed and wounded, and the Confederates 22,638, besides over 5,000 in missing on either side.[118] For Lee this indeed was a heavy price to pay for restocking his commissariat.

Though on the generalship of this campaign a book might be written, all I can attempt here is to touch upon a few of its salient points.

It was based upon two misconceptions—namely, that the Confederate soldier was invincible and that the Federal government could be terrified into accepting a peace of compromise. Strategically, the whole enterprise was hampered by the necessity to forage. Tactically it was

weak because the move north drew the Confederate Army out of the
wooded and broken country which was so unfavorable to the maneuvers
of large armies but which multiplied the resisting and striking power
of small armies. Whereas at Chancellorsville and again during the
Wilderness campaign of 1864, Lee and his men were at their best,
at Sharpsburg and at Gettysburg they were at their worst, because,
though a master of maneuver, the great Virginian persistently under-
estimated the effectiveness of the muzzle-loading rifle over open ground.

Though many separate blunders can be enumerated—such as the
detachment of Stuart, the failure of Ewell to take Cemetery Hill on
the 1st, the inadequacy of Longstreet's attacking columns on the 2d,
and the impossible charge on the 3d—the fundamental reason for the
Confederate defeat must be sought in the character of Lee himself.
Treating his enemy with too great a contempt, he treated his subordinates with too great a respect, so that he never got a personal grip
of his adversary. Men like Jackson gave him what by nature he lacked
—namely, a ruthless temperament; and men like Stuart, Ewell, and
Longstreet imposed their stronger personalities upon him. Several of
his subordinates remarked on this. For instance, Walter H. Taylor
writes:

First, that he was too careful of the personal feelings of his subordinate commanders, too fearful of wounding their pride, and too
solicitous of their reputation . . .
The traits of character alluded to, excessive generosity and perfect
subordination, while they adorned the life of General Lee, are not
compatible with the generally accepted notions of perfection in a
revolutionary leader.[119]

Again Fitzhugh Lee says:

Lee to the strong courage of the man united the loving heart of the
woman. His "nature was too epicene," said an English critic, "to be
purely a military man." He had a reluctance to oppose the wishes of
others, or to order them to do anything that would be disagreeable and
to which they would not consent . . . If Lee had issued by his chief of
staff his battle order for the 2nd in writing, as is customary, Longstreet
would have carried it out probably in good faith, and not have wasted
most valuable time in attempting to convince his commander it was
faulty.[120]

Foreigners also noticed this weakness, for weakness it was. For
instance, Fremantle says: "His only faults, so far as I can learn, arise
from his excessive amiability";[121] and Captain Mangold, a German

officer, says, "the defect in General Lee's military character was a too kindly consideration for incompetent officers, resulting from an excess of good-nature." [122]

Though it was this amiability which more than any other factor opened the road to Richmond, the ruthlessness of a very different general opened the road which led to Atlanta. These two cities were the hinges upon which the now creaking door of the Confederacy swung.

REFERENCES

[1] *The Story of the Civil War,* William Roscoe Livermore, Part III, Book I, p. 98.

[2] See *Battles and Leaders,* vol. III, pp. 239–240. Chesney (see his *Campaigns in Virginia and Maryland,* p. 34) informs us that Hooker was the only officer of mark in the Army of the Potomac who was ineligible as a future president.

[3] *The War of the Rebellion, etc.,* vol. XL, p. 597. Also see *The Campaign of Chancellorsville,* Major John Bigelow, p. 35.

[4] See *Memoirs of Robert E. Lee,* by A. L. Long, pp. 246–247.

[5] See *W.R.,* vol. XL, p. 693, and *Military Memoirs of a Confederate,* by E. P. Alexander, p. 319. Colonel Fremantle writes: "Before starting, the engine gives two preliminary snorts, which, with a yell from the official, of *'all aboard'* warn the passengers to hold on; for they are closely followed by a tremendous jerk, which sets the cars in motion. Every passenger is allowed to use his own discretion about breaking his arm, neck, or leg, without interference by the railway officials" (*Three Months in The Southern States,* p. 61).

[6] See Bigelow, p. 33.

[7] *W.R.,* vol. XL, p. 713.

[8] *Ibid.,* vol. XL, p. 736.

[9] *Ibid.,* vol. XL, p. 859.

[10] Bigelow, p. 433.

[11] *Ibid.,* p. 488.

[12] *W.R.,* vol. XXXV, p. 836.

[13] *From Manassas to Appomattox,* James Longstreet, p. 327.

[14] Walter H. Taylor says: "His design was to free the State of Virginia, for a time at least, from the presence of the enemy (*General Lee: His Campaigns in Virginia,* 1861–1865, p. 180). Grant was also of this opinion (see *Memoirs of Gen. W. T. Sherman* Written by Himself, vol. II, p. 224). Pollard says: "The fact was that, although many of General Lee's views were sound, yet, outside of the Army of Northern Virginia, and with reference to the general affairs of the Confederacy, his influence was negative and accomplished absolutely nothing" (*The Lost Cause,* p. 655). E. A. Pollard was a Southern journalist.

[15] Longstreet, p. 331.

[16] *W.R.,* vol. XLV, p. 868.

[17] *Ibid.,* vol. XLV, pp. 880–882.

[18] *Ibid.,* vol. XL, p. 814.

[19] For instance, General Hood writes: On the day before the Battle of Antietam, "My troops . . . were sorely in need of shoes, clothing and food. We had had issued to us no meat for several days, and little or no bread; the men had been forced to subsist principally on green corn and green apples" (*Advance and*

Retreat, p. 41). According to Fremantle, one of the principal objects in killing a Yankee was to get his boots (p. 171).

[20] General Heth says: "It is very difficult for anyone not connected with the Army of Northern Virginia to realize how straitened we were for supplies of all kinds, especially food" (*Southern Historical Society Papers,* vol. IV, p. 153—cited as *S.H.S.P.*).

[21] Long, p. 269.

[22] *R. E. Lee, a Biography,* Douglas Southall Freeman, vol. III, p. 19.

[23] Ewell had but one leg. He had served under Jackson and suspected him of being insane; he had once heard "Jackson seriously assert that he never took pepper with his food because it made his left leg weak" (Freeman, vol. III, p. 9).

[24] *S.H.S.P.,* vol. IV, p. 160. Chesney writes: "All ranks in Lee's army held the Federals in utter contempt" (p. 103). After the war Longstreet told Swinton, "The Army of Northern Virginia was in a condition to undertake *anything.*" Taylor adds: "In this opinion he but expressed the sentiment of the whole army; an overweening confidence possessed us all" (*Four Years with General Lee,* p. 101).

[25] *W.R.,* vol. XLIII, p. 30.

[26] *Ibid.,* vol. XLIII, p. 31.

[27] *Ibid.,* vol. XLIII, p. 34.

[28] *Ibid.,* vol. XLIII, p. 35.

[29] *Ibid.,* vol. XLIII, p. 38.

[30] *Ibid.,* vol. XLIII, p. 39.

[31] *Ibid.,* vol. XLIV, p. 296.

[32] *Ibid.,* vol. XLV, p. 914.

[33] Long, pp. 272–273.

[34] *W.R.,* vol. XLV, p. 925, and *ibid.,* vol. XLV, p. 931.

[35] See *ibid.,* vol. XLIII, p. 75.

[36] *Advance and Retreat,* p. 54.

[37] Fremantle, p. 244. He has also the following story to tell: "One female had seen fit to adorn her ample bosom with a huge Yankee flag, and stood at the door of her house, her countenance expressing the greatest contempt for the barefooted Rebs; several companies passed her without taking any notice; but at length a Texan gravely remarked, 'Take care, madam, for Hood's boys are great at storming breastworks when the Yankee colours is on them.' After this speech the patriotic lady beat a precipitate retreat."

[38] Long, p. 272.

[39] Taylor's *General Lee,* p. 185.

[40] *W.R.,* vol. XLV, p. 890.

[41] *Ibid.,* vol. XLV, p. 900.

[42] *An Aide-de-Camp of Lee, Papers of Colonel Charles Marshall,* p. 200.

[43] *W.R.,* vol. XLV, p. 913.

[44] *Ibid.,* vol. XLV, p. 914.

[45] *Papers of Colonel Charles Marshall,* p. 204. Longstreet (p. 344) says: "In my note to General Stuart enclosing General Lee's instructions was this item: 'P.S.—I think your passage of the Potomac by our rear at the present moment will, in a measure, disclose our plans. You had better not leave us, therefore, unless you can take the route in rear of the enemy.' "

[46] *W.R.,* vol. XLV, p. 923.

[47] *Ibid.,* vol. XLV, p. 927.

[48] *Papers of Colonel Charles Marshall,* p. 224.

[49] See *The Life and Campaigns of Major General J. E. B. Stuart,* by Major H. B. McClellan (Chief of Staff of the Cavalry Corps, Army of Northern Virginia),

pp. 319–321. A more recent account will be found in *Jeb Stuart* by John W. Thomason, chap. XVIII.

[50] Alexander (p. 375) writes: "In saving a large number of wagons, instead of burning them, and in delaying 12 hours to parole his prisoners, instead of bringing along the officers and letting the men go, Stuart committed fatal blunders." Fitzhugh Lee says (p. 266): "Without rations for men, and with horses exhausted, Stuart arrived at Carlisle the day Hill and Ewell engaged at Gettysburg . . . Stuart did not know until he received a dispatch from General Lee on the night of July 1st where he was, for the Union army had been between his march and his own army."

[51] *W.R.*, vol. XLIII, p. 55.

[52] *Ibid.*, vol. XLIII, p. 58.

[53] *Ibid.*, vol. XLIII, p. 60.

[54] *Ibid.*, vol. XLIII, p. 61.

[55] See *Report of the Joint Committee on the Conduct of the War*, 1865, vol. I, pp. 329–330.

[56] *W.R.*, vol. XLIV, p. 307.

[57] Longstreet, pp. 346–347. He dates this incident the 29th.

[58] Freeman, vol. III, p. 60.

[59] McClellan in his *Life of Stuart* (p. 119) says that Stuart left 3,000 cavalry behind him. Also: "It was not the want of cavalry that General Lee bewailed, for he had enough of it had it been properly used. It was the absence of Stuart himself that he felt so keenly; for on him he had learned to rely to such an extent that it seemed as if his cavalry were concentrated in his person, and from him alone could information be expected" (p. 336).

[60] *W.R.*, vol. XLIV, p. 321.

[61] Freeman, vol. III, pp. 63–64.

[62] *W.R.*, vol. XLV, p. 458.

[63] *Ibid.*, p. 349.

[64] Quoted by Longstreet, p. 357.

[65] Taylor's *General Lee*, p. 190.

[66] Longstreet, pp. 358–359. A slightly different version is to be found in *Battles and Leaders*, vol. III, p. 339.

[67] Long in *S.H.S.P.*, vol. IV, p. 66.

[68] For this conversation between Lee and Ewell, Early and Rodes see Freeman, vol. III, pp. 79–80.

[69] *W.R.*, vol. XLIV, p. 317.

[70] Alexander, p. 388.

[71] Chesney, p. 64. He adds: "In this yielding to the judgment of others, less responsible for the consequences—supported though they were by the excited and somewhat over-confident feeling of the whole army—we see the one weak point in the military character of the chief."

[72] Alexander (p. 388) says: "No orders whatever were given Longstreet that night." And Walter H. Taylor writes: "I cannot say that he [Longstreet] was notified, on the night of the 1st, of the attack proposed to be made on the morning of the 2nd, and the part his corps was to take therein." Further: "I can only say that I never before heard of the 'sunrise attack' you were to have made" (*Four Years with General Lee*, pp. 99, 101).

[73] Longstreet, p. 361.

[74] Long, p. 277.

[75] Longstreet, p. 362.

[76] *Papers of Colonel Charles Marshall*, p. 232.

[77] *General Lee of the Confederate Army*, Fitzhugh Lee, p. 277.

[78] Alexander, p. 391. The signal for attack is reminiscent of Malvern Hill. In connection with this, Colonel Fremantle's remark (p. 121) is interesting: "I had a long conversation with General Johnston, who told me that the principal evils which a Confederate general had to contend against is the difficulty of making combinations, owing to uncertainty about the time which the troops would take to march a certain distance, on account of their straggling propensities."

[79] See Lee's *Lee*, p. 281.

[80] See Longstreet, p. 365, and Alexander, p. 392.

[81] See Hood's *Advance and Retreat*, pp. 56–57, and Lee's *Lee*, p. 279.

[82] Longstreet, pp. 365–366.

[83] Fremantle, p. 262.

[84] Alexander, p. 392. See also McLaws in *W.R.*, vol. XLIV, pp. 366, 372.

[85] *W.R.*, vol. XLIII, pp. 616–617.

[86] Freeman (vol. III, p. 98) says that as Lee was less than two miles away, Longstreet could easily have referred this request to him. But the question really is, why was not Lee on the spot? It was vital to his plan that the First Corps attack should succeed; therefore he should have remained with Longstreet. (See also Alexander, p. 394.)

[87] Longstreet, pp. 373–374.

[88] Alexander, p. 397.

[89] Taylor's *Four Years*, p. 99.

[90] *Battles and Leaders*, vol. III, p. 314.

[91] *W.R.*, vol. XLIV, p. 320.

[92] Longstreet, p. 386.

[93] Freeman, vol. III, p. 111.

[94] Alexander, p. 416.

[95] Livermore, Part III, Book II, pp. 472–473.

[96] Alexander, p. 419.

[97] *Ibid.*, p. 419.

[98] *Battles and Leaders*, vol. III, pp. 371–372.

[99] Alexander, p. 421.

[100] *Battles and Leaders*, vol. III, pp. 373–374.

[101] Alexander had incorrectly been told that the cemetery was the point against which the assault was to be directed. This error was again due to verbal orders.

[102] The above account is taken from Alexander, pp. 423–424. Also see Longstreet, p. 392, and Lee's *Lee*, pp. 292–294.

[103] See Alexander in *Battles and Leaders*, vol. III, p. 365.

[104] Lee's *Lee*, pp. 296–297.

[105] Long, p. 290.

[106] *S.H.S.P.* vol. IV, p. 83.

[107] Taylor's *Four Years*, p. 107.

[108] *Ibid.*, p. 109.

[109] Lee's *Lee*, p. 295.

[110] See Fremantle, p. 274.

[111] *Ibid.*, p. 276.

[112] Lee's *Lee*, p. 304.

[113] Alexander, p. 432.

[114] General Imboden in *Battles and Leaders*, vol. III, p. 423.

[115] Longstreet, p. 429.

[116] *W.R.*, vol. XLIV, p. 311.

[117] The sufferings of the wounded were appalling. (See General Imboden in *Battles and Leaders*, vol. III, p. 424.)

[118] Livermore's *Numbers and Losses*, pp. 102–103.

[119] Taylor's *Four Years*, pp. 146–148.

[120] Lee's *Lee*, pp. 280–281.

[121] Fremantle, p. 255.

[122] Quoted from Lee's *Lee*, p. 301.

1861–1863

SYNOPSIS OF BACKGROUND EVENTS

W HILE the great battles, recorded in the last two chapters, were being fought, far away on the banks of the Mississippi the Confederacy was being threatened by a hitherto all but unknown man— Ulysses S. Grant.

Born on April 27, 1822, he graduated from West Point in 1843; distinguished himself in Mexico at Monterrey and Chapultepec, and in 1854 was compelled to retire from the army on the score of drunkenness. Four years later he was walking the streets of St. Louis looking for work. When the war broke out, it found him working as a clerk in a leather store at Galena, managed by his younger brothers. Appointed by Governor Yates to command the 21st Illinois Infantry, on September 4, having by then been made a brigadier general, he opened his head-western sector. From there, river communications ran to Vicksburg, New Orleans, Louisville, Pittsburg, Nashville, and Chattanooga, and the quadrilateral Humboldt-Corinth-Decatur-Nashville formed the waist quarters at Cairo. Cairo was the strategical pivot of the war on the of the railroads between the Northern and Southern states west of the Alleghany mountains. To protect it, the Confederates had erected strong works on the Mississippi, and had built Fort Henry on the Tennessee and Fort Donelson on the Cumberland Rivers, east of which they had pushed forces out into southern Kentucky.

Appreciating the importance of Paducah, which lay on the Ohio River some twenty-five miles east of Cairo and commanded the exits of the Tennessee and Cumberland Rivers, Grant occupied it on September 5. Then, on November 7, by chance rather than generalship, he won a small battle at Belmont, and a few days later Major General Henry Wager Halleck and Don Carlos Buell, respectively, were placed

251

in command of the Departments of Missouri and of the Ohio. Buell at once ordered General George H. Thomas to advance against General Zollicoffer in East Tennessee. Thomas defeated Zollicoffer at Mill Springs on January 19, 1862.

The importance of this battle was that it opened the road to the right flank of the Confederate forces under General Albert Sidney Johnston, then holding Kentucky. Appreciating that Johnston's distribution was overextended, Buell in vain suggested to Halleck a combined move on Nashville. Meanwhile Grant at Cairo had on January 6 requested Halleck's permission to strike a blow at the center of the railroad waist at Forts Henry and Donelson, with the object of separating the Confederate forces in Missouri from those in Kentucky. On the 23d he again asked permission, but with no further success. Nevertheless, Halleck, whose jealousy had been roused by Thomas's victory at Mill Springs, had already, on the 20th, telegraphed McClellan for authority to move against the forts, in order to "turn Columbus, and force the abandonment of Bowling Green." On February 1 he agreed to Grant's request for permission to assault Fort Henry, which, thanks to Foote's gunboats, surrendered on the 6th.

The result of this success was that Johnston abandoned Bowling Green, and, foolishly divided his army, sent 14,000 men to Nashville and 12,000 to Fort Donelson. Grant thereupon moved forward to surround Fort Donelson on its landward side, while the gunboats attacked it from the river. On the 16th the fort surrendered unconditionally.

This was Grant's first real success: it forced the Confederates back toward their sally port; it opened the road to the capture of Vicksburg, and by winning Kentucky and laying Tennessee open to invasion, it deprived the Confederacy of 175,000 potential recruits.

Meanwhile Albert Sidney Johnston fell back on Corinth, drawing in his scattered forces, whereupon Buell occupied Nashville on February 24. Buell suggested that from there a blow should be struck against the Memphis-Charleston Railroad. Halleck agreed, but, accusing Grant of insubordination, placed General C. G. Smith in command of the expedition.

Two things now occurred that influenced the trend of events in the West. The first was that, in the beginning of March, McClellan, as we have seen, was relieved of his office as commander in chief, and shortly thereafter Halleck was placed in command of all the Federal forces in the West. This brought Buell under his orders, and two days later Grant was reinstated.

The second event was, that, on March 7–8, General Curtis gained the state of Missouri by decisively defeating General Van Dorn at Pea Ridge. Thus relieved of all anxiety about the security of the western side of the Mississippi, Halleck decided to move his combined armies on Corinth.

Meanwhile Smith, after having carried out several minor raids, established himself at Savannah with Sherman's and Hurlbut's divisions at Pittsburg Landing and Lewis Wallace's at Crump's Landing. Grant arrived at Savannah on the 17th, under instructions from Halleck to act on the defensive, and not to bring about a general engagement until Buell arrived. Buell was then at Columbia, forty miles south of Nashville. Considering Smith's distribution to be faulty, Grant concentrated the whole army at Pittsburg and Crump's Landings, and there set about organizing and drilling his raw troops.

Grant expected Buell on the 24th or 25th, but Buell telegraphed him that owing to delays en route, he would be unable to arrive at Savannah before April 5. In spite of this delay, which enabled Johnston to collect and reorganize his forces at Corinth, Grant failed to entrench his position. Worse still, he established his headquarters at Savannah, and General Sherman, who was left in nominal command of the three forward divisions at Pittsburg Landing, failed to secure or adequately to patrol his front. On April 4, Grant was thrown from his horse and severely bruised; nevertheless, late on the 5th, he went to Savannah to meet Buell.

Meanwhile, on March 2, Johnston was reinforced by a division under General Beauregard, and on the 29th by another under General Bragg. Finding himself at the head of 45,000 troops, he determined to strike at Grant before Buell could join him.

On April 4 he moved out of Corinth hoping to fall upon Grant the following morning and drive him into the Tennessee; but his troops straggled so badly that he was unable to deliver his attack until the 6th.

Early that day he launched the attack which became known as the Battle of Shiloh. It was a complete surprise. The forward Federal divisions were routed, thousands of men falling back on the Landing, where a scene of pandemonium greeted Grant when he arrived from Savannah at 6 A.M.

It was a spectacle of complete defeat, and any ordinary general would forthwith have ordered a withdrawal. But Grant was no ordinary general; he was one of those rare men who are fortified rather than depressed by disaster. At once he sent forward ammunition, organized reserves, and then rode to the front. Johnston was killed at 2.30 P.M., by which hour the Confederate reserves were practically exhausted.

On the 7th the battle was renewed. When Beauregard, now in command of the Confederates, decided to retire, Grant did not pursue. This was his cardinal mistake, but the truth is, as Sherman replied to John Fiske when asked why there was no pursuit: "I assure you, my dear fellow, that we had quite enough of their society for two whole days, and were only too glad to be rid of them on any terms." The losses were heavy—13,573 Federals and 10,699—probably more—Confederates.

On April 11, Halleck himself arrived at Pittsburg Landing, and there assembled an army of over 100,000 men. On the 30th he moved on Corinth, occupying it on May 30th, having taken exactly thirty-one days to march twenty-one miles!

He made Grant his second-in-command, deprived him of all power over his men, and treated him in so intolerable a manner that he asked to be relieved of his duties in the field. Halleck agreed, whereupon Grant established his now emasculated headquarters at Memphis. There he was when, on July 11, came the "crowning mercy" for the North. McClellan's campaign against Richmond having failed, Lincoln called Halleck to Washington and appointed him general in chief of the entire land forces of the United States! Meanwhile, on June 10, Buell had set out on his march to Chattanooga.

Grant was still in command of the Department of West Tennessee; his forces, numbering some 46,000 men, were nominally in reserve should Buell require them. He had learned much while in disgrace. He had had two months wherein to think things over, and there can be little doubt that during this dismal period he analyzed his own mistakes, learned many lessons from them, and began to elaborate that strategy which was to win the war.

Watching the summer slip by, he grew fretful, and, on July 30, asked Halleck's permission to move against Van Dorn, then at Holly Springs and Grand Junction. Eventually Halleck agreed, and on September 18 and October 2–6 Grant won two brilliant engagements over his enemy at Iuka and Corinth.

The Battle of Memphis, won by Admiral Davis on June 6, 1862, had gained for the Federal cause the command of the upper Mississippi, and the occupation of New Orleans by General Butler on May 1, had opened the mouth of that same river. Now Grant's victory at Corinth, compelling the Confederates to retire southward, unbarred the way to

Vicksburg, the strongest point left on the Mississippi and the main link between the Confederate states west and east of that river. Halleck should have advanced on Vicksburg in June. Grant understood this, and three weeks after the Battle of Corinth he wrote as follows to him:

You never have suggested to me any plan of operation in this department . . . With small reinforcements at Memphis I think I would be able to move down the Mississippi Central road and cause the evacuation of Vicksburg.

On November 6, Halleck approved of this advance, and promised to send Grant 20,000 reinforcements.

At the time Grant received this encouraging news, the position which confronted him was as follows: Bragg, who had replaced Beauregard in June, now was opposing Buell in East Tennessee. Buell's danger lay in the exposure of his right flank, for even if he gained Chattanooga, a turning movement from the West—that is from Northern Alabama— might easily drive him out of that town. Grant saw that his projected campaign depended on Buell's advance, and that Buell's advance depended for its security on his own army moving south on Vicksburg, for by such a move he would draw Confederate reinforcements away from Buell. Realizing that he and Buell must co-operate, he therefore asked Halleck to inform him of the exact situation. The only answer he received was: "Fight the enemy when you please!"

On the Southern side, Bragg had succeeded Beauregard on June 27, and had found the bulk of his army at Tupelo. By that time Buell's van had reached Decherd, some thirty miles north of Bridgeport. There, on July 13, Forrest raided his communications at Murfreesboro and forced him to halt. Bragg, therefore, determined to regain East Tennessee by invading Middle Tennessee and Southern Kentucky. His plan was a bold one—to reinforce Kirby Smith at Cumberland Gap and direct him on to Louisville—Buell's base of operations—while he himself advanced from Chattanooga.

Once again a raid, this time at Gallatin, on the railway between Nashville and Bowling Green, compelled Buell to halt; whereupon Kirby Smith, advancing from Cumberland Gap, pushed back the weak enemy forces confronting him, and, on September 2, established his headquarters at Lexington, from where he threatened Louisville and Cincinnati. Meanwhile Bragg moved to Sparta; and Buell concentrated his army at Murfreesboro. A race north followed, Buell falling back on

Bowling Green and Bragg advancing to Glasgow. Next, instead of forcing Buell further back and bringing Kirby Smith down on his rear, Bragg cast all strategy aside, and decided to join up with Kirby Smith, not to fight a battle, but to inaugurate a secessionist state capital at Frankfort! Thus Buell was saved, and fell back on Louisville.

On October 1 he moved out of Louisville. Sending a small force toward Frankfort in order to protect his left flank, he advanced on Bardstown. This compelled Bragg to fall back, and, on September 8, an encounter took place at Perryville. Not wishing to risk a battle against numerically superior forces, Bragg withdrew into East Tennessee. On October 30, Buell—who had fallen into Halleck's disfavor—was replaced by General William S. Rosecrans, his Army of the Ohio being renamed the Army of the Cumberland.

The winter having now set in, Rosecrans decided not to advance south until he had repaired the railroads and re-established his depots. This accomplished, on December 26 he moved out of Nashville to be confronted by Bragg at Murfreesboro. There, on the last day of the year, a sanguinary battle was fought. Though its results were indecisive, Bragg's losses were so heavy that he decided on a withdrawal to Chattanooga, where he went into winter quarters.

Sometime before this, General John A. McClernand, one of Grant's subordinates and a political soldier, had brought pressure to bear on Washington to place him in command of a force to be collected at Memphis, from where he intended moving down the Mississippi and operating against Vicksburg. Hearing of this proposal, and believing that McClernand was unfit for an independent command, Grant decided to hasten forward an operation he was then preparing. On November 13 he had informed Halleck that his cavalry had entered Holly Springs, but that he did not intend to move further south until his line of communications was in working order. Now he decided to move as soon as possible; to send Sherman by river from Memphis to Vicksburg while he advanced from Grand Junction. In short, his plan was to draw General Pemberton, then in command at Jackson, toward Grenada, and by thus weakening the Confederate forces at Vicksburg facilitate Sherman's attack.

By December 12, when Grant was sixty miles south of Grand Junction, Sherman set out at the head of 32,000 men and landed them at Milliken's Bend on Christmas Day. On December 29 he fought the battle of Chickasaw Bluff and was repulsed. On January 2, McClernand

—who ranked him—arrived at Milliken's Bend and took over command of the expedition.

As Grant moved southward his supply difficulties increased. Being a general who realized the importance of supplies, he established a depot at Holly Springs, informing Halleck that, on account of his long line of communications, he would not be able to advance beyond Grenada until reinforced. Meanwhile Jefferson Davis, becoming thoroughly alarmed, appointed General Joseph E. Johnston to command all the Confederate forces distributed between the Blue Ridge Mountains and the Mississippi River. Arriving at Chattanooga, Johnston ordered Bragg to send out a force of cavalry to fall upon Grant's communications. Carrying out these orders, on December 20 Van Dorn made a dash for Holly Springs, surprised its garrison, and destroyed the depot.

This raid completely upset Grant's plan. Fearing McClernand's incompetence, he asked Halleck for authority to retire on Memphis and take command of the river expedition. This request being granted, on January 10, 1863, he returned to Memphis, and, on the 30th, arrived at Young's Point, at the mouth of the Yazoo River. There he took over command from McClernand.

CHAPTER VIII

THE VICKSBURG CAMPAIGN AND THE
BATTLE OF CHATTANOOGA, 1863

BECAUSE Vicksburg lay on the left bank of the Mississippi, its capture demanded that Grant should establish a base of operations on that bank either to the north or south of the fortress. Although from the first he was fully aware of the superiority of the southern approach, he could not attempt it until the winter rains were ended and the floods had subsided. But neither could he stand still, for the political conditions in the North were so precarious that he had to do something.[1] He was therefore compelled, as he says, to carry out "a series of experiments to consume time, and to divert the attention of the enemy, of my troops, and of the public generally." And further: "I myself never felt great confidence that any of these experiments resorted to would prove successful. Nevertheless I was always prepared to take advantage of them in case they did."[2]

The more important moves attempted were the opening up of the Yazoo Pass, the approach by way of Steel's Bayou and Deer Creek, the digging of a canal from the Mississippi to Lake Providence, and the opening up of Roundaway Bayou to the southwest of Milliken's Bend.

These various operations I do not intend to examine. All were extremely difficult, entailed immense labor, and though all failed in their object, undoubtedly provided admirable training for Grant's army.

On January 11, the day after Grant took over command, General James H. Wilson proposed to Rawlins, Grant's chief of staff, "to ignore all the canal schemes; run the gunboats and transports by the batteries under the cover of darkness; march the troops overland to the

258

bank of the river below; and then use the fleet for transferring them to the east side of the river at the first point where they could find a safe landing with a dry road to the highlands back of it; that accomplished, to march inland, scatter the enemy, and take Vicksburg in rear." [3]

Rawlins explained this scheme to Grant, and, though Sherman considered it impracticable, Grant gave no indication whether he was for or against it. The truth is that he could not afford to take risks; he could not afford even to agree that it was the only sound scheme and the one he intended to adopt directly the floods began to subside. He could not do so, because this was not so much Wilson's plan as his own,[4] and should Pemberton learn that he intended to adopt this line of advance, then most certainly he would prepare to meet it. All this bayou warfare, and some of it was quite desperate, was a gigantic bluff to deceive the enemy, to deceive the politicians, and to deceive his own troops, so that, when he moved, Pemberton might be surprised.

In the West, clamors were raised against Grant's slowness; his soldiers, it was rumored, were dying by thousands of swamp fever, and as Badeau writes: "He was pronounced utterly destitute of genius or energy; his repeatedly baffled schemes declared to emanate from a brain utterly unfitted for such trials; his persistency was dogged obstinacy, his patience was sluggish dullness." [5] Yet he had one friend who unfailingly supported him, a man he had as yet never met—Lincoln. When urged to recall him, the president would turn round and earnestly reply: "I can't spare this man; he fights." [6]

By the end of March the political necessity for an advance on Vicksburg had become paramount, and, as the waters on the Louisiana bank of the Mississippi began to recede, Grant decided to move his army south of the fortress. On April 4 he wrote to Halleck as follows:

There is a system of bayous running from Milliken's Bend, and also from near the river at this point [Young's Point] that are navigable for barges and small steamers, passing around by Richmond to New Carthage. The dredges are now engaged cutting a canal from here into these bayous. I am having all the empty coal and other barges prepared for carrying troops and artillery, and have written to Colonel Allen for some more, and also for six tugs to tow them. With them it would be easy to carry supplies to New Carthage and any point south of that. My expectation is for a portion of the naval fleet to run the batteries of Vicksburg, whilst the army moves through by this new route. Once there, I will move either to Warrenton or Grand Gulf, most probably the latter. From either of these points there are good roads to Vicksburg, and from Grand Gulf there is a good road to Jackson and the

Black River Bridge without crossing Black River . . . I will keep my army together, and see to it that I am not cut off from my supplies, or beat in any way, than in fair fight.[7]

When this plan became known to his subordinate commanders, Sherman, McPherson, and Logan opposed it, Sherman asserting that the

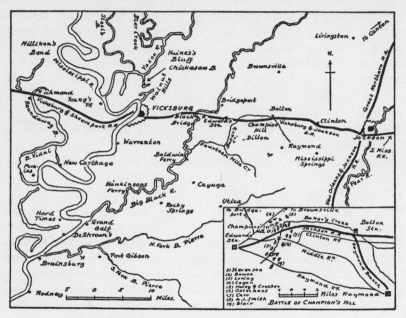

21. Map of the Vicksburg Campaign, 1863

only way to take Vicksburg was from the north, which meant a return to Memphis. But Grant saw that the political situation permitted no turning back. Though he had under his command some 97,000 officers and men,[8] only 51,000 were in the neighborhood of Vicksburg. They were organized in three corps, each approximately 17,000 strong— the Thirteenth under McClernand, the Fifteenth under Sherman, and the Seventeenth under McPherson. Opposed to Grant was General John C. Pemberton with an equal number [9] distributed as follows: 13,000 at Vicksburg, 4,000 about Haines's Bluff, 9,000 between Vicksburg and Port Gibson, 5,000 at Jackson, 10,000 in the state of Mississippi, and 11,000 at Port Hudson.

On April 6, New Carthage was occupied by McClernand's corps, followed by McPherson's and eventually by Sherman's. But in order to mystify the enemy, Steele's division of Sherman's corps was sent 150 miles upstream to march through the Deer Creek country and lay waste the land, while Colonel Grierson at the head of 1,800 cavalry was sent on a 600-mile raid through the state of Mississippi with a similar object.[10]

These two feints completely bewildered Pemberton, who reported to Richmond that the enemy was in constant motion, that Grant's principal effort was directed against Deer Creek, and that the rumors of troops having moved south along the western bank of the Mississippi were not to be believed.

On the night of the 16th, Admiral Porter ran a convoy of river steamers towing barges, escorted by seven ironclads, past the Vicksburg batteries. On the 20th the final orders for the move south were issued, McClernand's corps forming the right wing, McPherson's the center, and Sherman's the left wing. Two days later a second convoy loaded with rations successfully passed the batteries.

On the 24th, Grant reconnoitered Grand Gulf, and four days later McClernand's corps was assembled at Perkin's plantation, from where on the 29th it was moved by transport to Hard Times. There it was landed and re-embarked in readiness to move over to Grand Gulf. Porter then opened fire on the batteries. Finding that the bombardment had little effect, Grant decided to reland his troops and move the transports past the batteries under cover of night. Early on the morning of the 30th, McClernand's corps and one division of McPherson's re-embarked at De Shroon's and landed on the eastern bank of the river at Bruinsburg. Meanwhile Sherman with Blair's division and eight gunboats made a vigorous demonstration against Haines's Bluff in order to distract Pemberton.

When this landing was effected, Grant writes:

"I felt a degree of relief scarcely ever equalled since. Vicksburg was not yet taken it is true, nor were its defenders demoralized by any of our previous moves. I was now in the enemy's country, with a vast river and the stronghold of Vicksburg between me and my base of supplies. But I was on dry ground on the same side of the river with the enemy. All the campaigns, labors, hardships and exposures from the month of December previous to this time that had been made and endured, were for the accomplishment of this one object." [11]

Four months of ruse and feints, of wrestling with swamps, bayous, and forests, of labors seldom equaled in war, were the mist which covered this landing. Pemberton had been completely misled. His forces were concentrated between Grand Gulf and Haines's Bluff; his left flank was but lightly guarded, and was turned by the first flight of the invading army. By 2 A.M. on May 1, McClernand's leading division had advanced eight miles east of Bruinsburg. There it came into contact with the enemy, who attempted to hold up Grant's advance on the Bayou Pierre until reinforcements could arrive from Vicksburg. But this was a vain hope, for the Battle of Port Gibson opened at dawn, and resulted in the turning of the Confederates' right flank. Thereupon they retired northwards, with McPherson in pursuit. On the 3d he drove the enemy forces over the Big Black River, with the result that Grand Gulf, now threatened in rear, had to be evacuated. A bridgehead thus secured, Grant moved forward his depots from Bruinsburg to Grand Gulf.

Grant was now faced by a problem almost unique in the history of war. He was operating in a hostile country with his enemy's main forces located between his base of supply at Memphis and his base of operations at Grand Gulf. Though the fleet commanded the Mississippi, his line of supply was no certain one since every convoy had to pass the Vicksburg batteries. Vicksburg was not only exceedingly strong, but was connected by railroad with Jackson—an important junction forty-five miles to its east—and therefore, could be rapidly reinforced. There was also the danger that, should the Confederates concentrate an army at Jackson, Grant might be caught between two fires.

Though Pemberton was greatly outnumbered, according to all the rules of war his position was by no means hopeless: his enemy was operating in hostile country, and presumably would have to make large detachments in order to protect his line of supply. Furthermore, the country was broken and wooded, and therefore admirably suited to defensive warfare. To hold Grant at Vicksburg while forces were concentrating at Jackson did not appear to Pemberton to be a difficult task.

Grant's problem was the reverse, in fact it would be difficult to devise a more desperate one. The whole of his strategy pivoted on the question of supply. At first he proposed [12] sending 15,000 men to co-operate with General Banks against Port Hudson, with the object of capturing that place and then shifting his base of supply from Memphis to New Orleans. But when informed that Banks could not begin to move until May 10,[13] appreciating the importance of the time factor, he says: "I therefore determined to move independently of Banks, cut loose from my base, destroy the rebel forces in rear of Vicksburg and invest or capture the city." [14] In brief—to attack the enemy in rear. Simultaneously, by cutting loose from his base he protected himself against an attack in rear by leaving himself without a rear to be attacked. This decision completely bewildered Pemberton, who, failing to grasp the audacity of Grant's strategy, and not believing that he would dare to advance without first securing his communications, based his own operations on the assumption that so bold a plan was impossible.

Besides the strategical soundness of Grant's decision, so long as his army could be fed, the political situation demanded that not a minute should be lost. The battle of Chancellorsville had just been fought, and were Grant not to act at once, he ran every chance of being recalled and his army of being broken up, for Washington had been thrown into a panic by Lee's bold maneuver. As it was, directly Halleck learnt of his move,[15] he at once sent him orders to return and co-operate with Banks. Fortunately for Grant, as there was at this time no telegraph line in operation south of Cairo, this order did not reach him until after his movement had begun; consequently he could not obey it. "Had the general-in-chief, however, been able to reach his subordinate, the Vicksburg campaign would never have been fought." [16]

Grant's position at this moment was indeed unusual. He was opposed—so he calculated at the time—by a force double his own. He knew that the government, reeling under Hooker's defeat at Chancellorsville, must be aghast at the news that he was not only about to plunge into the wilds of the Mississippi, but to cut loose from his communications in the face of two hostile armies, one pivoted on a powerful fortress and the other on an important railroad junction. His army was without proper transport; ". . . the ammunition train was a curious assemblage of fine carriages, farm waggons, long coupled waggons with racks for carrying cotton bales—every vehicle, indeed, that could be found on the plantations which had been used either for work or pleasure. These vehicles were a nondescript outfit, drawn by oxen and mules, wearing plough harness, or straw collars and rope lines." [17]

On April 29, Grant had ordered Sherman to cease his demonstration against Haines's Bluff, and to march with all haste to Hard Times. On May 3 he directed [18] him to organize a supply train of 120 vehicles, and ferry them over to Grand Gulf, where they were to be loaded with 100,000 rations from the transports. This would give five days' rations for Sherman's corps, and two days' for McClernand's and McPherson's,[19] which had already three days' rations with them. These were all the rations Grant intended to carry.

Sherman expostulated. It seemed to him quite impossible to supply the army over a single road. He urged Grant to "stop all troops till your army is partially supplied with waggons, and then act as quickly as possible, for this road will be jammed, as sure as life."[20] To this Grant replied: "I do not calculate upon the possibility of supplying the army with full rations from Grand Gulf. I know it will be impossible without constructing additional roads. What I do expect is to get up what rations of hard bread, coffee, and salt we can, and make the country furnish the balance."[21]

What did Grant plan, once he was on dry ground at Port Gibson? His obvious course would have been to have marched direct upon Vicksburg. He was but twelve miles from Warrenton, and the sole formidable obstacle which lay across his path was the Big Black River. A *bon général ordinaire* would undoubtedly have moved north; not so Grant. He knew that a Confederate force under Gregg—of what strength he was uncertain—was collecting toward the east and northeast of Vicksburg. Were he himself to advance on Vicksburg, this force would certainly move there also and he might be outnumbered. So, instead, he decided not to push in between the two armies before they could co-operate, but to move against Jackson in order to draw the Confederate forces east of Vicksburg toward that all-important junction, defeat them in its vicinity before Pemberton could sally out of his fortress, and then destroy the railroad at Jackson. By doing this he would not only protect his rear when the time came for him to advance against Vicksburg, but he would simultaneously cut Vicksburg off from its base of supply. In short, his idea, rather than plan, was to maneuver against the Vicksburg line of communications in order to isolate the fortress, and simultaneously destroy that force of the enemy which was so placed that it could operate against his rear.

Success, however, depended not so much on the boldness of this idea, as upon the rapidity of its execution. Since Napoleon exclaimed, "It may be that I shall lose a battle, but I shall never lose a minute," no man has understood better than Grant the value of time. His dispatches teem with indications of this. Here are a few examples: To Sherman, on May 3, he wrote: "It is unnecessary for me to remind you of the overwhelming importance of celerity in your movements."[22] To Hurlbut, on the 5th: "Send Lauman's division to Milliken's Bend . . . Let them move by brigades, as fast as transportation can be gotten." [23] To the commissary at Grand Gulf: "There must be no delay on account of either lack of energy or formality," load up "regardless of requisitions or provision returns." To an officer of his staff: "See that the commissary at Grand Gulf loads all the wagons . . . Issue any order in my name that may be necessary to secure the greatest promptness in this respect . . . Every day's delay is worth two thousand men to the enemy." And again on the 6th: Rush "forward rations with all dispatch . . . How many teams have been loaded with rations and sent forward? I want to know as near as possible how we stand in every particular for supplies. How many wagons have you ferried over the river? How many are still to bring over? What teams have gone back for rations?" [24]

Grant's tremendous energy electrified his men, until activity became universal. McPherson was pushed up to Hankinson's Ferry to protect the left flank; reconnaissances were sent out daily to examine the roads and country, and foraging parties swarmed over the cultivated areas collecting supplies.

Grant's plan was to keep the Big Black on his left, or strategic, flank, using it as a shield; to advance Sherman's and McClernand's corps under cover of it to the Vicksburg-Jackson railway between Edward's Station and Bolton, while McPherson's corps was to move by way of Utica to Raymond and thence on to Jackson.

On the 7th the move forward began. On the 12th Sherman and McClernand reached Fourteen Mile Creek, and McPherson, encountering Gregg's brigade two miles west of Raymond, drove it back, and bivouacked on the outskirts of the town. Grant now had gained the position he wanted; his left flank rested on the Big Black, and his right was secured by Gregg's defeat.

Although to Pemberton Grant's move south was not altogether unexpected it would seem that he believed it to be no more than another feint. Hearing that Grant had landed, on May 1 he telegraphed Johnston for reinforcements.[25] Johnston ordered him to unite all his troops against Grant, while Jefferson Davis, believing that the movement was nothing more than a raid,[26] instructed him to hold on to Vicksburg and Port Hudson. These orders were contradictory, and as Pemberton was under the impression that Grant must, within a few days, fall back in order to replenish his supplies, he was inclined to follow the second.

He decided, therefore, to hold the line of the Big Black so that, when the opportunity arose, he could fall upon Grant's (nonexistent) line of supply, and keep open the Vicksburg-Jackson railway—his own line of communications.

On the 3d, Pemberton assembled the bulk of his forces between Vicksburg and the Big Black. On the 11th he ordered Gregg, if attacked, to retire toward Jackson, but should Grant move on Edward's Station, to fall upon his flank and rear. On the 12th, as we have seen, Gregg was compelled by McPherson to adopt the first course. The next day Pemberton ordered three divisions—Bowen's, Loring's, and Stevenson's—to advance on Edward's Station on the following day. At the same time Johnston arrived at Jackson from Tullahoma, found the railway occupied by Sherman, and telegraphed to Richmond—"I am too late." [27] Then he ordered Pemberton to attack Grant in rear. "I have arrived," he wrote, "and learned that Major-General Sherman is between us . . . It is important to re-establish communications that you may be reinforced. If practicable, come up on his rear at once. The troops here could co-operate . . . Time is all important." [28] Pemberton, still of opinion that Grant must fall back were he to strike at his line of supply, set aside Johnston's order, informing him that, early on the 17th, 17,000 men would move on Dillon's: "The object is to cut the enemy's communications and force him to attack me . . ." [29]

Meanwhile, on the 12th, McPherson's corps was ordered to move on Clinton to destroy the railway, whilst Sherman and McClernand converged on Raymond. These movements were preparatory to the occupation of Jackson; for as Grant says: "As I hoped in the end to besiege Vicksburg, I must first destroy all possibility of aid. I therefore determined to move swiftly towards Jackson." [30] During the night of the 13th and on the morning of the 14th it rained in torrents, nevertheless Grant pushed on at top speed.

On the 14th, McPherson moved from Clinton toward Jackson, and Sherman from Mississippi Springs toward the same spot; McClernand protecting the rear of these two divisions by sending a brigade to Clinton and by occupying Raymond. The attack on Jackson was at first delayed by the rain, because it was feared that ammunition might be spoilt if the men opened their cartridge boxes.[31] At 11 A.M. the battle opened, and at 4 P.M. the town was carried.

Forced out of Jackson, Johnston withdrew up the Canton road, and, on the 15th, wrote to Pemberton as follows: "The only mode by which we can unite is by your moving directly to Clinton, informing me, that we may move to that point with about 6,000." [32]

At this time the situation of the Confederate forces was ludicrous: Johnston was moving north to unite with Pemberton, and Pemberton was moving east and southeast from Edward's Station to cut Grant's imaginary communications. On the night of the 14th, Pemberton had 9,000 men about Vicksburg, which was not threatened, and some 14,000 were moving on Edward's Station; Johnston—now near Calhoun—headed 12,000, with 10,000 reinforcements on their way to join him. Thus we see 45,000 men in three detachments faced by an equal force, concentrated and ready to strike at any one in overwhelming strength. Pemberton, who, on the night of the 15th, had arrived in the neighborhood of Raymond, there received Johnston's second order to unite with him. Fearing to disobey it, he abandoned his attack on Grant's line of communications and decided to turn north.

Unfortunately for both Johnston and Pemberton, Johnston's dispatch of the 13th was carried by three separate messengers, one of whom happened to be a Federal soldier enlisted in the Confederate army. This man took his copy to General McPherson, who forwarded it to Grant on the evening of the 14th. Assuming that Pemberton would obey the order contained in it, and that he was now moving from Edward's Station to unite with Johnston, Grant at once issued orders for the 15th: McPherson to move back to Bolton, "and make all dispatch in getting there"; Sherman's corps, less Blair's division, to remain at Jackson, and destroy the railways.[33] By the evening Grant had concentrated in all about 32,000 men between Bolton and Raymond, and that night he opened his headquarters at Clinton.

Early on the 16th, Pemberton informed Johnston that, as he considered he could not move on Clinton, he would return to Edward's Station and take the Brownsville road. Meanwhile Grant, learning from two men employed on the Vicksburg-Jackson railroad that Pemberton with some 25,000 men had marched eastward the night before, ordered up Steele's division of Sherman's corps, which was on the road within an hour. McPherson's corps, on the right, he directed to advance by the Clinton road on Champion's Hill; and McClernand's corps, on the left, to move by the Middle and Raymond roads on Edward's Station. By 7.30 A.M., skirmishing having begun, Grant rode forward and joined McPherson's corps, and later on he ordered McClernand to push forward and attack.

Pemberton's position was a strong one. Not only did his front command the three roads along which Grant's leading divisions were advancing, but his left was protected by Champion's Hill and Baker's Creek, as well as by a number of precipitous ravines, woodland, and much undergrowth, "difficult," as Grant says, "to penetrate with troops even when not defended." This difficulty soon became apparent. An examination of it is illuminating, for it explains why so many opportunities were lost a year later in the Wilderness of Virginia.

Though Smith's division on the Raymond road was the first to encounter the enemy, its advance was painfully slow. Osterhaus's, on the Middle road, did no better. These divisions were confronted by a well-placed but weak force, and had McClernand ordered a charge, he would have cleared his front in a few minutes. The ground was, however, thickly wooded, and not being able to ascertain the strength of the enemy, he groped his way forward with extreme caution. Throughout the day he never made his strength felt. Meanwhile, on the right, Hovey's division had become closely engaged, and to protect its right flank, Logan's division was pushed beyond it to attack Champion's Hill from the north. Still pressed in front, Hovey was reinforced by Crocker.

The situation was now as follows: Hovey, in spite of Crocker's assistance, could make little impression on Champion's Hill; on Hovey's left, McClernand, failing to assault, in no way restricted the enemy's freedom of movement. Logan, although neither he nor Grant were aware of it, had worked his way behind the enemy on Champion's Hill and was actually in line parallel to their rear, and in command of the only road by which Pemberton could retreat. At the same time, a brigade of McArthur's division, which a few days before had crossed over to Grand Gulf, was coming up on McClernand's left flank. Thus, although Grant had not realized it, Pemberton's army was to all intents and purposes surrounded when Hovey once again called for reinforcements. Grant, fearing that his front might be broken, ordered McPherson to disengage part of Logan's division and move it round to Hovey's support. The assault which was then made was successful principally because the enemy's line of retreat was now opened. Grant at once sent forward Osterhaus's and Carr's divisions in pursuit, ordering them to push on to the Big Black, and to cross that river if they could. That night McPherson's command bivouacked six miles west of the battlefield, and Carr and Osterhaus at Edward's Station. The losses in this battle were as follows: Grant's army, 2,438 and Pemberton's, 4,082.[34]

Defeated at Champion's Hill, Pemberton abandoned his intention to move north and unite with Johnston. It is true that he could no longer move by the Brownsville road, but he could have retired under cover of darkness across the Big Black, burned the bridges and, abandoning Vicksburg, have saved his army by moving north and then east toward Canton. Instead, he fell back on the Big Black and reported to Johnston that he had about sixty days' rations in Vicksburg, but that, when Grant advanced, he would be compelled to abandon Haines's Bluff. Johnston replied: "If it is not too late, evacuate Vicksburg and its dependencies, and march to the north-east." [35] This message was received by Pemberton at noon on the 18th. He at once assembled a council of war which decided that as Vicksburg was "the most important point in the Confederacy," it could not be abandoned.[36]

Early on the 17th, Grant continued his pursuit, and about midday, he broke the Confederate line. For the Confederates, as Pemberton says: "It very soon became a matter of *sauve qui peut.*" [37] His army greatly demoralized, he withdrew to Vicksburg.[38] Many stragglers had already made their way there; the bridge over the Big Black was burned and Haines's Bluff was abandoned.

On the morning of the 18th, Sherman, making use of the sole pontoon train in Grant's army, crossed the Big Black at Bridgeport, and that night, accompanied by Grant, reached Walnut Hill. The true goal of the campaign was won—namely, high, dry ground free from enemy interference, upon which a supply base could be established. Turning to Grant, Sherman exclaimed: "Until this moment, I never thought your expedition a success. I never could see the end clearly, until now. But this is a campaign; this is a success, if we never take the town." [39] Indeed, it was an amazing success, the greatest in Grant's life, and from a strategical point of view one of the greatest in military history.

Handing Haines's Bluff over to the navy, Grant at once re-established his line of supply. He then issued orders to carry the fortress by storm at 2 P.M. on the 19th, "relying," as he says, "upon the demoralization of the enemy in consequence of repeated defeats outside of Vicksburg." [40] The assault failed, however, for though during the last two days the Confederates "had run like sheep . . . now they were in intrenchments which had been prepared long before . . . they felt at home. Their demoralization was all gone. . . ." [41] There was every excuse for the failure of this first assult, but there was little or none for the failure of the second. Of it Grant says: "The attack was ordered to commence on all parts of the line at ten o'clock A.M. on the 22d with a furious cannonade from every battery in position. All the corps commanders set their time by mine so that all might open an engagement at the same minute." [42] Every possible preparation was made, and it might have succeeded had Grant concentrated on one point instead of ordering an assault all along the line.

Suddenly . . . as if by magic every gun and rifle stopped firing. . . . The silence was almost appalling, at the sudden cessation of the firing of as many field guns [about 180], and the crackling of so many thousands of sharpshooters' rifles. But the silence was only for a short time. Suddenly, there seemed to spring almost from the bowels of the earth, dense masses of Federal troops, in numerous columns of attack, and with loud cheers and huzzahs, they rushed forward, at a run with bayonets fixed, not firing a shot, headed for every salient advanced position along the Confederate lines . . . As they came within easy range (almost as soon as they started) the Confederate troops, not exceeding 9,938 men, along the 3½ miles of assault, deliberately rose and stood in their trenches, pouring volley after volley into the advancing enemy; at the same time the troops in reserve advanced to the rear of the trenches, and fired over the heads of those in the trenches. Every field gun and howitzer belched forth continuously and incessantly double-shotted discharges of grape and canister . . .[43]

This description of the assault, written by General S. D. Lee, speaks for itself. It failed, because it was launched on so wide a front that no concentrated covering fire could support it. Unfortunately McClernand, believing that his troops had gained a secure footing in the enemy's entrenchments, sent urgent appeals to Grant for aid. Then a second assault was ordered, which failed as disastrously as the first.

As the fortress could not be stormed, Grant resorted to siege tactics. The entrenched camp of Vicksburg was some four miles in length and two in breadth, its outer line of works extending over seven miles. Grant's lines were twice as long. Moreover, he had to prepare his rear against attack, because Johnston was assembling a powerful army in the neighborhood of Canton. On May 29, Grant informed Halleck that unless Banks could come to his assistance, large reinforcements would be required. These demands were promptly met by the general in chief, and a month later Grant's army numbered 71,141 men and 248 guns.[44]

The siege was prosecuted methodically. A line of circumvallation was dug from Haines's Bluff to Warrenton, and one of contravallation from the Yazoo to the Big Black River. This latter line was held by Sherman and some 30,000 men.

On July 3, at 10 A.M., white flags appeared on the Confederate works, and an aide-de-camp crossed over to the Federal lines bearing a letter from Pemberton asking for an armistice. Grant sent in reply a demand for "unconditional surrender." When Pemberton refused, Grant modified his demand to a surrender on terms. There were several reasons for this. In the first place, had he insisted upon unconditional surrender, the prisoners could not have been paroled and would have had to be transported to Cairo at much inconvenience to the army. Secondly, the moral effect of a surrender on July 4 [45] could not fail to be of enormous political significance.

At 10 A.M. on Saturday, July 4, the garrison of Vicksburg, some 31,000 men in all, stacked their arms in front of their conquerors. Laying their colors upon the heaped-up arms, they returned to the town—and proceeded to fraternize with the Federal soldiers.

On July 1, Johnston and 27,000 men were encamped between Brownsville and the Big Black. On the 4th, immediately after Pemberton's surrender, Sherman, at the head of 40,000 men, moved out against him. Two days later he crossed the Big Black. Johnston retired to Jackson, hoping that the scarcity of water would compel his antagonist to make an assault, but evacuated it on the 16th. Sherman decided not to follow up his retreating enemy, as he would have to cross ninety miles of waterless country. Therefore on the 25th he returned to Vicksburg.

The losses in this campaign are instructive, because quite unjustly Grant came down in history as a butcher. Since April 30 he had won five battles, had taken Vicksburg, and had occupied Jackson at a cost to himself of 1,243 killed, 7,095 wounded, and 535 missing, a total of 8,873 casualties. [46] He had killed and wounded about 10,000 Confederates, and had captured 37,000; [47] among these were 2,153 officers including 15 generals. Also, 172 cannon fell into his hands.

The disparity between the losses of the contending forces was entirely due to Grant's strategy. Founding his plan on surprise, and accepting risks which surprise alone justified, in the first eighteen days after he crossed the Mississippi, he defeated his enemy at Port Gibson, established a temporary base at Grand Gulf, marched 200 miles, and won the battles of Raymond, Jackson, Champion's Hill, and the Big

Black River—these four within a space of six days. During the whole of this period his men had but five days' rations, and for the rest had to live upon the country. Well may Greene say: "We must go back to the campaigns of Napoleon to find equally brilliant results accomplished in the same space of time with such small loss." [48]

At 7 A.M., on July 9, Port Hudson surrendered unconditionally to General Banks, and a week later "the steam-boat *Imperial* quietly landed at the wharf in New Orleans, arriving direct from St. Louis, laden with a commercial cargo, having passed over the whole course of that great thoroughfare of commerce undisturbed by a hostile shot or challenge from bluff or levee on either side." [49] The South had been cleft; Vicksburg and not Gettysburg was the crisis of the Confederacy.

Two days after this event, Grant suggested to Halleck that an expedition should set out from Lake Pontchartrain with the object of taking Mobile.[50] Operations from that point against the rear of Bragg's army, he thought, might induce him to detach troops from Chattanooga and so facilitate a Federal advance on that town. As an alternative Grant suggested an advance through Georgia in order to lay waste the country from which Lee in Virginia was drawing most of his supplies. Though he repeated this proposal during August and September, Halleck would not listen to it, because, for purely political reasons, Lincoln had set his mind upon two projects. The first was the reopening of trade in the conquered Mississippi territories, and the second the occupation of Texas, which was threatened by the machinations of Louis Napoleon of France. On October 11, Halleck wrote to Grant saying: "I regret equally with yourself that you could not have forces to move on Mobile, but there were certain reasons which I cannot now explain, which precluded such an attempt." [51]

The Mobile operation forbidden, Grant's magnificent army was broken up. The Ninth Corps was sent to Kentucky; 4,000 men to Banks in Louisiana, 5,000 to Schofield in Missouri; a brigade to Natchez, while the remainder was employed in the thankless task of hunting down guerrilla bands.[52] On August 7, Grant was instructed further to deplete his army by sending the Thirteenth Corps to General Banks. To arrange this move he went to New Orleans, where he met with a serious accident, his horse shying at a locomotive and throwing him. Then, on September 13, he received an urgent telegram from Halleck ordering him to send all "available forces to Memphis and thence to Corinth and Tuscumbia, to co-operate with Rosecrans." [53]

When Grant was operating against Vicksburg, he was anxious that Rosecrans, whom we left at Murfreesboro, should advance against Bragg in order to prevent him from reinforcing Johnston. One June 3, Burnside with the Army of the Ohio, who was to advance from Lexington, Kentucky, and co-operate with Rosecrans, was ordered to send large reinforcements to Grant. Thus it was not until June 23 that Rosecrans resumed his long-interrupted move against Bragg, Burnside advancing on Knoxville on August 16. Thereupon Bragg evacuated Tullahoma on July 1, and crossed the Tennessee. Once Burnside was in a position to co-operate, Rosecrans decided to feint at Bragg's right and cross the Tennessee below Chattanooga. Bragg was completely deceived by this maneuver, and, on September 9, Rosecrans took possession of the town.

Thus far Rosecrans's strategy left nothing to be desired, but thinking that Bragg was in full retreat, he pushed on in pursuit, and with his army in no way prepared to offer battle he suddenly found himself confronted by a concentrated enemy. In order to extricate himself, on September 19–20 he was compelled to fight the battle of Chickamauga,[54] in which he was badly beaten and saved from complete destruction only by the gallant defensive action of General Thomas—the "Rock of Chickamauga." Retiring on Chattanooga, he abandoned Lookout Mountain which commanded the town. This battle was one of the most bloody of the war; 55,000 to 60,000 Federals met from 60,000 to 70,000 Confederates, the former losing 16,336 and the latter 20,950 in killed, wounded, and missing.[55] At Chattanooga, Rosecrans was besieged.

This disaster awoke Lincoln from his dreams of campaigning in Texas and of peaceful trading, to the immense strategical importance of Chattanooga, where Rosecrans was now locked up. Hitherto the Departments of the Tennessee, Cumberland, and Ohio had been commanded respectively by Grant, Rosecrans, and Burnside, and Halleck at Washington was incapable of establishing co-operation between them. Now they were fused into the Military Division of the Mississippi.

On September 29, Halleck telegraphed Grant to send all possible reinforcements to Rosecrans, and on October 3 he wrote: "It is the wish of the Secretary of War that, as soon as General Grant is able to take the field, he will come to Cairo and report by telegraph." [56] To which Grant, still crippled, replied from Columbus: "Your dispatch of the 3rd, directing me to report at Cairo, was received at 11.30 A.M. the 9th inst. I left same day with my staff and headquarters, and have just

reached here, *en route* for Cairo." [57] From Cairo he was ordered to
Louisville, and on his way there, at Indianapolis, he met Stanton
"pacing the floor rapidly in his dressing-gown." Stanton at once placed
him in command of all troops between the Alleghanies and the Mississippi—a course suggested by Grant nearly a year before.

Grant at once assumed command, and having assigned the Department of the Cumberland to General Thomas, on the 19th he set out by
rail for Chattanooga. The last forty miles of this journey had to be
made on horseback. General Howard tells us that "at times it was
necessary to take the General from his horse. The soldiers carried him
in their arms across the roughest places. Yielding to no weakness or
suffering, he pushed through to Chattanooga, reaching General Thomas
the evening of October 23rd." [58]

Before Thomas took command, the condition of the Army of the
Cumberland could be described only as deplorable. Rosecrans had quar-
reled with Halleck, and now occupied an all but untenable position.
His back was against the Tennessee River, his left rested on Citico
Creek, his front faced Missionary Ridge,[59] which rose to a height of
some 300 to 400 feet above the plain. This ridge was separated from
Lookout Mountain, on his right, by the Rossville Gap, through which
ran Chattanooga River. This mountain, 2,400 feet high, dominated the
town of Chattanooga and the railway which ran thence up Lookout
Valley to Decatur and Trenton. The Confederate entrenchments began on the north end of Missionary Ridge, ran along the ridge, spanned
Chattanooga Valley, and ended on Lookout Mountain. The importance
of this mountain lay in the fact that it commanded the railway. It had
been abandoned by Rosecrans because he considered that his weakened
army was not strong enough to hold it. General William F. Smith is
of opinion that he was right in abandoning it, for had he not done so
he would have "diminished his force in the front by about 8,000." Personally,[60] I consider either that Lookout Mountain should have been
held or Chattanooga evacuated, because to remain there with the mountain in the hands of the enemy was to risk not only the loss of the
town, but also the loss of the army. Colonel Livermore supports me in
this, giving it as his opinion that Rosecrans abandoned the mountain
only because he exaggerated Bragg's strength. On October 1, Bragg
had 41,972 [61] men on a line seven miles long, and Rosecrans 38,928,[62]
"equal to 6,500 men per mile of a possible line of six miles from Citico
Creek across the point of Lookout Mountain to Lookout Creek."

Further, he says: "The example of the Confederate defence for six weeks of seven miles of intrenchments at Vicksburg five months before with 22,000 effectives against a force as large as, or greater than Bragg's . . . would have amply justified Rosecrans in the attempt to hold the line from Citico to Lookout Creek." [63]

Although he lost his railroad communications, which on September 30 were raided by Wheeler and his cavalry, who destroyed 400 wagons with their loads and teams [64]—a crippling blow to the transportation of the army—Rosecrans made no efforts to run boats down the river. There were two steamers at Chattanooga, which could have brought up 200 tons of supplies daily from Bridgeport to a point near Williams Island, whence the wagon haul was but four or five miles to the town.[65] Instead, supplies were hauled over a circuitous and mountainous route north of the river, a distance of sixty to seventy miles. The result was that neither could the troops be properly rationed nor the animals fed. Boynton says: "Thousands of horses and mules . . . died from want of food. There were Brigade headquarters where the officers lived chiefly on parched corn, there were regimental headquarters where the daily food was mush or gruel; there were officers of high rank, who lived for days on sour pork and wormy mouldy bread." [66] This statement is corroborated by General Smith and by Grant.[67] The latter informs us that nearly 10,000 horses and mules died, and "not enough were left to draw a single piece of artillery or even the ambulances to convey the sick . . . the beef was so poor that the soldiers were in the habit of saying . . . that they were living on 'half rations of hard bread and beef dried on the hoof.' " [68]

It would be difficult to find a more perfect example of an army paralyzed by the inefficiency of its commander, who, in this case, had completely collapsed under the shock of defeat. Dana, writing to the War Department on October 16, said: "Nothing can prevent the retreat of an army from this place within a fortnight . . . General Rosecrans seems to be insensible to the impending danger, and dawdles with trifles in a manner which can scarcely be imagined . . . all this precious time is lost because our dazed and mazy commander cannot perceive the catastrophe that is close upon us, nor fix his mind upon means of preventing it. I never saw anything which seemed so lamentable and hopeless." [69] Such was the state of affairs when Grant arrived at Chattanooga on the evening of October 23.

Grant's immediate problem was to establish a workable line of supply. He at once saw that the key to it lay in securing command of Lookout Valley. Had Bragg grasped that this valley was the key to Chattanooga he would have held it in force, as well as the passes over Raccoon Mountain. Grant's problem would then have been an impossible one to solve.

Hooker was then at Bridgeport, where Rosecrans, on October 1, had ordered him to bridge the river. To bring him forward was useless unless a footing could be gained on the left bank of the Tennessee near Brown's Ferry and the enemy driven from the hills commanding that point. On the 19th, General Smith had reconnoitered Brown's Ferry, and had come to the conclusion that it was the most suitable place at which to cross the river. Immediately after his arrival on the 23d, Grant approved of Smith's scheme, and on examining the ferry the following morning he decided to force a crossing on the 27th.

At 3 A.M. that day 1,500 men under the command of Smith left Chattanooga in fifty-two boats, hugging the right bank until they reached a signal light indicating the point at which they were to cross the river and land. The men then bent to their oars, landed, and rushing the weak Confederate pickets occupied the hills on the left bank and entrenched them. So thoroughly was this work done that at 3.30 P.M. Smith was able to telegraph General Thomas's chief of staff : "This place cannot be carried now." [70] In this way was Chattanooga saved at a cost of four men killed and seventeen wounded.

That night Hooker's advanced guard entered Lookout Valley, and at 3 P.M. on the 28th the head of the main body reached Wauhatchie. At 11 P.M. General Thomas telegraphed Halleck that "the wagon-road is now open to Bridgeport. We have, besides two steam-boats, one at Bridgeport and one here, which will be started tomorrow . . . By this operation we have gained two wagon-roads and the river to get supplies by, and I hope in a few days to be pretty well supplied . . ." [71] Thus, within five days of Grant's arrival at Chattanooga, the road to Bridgeport was opened, and within a week the troops were receiving full rations, were being reclothed and resupplied with ammunition, "and a cheerfulness prevailed not before enjoyed in many weeks. Neither officers nor men looked upon themselves any longer as doomed." [72]

On the night of the 28th–29th, Longstreet made a night attack on Hooker at Wauhatchie which was easily repulsed. The Federals were assisted by their mules which took fright and stampeded toward the enemy, who in their turn broke and fled, imagining that a cavalry charge was upon them. By 4 A.M. on the 29th the battle was over, and the "Cracker Line" was never again disturbed. [73]

Having secured a workable line of supply, Grant's next task was to bring up Sherman's corps from Corinth. On October 27 "a dirty black-haired individual, with a mixed dress and strange demeanour" approached Sherman's house in Iuka. It was Corporal Pike, who had paddled down the Tennessee under the enemy's fire, with a message to Sherman ordering him to move with all possible haste to Bridgeport. Acting upon these instructions, Sherman arrived at Bridgeport on November 13. Meanwhile Burnside's position at Knoxville was causing high alarm in Washington, and Grant was plied with dispatch after dispatch urging that action be taken to relieve the presure on him.

Longstreet had quarreled with Bragg, and either to put an end to this bad feeling, or believing that Longstreet could move on Knoxville—a hundred miles away—destroy Burnside, and withdraw to Chattanooga before Grant was ready to attack, President Davis instructed Bragg to send him to Knoxville. Longstreet set out on November 4. Grant, hearing of this on the 7th, ordered [74] Thomas to attack Bragg and so force Longstreet to return. Thomas replied that he could not comply with this order as he was unable to move a single piece of artillery. Grant then directed him to take "mules, officers' horses, or animals wherever he could get them." [75]

Thomas, much perturbed by this order, rode out on the 7th with General Smith to examine the approaches leading from the mouth of the South Chickamauga toward Missionary Ridge. On this reconnaissance Smith pointed out to Thomas that the ground lent itself to a turning operation against Bragg's right flank. If successful, such a move would not only threaten his rear, but separate him from Longstreet in East Tennessee. On their return they informed Grant of their conclusions, whereupon he at once countermanded his order. [76]

Having studied this new proposal, Grant ordered Smith to explore the country and to prepare bridging material for a second bridge at Chattanooga, or at Brown's Ferry, as well as a bridge across the South Chickamauga. On the 14th, Grant informed [77] Burnside that Sherman would cross South Chickamauga Creek in a few days' time, and that a general attack would then be launched on Bragg. Two days later Grant took Thomas, Smith, and Sherman out to a position overlooking the mouth of the creek. Sherman, after carefully examining the ground, shut up his long glass with a snap and said—"I can do it." [78]

Grant's idea was to effect a double envelopment with the forces under Sherman and Hooker pivoted on Thomas's army. Sherman was to attack Bragg's right, envelop it, and threaten or seize the railway in Bragg's rear. This would compel Bragg either to weaken his center, or lose his base at Chickamauga Station.[79] Hooker was to advance from Lookout Valley to Chattanooga Valley, move on Roseville, and threaten Missionary Ridge from the left. Thomas was to hold the center, move forward in conjunction with Sherman, obliquing to the left in order to form a continuous battle front. [80]

Grant's main difficulty was that from Lookout Mountain and Missionary Ridge Bragg could watch every move that took place in or around Chattanooga. Therefore, in order to mislead Bragg and convince him that Grant's intention was to attack his left, Sherman was ordered to cross the river at Bridgeport, move his leading division by the Trenton road, and then throw some troops onto Lookout Mountain. (This move was effected and a brigade was encamped on the mountain on the on the 18th.) [81] Sherman's remaining forces were to take the Brown's Ferry road, move towards South Chickamauga Creek as if their intention were to advance on Knoxville, and then hide themselves in the hills opposite the mouth of the creek, where they could not be observed from Lookout Mountain. One brigade of this force was to move on to the North Chickamauga, where 116 pontoons were in readiness to be floated down the river in order to effect a landing on the left bank. "All things," said Sherman, were "prearranged with a foresight that elicited my admiration." [82]

These movements partially misled Bragg, and had not the rain and the shocking state of the roads delayed Sherman, they might well have completely succeeded. At 9.45 P.M. on the 20th, Hardee, in command of Bragg's left, ordered the passes over Lookout Mountain to be blocked and said to a subordinate commander: "Direct your advanced brigade to make obstinate defense, so as to give time to send reinforcements. Be constantly on the alert. General Bragg is under conviction that a serious movement is being made on our left." [83] Unfortunately for Grant, Sherman's command was not ready to cross on the night of the 22d,[84] and on the afternoon of the 21st the march of his division from Trenton toward Wauhatchie was observed. The result was that, on the afternoon of the following day, Bragg began to move troops to his right. [85]

On the night of the 22d, a deserter came into the Federal lines and reported that Bragg was falling back. His story was that two divisions had been sent toward Sherman, who was expected to attack Steven's Gap—over Lookout Mountain—and that the greater part of Bragg's army was massed between his headquarters and the mountain. This move—assuming the information to be correct—fell in exactly with Grant's plan of drawing Bragg away from the point selected for Sherman's attack. Whether he realized this at the time is unknown, but he had received news [86] that Knoxville had been attacked and as he was being appealed to daily by the authorities in Washington to do something to assist Burnside, he apparently thought that Bragg's move was a ruse to cover the sending of more troops to Knoxville. Furthermore, on the 20th he had received the following cryptic message from Bragg: "As there may still be some non-combatants in Chattanooga, I deem it proper to notify you that prudence would dictate their early withdrawal." [87] Grant knew that this letter was meant to deceive him, but coupling it with the information furnished by the deserter, his anxiety about Knoxville, [88] as well as the fact that Sherman could not cross the Tennessee until the night of the 23d–24th and that the flooded river was threatening destruction to the bridges, he ordered [89] Thomas to make a reconnaissance in force on the morning of the 23d in order to verify Bragg's position. This was done, Thomas moving forward and establishing his lines parallel to Bragg's, within a mile of the western flank of Missionary Ridge. This movement materially changed the task allotted to Thomas in Grant's order of the 18th; [90] also it awoke Bragg to the danger threatening his right flank. On the night of the 23d, Bragg ordered Walker's division to move from near Lookout Mountain to Missionary Ridge, [91] and a brigade to occupy a position near the mouth of the South Chickamauga. [92]

By the night of the 23d Sherman's command, with the exception of Osterhaus's division which was still west of Brown's Ferry was ready to move. Osterhaus was ordered to report to Hooker should he not be able to cross by 8 A.M. on the 24th. At midnight Sherman's landing force, under General Smith, advanced downstream from the North Chickamauga. At two o'clock the following morning a landing was effected near the mouth of the South Chickamauga, when the work of ferrying over Sherman's infantry at once began. By daylight two divisions had crossed. A bridge, 1,350 feet in length was then thrown over the Tennessee and another across the South Chickamauga, and a brigade of cavalry was moved over under orders to proceed to the vicinity of Charleston and destroy the railroad.

At 1 P.M. Sherman began his advance in three divisional columns with the left leading and covered by the South Chickamauga, while the right was echeloned back in order to refuse that flank. At 3.30 P.M. the heads of the columns reached a detached hill north of Missionary Ridge, where Sherman, instead of pushing on to the tunnel, ordered his division to halt and entrench for the night. "This," General Smith, among others, proclaims, "was the blunder of the battle." [93]

For a moment I will examine Sherman's problem, for although it has been debated by several historians, in my opinion it has not been very carefully analyzed.

The date was November 24; therefore by half-past four it would be getting dark. Throughout the day drizzling rain fell, and the clouds were low. [94] Even before four o'clock it was so dark on Lookout Mountain that Hooker had to suspend his advance. [95] Though we are told that the whole of Sherman's cavalry was over both bridges by 3.30 P.M.,[96] we are not told when his artillery began to cross. However, it could not have been much before 2 P.M.—probably later—because during the night of the 23d–24th, Thomas, having no artillery horses, had to borrow Sherman's in order to move forward forty guns of the Army of the Cumberland on the north side of the Tennessee "to aid in protecting the approach to the point where the south end of the bridge was to rest." [97]

In short, Sherman's position seems to have been as follows: Tunnel Hill was one and a half miles away; visibility was poor; night was approaching, and only part of his artillery was up. Should he decide to advance to the tunnel, which might, so far as he knew, be strongly held, he could not arrive there until dark. Once there, his right flank would be a mile and a half to two miles from Thomas's left flank, and well in advance of it. If attacked in flank, he risked being rolled up and thrown back into the South Chickamauga. In any case, in the dark, he would have found it extremely difficult to select a tactically sound position to entrench. I do not say that he should not have risked an advance, yet I do consider that these circumstances should be carefully weighed before Sherman is condemned. In my opinion, Sherman's blunder was not that he halted where he did, but that apparently he did not make it clear to Grant that he was not on the northern end of Missionary Ridge, because that night Grant wrote to Thomas saying: "General Sherman carried Missionary Ridge as far as the tunnel with only slight skirmishing. . ." [98]

While Sherman was advancing, Thomas stood fast. Brown's Ferry bridge broke before Osterhaus's division could cross over, and at 12.30 A.M. on the 24th, Thomas, under instructions from Grant, ordered Hooker to "take the point of Lookout." [99]

Early on the 24th, Hooker advanced. Working his way through the mist, he climbed the mountain as far as the base of the "upper palisade," that is, to the foot of the precipitous wall of rock which tops the mountain. During the night he worked forward small parties of sharpshooters who drove the enemy off the summit. "Just before sunrise a group of soldiers stepped out on the rock which forms the overhanging point of the mountain. They carried a flag but held it furled, waiting for the sun. The instant the rays broke full upon them they loosened its folds, and the waiting thousands below beheld the stars and stripes." [100]

That evening Grant reported his position to Washington, and the following day he received replies from both Lincoln and Halleck. The former bade him "Remember Burnside" and the latter answered: "I fear that Burnside is hard pushed, and that any further delay may prove fatal," which was scarcely encouraging, and shows how persistently Grant was pressed to move.

A little after midnight he ordered [101] Sherman to advance as soon as it was light and to Thomas he wrote: "Your attack, which will be simultaneous, will be in co-operation. Your command will either carry the rifle-pits and ridge directly in front of them, or move to the left, as the presence of the enemy may require." [102] Further: "If Hooker's present position on the mountain can be maintained with a small force, and it is found impracticable to carry the top from where he is, it would be advisable for him to move up the valley with the force he can spare and ascend (i.e., to the top of Lookout Mountain) by the first practicable road." [103] Obviously "top of Lookout Mountain" was a slip for "top of Missionary Ridge," [104] and Thomas, recognizing this, at 10 A.M. on the 25th ordered Hooker to march "on the Rossville road towards Missionary Ridge," [105]—that is toward its southern extremity. A little later on, Grant, who then was with Thomas at Orchard Knob, decided that Thomas should not move forward with Sherman but wait until Hooker had reached Missionary Ridge [106]—obviously in order to take advantage of Hooker's success of the 24th, were it followed by an equal success this day.

One of the results of Thomas's reconnaissance of the 23d was that Bragg moved a division from Lookout Mountain to Missionary Ridge. Although this move facilitated Hooker's advance, it was destined to delay Sherman's. On the morning of the 23d, Cleburne's division and one brigade of Buckner's were at Chickamauga Station en route to join Longstreet.[107] Immediately after Thomas attacked, Bragg ordered Cleburne to place his division immediately in rear of Missionary Ridge. Early on the 24th, as Sherman was still crossing the Tennessee, Bragg ordered Cleburne to send a brigade to the East Tennessee and Georgia railroad bridge over the South Chickamauga in order to protect his line of retreat. Next, at 2 P.M., he ordered him to move his remaining three brigades to the northern end of Missionary Ridge, near the railway tunnel, and "preserve the bridge in [his] rear at all hazards." [107] Actually, when Sherman arrived at the position he occupied on the night of the 24th–25th, Cleburne had only one brigade entrenched between him and the tunnel.[108] On the morning of the 25th, Cheatham's division and a brigade from Stevenson's arrived from Lookout Mountain, the rear of Stevenson's division not coming up until later in the day. [109]

The morning of the 25th was clear and bright, and consequently Grant from Orchard Knob had a full view of the left of the battlefield. Sherman advanced at daylight as ordered, and after a two hours' contest, Grant from his observation post saw "column after column of Bragg's forces moving against him." Thereupon he ordered Thomas to send Baird's division to reinforce Sherman, but it turned out that it was not required. Simultaneously "Bragg at once commenced massing in the same direction." [110] "This," says Grant, "was what I wanted. But it had now got to be late in the afternoon, and I had expected before this to see Hooker crossing the ridge in the neighbourhood of Rossville, and compelling Bragg to mass in that direction also." [111]

Meanwhile Sherman could not understand what was delaying Thomas's advance. At 12.45 P.M. he asked, "Where is Thomas?" [112] To which Thomas replied: "I am here, my right is closing in from Lookout Mountain toward Missionary Ridge." [113] Grant was still holding Thomas back, for the circumstances of battle had compelled him to modify his original plan. Sherman having been checked, there was now little hope left of turning Bragg's right; but directly Hooker turned Bragg's left, Bragg would be compelled to denude his center in order to reinforce his left. This was the movement Grant was waiting for before he launched Thomas against the enemy's weakened center.

Hooker had advanced early on the 25th, but the retiring Confederates had burned the bridge over Chattanooga Creek. This delayed his crossing for several hours and resulted in his not reaching Rossville Gap until after 3 P.M. When he did, he carried it immediately and swept on to Missionary Ridge. He did not, however, report his success to Thomas.

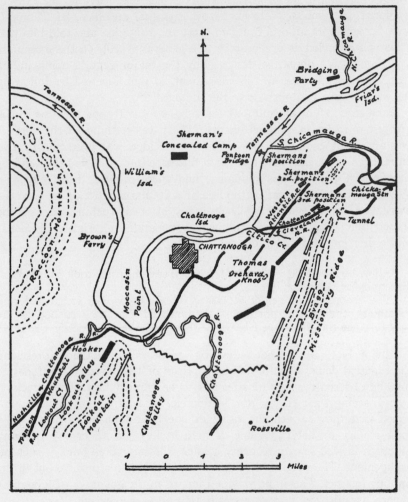

22. Battle of Chattanooga, November 23–25, 1863

As Grant considered that Sherman's position was critical, at 3.30 P.M. he ordered Thomas to advance and carry the "rifle pits" at the foot of the ridge. [114] This, considered in connection with Grant's instructions issued to Thomas a little after midnight on the 24th, was obviously to be the first step toward carrying the ridge itself. In spite of the quibbles raised over this order by a number of historians, and more particularly by General Smith, the *Official Records* of the war leave its meaning in no doubt. General Baird in his report says that an officer of Thomas's staff brought him an oral order to carry the rifle pits, and told him that "this was intended as preparatory to a general assault on the mountain, and that it was doubtless designed by the major-general commanding that I should take part in this movement, so that I would be following his wishes were I to push on to the summit." [115]

Dana says: "The storming of the ridge by our troops was one of the greatest miracles in military history." [116] It was nothing of the sort; it was an act of common sense. Missionary Ridge was protected by two entrenched lines, each held by men at one pace intervals, and the artillery fire from the ridge was plunging, and therefore not fully effective. When the first line—that is, the line of rifle pits mentioned by Grant—was taken, its defenders fell back, many of them rushing through the second line. General Manigault, who commanded a brigade of Hindman's division (Confederate) says:

"All order was lost, and each striving to save himself took the shortest direction for the summit . . .
"The troops from below at last reached the works exhausted and breathless, the greater portion so demoralized that they rushed to the rear to place the ridge itself between them and the enemy." [117]

Obviously Grant intended the ridge to be taken, but not foreseeing the eventual demoralization of the garrison of the forward Confederate line, he ordered the line of rifle pits to be carried first. The attacking troops, seeing their enemy run, instinctively ran after him; thus it happened that they carried the ridge in one bound instead of two. The impossibility of holding a line of men back when an enemy is flying before it is well known to every soldier who has taken part in such an engagement. The continued advance was not due to a miracle but to the fighting instinct. This in no way detracts from the gallantry of Thomas's superb assault, yet it does explain it.

This charge having succeeded, Hooker's advance, which had already made itself felt, proved the decisive act of the battle. Shattered in front, Bragg could not possibly meet this flank attack. Instead of winning the battle with his left, as originally intended, Grant won it with his right. That he should have done so after having made the mistake of ordering a reconnaisance by Thomas on the 23d does not reflect adversely on his generalship; instead it shows that his plan and distribution were flexible —that is, that they could be adapted to changing circumstances.

The pursuit was at once taken up but abandoned on the 28th, for Grant's immediate problem was the relief of Burnside. On the 29th, having ascertained that Bragg was in full retreat, Grant ordered Sherman to march on Knoxville. [118] Sherman arrived there on December 6, to find that Longstreet had raised the siege on the 4th and retired to the Holston Valley. On the 30th, Grant moved his headquarters to Nashville, leaving Thomas in command of the sally port—now firmly in Federal hands.

In this battle Grant's losses were 5,815 men out of a total force of about 60,000.[119] Bragg, who after Longstreet's departure had no more than 33,000 troops in line, lost 6,175 stands of arms, 40 guns, and 5,471 prisoners. [120] His killed and wounded numbered about 3,000.

REFERENCES

[1] Lincoln and Halleck were urging him on. See *The War of the Rebellion, Official Records*, vol. XXXVI, p. 10.

[2] *Personal Memoirs of U. S. Grant*, vol. I, p. 446.

[3] Letter of General Wilson, October 31, 1911, quoted by Colonel W. B. Livermore in *The Story of the Civil War*, Pt. III, Bk. I, p. 234.

[4] "I had in contemplation the whole winter the movement by land to a point below Vicksburg from which to operate, subject only to the possible but not expected success of some one of the expedients resorted to for the purpose of giving us a different base. This could not be undertaken until the waters receded. I did not therefore communicate this plan, even to an officer of my staff, until it was necessary to make preparations for the start." (Grant's *Memoirs*, vol. I, pp. 460–461.)

[5] *Military History of Ulysses S. Grant*, A. Badeau, vol. I, p. 180.

[6] *Lincoln and Men of War Times*, McClure, p. 179.

[7] *W.R.*, vol. XXXVI, p. 26.

[8] *Ibid.*, vol. XXXVIII, p. 249. As is usual in this war it is most difficult to estimate correct strengths. F. V. Greene in *The Mississippi* (p. 136) estimates Pemberton's force at over 50,000, and states that Grant began his campaign with about 41,000, and at no time prior to the siege had over 45,000. Grant in his *Memoirs* (vol. I, p. 481) says that, on May 7, he had 33,000, and that his enemy had nearly 60,000. In *Battles and Leaders* (vol. III, p. 549), it is stated that Grant's effective force ranged from 43,000 at the opening to 75,000 at the close of the campaign.

[9] *W.R.*, vol. XXXVIII, p. 702.

[10] See Badeau, vol. I, p. 189.

[11] Grant's *Memoirs*, vol. I, pp. 480–481.

[12] *W.R.*, vol. XXXVIII, p. 192.

[13] *Ibid.*, vol. XXXVI, p. 30.

[14] Grant's *Memoirs*, vol. I, pp. 491–492.

[15] According to Grant, Halleck "was too learned a soldier to consent to a campaign in violation of all the principles of the art of war." (*Ulysses S. Grant*, W. C. Church, p. 163. See also Badeau, vol. I, p. 221, and *W.R.*, vol. CIX, p. 406.)

[16] Badeau, vol. I, p. 221.

[17] Church, p. 164.

[18] *W.R.*, vol. XXXVIII, p. 268.

[19] If this is correct, then it would appear that, as Grant says, his total force numbered 33,000: 55,000 rations for Sherman's corps and 22,000 each for the remaining two gives an average corps strength of 11,000 strong.

[20] *W.R.*, vol. XXXVIII, p. 285.

[21] *Ibid.*, vol. XXXVIII, p. 285.

[22] *Ibid.*, vol. XXXVIII, p. 268.

[23] *Ibid.*, vol. XXXVIII, p. 274.

[24] Badeau, vol. I, pp. 223–224.

[25] *W.R.*, vol. XXXVIII, pp. 807, 810, and 817; also *W.R.*, XXXVI, pp. 214 and 259.

[26] *Ibid.*, vol. XXXVI, p. 327.

[27] *The Rise and Fall of the Confederate Government*, Jefferson Davis, vol. II, p. 404.

[28] *W.R.*, vol. XXXVIII, p. 870.

[29] *Ibid.*, vol. XXXVI, p. 262.

[30] Grant's *Memoirs*, vol. I, p. 499.

[31] This was before the introduction of the metallic cartridge case.

[32] *W.R.*, vol. XXXVIII, p. 882.

[33] *Ibid.*, vol. XXXVIII, pp. 310–312.

[34] Livermore, Pt. III, Bk. II, p. 310.

[35] *W.R.*, vol. XXXVI, p. 241, and vol. XXXVIII, p. 888.

[36] *Ibid.*, vol. XXXVIII, p. 890.

[37] *Ibid.*, vol. XXXVI, p. 367.

[38] General Loring's division, unable to cross the Big Black, retreated on Jackson to join up with Johnston.

[39] Badeau, vol. I, p. 281.

[40] *W.R.*, vol. XXXVI, p. 54.

[41] F. V. Greene, p. 170.

[42] Grant's *Memoirs*, vol. I, p. 531.

[43] *Publications of the Mississippi Historical Society*, vol. III, p. 60.

[44] Greene, p. 188.

[45] Pemberton also realized this. He says: "I believed that upon that day I should obtain better terms. Well aware of the vanity of our foes . . ." (*W.R.*, vol. XXXVI, p. 285).

[46] Badeau, vol. I, p. 399. *W.R.*, vol. XXXVII, p. 167 gives—9,362.

[47] *W.R.*, vol. XXXVI, p. 58.

[48] Greene, pp. 170–171. Grant's losses during the first eighteen days were about 3,500.; Pemberton's, 8,000 and 88 guns.

[49] *Abraham Lincoln: A History*, by J. B. Nicolay and J. Hay, vol. VII, p. 327.

[50] *W.R.*, vol. XXXVIII, pp. 529–530.

[51] *W.R.*, vol. LIII, p. 274. These reasons were events in Mexico and the re-establishment of authority in Western Texas.

[52] It must never be overlooked that throughout this war the difficult problem of the guerrilla faced Grant and other Federal commanders. In the east this form of warfare was to a certain extent organized; in the west it was murder, robbery,

and terrorism. When caught, guerrillas were usually shot. General Crook and some cavalry once fell in with a party of twenty guerrillas. He shot twelve and the rest were captured. "He regrets to report that on the march to camp the eight prisoners were so unfortunate to fall off a log and break their necks." This was in Tennessee (*Papers of the Military Historical Society of Massachusetts*, vol. XIV, p. 81—cited as *M.H.S.M.*).

[53] *W.R.*, vol. LII, p. 592.

[54] "The River of Blood"—in Indian.

[55] *Battles and Leaders*, vol. III, pp. 673-676, and *The Army of the Cumberland*, H. M. Cist, p. 228.

[56] *W.R.*, vol. LIII, p. 55.

[57] *Ibid.*, vol. LIII, p. 375.

[58] Church, p. 199.

[59] Called so by the Indians who, in former times, allowed the missionaries to pass no further west. Rossville was named after the Cherokee chief John Ross. Chattanooga is Indian for "The Eagle's Nest."

[60] *M.H.S.M.*, vol. VIII, p. 156.

[61] *W.R.*, vol. LIII, p. 721.

[62] *Ibid.*, vol. LII, pp. 914-915.

[63] *M.H.S.M.*, vol. VIII, pp. 285-286.

[64] *W.R.*, vol. LIII, pp. 114, 231.

[65] *W.R.*, vol. LII, p. 890; vol. LIII, p. 102; and vol. LIV, pp. 67 and 74.

[66] *Sherman's Historical Raid*, by H. V. Boynton, p. 69. This was written in 1875, and it is strange to find this same officer writing in 1892: "At no time did the men suffer, and at no time were the troops of the Cumberland either discouraged or demoralized" (*M.H.S.M.*, vol. VII, p. 381).

[67] *M.H.S.M.*, vol. VIII, p. 167.

[68] Grant's *Memoirs*, vol. II, p. 25, and *W.R.*, LVI, p. 216. See also *Battles and Leaders*, vol. III, p. 719.

[69] *W.R.*, vol. L, pp. 218-219. See also pp. 202, 215.

[70] *Ibid.*, vol. LIV, p. 54.

[71] *Ibid.*, vol. LIV, p. 41.

[72] Grant's *Memoirs*, vol. II, p. 38.

[73] On the 29th, Grant inspected the pickets, and as he was under fire he took only a bugler with him. On passing a post, he heard a soldier shout: "Turn out the guard, for the commanding general." He replied: "Never mind the guard"; barely had he uttered these words, than a little way off a Confederate sentry called out: "Turn out the guard for the commanding general—General Grant!" Grant saluted and rode on—truly a picturesque war.

[74] *W.R.*, vol. LVI, p. 634.

[75] *Ibid.*, vol. LVI, p. 73.

[76] *Ibid.*, vol. LV, p. 29, and *Battles and Leaders*, vol. III, p. 716.

[77] *Ibid.*, vol. LV, p. 30.

[78] *M.H.S.M.*, vol. VIII, p. 195, and Grant's *Memoirs*, vol. II, p. 58.

[79] Grant's *Memoirs*, vol. II, p. 55.

[80] *W.R.*, vol. LV, pp. 130, 131, 154, 184, and *Battles and Leaders*, vol. III, p. 716.

[81] *W.R.*, vol. LV, p. 583.

[82] *Ibid.*, vol. LV, p. 571.

[83] *Ibid.*, vol. LV, p. 668.

[84] Originally ordered for the 21st, see *ibid.*, vol. LV, p. 31.

[85] *Ibid.*, vol. LV, p. 671.

[86] *Ibid.*, vol. LVI, p. 206.

[87] *Ibid.*, vol. LV, p. 32.

[88] Grant says: "Hearing nothing from Burnside [the telegraph was cut], and hearing much of the distress in Washington on his account I could no longer defer operations for his relief. I determined, therefore, to do on the 23rd, with the Army of the Cumberland, what had been intended to be done on the 24th" (Grant's *Memoirs*, vol. II, p. 62).

[89] *W.R.*, vol. LV, p. 32.

[90] *Ibid.*, vol. LV, p. 31.

[91] *Ibid.*, vol. LV, p. 718.

[92] *Ibid.*, vol. LV, pp. 745–746.

[93] *M.H.S.M.*, vol. VIII, pp. 202 and 228.

[94] Grant's *Memoirs*, vol. II, p. 68.

[95] *Ibid.*, vol. II, p. 72.

[96] *Ibid.*, vol. II, p. 69.

[97] *Ibid.*, vol. II, p. 66.

[98] *W.R.*, vol. LV, p. 44.

[99] *Ibid.*, vol. LV, p. 106.

[100] *M.H.S.M.*, vol. VII, p. 391. See also *W.R.*, vol. LV, p. 122.

[101] *W.R.*, vol. LV, p. 40.

[102] *Ibid.*, vol. LV, p. 44.

[103] *Ibid.*, vol. LV, p. 44.

[104] See footnote *M.H.S.M.*, vol. VIII, p. 232, and Grant's *Memoirs*, vol. II, p. 75.

[105] *W.R.*, vol. LV, p. 115.

[106] Grant's *Memoirs*, vol. II, p. 75, and *W.R.*, vol. LV, pp. 34, 96, 112, and 113.

[107] *W.R.*, vol. LV, p. 745.

[108] *M.H.S.M.*, vol. VIII, p. 205.

[109] *W.R.*, vol. LV, pp. 701, 726.

[110] *Ibid.*, vol. LV, p. 34.

[111] Grant's *Memoirs*, vol. II, p. 78.

[112] *W.R.*, vol. LV, p. 44.

[113] *Ibid.*, vol. LV, p. 44.

[114] *Ibid.*, vol. LV, p. 34. Thomas, always slow, delayed to do so, and nearly an hour later Grant himself ordered the advance (Grant's *Memoirs*, vol. II, p. 79).

[115] *W.R.*, vol. LV, p. 508. See also *Battles and Leaders*, vol. III, pp. 724–726, for Brigadier General Joseph E. Fullerton's account.

[116] *W.R.*, vol. LV, p. 69.

[117] *Military Memoirs of a Confederate*, by E. P. Alexander, p. 478.

[118] On the 27th, Grant instructed Thomas to send Granger's corps to Knoxville. On the 29th, finding that it had not yet started, he sent Sherman instead (Grant's *Memoirs*, vol. II, pp. 90–92).

[119] *Battles and Leaders*, vol. III, p. 711.

[120] H. M. Cist, p. 258.

1863–1864

SYNOPSIS OF BACKGROUND EVENTS

G RANT'S victory at Chattanooga opened the road to Atlanta— the back door of Lee's army in Virginia. Of his plans for the future, he wrote:

I expected to retain the command I then had, and prepared myself for the campaign against Atlanta. I had great hopes of having a campaign made against Mobile from the Gulf. I expected after Atlanta fell to occupy that place permanently, and cut off Lee's army from the west by way of the road running through Augusta to Atlanta and thence southwest. I was preparing to hold Atlanta with a small garrison, and it was my expectation to push through to Mobile if that city was in our possession; if not, to Savannah; and in this manner to get possession of the only east and west railroad that would then be left to the enemy.

On December 7, from Chattanooga he set this plan before Halleck, writing as follows:

. . . I take the liberty of suggesting a plan of campaign that I think will go far towards breaking down the rebellion before spring . . .
I propose, with the concurrence of higher authority, to move by way of New Orleans and Pascagoula on Mobile. I would hope to secure that place, or its investment, by the last of January. Should the enemy make an obstinate resistance at Mobile, I would fortify outside and leave a garrison sufficient to hold the garrison of the town, and with the balance of the army make a campaign into the interior of Alabama and possibly Georgia. The campaign, of course, would be suggested by the movements of the enemy. It seems to me that the move would secure the entire State of Alabama and Mississippi and a part of Georgia, or force Lee to abandon Virginia and North Carolina. Without his force the enemy have not got army enough to resist the army I can take . . .

On the 21st, Lincoln agreed to this plan, but only on the proviso that Longstreet should first be ejected from Tennessee. Grant, realizing that, because of the severity of the winter a direct advance against Long-street was out of the question, decided to move Sherman on Meridian. On January 15, 1864, he informed Halleck that Sherman was then concentrating at Vicksburg, that he would move on Meridian and thoroughly destroy the railways, after which he would return "unless opportunity of going into Mobile with the force he has, appears perfectly plain." In this same letter he wrote:

I look upon the next line for me to secure to be that from Chattanooga to Mobile; Montgomery and Atlanta being the important intermediate points. To do this, large supplies must be secured on the Tennessee river, so as to be independent of the railroads from here [Nashville] to the Tennessee for a considerable length of time. Mobile would be a second base. The destruction which Sherman will do to the roads around Meridian will be of material importance to us in preventing the enemy from drawing supplies from Mississippi and in clearing that section of all large bodies of rebel troops. I do not look upon any points except Mobile in the south, and the Tennessee river in the north, as presenting practicable starting points from which to operate against Atlanta and Montgomery.

Thus was outlined the idea which, as we shall see in the next chapter, was carried out by Sherman in his grand wheel against Lee's rear.

A copy of this letter was sent to Sherman, and, on January 19, Grant informed Thomas that he was to co-operate in this movement, and that he particularly wanted him "to keep up the appearance of preparation for an advance from Chattanooga."

In short, Grant was preparing to cast his net over an area a thousand miles in extent. Thomas, in the center, was confronted by Joseph E. Johnston, who had relieved Hardee, who in turn had relieved Bragg. Schofield, now in command of the Department of the Ohio, was holding Longstreet in East Tennessee. Sherman was about to move out of Vicksburg eastward through Mississippi and Alabama, and by threatening Johnston's rear while Thomas operated against his front, compel the Confederate government to call upon Longstreet to evacuate East Tennessee, and come to Johnston's assistance.

A prettier piece of strategy has seldom been devised. Not only would it force the Confederates to evacuate East Tennessee, but it would also prepare the way for an eventual move against Mobile, Montgomery, and Atlanta from the west.

On February 3, Sherman set out from Vicksburg, General William Sooy Smith and 7,000 cavalry having on the 1st been ordered to advance from Memphis and join him at Meridian. However, Smith, an indifferent soldier, delayed his move until the 11th, and failing to accomplish his task, turned back on the 22d. On the 14th, Sherman entered Meridian. He so completely destroyed the railroad there that when Hood cut loose from Atlanta in the autumn, he was detained in Florence-for nearly a month, wagoning his supplies round the breaks. This delay enabled Thomas to collect his scattered forces and destroy him at Nashville.

This raid caused great excitement throughout the Confederacy. Troops were sent from Mobile and from Johnston's army to bring Sherman to book. But Sherman, not waiting for their arrival, fell back and reached Canton on the 28th.

On the 12th, Thomas was ordered to make a reconnaissance in force toward Dalton, but the usual delays followed and he did not leave Chattanooga until the 22d. Longstreet having fallen back, Schofield followed him up, but the roads were so bad that he was unable to proceed far. Such was the situation which faced Grant in the West, when, on March 3, he was called to Washington to replace Halleck as commander in chief.

CHAPTER IX

THE ATLANTA CAMPAIGN AND THE
BATTLE OF NASHVILLE, 1864

HAVING arrived in Washington, on March 9 Grant received his commission as lieutenant general, a grade restored by Congress on February 26, and on the following day he went to the front. From that date until May 4, when he crossed the Rapidan, he had approximately eight weeks wherein to examine the political and military situation in the East; concentrate large numbers of scattered troops; organize them into a number of powerful armies; distribute them according to the demands of strategy; and elaborate a plan of campaign for all the forces of the Union.

Two circumstances accentuated his difficulties. The first was that he was personally unknown to the Army of the Potomac, to Lincoln, and to most of the politicians at Washington. Secondly, he was to be faced not by a Pemberton or by a Bragg, but instead by Robert E. Lee, who had broken McClellan, Pope, Burnside, and Hooker.

Grant found the Army of the Potomac, under Meade, on the northern bank of the Rapidan facing Lee. On its right, in the Shenandoah Valley, was an army under Sigel, and on its left another under Butler, based on Norfolk. In the West, Thomas with the Army of the Cumberland was at Chattanooga; Sherman, heading the Army of the Tennessee, was moving from Vicksburg to join him, and Schofield, in command of the Army of the Ohio, was still operating against Longstreet in East Tennessee; while an army of some 30,000 men under Banks was moving up the Red River toward Shreveport. All these forces, as Grant said, were acting independently and without concert, "like a balky team, no two ever pulling together." [1]

Though the armies of both sides had now become veteran forces, the politicians had as yet learned little from the war. Not only did they work at cross purposes, but the councils at Washington, as Swinton writes, continued to rule alternately by "an uninstructed enthusiasm and a purblind pedantry." [2] The masses of the people were eager for leadership, and ready to undergo all privations; nevertheless "the politicians feared that strong measures would lose votes, and therefore deemed it a political necessity to coax and bribe men to serve their country instead of compelling their service as a sacred duty." [3] Their fearfulness and lack of policy had so encouraged the peace party in the North that Grant understood that the problems which confronted him were as much political as military. In order to save the North from a moral dry rot, he had not merely to win the war in the most economical way, but to crush the rebellion in the shortest possible time. Therefore he made up his mind to concentrate his forces and develop an unceasing offensive. This demanded unity of direction, and, having been appointed generalissimo, he intended to act as such. Further still, he saw that the fulcrum of his strategy was the fixing of Lee. Therefore he determined, though leaving the detail of executive command to Meade, to become *de facto* commander of the Army of the Potomac.

In this resolution he was firmly supported by Lincoln who, having learned his lesson, said that all he "wanted, or had ever wanted, was someone who would take the responsibility and act." [4]

Lincoln immediately agreed to a rapid reshuffle of commanders. Halleck was to become chief of staff and remain in Washington; Meade to continue in command of the Army of the Potomac; Sherman to take over the Department of the Mississippi, and McPherson to command the Army of the Tennessee. This decided upon, Grant reduced the number of military departments and nominated their commanders. [5] The bulk of the troops, other than those required for protective purposes, he merged into three main armies: the Army of the Potomac, to confront Lee; Sherman's army, to operate against Johnston; and Butler's based on Fort Monroe, to co-operate with Meade and eventually unite with him.

Now that he had established a firm base of operations at Chattanooga and a subsidiary one along the Mississippi, Grant's plan was to fix Lee in Virginia, while Sherman from Chattanooga maneuvered against his rear.

In order to protect Washington, the simplest operation was to place the Army of the Potomac between Lee and the capital. Grant at first favored a coastal movement to the south of the James, but for political reasons he discarded this idea [6] and decided on a direct forward movement. On April 9 he wrote to Meade:

Lee's army will be your objective point. Wherever Lee's army goes, you will go also. The only point upon which I am in doubt is whether it would be better to cross the Rapidan above, or below him . . . [7]

He decided on the second line of advance in spite of the tactical difficulties offered by the Wilderness, because the Federal command of the sea facilitated the supply of Meade's army. Next, turning to his flanking forces, he set Sigel two problems: to operate against the Virginia and Tennessee Railroad, and to menace the Virginia Central at Staunton. Meanwhile Butler was to operate against Richmond and so prevent Lee from reinforcing his army along the Rapidan. Lastly, he turned to the grand maneuver which was to be directed against Lee's rear by Sherman. On this subject he wrote: "There could have been no difference of opinion as to the first duty of the armies of the Military Division of the Mississippi. Johnston's army was the first objective, and that important railroad center, Atlanta, the second." [8] Once Atlanta was occupied, the range of the Alleghanies would be turned. On April 4 he sent the following instructions to Sherman:

You I propose to move against Johnston's army, to break it up, and to get into the interior of the enemy's country as far as you can, inflicting all the damage you can against their war resources. I do not propose to lay down for you a plan of campaign; but simply to lay down the work it is desirable to have done and leave you free to execute it in your own way. Submit to me, however, as early as you can, your plan of operations.[9]

Again on the 18th he wrote to Sherman explaining that, should the two main attacks promise great success, the enemy might abandon one part of his line of defense and seek to unite his forces at some central point, hoping that "the Federal army meeting with no resistance will rest perfectly satisfied with their laurels." Then he added: "But you have had too much experience in traveling light, and subsisting on the country to be caught by any such ruse. I hope my experience has not been thrown away. My directions, then, would be, if the enemy in your front shows signs of following Lee, follow him up to the full extent of your ability." [10]

To assist Sherman, Grant intended to move on Mobile by land, while the navy closed the harbor. From Mobile his idea was to advance northward toward Montgomery, and distract Johnston by threatening his rear, Sherman meanwhile pressing him in front. This part of his general plan depended on whether General Banks—then engaged with 40,000 men on the Red River campaign in Louisiana—would be able to co-operate. Therefore, on March 15, he had written to Banks as follows: "It will, however, be my desire to have all parts of the Army, or rather all armies, act as much in concert as possible . . . I look upon the conquering of the organized armies of the enemy as being of vastly more importance than the mere acquisition of territory." [11] He instructed Banks to take Shreveport as rapidly as possible, after which he was to send Sherman 10,000 men under General A. J. Smith, and to hold 25,000 in readiness to move against Mobile. On the 31st he sent him orders to [12] concentrate the latter force, but on April 8, Banks was attacked and decisively defeated. The result was that Sherman had to face Johnston alone. The interesting point to note is that Banks was to give the same assistance to Sherman which Butler was to give to Meade. While Meade immobilized Lee in order to enable Sherman to maneuver, Butler was to distract Lee, as Banks was intended to distract Johnston, by subsidiary rear maneuvers and attacks. Not often has so perfect a plan of developing mobility from a protected offensive base been devised; for, as Grant said to Meade on April 9: "So far as practicable, all armies are to move together, and towards one common center," [13] the whole pivoting on the Army of the Potomac.

As Grant's Wilderness campaign does not concern us here, suffice it to say that it opened on May 4, and that after six weeks of desperate fighting it resulted in Lee's checking his determined adversary at Old Cold Harbor and compelling him to swing south and cross the James. But, through the bunglings of Grant's subordinates, Petersburg—the key to Richmond—was not occupied. From thence onward until the end of March, the following year, the Army of the Potomac was engaged in siege warfare.

Four days before Grant transferred his headquarters from Chattanooga to Nashville—that is, on December 16, 1863—Jefferson Davis most reluctantly was compelled to order Bragg to turn the command of his army over to General Joseph E. Johnston, [14] whom he not only detested, but consistently impeded. Next, on December 18, he urged Johnston to adopt an offensive policy in combination with Longstreet, then 200 miles away in East Tennessee.[15] This of course was impossible unless reinforcements were sent him, because his army—36,000 strong—was in a shocking condition. The men were dispirited, half naked, and lacked 6,000 rifles; the artillery horses were broken down, the guns mainly too light, and ammunition lacking.

Setting to work, Johnston organized this rabble—the wreckage of Chattanooga—into three corps under Hardee, Hood,[16] and Polk. By the end of April he had succeeded in raising their combined strengths to 43,000 officers and men,[17] and 144 guns. These he posted about Dalton, which lies some thirty miles to the southeast of Chattanooga. The railway from Dalton to Chattanooga runs through the Rocky Face Hills at Mill Creek Gap (also called Buzzard's Roost) by way of Tunnel Hill and Ringgold. This range is flanked on its southwestern extremity by Milk Mountain, which in turn is flanked by Horn Mountain and separated from it by Snake Creek Gap, through which a road ran to Resaca and Calhoun on the Western and Atlantic Railroad.

While Johnston was preparing for the inevitable contest, Sherman relieved Grant and took command of the Military Division of the Mississippi, which embraced the Departments of the Ohio, Cumberland, Tennessee, and Arkansas, respectively commanded by Generals Schofield, Thomas, McPherson, and Steele. This changing brought into full daylight probably the most remarkable of the many remarkable leaders of this war.

William Tecumseh Sherman was born at Lancaster, Ohio, on February 8, 1820, and was now in his forty-fifth year. Entering West Point in 1836, he graduated sixth in order of merit in 1840, and during the Mexican War saw service in California. He was a man of marked individuality and fertile imagination, bold in action and outspoken in speech. Ropes says that "He possessed all the peculiarly American characteristics," [18] and Major George W. Nichols—one of his aides-de-camp—writes of him: "He is a Democrat in the best sense of that word. There is nothing European about him. He is a striking type of our institutions . . ." [19] which I take to mean that he was out and out typical of the new America which at this time was emerging from the chrysalis of the old. He broke away from all the conventions of nineteenth-century warfare, took the public into his confidence, at heart despised the people and above all the popular press, and with steel waged war as ruthlessly as Calvin had done with word.

An imaginative strategist, he was also an imaginative tactician, and

above all a marvelous quartermaster. "No general ever lived," writes
Ropes, "who realized more fully than General Sherman the importance
of knowing just where every pound of beef and every ounce of am-
munition was to come from . . ." [20] And, most fortunately for the
Federal cause, Grant trusted him as completely as he trusted Grant.
They worked together as closely as Marlborough and Eugene.

On April 10 he received Grant's instructions of April 4, and on the
same day answered them as follows: "Your two letters of April 4th
are now before me, and afford me infinite satisfaction. That we are
now all to act in a common plan on a common center, looks like en-
lightened war." [21] The forces at his disposal were as follows: [22]

Army of the Cumberland—Major General Thomas

Infantry	.	.	.	.	.	.	54,568 men	
Artillery	.	.	.	.	.	.	2,377 "	and 130 guns
Cavalry	.	.	.	.	.	.	3,828 "	

Army of the Tennessee—Major General McPherson

Infantry	.	.	.	.	.	.	22,437 "	
Artillery	.	.	.	.	.	.	1,404 "	and 96 guns
Cavalry	.	.	.	.	.	.	625 "	

Army of the Ohio—Major General Schofield

Infantry	.	.	.	.	.	.	11,183 "	
Artillery	.	.	.	.	.	.	679 "	and 28 guns
Cavalry	.	.	.	.	.	.	1,697 "	

To these must be added three cavalry divisions commanded by Generals Stoneman, Garrard, and Kilpatrick, numbering in all 11,326
officers and men. Together with the personnel of the three armies this
made a grand total of 110,123—over twice the enemy's strength.

On April 28, Sherman moved his headquarters to Chattanooga. Six
days later Thomas was established at Ringgold with his left at Catoosa
and his right at Leet's Tan-yard; Schofield was at Red Clay on Thomas's
left, while McPherson was moving into Chattanooga and thence on to
Gordon's Mill.[23]

The theater of war in which Sherman was now called upon to operate
was an exceedingly difficult one, and Johnston had every intention of
using it defensively. Dalton he fortified strongly, as he judged rightly
from the nature of the country that Sherman would be compelled to
advance along the railway. Seeing that Sherman must assume the
offensive, and knowing him to be of an impulsive nature, Johnston

trusted that he would exhaust his strength in useless assaults until such time as he himself was reinforced, when he would be in a position to meet him on more equal terms. In this he was to be disappointed; although Sherman was pre-eminently a fighting general, he was by no means a reckless one. Foreseeing that his communications would absorb many men, Sherman determined not to do what Johnston wished, but instead, by constant maneuvers, to keep a grip on him while Grant was hammering Lee in the East. Therefore he planned that while Thomas and Schofield pinned Johnston to his entrenchments, McPherson should turn his left through Snake Creek Gap, and cut in behind him at Resaca. Should this operation prove successful, the chances were that the campaign would be ended in a single battle.

The idea behind this maneuver must be credited to Thomas, for it was he who suggested it to Sherman some time before the campaign opened. He proposed to march his army through the Gap,[24] and so concentrate an overwhelmingly strong force against Johnston's rear. Sherman, however, seems to have considered so large a force unnecessary; why, it is difficult to say, unless it was that he distrusted Thomas's generalship. Selecting the Army of the Tennessee instead, on May 5 he sent McPherson the following order:

I want you to move . . . to Snake Gap, secure it and from it make a bold attack on the enemy's flank or his railroad, at any point between Tilton and Resaca . . . I hope the enemy will fight at Dalton, in which case he can have no force there [?at Resaca] that can interfere with you. But, should his policy be to fall back along the railroad, you will hit him in flank. Do not fail in that event to make the most of the opportunity by the most vigorous attack possible.[25]

On the 8th, McPherson advanced through Snake Creek Gap unopposed. Hearing of this move on the 9th, Johnston sent three divisions to Resaca, whereupon McPherson, finding the position too strong to be attacked, fell back to the entrance of the gorge.

Sherman blamed him for doing so, saying that although "he was perfectly justified by his orders," he missed "an opportunity [which] does not occur twice in a single life." [26] Ropes thinks otherwise; he says: "Sherman lost, at the very outset, the best and perhaps the only chance he had during the whole summer of inflicting a decisive defeat upon his antagonist. Had he followed Thomas's advice . . . he might have ended the campaign with a sudden and brilliant victory. But he missed this

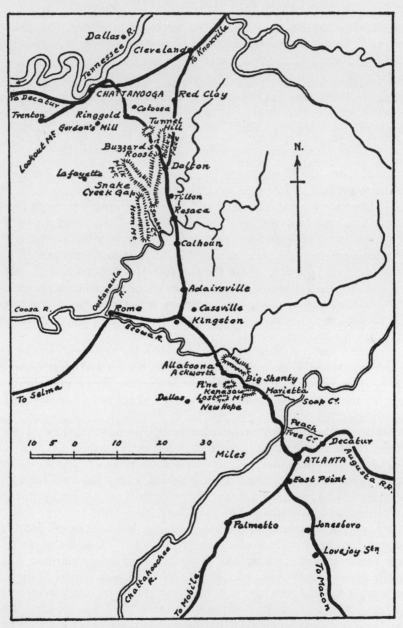

23. Map of the Atlanta Campaign, 1864

opportunity, and his wary and skilful opponent presented him with no other." [27] In this Ropes is supported by Johnston, who in a conversation with Robert M. Hughes, said:

I would have given all the money I had, and all I ever expected to have, if McPherson had given me such a chance. I could easily have stolen a night march upon Sherman and fallen upon McPherson with such superior force as to crush him. The fact that I transferred Hood's three divisions on the night of the 9th proves its feasibility. I have always thought that McPherson acted exactly as he should have done. [28]

On the 10th the Confederates held firm, but the next day increasing pressure persuaded Johnston to order a withdrawal. On the 12th and 13th, Sherman pushed Thomas's and Schofield's armies through Snake Creek Gap and deployed them before Resaca. They closed in on the town on the 14th, and the next day Johnston withdrew over the Oostenaula River. Sherman pursued him to Adairsville and pushed him back south of Cassville, where the Confederates formed line of battle.

Here Sherman deployed his three armies to attack at dawn on the 20th; but, when day broke, once again his wily enemy had disappeared. Thereupon Sherman called a halt in order to repair the railroad and replenish his supplies.

Knowing that the Allatoona Pass would be strongly held, on the 23d Sherman ordered Thomas, with Schofield on his left and McPherson on his right, to move on Dallas in order to outflank it. This meant abandoning the railway; consequently twenty days' supplies had to be carried on the wagons.

On the 25th they approached the densely wooded country of New Hope where they engaged in stiff fighting until June 4. On that day Johnston again fell back, which enabled Sherman to regain his rail communications at Allatoona. After a halt of several days, on June 10th he pushed on to Big Shanty, from where he could see his enemy strongly entrenched about Kenesaw, Pine, and Lost Mountains.

Up till now the tactics adopted by both sides had been novel. Johnston described them as a "race of flying breastworks." Sherman says: "All this time a continual battle was in progress by strong skirmish lines, taking advantage of every species of cover, and both parties fortifying each night by rifle-trenches, with head-logs, many of which grew to be as formidable as first-class works of defense." [29] These trenches were used as shields and hundreds if not thousands of miles were dug during this campaign.

But now Sherman decided to abandon them. He was afraid that, because of the bad weather, Johnston might seize the opportunity to detach troops to Lee. Another motive, as he wrote, was that "The enemy and our own officers had settled down into a conviction that I would not assault fortified lines." [30] His decision was a mistake and it cost him dear, for on the 27th he launched three useless assaults on the Kenesaw position, losing 2,500 in killed and wounded. Having learnt his lesson, on July 2 he reverted to outflanking tactics. Johnston thereupon retired to the Chattahoochee River and Sherman occupied Marietta the next day. Once again he decided to cut loose from the railway, which he did on the 9th, Schofield crossing the Chattahoochee at Soap Creek. Johnston also crossed and fell back on Peachtree Creek. But on the 17th, as Johnston was making ready to attack his enemy, he was suddenly withdrawn from his command and to the consternation of his army and the joy of his enemy [32] replaced by General J. B. Hood.[33]

Hood was a bold, brave, and bone-headed tactician to whom trenches and breastworks were anathema; in his opinion they demoralized the men.[34] Consequently, on the 20th, he launched a fierce attack on Sherman at Peachtree Creek, only to be repulsed at a loss of 4,796 men.[35] Rightly or wrongly, he placed the blame of his failure on the shoulders of General Hardee.[36] In this battle McPherson, at the early age of thirty-four, was killed and succeeded by General O. O. Howard.

Hood next fell back on Atlanta, from where on the 22d he launched yet another battle. He made in all seven assaults which were repulsed at a cost of some 10,000 in killed and wounded.[37] This time he laid the blame on Johnston's policy "which had wrought such demoralization amid rank and file as to render the men unreliable in battle." [38] He informs us that this attack " . . . greatly improved the morale of the troops . . ." [39] a statement which may well be doubted.

Having beaten off Hood, Sherman decided to move the Army of the Tennessee "boldly against the railroad below Atlanta, and at the same time to send all the cavalry around by the right and left to make a lodgment on the Macon road about Jonesboro." [40] This led to Hood's launching yet a third battle near Ezra Church on the 28th. After six successive assaults he was again repulsed, at a loss of probably 5,000 men. By now Richmond had its bellyful of the offensive, and on August 5, Jefferson Davis wrote to Hood saying: "The loss consequent of attacking him [Sherman] in his entrenchments requires you to avoid that, if practicable." [41]

Sherman now set out to operate against the Macon railroad to the south of Atlanta. On September 1, Hood was compelled to evacuate Atlanta and withdraw to Lovejoy Station. Thereupon "the gate city of the South" was occupied by his enemy, Sherman soon after sending Newton's division back to reinforce his line of communication.

The casualties of this long-drawn-out campaign were heavy. Sherman's amounted to 4,428 killed, 22,882 wounded, and 4,442 missing;[42] while between them Johnston and Hood lost 3,044 killed, 21,996 wounded, and 12,983 prisoners.[43]

Once Atlanta was his, Sherman decided to evacuate its entire civil population and convert it into "a pure military garrison or depot." On September 4 he wrote to Halleck, saying: "If the people raise a howl against my barbarity and cruelty, I will answer that war is war, and not popularity-seeking. If they want peace they and their relatives must stop the war."[44] He wrote again in a somewhat similar strain on the 20th. Halleck replied on the 28th:

Let the disloyal families of the country, thus stripped, go to their husbands, fathers, and natural protectors, in the rebel ranks . . . I would destroy every mill and factory within reach which I did not want for my own use . . .

I have endeavoured to impress these views upon our commanders for the last two years. You are almost the only one who has properly applied them.[45]

As we shall soon see, Sherman needed no encouragement in this particular form of warfare.

Having settled with the unfortunate citizens of Atlanta, on September 20 he suggested to Grant that if Savannah could be occupied, he "would not hesitate to cross the State of Georgia with sixty thousand men, hauling some stores, and depending on the country for the balance. Where a million of people find subsistence, my army won't starve . . ."[46] Thus was launched the idea of his eventual march to the Atlantic shore.

While Sherman's active mind was pouring forth suggestions to Grant, Hood was also considering his future movements. It was clear to him that he must abandon his present line of retreat as he was now on the edge of the highlands, and once in the open country he would be at the mercy of Sherman's superior forces. To cover Selma, Montgomery, Columbus, and Macon, and to threaten a Federal advance from

Atlanta on Augusta, he withdrew on September 20 to Palmetto Station and there entrenched. Sherman, reporting this move, noted: "He is eccentric, and I cannot guess his movements as I could those of Johnston, who was a sensible man and only did sensible things." [47] He was not, however, left long in doubt. Jefferson Davis, journeying from Richmond to visit Hood, publicly announced at a number of places that Atlanta was to be recovered; that Sherman would meet the fate of Napoleon in his retreat from Moscow, etc. To the Tennessee troops he said: "Be of good cheer, for in a short while your faces will be turned homeward, and your feet pressing Tennessee soil." [48]

The result of this proclamation was that Sherman ordered [49] Thomas back to Chattanooga. It was a wise precaution, because, on the 29th, Hood crossed the Chattahoochee, and by October 2 it was obvious that his intention was to strike at the railway in the vicinity of Marietta. Leaving one corps to hold Atlanta, Sherman set off in pursuit. He soon found that there was little chance of bringing Hood to battle, and his thoughts returned to his proposed march on Savannah. On the 9th he wrote to Grant as follows: "It will be a physical impossibility to protect the roads, now that Hood, Forrest, Wheeler, and the whole batch of devils are turned loose without home or habitation . . . By attempting to hold the roads we will lose 1,000 men monthly, and will gain no result. I can make the march and make Georgia howl." [50] And again on the 11th: "Instead of guessing at what he means to do, he would have to guess at my plans . . . I can make Savannah, Charleston, or the mouth of the Chattahoochee." [51]

By October 13, Sherman's pursuit of Hood had taken him back to Snake Creek Gap from where he had set out in May. For a time Hood was inclined to make a stand and accept battle. Finding however that the temper of his officers and men was against such a proposal, he abandoned the idea. "In this dilemma," he writes, "I conceived the plan of marching into Tennessee with a hope to establish our line eventually in Kentucky . . . unless withheld by General Beauregard or the authorities at Richmond." [52]

Oblivious of Hood's intention, Sherman pressed on until the 19th, when he saw that his chance of bringing his extremely mobile adversary to book was hopeless. That day he informed Thomas that he intended to abandon the pursuit, and "make a hole in Georgia and Alabama," and added: "If you can defend the line of the Tennessee in my absence of three months, it is all I ask." [53] Again on the 20th he wrote: "To pursue Hood is folly, for he can twist and turn like a fox, and wear out any army in pursuit." [54]

As it will be remembered, the primary object of Sherman's campaign was to destroy Johnston's army, now Hood's. Grant, who never liked changing the idea of a campaign, on November 1 wrote to Sherman as follows:

Do you not think it advisable now that Hood has gone so far north to entirely settle him before starting on your proposed campaign? With Hood's army destroyed you can go where you please with impunity. I believed, and still believe, if you had started south while Hood was in the neighbourhood of you he would have been forced to go after you. Now that he is so far away, he might look upon the chase as useless, and will go in one direction whilst you are pushing in the other. If you can see the chance for destroying Hood's army, attend to that first, and make your other move secondary. [55]

Hood's advance was strategically sound, as can be judged from this dispatch, because it was upsetting his enemy's plans. Had it been possible for Kirby Smith in Arkansas to have reinforced him—and in spite of the Federal command of the Mississippi this was not altogether impossible—he would have been right in moving as he eventually did on Nashville. Not being reinforced, he should have terrorized Tennessee, and then turning south have followed up Sherman, waging a guerrilla war on his foraging parties.

Grant, at a distance, as usual avoided giving a direct order, and instead asked the question: "Do you not think it advisable to follow up Hood?" Strategically, on the map, it appeared essential; but Grant knew that war is not made solely on maps and he wanted Sherman to consider the question from every angle. This he did most ably. On November 2 he pointed out that no single army could catch Hood, and that Thomas would have a force strong enough to hold him. Then he wrote: "I am convinced the best results will result from defeating Jeff Davis' cherished plan of making me leave Georgia by manoeuvring . . . If I turn back the whole effect of my campaign will be lost." [56] He saw that Hood's army was his primary objective only so long as it covered Georgia, the Carolinas, and Lee's rear, and *because* it covered them. Now that they were no longer covered, these vital localities in themselves became his primary objective; and so long as he could guarantee the security of the country in his rear, he would have violated the principle of direction had he continued in pursuit of Hood. On the 6th he again wrote to Grant saying:

On the supposition always that Thomas can hold the line of the Tennessee . . . I propose to act in such a manner against the material resources of the South, as utterly to negative Davis' boasted threats and promises of protection. If we can march a well-appointed army right through his territory, it is a demonstration to the world, foreign and domestic, that we have a power which Davis cannot resist. This may not be war, but rather statesmanship; nevertheless, it is overwhelming to my mind that there are thousands of people abroad and in the South, who will reason thus: If the North can march an army right through the South, it is proof positive that the North can prevail in this contest, leaving only open the question of its willingness to use that power.

Now Mr. Lincoln's election, which is assured, coupled with the conclusion thus reached, makes a complete, logical whole. Even without a battle the results, operating upon the minds of sensible men, would produce fruits more than compensating for the expense, trouble and risk." [57]

But Grant was already convinced, for on this same day he wrote to Sherman: "With the force, however, you have left with General Thomas, he must be able to take care of Hood and destroy him. I really do not see that you can withdraw from where you are, to follow Hood, without giving up all we have gained in territory. I say, then, go on as you propose." [58]

Returning to Atlanta, on November 12 Sherman ordered all his railroad and telegraph communications with his rear to be broken. Then, on the 15th, he fired the town and set out for Milledgeville, the capital of Georgia. "Behind us," he writes, "lay Atlanta, smouldering and in ruins, the black smoke rising high in air, and hanging like a pall over the ruined city." [59]

I do not intend here to describe the famous march which now took place; it has been depicted in many books, notably in those written by Sherman's staff officers—Major Ward Nichols and Major Henry Hitchcock.[60] Instead, I will touch upon the new type of war inaugurated by Sherman.

Nothing like it had been seen in the West since the maraudings of Tilly and Wallenstein during the Thirty Years' War; it was something utterly novel from the point of view of the eighteenth century, though during the Napoleonic Wars it cropped out occasionally. True, Southern guerrillas, as Sherman notes, had shown and continued to show much brutality. But the atrocities they perpetrated were individual acts and not a matter of policy. With some justice Jefferson Davis calls Sherman the "Attila of the American Continent." [61] Yet Sherman was not alone in his ruthlessness; in this war, the outlook of the North was materialistic and consequently brutal, or if the reader prefers, "modern." I have already quoted Nichols's description of Sherman as "a Democrat in the best sense of that word." Actually he meant, in the fullest sense. Sherman was, in fact, a most skillful and able mob leader. Nichols informs us that his army was followed by 20,000 camp followers,[62] as Wallenstein's was, or Toukhatchevski's in 1920, when he invaded Poland.

Terror was the basic factor in Sherman's policy; he openly says so. Here are a few quotations:

Until we can repopulate Georgia, it is useless to occupy it; but the utter destruction of its roads, houses and people will cripple their military resources . . . I can make the march, and make Georgia howl.[63]

Should I be forced to assault . . . I shall then feel justified in resorting to the harshest measures, and shall make little effort to restrain my army. [To General Hardee in command at Savannah.] [64]

. . . we can punish South Carolina as she deserves . . . I do sincerely believe that the whole United States, North and South, would rejoice to have this army turned loose on South Carolina to devastate that State, in the manner we have done in Georgia . . .[65]

We are not only fighting hostile armies, but a hostile people, and must make old and young, rich and poor, feel the hard hand of war . . . The truth is the whole army is burning with an insatiable desire to wreak vengeance upon South Carolina. I almost tremble for her fate . . .[66]

Like Nichols, Sherman believed that his army was "God's instrument of justice." [67] Hitchcock says much the same thing: "It is war now that it may not be war *always*. God send us peace—but there is no peace save in *complete submission to the Government:* and this seems impossible save through the terrors of war." [68] Also: "Sherman is perfectly right—the only possible way to end this unhappy and dreadful conflict . . . is to make it *terrible beyond endurance.*" [69]

The basic factor in this policy of frightfulness was that, though in his orders issued on November 9 soldiers were forbidden to enter civil dwellings "or commit any trespass," the army was instructed to "forage liberally"—which to the men meant indiscriminately. A good example of how they translated the word "liberally" is given by Sherman himself: "It was at this very plantation that a soldier passed me with a ham on his musket, a jug of sorghum—molasses—under his arm, and a big piece of honey in his hand, from which he was eating, and, catching my eye, he remarked *sotto voce* and carelessly to a comrade, 'Forage liberally on the country,' quoting from my general orders." [71]

Sherman apologizes for such and much worse acts by saying:

No doubt, many acts of pillage, robbery, and violence, were committed by these parties of foragers, usually called "bummers"; for I have since heard of jewelry taken from women, and the plunder of articles that never reached the commissary; but these acts were exceptional and incidental. [72]

This is quite untrue, for little or no restraint was put on the men, and literally thousands left the ranks in search of plunder. To support this contention it is not necessary to quote hostile evidence, such as that of Jefferson Davis; [73] for sufficient is supplied from Federal sources. Nichols tells us:

Yesterday we passed the plantations of a Mr. Stubbs. The house, cotton gin, press, corn-ricks, stables, everything that could burn was in flames, and in the door-yard lay the dead bodies of several bloodhounds, which had been used to track and pull down negroes and our escaped prisoners. And wherever our army has passed, everything in the shape of a dog has been killed . . . [74]

Again:

Wherever the army halted, almost every inch of the ground in the vicinity of the dwellings was poked by ramrods, pierced with sabres, or upturned with spades . . . If they "struck a vein" a spade was instantly put in requisition, and the coveted wealth was speedily unearthed. Nothing escaped the observation of these sharp-witted soldiers. [75]

In turn Hitchcock writes:

Soldiers "foraged liberally"—took all her peanuts drying on roof of shed: and, as we left the house, after riding some distance, saw her barn, old and rickety, on fire. [76]

One result of this unrestricted foraging—really brigandage—was a lapse of discipline; the army became a rabble. Hitchcock jots down: "Not so much shooting on the flanks to-day, but soldiers all the time 'foraging' and straggling. To a novice there seems much more of this than consistent with good discipline." [77]

Sherman himself was totally impotent to stop the wanton pillaging he had unloosed by his foolish word "liberal." Here are a few instances:

"There," said Sherman, "are the men who do this. Set as many guards as you please, they will slip in and set fire. That Court House was put out—no use—dare say whole town will burn . . . didn't order this, but can't be helped. I say *Jeff. Davis burnt them.*" [78]

". . . an elderly lady seeing Gen. S. pass, ran out to gate and begged for a guard. General answered . . . couldn't do it, army was marching and couldn't stop men . . . At night . . . he said, 'I'll have to harden my heart to these things. That poor woman to-day—how could I help her? There's no help for it. The soldiers will take all she has. Jeff. Davis is responsible for all this.' " [79]

"General advised V. very kindly (in tone) to bring all he could, of corn, wheat, etc., into *his house,* for safety from the soldiers . . ." [80]

What a confession of impotence!

On December 21, Savannah fell to Sherman's pillaging horde, now followed by thousands of plundering Negroes. The next day he presented that city as a Christmas gift to President Lincoln.[81] Then the Carolinas were devastated and gutted.[82]

In Georgia, Sherman estimated the entire damage done at $100,000,-000, of which only $20,000,000 "inured to our advantage," the remainder being "simple waste and destruction." [83]

This savagery was resented by many of his own officers, notably Generals Jeff. C. Davis, Slocum, Hawley, and Kilpatrick,[84] and Hitchcock, himself, considered it morally wrong.[85] Ropes, the historian, points out clearly and correctly that "Military operations are not carried on for the purpose of inflicting punishment for political offences," and, therefore, "if Sherman purposely destroyed, or connived at the destruction of, property, which was not needed for the supply of his army or of the enemy's army, he violated one of the fundamental canons of modern warfare; and . . . conducted war on obsolete and barbarous principles."

The depredations of Sherman's army, he rightly points out, had little influence on Grant's operations in Virginia. Lee was not seriously affected by the devastation of Georgia, for he remained in his lines at Petersburg and Richmond until the Battle of Five Forks. In Ropes's opinion, it would have been tactically more profitable as well as strategically sounder for Sherman to have stuck to Hood instead of turning away from him. Ropes maintains that it was Thomas's victory at Nashville, and not the march through Georgia and the Carolinas, which settled the war in the West.[86] To that decisive battle I will now turn.

Suspecting that Sherman would "cut loose and move south," on October 15–16 Hood, as he tells us, conceived the plan of advancing into Tennessee, passing through the Cumberland Gaps to Petersburg, and attacking Grant in the rear "at least two weeks before Sherman could render him assistance." This move, he believed "would defeat Grant,

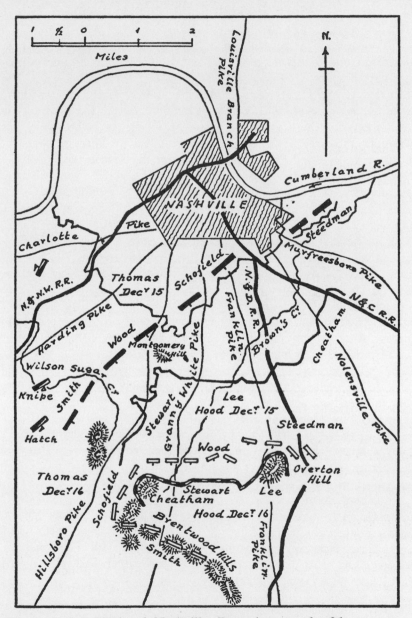

24. Battle of Nashville, December 15–16, 1864

and allow General Lee, in command of our combined Armies, to march upon Washington or turn about and annihilate Sherman." [87] He submitted this idea to Beauregard, who on the 21st authorized him to proceed with his plan.

Next day, with twenty days' rations "in the haversacks and wagons," Hood set out for Florence on the Tennessee River, the head of his column entering the town on the 31st. On November 13 he opened his headquarters there and the next day was joined by Forrest. Then, on the 17th, he received the following order from Beauregard's A.A.G.: "General Beauregard desires me to say that he desires you will take the offensive at the earliest practicable moment, striking the enemy whilst thus dispersed, and by this means distract Sherman's advance into Georgia." [88]

As we have seen, Thomas had been sent back to Nashville on September 29, and, on October 10, Sherman had ordered him to concentrate all troops within reach "at some converging place, say Stevenson." [89] Three days later similar orders had been sent him by Grant through Halleck,[90] and, on the 19th, Schofield's corps had been sent back to reinforce him. Thomas, however, instead of falling back, and concentrating—which obviously was the correct thing to do—had preferred to hold the Tennessee from Decatur to Eastport.[91] On the 25th, Hood had appeared in force before the former of these towns, and then, on the 29th, marched to Florence. Again Thomas was ordered to concentrate;[92] yet again he refused to abandon his advanced posts.

At this time Hood was at the head of 41,185 infantry and artillery as well as 12,753 cavalry,[93] mainly under Forrest; and though Thomas's army numbered in all close upon 60,000 men, so many were detached that under his immediate command he could muster no more than 22,000 infantry and 4,300 [94] cavalry—many dismounted.

As Hood advanced, Thomas ordered Schofield at Chattanooga to fall back on Columbia. Hood, seeing his chance to annihilate him, at once set out in pursuit, catching up with him on November 27th when, by a clever maneuver against his rear at Spring Hill, he would undoubtedly have attained his object had not General Cheatham utterly failed him. Van Horne writes:

Rarely has an army escaped so easily from a peril so threatening. It has been accepted as true that General Hood ordered one corps general and then another to attack the national troops when passing so near the front of his army at Spring Hill; but these generals disobeyed his orders, so plainly imperative from the situation itself, as well as from the voice of the commander-in-chief. From whatever cause the failure resulted, the opportunity of the campaign was lost to the Confederate army.[95]

Hood laments that he could not succeed "in arousing the troops to action, when one good division would have sufficed to do the work." [96]

Having escaped, Schofield withdrew to Franklin, hotly followed by Hood, who caught him up on the afternoon of the 30th and decided forthwith to drive him into the Big Harpeth river, which flowed in his rear.

At 11 P.M. that day a desperate attack was launched on the Federal front, the battle continuing until 9 P.M. "It was reported," writes Hood, "that soldiers were even dragged from one side of the breastworks to the other by men reaching over hurriedly and seizing their enemy by the hair or the collar." [97] At length, under cover of night, leaving their dead and wounded on the field, the Federals slipped back to Nashville. For Hood it was a bitter disappointment and it cost him 6,300 casualties to Schofield's 2,326.[98] This, as Hood says, left him with an effective force of 23,053 men. Therefore, still determined to march on Nashville, he decided, when once contact was made with Thomas, "to entrench, to accept the chances of reinforcements from Texas, and, even at the risk of an attack in the meantime by overwhelming numbers, to adopt the only feasible means of defeating the enemy with . . . reduced numbers, viz., to await his attack, and, if favoured by success, to follow him into his works." [99]

Moving forward on December 1, the next day he formed his line of battle in front of Nashville. S. D. Lee's corps was placed in the center across the Franklin Pike, Stewart moving up on his left and Cheatham on his right "their flanks extending as near the Cumberland as possible, whilst Forrest's cavalry filled the gap between them and the river." [100]

Now was Thomas's chance. He should have advanced at once and have overwhelmed his enemy; instead on December 1 he wrote to Halleck that he intended to retire to the fortifications round Nashville until his cavalry were equipped.[101] Hood's army was by now reduced to 44,000 men; [102] yet, on November 20, Thomas had "present for duty" 71,463.[103] Therefore, even when Schofield's casualties are deducted, he outnumbered his adversary by nearly two to one. Why, then, did not he assume the offensive? The answer must be sought in his cautious nature.

At West Point his fellow cadets had nicknamed him "Slow Trot," and as so often is the case, youth, with unerring accuracy, appreciated his predominant characteristic. A Virginian by birth, born in 1816, he was a man of firm and fervent loyalty, deliberate, cautious, and sure. He once said to a battery commander who had carelessly allowed his harness to break, that "the fate of a battle may depend on a buckle," and he undoubtedly believed that such small things were of paramount importance in war.[104] Of his present delay, Colonel Stone, his assistant adjutant general, says: "He realised too keenly the importance of victory to allow anything that might help to secure it to be neglected. Compared with the destruction of Hood's army nothing else was of any account." [105] Yet the way to destroy it was to attack and at once. because Hood might change his mind and at any moment slip away.

Meanwhile, at Washington, the fruits of Sherman's abandonment of his pursuit of Hood, coupled with Hood's advance into Tennessee, were causing an exaggerated anxiety, bordering on panic. On December 2, Stanton informed Grant that "the President feels solicitous about the disposition of Thomas to lay in fortifications for an indefinite period, 'until Wilson [his cavalry general] gets equipped.' " Grant thereupon telegraphed Thomas: "Should he [Hood] attack you it is well, but if he does not you should attack him before he fortifies"; and again: "After the repulse of Hood at Franklin it looks to me that instead of falling back to Nashville we should have taken the offensive against the enemy." To which Thomas replied: "I earnestly hope . . . that in a few more days I shall be able to give him a fight."

On the 5th, Grant again telegraphed Thomas: "It seems to me, whilst you should be getting your cavalry . . . Hood should be attacked where he is. Time strengthens him, in all probability, as much as it does you." Thomas answered: "As soon as I get up a respectable force of cavalry I will march against Hood." Grant, losing patience, telegraphed: "Attack Hood at once, and wait no longer for a remount of your cavalry. There is great danger in delay resulting in a campaign back to the Ohio River." Thomas's reply was: "I will make the necessary disposition and attack Hood at once . . . ," but no move was made.

On the 7th, Stanton telegraphed Grant: "Thomas seems unwilling to attack because it is hazardous, as if all war was anything else but hazardous. If he waits for Wilson to get ready, Gabriel will be blowing his last horn." Thereupon Grant telegraphed Halleck: "If Thomas has not struck yet he ought to be ordered to hand over his command to

Schofield." Halleck replied: "If you wish General Thomas relieved, give the order." Understanding from this that Lincoln did not support his removal, Grant telegraphed Thomas: "Now is one of the fairest opportunities ever presented of destroying one of the three armies of the enemy." To which Thomas again answered that his cavalry were not as yet in a condition to move.

On the 9th, Halleck telegraphed Thomas: "If you wait till General Wilson mounts all his cavalry, you will wait till doomsday, for the waste equals the supply." Thereupon Thomas replied that the weather had broken, and that the roads were impassable. Before this telegram was received, Grant had asked Halleck to replace Thomas by Schofield. This order was made out but not sent, and Grant learning from Thomas that the roads now were covered with sheets of ice, suspended the relieving order and again urged him on.

On the 11th, Grant telegraphed Thomas: "If you delay attacking longer the mortifying spectacle will be witnessed of a rebel army moving for the Ohio River, and you will be forced to act, accepting such weather as you find. Let there be no further delay." Thomas wired in reply: "I will obey the order as promptly as possible, however much I may regret it"; and the next day to Halleck he telegraphed: "Under the circumstances, I believe that an attack at this time would only result in a useless sacrifice of life." At length Grant could tolerate Thomas's inaction no longer. On the 13th he ordered General Logan to proceed to Nashville and take over command of the Army of the Cumberland. The following day he set out from City Point to assume personal control. Then, on arriving at Washington on the 15th, he learnt that Thomas at last had attacked.[106]

While this battle of words was being fought, on the 3d Hood's advanced troops had gained contact with the Federal outposts. They took up a line extending from a little west of the Hillsboro Pike about Sugar Tree Creek, across the Nolensville Pike to the Chattanooga Railroad; the whole of the right flank was covered by Brown's Creek. Weak though he was, Hood sent Bate's division of Cheatham's corps to reduce Murfreesboro. Next he reinforced him with a division of Lee's corps and on the 8th and 9th sent a considerable force of cavalry out to break the Louisville-Nashville Railroad. Thomas must have known of these detachments, which makes it all the more remarkable that he did not attack Hood during their absence.

On the 14th the respective orders of battle were as follows:

Major General George H. Thomas

Fourth Corps, Brig. Gen. Thomas I. Wood: 1st Division—Kimball; 2d Division—Elliott; 3d Division—Beatty.

Twenty-Third Corps, Maj. Gen. John M. Schofield: 2d Division—Couch; 3d Division—Cox.

Army of the Tennessee, Maj. Gen. Andrew J. Smith: 1st Division—McArthur; 2d Division—Garrard; 3d Division—Moore.

Provisional Detachment, Maj. Gen. James B. Steedman.

Cavalry Corps, Maj. Gen. James H. Wilson.

In all, about 55,000 officers and men.[107]

Major General John B. Hood

Lee's Corps, Lieut. Gen. S. D. Lee: Johnson's division; Stevenson's division; Clayton's division.

Stewart's Corps, Lieut. Gen. A. P. Stewart: Loring's division; French's division; Walthall's division.

Cheatham's Corps, Maj. Gen. B. F. Cheatham: Brown's division; Cleburne's division; Bate's division.

Cavalry Corps, Brig. Gen. James R. Chalmers.

In all about 35,000 officers and men.[108]

In brief, Thomas's plan of attack was first to feint at his enemy's right, and then deliver the main blow against his left. To carry this out he issued the following instructions:

(1) Steedman, on the left of the line, to make "a most positive" feint against the enemy's right, in order to divert his attention from his left.

(2) Smith to make a vigorous attack on the enemy's left.

(3) Wilson to support Smith on the right with two dismounted cavalry divisions, and to send a third to the Charlotte Pike in order to protect the right rear until the enemy's left flank were turned.

(4) Wood to support Smith on the left.

(5) Schofield to remain in reserve.

(6) The troops to move forward at 6 A.M. on the 15th.[108]

When dawn broke a dense fog lay heavy on the field over which, before forty-eight hours ran out, was to be fought one of the most decisive battles of the war. At six o'clock all the troops advanced. When they were in position, at about 8 A.M. orders were sent to Steedman to open the battle. He at once moved south from the Murfreesboro turnpike and drove his enemy back from the Nashville-Chattanooga Railroad, but was unable to hold it. Nevertheless, his assault was made with such vigor that Hood was deceived and drew troops from his center and left to reinforce his right.

A little later McArthur's division of Smith's corps threw out its skirmishers and advanced west of the Harding Road against two redoubts sited on hilltops west of the Hillsboro Pike, Hatch's dismounted cavalry division moving around their left flank. Both redoubts were carried. Meanwhile Schofield was ordered to move up on Smith's right to attack the enemy's left, which rested on a group of hills near the Hillsboro Pike. This advance was completely successful, Garrard's division of Smith's corps crossing the pike while Schofield carried a series of small hills overlooking the Granny White Pike.

So soon as Smith became engaged, Wood moved forward toward Montgomery Hill, the salient in Hood's line. Though the position was both strong by nature and well entrenched, his men carried it under cover of a vigorous bombardment. At 5 P.M. he was ordered to move forward on the Franklin Pike, but was unable to reach it before night fell.

The result of this day's fighting was that the Confederates were driven completely out of their works and forced back toward the Brentwood Hills, their left thrown back *en potence* half a mile to the west of the Granny White Pike, their right resting on Overton Hill. Thus they still covered two lines of retreat to Franklin—namely, the Granny White and Franklin turnpikes.

Hood, who seems to have been incapable of gauging the morale of his men, had no intention of giving up the fight. Once his new line was taken up, he moved Cheatham's corps from his right to his left and Lee's from his center to his right,[110] with the result that few of their men can have obtained any rest at all. This, I think, explains their rapid collapse on the second day of the battle. Meanwhile Thomas made ready to push the attack should his enemy be found still in position, or to pursue him should he retire. In the first eventuality, his plan was to assault both of his enemy's flanks, in spite of their great natural strength, in order to gain command of the Granny White and Franklin Pikes, a move which would inevitably be followed by a complete debacle. Schofield and Smith were to attack the Brentwood Hills while Wood and Steedman attacked Overton Hill.

At dawn on the 16th, Wilson's cavalry was pushed out beyond the extreme left of the Confederate line and gained a lodgment on the Granny White Pike. This left only the Franklin Pike as a line of retreat to Hood. Meanwhile, on the left, Overton Hill was reconnoitered. Considerable time was consumed in making ready and in preparing the assault by a converging bombardment; so it was not until 3 P.M. that the columns of attack, covered by a line of skirmishers, moved forward. In spite of the steepness of the ascent, which probably assisted rather than impeded their advance, since most of the enemy's shot and shell passed over their heads, they managed to reach the Confederate parapets. There they were met by so well-sustained a fire that they were thrown back to the foot of the hill.

During the time Steedman and Wood were making ready, General McArthur, who commanded the 1st Division of the Army of the Tennessee, tired of waiting, obtained permission from General Smith to carry the hill which faced Couch's division of Schofield's corps. Then occurred a somewhat unusual maneuver. Withdrawing his right brigade under McMillen, McArthur marched it by the flank in front of Couch's position, from where it moved down the slope and up the hillside, on the top of which was a redoubt held by Bate's division of Cheatham's corps. Fortunately for McMillen, as his men were advancing, Hatch's division of dismounted cavalry, which meanwhile had been pushing its way through the woods, gained two hilltops which commanded Bate's rear, and at the moment McMillen began his charge, Hatch's men opened so heavy a fire with their repeating rifles, that, caught between two fires, the Confederates broke back in panic.

Of this extraordinarily fortunate and really fortuitous combination of bullet and cold steel, Colonel Henry Stone, of Thomas's staff, writes:

It was more like a scene in a spectacular drama than a real incident in war. The hillside in front, still green, dotted with the boys in blue swarming up the slope; the dark background of high hills beyond; the lowering clouds; the waving flags; the smoke slowly rising through the leafless tree-tops and drifting across the valleys; the wonderful outburst of musketry; the ecstatic cheers; the multitude racing for life down into the valley below—so exciting was it all, that the lookers-on instinctively clapped their hands, as at a brilliant and successful transformation scene, as indeed it was. For, in those few minutes, an army was changed into a mob, and the whole structure of the rebellion in the South-west, with all its possibilities, was utterly overthrown.[111]

As the noise of this remarkable assault swept over the battlefield, Wood and Steedman without waiting for orders once again moved against Overton Hill, and this time swept all before them, the Confederate right falling back in complete confusion. Then, as soon as Wilson's dismounted troopers had regained their saddles, Hatch's and Knipe's cavalry divisions set out in a pursuit which, however, was halted by nightfall.

The victory was complete and rendered annihilating by the pursuit which was once again taken up on the morning of the 17th and pressed until the 26th, when it was found that Hood had succeeded in carrying the fragments of his army over the Tennessee River at Bainbridge. Exclusive of stragglers and 2,000 deserters, Hood lost in prisoners 4,462 men.[112]

The remainder of this the greatest war in American history is worth telling, if only to bring it to its dramatic conclusion.

While the above events were unfolding themselves in the West, in the East Grant waged a ceaseless war against the Petersburg railways; Sigel failed in the Valley and Early's corps once again moved on Washington. In order to close that "race course," for good and all, on August 7 Grant sent General Philip H. Sheridan to take over the command of that region and systematically devastate it. Following out his orders, Sheridan defeated Early on September 19 at Opequon Creek and again at Cedar Creek exactly a month later.

For 1865, Grant's plan was to draw the net closer and closer round his adversary. His first problem was to occupy the remaining seaports —Charleston, Mobile, and Wilmington, the last being the most important. Its entrance was protected by Fort Fisher, which fell on January 15. The capture of that fort was, says Vice-President Stephens, a blow equal to the loss of Vicksburg.

With Hood disposed of and Fort Fisher in Federal hands, Grant, fearing that Lee might attempt to break away and unite with Joseph E. Johnston—once again opposing Sherman—decided to watch rather than attack him, holding his army in readiness to spring upon Lee should he abandon Richmond. Next he decided to close in on Lee with four columns. Sherman was to advance on Branchville and eventually on Raleigh;[113] Schofield was to be transferred from Tennessee to North Carolina, secure Wilmington, and then occupy Goldsboro, in order to open a base of supplies for Sherman;[114] Sheridan was to move on Lynchburg; Thomas was to move on Selma, sending a strong force of cavalry under General Stoneman toward Columbia, and Canby to occupy Mobile.

Thomas's movement failed, owing to the slowness with which it was executed. Schofield, however, occupied Wilmington on February 22, and Sherman advanced north on February 1. After a march of 425 miles he joined hands with Schofield at Goldsboro on March 23. Meanwhile Sheridan set out toward Staunton, annihilated the remnants of Early's army, occupied Charlottesville, and then turning south rejoined the Army of the Potomac on March 19.

Lee's situation was now desperate. On February 19 he had already warned his [115] government that Richmond might have to be abandoned. Hearing [116] from Johnston on March 23 that Sherman had joined Schofield, two days later, apparently to disengage himself, he attacked Fort Steadman, which lay a little to the east of Petersburg, and failed hopelessly because of faulty staff arrangements.[117] The initiative was now entirely Grant's. Not waiting for Sherman, who was unable to advance on the Roanoke until April 10, he decided to strike at once.

His plan was to hold the trenches north of the James with one corps—the Twenty-Fifth; mass two—the Ninth and Sixth—in the Petersburg area ready to break the enemy's front should Lee strip it; while the remainder, in all 66,000 men, preceded by Sheridan and 14,000 cavalry, were to move west and turn Lee's right flank.[118]

Hearing that Lee was concentrating on his right, in spite of the rain which in many places rendered the roads impassable for wheeled traffic, on the 30th Grant ordered Sheridan to seize the road junction at Five Forks. Sheridan accomplished this by decisively beating General Pickett on April 1. The result of this battle was to place the South Side Railroad at Grant's mercy, and thus seal the fate of Petersburg.

Learning of Sheridan's success, Grant ordered an assault along the whole Petersburg front in order to prevent a concentration against Sheridan, and to enable him to advance on the South Side Railroad. The attack took place at 4 A.M. on April 2, the Confederate works west of Petersburg being penetrated and Lee's army cut in two. Sheridan drove all west of Lee's center beyond the Appomattox, and Grant, wheeling his left flank inward, forced all east of it into Petersburg. Early on the 3d the Federal troops occupied Petersburg and Richmond at length was abandoned.

Correctly surmising that Lee would follow the Danville Railroad in order to gain the Roanoke, Grant decided not to follow him and become involved with his rearguards, but instead to get ahead of him and intercept his line of retreat.[119] On the 3d, before leaving Petersburg, he had written to Sheridan saying: "The first object of present movement

will be to intercept Lee's army and the second to secure Burkesville."
Therefore Sheridan continued his movement westwards, cutting in on
Lee's line of retreat on Danville; whereupon Lee switched toward
Farmville. He was now to all intents and purposes hemmed in; on his
left was Sheridan and the Sixth Corps, on his right the Fifth Corps, and
in his rear the Second. Nevertheless, he pushed on, deciding to cross to
the left bank of the Appomattox at Farmville and gain Danville by
the road leading through Appomattox Court House.

As the Army of Northern Virginia straggled onward to its doom,
Grant ordered the Second and Sixth Corps to move north of the Appomattox and press the enemy's rear, while Sheridan, the Fifth and
Ord's Corps [120] were directed on to Appomattox Station,[121] as information had been received that Lee intended to resupply his army at that
place. On the evening of the 8th, Sheridan reached Appomattox Station, from where he pushed Lee's advanced troops back toward the
Court House. On the morning of the 9th, Lee advanced to attack him,
whereupon Sheridan's cavalry, "parting to right and left," disclosed the
Fifth and Ord's Corps in line behind them. Simultaneously the Second
and Sixth Corps arrived in rear of Lee's men. The white flag was then
raised,[122] and a little later, at McLean's house, in "a naked little parlor
containing a table and two or three chairs," Robert E. Lee at the head
of 7,872 infantry with arms, 2,100 cavalry, 63 guns, and not a single
ration, surrendered to Ulysses S. Grant.

Though the influences of this war were as profound and as epoch-
shattering as those which sprang out of the War of American Independence, they were lost upon Europe and the world in general.
Whereas out of the first of these civil wars emerged a new political
theory, out of the second came a new military theory—new at least for
the nineteenth century—which finds its clearest exemplification in a
comparison between the methods employed by Lee and Sherman. Lee,
as Rhodes says,[123] in all essential characteristics resembled Washington, and resembling him, belonged to the eighteenth century, therefore
to the agricultural age of history. Sherman and to a lesser extent Grant,
Sheridan, and most of the Northern generals, spiritually and morally
belonged to the age of the industrial revolution. As Stephen Vincent
Benét says of this war, it was:

> The pastoral rebellion of the earth
> Against machines, against the Age of Steam—
> The Hamiltonian extremes against the Franklin mean.[124]

The one side represented "contentedness," the other, "efficiency." And as efficiency is governed by a single law—that every means is justified by the end—no moral or spiritual conceptions, conventions or customs can be allowed to stand in its way. So far as war is concerned, Sherman must forever rank as the first of the modern totalitarian generals. He universalized war, waged it on his enemy's people and not only on armed men, and made terror the linchpin of his strategy. To him, more than to any other man, must be attributed the hatred that grew out of this war, a hatred that is not dead even today.

This war was epoch-making not only politically but also tactically. Of supreme tactical importance was the fact that the rifle rendered the defense the stronger form of war. This fact is noted by two independent witnesses. Colonel Lyman says: "Put a man in a hole, and a good battery on a hill behind him, and he will beat off three times his number, even if he is not a very good soldier." [125] And Frank Wilkeson writes: "Before we left North Anna I discovered that our infantry were tired of charging earthworks. The ordinary enlisted men assert that one good man behind an earthwork was equal to three good men outside it." [126]

In fact the whole technique of fighting had changed unnoticed. For instance, the cavalry charge was rendered impotent; the rifle-cannon came more and more to the fore, and the dethronement of the bayonet was complete. "I don't think a single man of them was bayonetted," [127] writes one eyewitness. General Gordon says: "The bristling points and the glitter of the bayonets were fearful to look upon as they were levelled in front of a charging line; but they were rarely reddened with blood. The day of the bayonet is passed . . ." [128] Finally, Surgeon Major G. Hart writes that he saw few bayonet wounds "except accidental ones . . . I think half-a-dozen would include all the wounds of this nature that I ever dressed." [129]

It is easy to criticize the tactical ability of Grant, Lee, and other generals in this war, but it should be remembered that they had no precedents to guide them. To all intents and purposes the rifle was a new weapon. When we do criticize, we should remember that in 1914—fifty years after the Civil War ended—nine out of ten professional soldiers still believed in the bayonet. It was because the inefficacy of the bayonet in this type of warfare was not understood that between 1861 and 1865 scores of assaults were attempted and over 90 per cent of them failed.

The war that was fought by Grant and Lee, Sherman and Johnston,

Thomas and Hood, was a novel war—the war of the rifle bullet. It was a war that closely resembles the World War fifty-three years later. No other war, not even the Russo-Japanese War of 1904–1905, offers so exact a parallel. It was a war of rifle bullets and a war of trenches, of slashings, of abattis, and even of wire entanglements, an obstacle the Confederates called "a devilish contrivance which none but a Yankee could devise," because at Drury's Bluff they had been trapped in it and "slaughtered like partridges." [130] It was a war of astonishing modernity: of wooden wire-bound mortars, hand grenades, winged grenades, rockets, and many forms of booby traps. Magazine rifles were introduced and also Requa's machine gun. Balloons [131] were used by both sides, though the Confederates did not think much of them.[132] Explosive bullets are mentioned,[133] also a flame projector,[134] and in June, 1864, General Pendleton asked the chief ordnance officer at Richmond whether he could supply him with "stink-shell" which would give off "offensive gases" and cause "suffocating effect." The answer he got was: " . . . stink-shells, none on hand; don't keep them; will make if ordered." [135] Nor did modernity halt here: armored ships and armored trains, land mines and torpedoes [136] were used, also lamp and flag signaling and the field telegraph. A submarine was built by Horace L. Huntly at Mobile—twenty feet long, five deep, and three and a half wide—which was "propelled by a screw worked from the inside by seven or eight men." [137] On February 17, 1864, she sank U.S.S. *Housatonic* off Charleston and went down with her.

Had the nations of Europe but studied the lessons of this war and taken them to heart, they could not in 1914–1918 have perpetrated the enormous tactical blunders of which that war bears record.

REFERENCES

[1] *Military History of Ulysses S. Grant*, by A. Badeau, vol. II, p. 8.
[2] *Campaigns of the Army of the Potomac*, W. Swinton, p. 403.
[3] *Papers of the Military Historical Society of Massachusetts*, vol. IV, p. 183.
[4] *Battles and Leaders of the Civil War*, vol. IV, p. 100.
[5] For the full list, see Badeau, vol. II, pp. 29–32.
[6] Grant writes: "If the Army of the Potomac had been moved bodily to the James River by water, Lee could have moved part of his forces back to Richmond, called Beauregard from the south to reinforce it, and with the balance have moved on to Washington." (*Personal Memoirs of U. S. Grant*, vol. II, p. 141.)
[7] *The War of the Rebellion, Official Records*, vol. LX, p. 827.
[8] *Battles and Leaders*, vol. IV, p. 99.
[9] *W.R.*, vol. LIX, p. 246.

[10] *Ibid.*, vol. LIX, p. 409.

[11] *Ibid.*, vol. LXII, p. 610.

[12] *Ibid.*, vol. LXVII, p. 15.

[13] *Ibid.*, vol. LX, p. 827.

[14] Joseph E. Johnston was born on February 3, 1807, and educated at West Point. He had seen much service—namely in the Black Hawk War in 1832; the Florida War in 1836 and in the Mexican War, during which he was present at Palo Alto, Resaca de la Palma, Vera Cruz, Cerro Gordo, Molino del Rey, and Chapultepec.

[15] For criticism of this impossible order, probably suggested by Bragg—then Davis's chief of staff—see *W.R.*, vol. XXXII, Pt. 3, p. 839, and *History of the Army of the Cumberland*, by Thomas B. Van Horne, vol. II, pp. 26–27.

[16] He wanted W. H. C. Whiting or M. Lovell; but, as Hood was one of Jefferson Davis's favorites, he was sent instead.

[17] *Atlanta*, J. D. Cox, p. 25. Ropes says, 60,000 (see *M.H.S.M.*, vol. X, p. 135).

[18] *M.H.S.M.*, vol. X, p. 127.

[19] *The Story of the Great March*, by George Ward Nichols, p. 80.

[20] *M.H.S.M.*, vol. X, p. 137.

[21] *W.R.*, vol. LIX, p. 312. Sherman writes in his *Personal Memoirs of Gen. W. T. Sherman* (vol. II, p. 25, fourth edition): My armies "were to be directed against the rebel army commanded by General Joseph E. Johnston, then lying on the defensive, strongly intrenched at Dalton, Georgia; and I was required to follow it up closely and persistently, so that in no event could any part be detached to assist General Lee in Virginia; General Grant undertaking in like manner to keep Lee so busy that he could not respond to any calls of help by Johnston. Neither Atlanta, nor Augusta, nor Savannah, was the objective, but the 'army of Jos. Johnston,' go where it might."

[22] Sherman's *Memoirs*, vol. II, pp. 23–24.

[23] See *ibid.*, vol. II, pp. 30–31.

[24] *Atlanta*, p. 31.

[25] *W.R.*, vol. LXXV, pp. 39–40.

[26] Sherman's *Memoirs*, vol. II, p. 34.

[27] *M.H.S.M.*, vol. X, p. 135.

[28] *General Johnston*, by Robert M. Hughes, p. 231.

[29] Sherman's *Memoirs*, vol. II, p. 45.

[30] *W.R.*, vol. LXXII, p. 68.

[31] See Hughes's *Johnston*, pp. 250–251.

[32] See Sherman's statement in *Battles and Leaders*, vol. IV, p. 253.

[33] The dismissal of Johnston was due to a shabby intrigue in which the chief conspirators were Bragg, Hood, and particularly Seddon, the Secretary of War (see *The Rise and Fall of the Confederate Government*, by Jefferson Davis, vol. II, pp. 560–561). Lee was not implicated in it. (See Joseph E. Johnston in *Battles and Leaders*, vol. IV, p. 277, and Taylor's *Four Years with General Lee*, p. 139.)

[34] See *Advance and Retreat*, by J. B. Hood, pp. 162–183.

[35] *Battles and Leaders*, vol. IV, p. 253. The Federal losses were 1,710.

[36] See *Advance and Retreat*, p. 168. In practically every one of his failures he finds a convenient scapegoat.

[37] *Atlanta*, pp. 175 and 176; also Sherman's *Memoirs*, vol. II, p. 84. The Federal losses were 3,521.

[38] *Advance and Retreat*, p. 153.

[39] *Ibid.*, p. 181.

[40] Sherman's *Memoirs*, vol. II, p. 87.

[41] *W.R.*, vol. LXXVI, p. 946.

[42] Sherman's *Memoirs*, vol. II, p. 132.

[43] *Narrative of Military Operations during the Late War between the States*, by Joseph E. Johnston, pp. 576–577.

[44] Sherman's *Memoirs*, vol. II, p. 111.

[45] *Ibid.*, vol. II, pp. 128–129.

[46] *W.R.*, vol. LXXVIII, p. 412.

[47] *M.H.S.M.*, vol. VIII, p. 506. In *W.R.*, vol. LXXVIII, he says: "I do not see what he designs by this movement."

[48] Badeau, vol. III, p. 51. See also Sherman's *Memoirs*, vol. II, p. 141.

[49] *W.R.*, vol. LXXVIII, pp. 464–465, and Sherman's *Memoirs*, vol. II, p. 144.

[50] *W.R.*, vol. LXXIX, p. 162.

[51] *Ibid.*, vol. LXXIX, p. 202. That is the Appalachicola.

[52] *Advance and Retreat*, pp. 263–264. On October 2, Jefferson Davis had placed Beauregard in command of the military departments then controlled by Generals Hood and Taylor. Hood says, Davis "was averse to my going into Tennessee" (p. 273). Davis writes: "I must say after the event, as I did before it, that I consider this movement into Tennessee ill-advised" (vol. II, p. 570). Should Sherman discontinue his pursuit and march towards the coast, he wanted Hood to follow him up and prevent him from foraging (p. 567). This was sound advice.

[53] *W.R.*, vol. LXXIX, p. 365.

[54] *Ibid.*, vol. LXXIX, p. 378.

[55] *Ibid.*, vol. LXXIX, p. 576.

[56] *Ibid.*, vol. LXXIX, pp. 594–595.

[57] *Ibid.*, vol. LXXIX, p. 660.

[58] *Ibid.*, vol. LXXIX, p. 594.

[59] Sherman's *Memoirs*, vol. II, p. 178.

[60] See *ibid.*, vol. II, p. 178.

[61] Jefferson Davis, vol. II, p. 279.

[62] *The Story of the Great March*, by George Ward Nichols, p. 130.

[63] *W.R.*, vol. LXXIX, p. 162.

[64] *Ibid.*, vol. XCII, p. 737.

[65] *Ibid.*, vol. XCII, p. 743.

[66] *Ibid.*, vol. XCII, p. 799.

[67] Nichols, p. 101.

[68] *Marching with Sherman*, by Henry Hitchcock, p. 53.

[69] *Ibid.*, p. 35.

[70] Sherman's *Memoirs*, vol. II, p. 175.

[71] *Ibid.*, vol. II, p. 181. (See also Hitchcock, p. 69.)

[72] *Ibid.*, vol. II, pp. 182–183.

[73] See Jefferson Davis, vol. II, pp. 632–633. Also the letter of the Revd. Dr. John Bachman (*ibid.*, pp. 709–717).

[74] Nichols, pp. 51–52. Hitchcock (p. 143) says: "At one place I am told they killed five or six full grown dogs and as many more pups, and to the woman interceding for the latter as harmless they replied that the pups would soon be dogs if not killed."

[75] Nichols, p. 73.

[76] Hitchcock, p. 82.

[77] *Ibid.*, p. 83.

[78] *Ibid.*, p. 53.

[79] *Ibid.*, p. 77.

[80] *Ibid.*, p. 83.

[81] Sherman's *Memoirs*, vol. II, p. 231.

[82] See Nichols, pp. 189–190. He writes: "History, however, will be searched in vain for a parallel to the scathing and destructive effect of the invasion of the Carolinas . . . Often [the houses] were burned apparently from a petty feeling of spite . . . Day by day our legions of armed men surged over the land, destroying its substance . . . on every side, the head, centre and rear of our column might be traced by columns of smoke by day, and the glare of fires by night." (Also see pp. 86, 93, 102, and 116.)

[83] *W.R.,* vol. XCII, p. 13. "In nearly all his [Sherman's] dispatches after he had reached the sea, he gloated over the destruction of property" (Rhodes' *History of the United States,* vol. V, p. 22).

[84] See Hitchcock, pp. 86–87.

[85] *Ibid.,* pp. 92–93.

[86] *M.H.S.M.,* vol. X, pp. 148–151.

[87] *Advance and Retreat,* pp. 267–268.

[88] *Ibid.,* p. 277.

[89] *W.R.,* vol. LXXIX, p. 191.

[90] *Ibid.,* vol. LXXIX, p. 252.

[91] Schofield was at Chattanooga. For Thomas's various detachments, see Van Horne, vol. II, p. 186.

[92] *W.R.,* vol. LXXIX, p. 497.

[93] *The March to the Sea, Franklin and Nashville,* J. D. Cox, p. 12. In *Battles and Leaders,* vol. IV, p. 435, Hood gives his strength as 30,600.

[94] Van Horne, vol. II, p. 186.

[95] *Ibid.,* vol. II, p. 196.

[96] *Advance and Retreat,* p. 287.

[97] *Ibid.,* p. 294.

[98] Cox, pp. 96–97. See also Van Horne, vol. II, p. 202.

[99] *Advance and Retreat,* pp. 299–300.

[100] *Ibid.,* p. 300.

[101] *W.R.,* vol. XCIV, p. 3.

[102] This is Cox's figure (p. 101). According to *Battles and Leaders,* vol. IV, p. 474–39,000. Hood, as we have seen, says 23,053, and in *Battles and Leaders* (vol. IV, p. 435) he repeats that figure—23,000. Probably, he had 35,000.

[103] *W.R.,* vol. XCIII, p. 52.

[104] For his character, see *M.H.S.M.,* vol. X, pp. 199–200. He was also called "Old Safety." "Maj.-Gen. George H. Thomas, if it can be so put with due respect, may be called the elephant of our army animals—slow, ponderous, sagacious, not easily roused to wrath, but when aroused terrible and invincible" (Ingersoll in *Iowa and the Rebellion,* p. 644).

[105] *M.H.S.M.,* vol. VII, p. 496.

[106] This correspondence will be found in *W.R.,* vol. XCIV, pp. 15, 16, 17, 18, 55, 70, 84, 96, 97, 114, 116, 143, 155, and 180.

[107] Cox, p. 219, gives 70,270; but all these were not present.

[108] *Ibid.,* p. 222—36,440.

[109] See Van Horne, vol. II, pp. 226–227.

[110] See *Battles and Leaders,* vol. IV, p. 437.

[111] *Ibid.,* vol. IV, p. 464.

[112] See *Numbers and Losses in the Civil War,* Thomas L. Livermore, p. 133.

[113] *W.R.,* vol. XCII, pp. 797, 820.

[114] *Ibid.,* vol. XCIX, p. 190.

[115] *Ibid.,* vol. XCVIII, p. 1044.

[116] *Ibid.,* vol. XCIX, pp. 1453–1454, and vol. C, p. 682.

[117] See *Reminiscences of the Civil War,* John B. Gordon, pp. 397–408.

[118] See *W.R.,* vol. XCVII, pp. 234 and 266, and Grant's *Memoirs,* vol. II, p. 437.

[119] Grant's *Memoirs,* vol. II, p. 456.

[120] This corps was formed out of Butler's army, Ord relieving Butler in December, 1864.

[121] *W.R.,* vol. XCVII, pp. 621, 633.

[122] *Ibid.,* vol. XCV, pp. 1109–1110.

[123] Rhodes, vol. III, p. 413.

[124] *John Brown's Body,* Stephen Vincent Benét, p. 375.

[125] *Meade's Headquarters,* 1863–1865, Colonel Theodore Lyman, p. 224.

[126] *The Soldier in Battle, or Life in the Ranks of the Army of the Potomac,* Frank Wilkeson, p. 99.

[127] *Life in the Confederate Army,* William Watson, p. 217.

[128] Gordon, pp. 5–6. See also *Memoirs of the Confederate War for Independence,* Heros von Borcke, vol. I, p. 63 and vol. II, p. 50.

[129] *M.H.S.M.,* vol. XIII, p. 265.

[130] *Battles and Leaders,* vol. IV, p. 212.

[131] *Encyclopaedia Britannica,* Eleventh Edition, vol. XVII, p. 239.

[132] *The Times,* Special Correspondent, January 1, 1863.

[133] *Campaigns and Battles of the Army of Northern Virginia,* by George Wise, p. 160.

[134] *Meade's Headquarters,* p. 284.

[135] *W.R.,* vol. LXIX, pp. 888–889.

[136] *Battles and Leaders,* vol. II, p. 636.

[137] *M.H.S.M.,* vol. XIV, pp. 450–453.

1865–1898

SYNOPSIS OF BACKGROUND EVENTS

ON April 14, 1865—that is, five days after Lee's surrender at Appomattox Court House and on the fourth anniversary of the fall of Fort Sumter—at ten o'clock in the evening, Abraham Lincoln was shot dead by John Wilkes Booth, a fanatical Secessionist, in Ford's Theater at Washington. For the South, as for the North, this shot was fatal, because the man it killed—he who more than any other had won the war—was the man who above all others could best have won the peace that was now to follow it.

The problem that then faced Vice-President Andrew Johnson, who forthwith succeeded Lincoln, was immense. The entire economic foundation of the United States had been upheaved and its social life disrupted. The South was devastated, bankrupt, and riddled with hatred; all had been staked and all had been lost. How were her states to be readmitted into the Union? There, also, 4,000,000 slaves were to be found; yet the Thirteenth Amendment, abolishing slavery, had not yet been ratified, and seemingly could not be without the assent of the Southern states. What was to be done with these unfortunate people? Further, what was to be the legal basis of reconstruction, since the Constitution made no provision for secession? How was inflation to be tackled? And, finally, how were foreign relations to be dealt with, particularly as concerned France, then involved in a wild-goose chase in Mexico?

Lincoln, who had believed in a policy of amnesty, might have found the key answer to these many questions; but the tempestuous Andrew Johnson could not. The result was that the resentment of the North toward the South automatically became the keystone of reconstruction. A series of Reconstruction Acts were forced through Congress, by which the "Rebel States" were divided into five military districts "and a registration of voters was decreed, from which a rigid oath was to exclude all classes meant to be disfranchised by the Fourteenth Amendment, while negroes were to be included."

Though the Negroes formed the voting body, control was in the hands "of white residents of Northern origin, the 'carpet-baggers,' and of a few Southern whites or 'scalawags.'" Most of these people were rapacious scoundrels.

Outmatched in number and angered by Negro supremacy, in 1866 certain Southerners formed a secret society—the Ku Klux Klan, which established a rule of terror as a means of retaliation. The general result was that the whole South was precipitated into anarchy, "the lowest elements on both sides exhibiting the worst passions of humanity. Murder, violence, and a consuming race-hatred seemed pitted against utterly unscrupulous misgovernment and tyranny."

In 1868, General Ulysses S. Grant was unanimously chosen as Republican nominee for the Presidency and was elected by an overwhelming majority. The country was committed to a policy of high protection. Furtively, expansion again raised its head; in 1868, Alaska was purchased from Russia, and projects were set on foot to acquire the Danish West Indies and the island of San Domingo.

Meanwhile an enormous industrial development set in, carrying with it intense corruption, "the Democratic Tammany Hall and the Republican customs-house plundering New York city with equal impudence." The result was the panic of 1873. Then, at length, "dead issues" began to die, and a new way of life began to emerge from the chaos. Hordes of foreign immigrants created new problems, so did the growth of factories and the rise of a labor class. When Grover Cleveland was inaugurated as president in 1885, "The long Republican control, lasting since Lincoln, was broken; and the accession of a Democratic President elected by the votes of the 'solid South,' with the aid of a comparatively few Northerners, over one of the leaders of the Reconstruction period, presented the very result which the Radicals of 1867 meant to render impossible."

New men now appeared and with them came new outlooks. Most of the great territories—the acquisition of which had so largely helped to precipitate the Civil War—had now become states and were daily increasing their populations. But, although the Frontier period was fast closing, the country had not yet reached the limit of its expansion. Soon was it to extend over the seas. This was not a sudden impulse; it was part and parcel of the spirit of the American Revolution.

As early as the year 1809, Jefferson had made an effort to acquire the Island of Cuba, and fourteen years later John Quincy Adams considered its annexation indispensable. During the first Presidency of Grant, the question cropped up again with the outbreak of the ten years' revolutionary war in Cuba. This was a war of deliverance from the stranglehold of Spain, which degenerated into a war of banditti, Negroes, mulattoes, Chinese, and deserters controlled by rebels who, "having a holy horror of the smell of gunpowder," had fled to New York, Key West, and New Orleans, where they found not only safe but profitable harbors. Grant's contemporary. Giuseppe Mazzini, wrote: "I am profoundly saddened by the attitude of indifference which the United States has shown towards Cuba. The last act of the great American drama [colonial emancipation] is being played on the stage of that island. Cuba's revolt against Spain is the direct outgrowth of your war for independence. It is not logical, nor is it good, nor is it proper that the United States, having unfurled a banner, should now callously abandon to destruction those who have followed in their footsteps."

When these words were written, the most tremendous European expansion was in progress, an expansion which a few years later stirred the United States. Africa was being divided up between the Western nations, whose greeds were wrapped up in humanitarian tinsel. In 1885, Germany, having made a treaty with Samoa, came into conflict with American interests there. This friction led to a compromise and eventually, in 1899, to a division of that group of islands, the United States receiving Tutuila and its dependencies and the Germans occupying the rest. Earlier, in 1891, there had been a dispute with Chili, and during the following year American marines were landed in Hawaii and the native monarchy was replaced by a republic. Finally, in 1898, the United States annexed the Islands. In 1895 the U. S. A. and Great Britain clashed over the question of the Venezuelan frontier, which was settled by arbitration in 1897. That same year William McKinley was chosen president. In his inaugural address, after chanting a paean to this settlement, he declared that peace was "preferable to war in almost every contingency." With the McKinley administration, we come to yet another conflict, this time once again with Spain.

Though the Ten Years' War, which ended in 1878, was disastrous for both Cubans and Spaniards alike, Spanish pride remained intransigent and seventeen years of misrule followed. The bureaucracy continued to be a closed preserve for imported officials; taxes were increased and from them the bureaucrats reaped their blackmail. There was no security of person or property and the judiciary remained in the hands of the military authorities. Further still, as Admiral Chadwick informs us: "Four-fifths of Cuba's wealth was in sugar, for which the United States was practically her one purchaser. When the reciprocity of a few years ended, in 1894, the island, ground between the millstones of both American and Spanish protection, was naturally deeply disturbed by the revulsion from wealth to comparative poverty . . . The greed of American and Spanish protectionists was, in fact, at the bottom of Cuban revolt and largely responsible for the loss of hundreds of millions of money and the many thousands of lives which the war involved."

So it came about that on February 24, 1895, a fresh rebellion broke out. Spain's difficulties were accentuated by a simultaneous rising in the Philippines. In Cuba, the leader of the insurrection was Maximo Gomez who, in order to blockade the Spanish forces, set out to lay waste the plantations and destroy the railways in the Provinces of Havana and Matanzas. So serious did the situation become that General Calleja, the governor, was relieved by Martinez Campos who, failing in the field, was replaced in January of the following year by General Valeriano Weyler.

Under him were assembled no less than 196,000 soldiers, although, at any one time, the insurgents never exceeded an eighth of that force. His policy on the whole was an able one. It was to run lines of trenches protected by wire entanglements right across the island from north to south, and gradually clear the islands by driving the insurgents westward from area to area. By this means he probably would have succeeded in quelling the rebellion had not a violent campaign of propaganda been launched against him in the United States. There his ruthlessness stirred up violent philanthropic opposition, largely stimulated by the 150 Cuban revolutionary clubs in the States, and financial and economic interests determined that the rebels should win because the American stakes were large. President Cleveland, in his annual message of December 7, 1896, said: "It is reasonably estimated that at least from $30,000,000 to $50,000,000 of American capital are invested in plantations and in railroad, mining, and other business enterprises on the island. The volume of trade between the United States and Cuba, which in 1889 amounted to about $64,000,000, rose in 1893 to about $103,000,000, and in 1894 . . . amounted to nearly $96,000,000." In

1894 the imports from Cuba to the United States stood at $76,000,000, in 1896 at $40,000,000, and in 1897 at $18,000,000; whereas the exports of the United States to Cuba between 1894 and 1897 fell from $24,000,-000 to $8,000,000.

So, at length, the United States intervened, with the result that toward the end of 1897 the Spanish government recalled General Weyler and appointed in his stead General Ramon Blanco. Then, on January 24, 1898, as a mark of friendship President McKinley decided to send the battleship *Maine* to Havana.

Meanwhile, in Spain, Queen Regent Maria Cristina and her government, instead of preparing for war, pinned their hopes on intervention, much as the Confederates had done in 1861. Their plan was to show that although the question at issue was an American one, it was also a matter which should seriously concern the European Powers, because, as the loss of Cuba would wreck the Spanish monarchy, the downfall of the Spanish monarchy would in its turn rock the thrones of Great Britain, Austria, Germany, Russia, and Italy.

This was a clever move, which undoubtedly would have succeeded had the so-called Concert of Europe been anything more than a political façade behind which the Greater Powers maneuvered against each other. This is clearly shown in a report sent by Andrew W. White, American ambassador in Berlin, to his government on January 7, 1898, which reads as follows:

On the Continent there has never been a time, probably, when ill will towards the United States has been so strong as at present. Nevertheless, I do not believe that a coalition will be formed against us. The interests of European nations are so diverse, and in many respects so mutually hostile, that it would be very difficult to organize a coalition of them against us. This is the more true, because feeling is more intense about the questions dividing Europe, than it is about those between America and Europe.

Strangely enough, the Power which supported Spain most firmly was not one of the monarchies, but the Republic of France. The reason for this was that the French holdings in Spanish properties and in public debts, etc., amounted to about $1,000,000,000. Nevertheless, Horace Porter, American ambassador in Paris, was of opinion that no aggressive step would be taken by the French.

The Spanish plot, however, was finally wrecked by the attitude of Great Britain, whose age-old policy was to keep Europe divided, and who in recent years had turned more and more toward the U. S. A. in order to balance the rising power of Germany. That this was realized by William II is clear; for, according to Orestes Ferrara (see his book *The Last Spanish War, Revelations in "Diplomacy"*) on one of the documents of this period the German Emperor wrote:

England wishes to play the same game as when, last year, she confessedly promoted the Greco-Turkish war. She suggests measures to be taken by all the Powers, and seems to be taking part in them, until the belligerent has been thoroughly compromised by them. Then she retires, beats her breast like a Pharisee, declares that she has had nothing to do with it, allies herself secretly with one of the contending parties—the strongest, of course—and excites him against the Continental Powers! And all the time she is begging for commercial favours at their expense.

Such was the position in Europe, when at 9.40 P.M. on February 15 the *Maine* blew up in Havana harbor, with the loss of 2 officers and 258 men. A frantic war clamor swept the United States, where few stopped to realize that this disaster was even more disadvantageous to Spain than to America. How, or rather why this battleship was sunk has never been revealed. That the loss was due to an external explosion was proved; yet who was responsible remains a mystery, though conjecture points to those interests which had been secretly working for war—certainly neither the government of Spain nor that of America.

The furor culminated in the following resolutions, passed on April 19 by the Senate and House of Representatives in Washington:

First. That the people of the island of Cuba are, and of right ought to be, free and independent.
Second. That it is the duty of the United States to demand . . . that the government of Spain at once relinquish its authority and government in the island of Cuba . . .
Third. That the President of the United States be . . . directed and empowered to use the entire land and naval forces of the United States . . . to carry these resolutions into effect.
Fourth. That the United States hereby disclaims any disposition or intention to exercise sovereignty, jurisdiction, or control over said island except for the pacification thereof . . .

These resolutions were signed by the president at 11.24 A.M. on April 20, and, eleven minutes later the Spanish minister at Washington requested his passports, leaving that evening for Canada. Two days later Admiral Sampson's fleet was ordered to blockade the Cuban coast, and two days later still Admiral Dewey received orders to proceed to the Philippines and destroy the Spanish squadron there. Lastly, on the 25th, it was enacted by the American Congress: "That war be, and the same is hereby declared to exist, and that war has existed since the 21st of April, A.D., 1898, including said day, between the United States of America and the kingdom of Spain."

CHAPTER X

THE BATTLES OF EL CANEY–SAN JUAN HILL
AND SANTIAGO DE CUBA, 1898

IN this war, which was destined to bring to an end that vast empire which Columbus had founded and Cortés, Pizarro, and others had conquered, the object of the United States was clear—to liberate Cuba from the dominion of Spain. But the means to accomplish that end were vague. At first they consisted of no more than a blockade of the Cuban coast and the assistance of the insurgents with munitions and arms. Then it was decided to dispatch to Cuba an expeditionary force of some 5,000 regular troops, under the command of Major General William R. Shafter. But when it was heard that Admiral Pascual Cervera y Topete was sailing westward from Spain, this project was abandoned because, as should have been obvious from the start, it was necessary to secure command of the sea before any land attack could be launched. As Captain Alfred T. Mahan writes: "The issue of the war, as a whole and in every locality to which it extended, depended upon naval force." [1] Therefore, though the quarrel was on land, once again the sea was to be the decisive element.

In the United States, this necessity was complicated by the mental unpreparedness of the people for war. As Frederic L. Paxson says: "The strategic certainty of the Navy Department was disturbed by the nervousness of the seaboard cities. From Savannah to Portland there was apprehension of a Spanish bombardment. Mythical Spanish warships were daily reported in the newspapers, and nearly as often delegations of Congressmen waited upon the Secretary of the Navy to remind him of his duty to protect their constituents." [2] This nervousness led to the division of the American armored warships into two fleets widely separated from each other. The Flying Squadron under Commodore W. S. Schley was assigned to coastal defense, and the Main Fleet, commanded by Admiral W. T. Sampson was sent to blockade Cuba.

Though neither side was ready for a naval war, the Spaniards were totally unprepared. The sole chance their fleet had of fulfilling its mission was to assume a strategical defensive attitude from the start, leaving it to the numerous Spanish land forces in Puerto Rico and Cuba to bear the brunt of the fighting. By this means time might have been gained wherein to put the fleet in order for offensive action. Admiral Cervera considered the naval situation hopeless, and begged in vain for a plan of action. So ignorant was the Spanish government that General Beranger, Secretary of the Navy, held the opinion that the Spanish fleet would fight triumphantly and "conquer the sea," because "as soon as fire is opened the crews of the American ships will commence to desert, since we all know that among them are people of all nationalities. Ship against ship, therefore, a failure is not to be feared." [3]

As it happened, the exact opposite was true. The Spanish fleet lacked guns,[4] ammunition, coal,[5] and even bread. But of their adversary, H. W. Wilson writes: "In training, discipline, education, and seamanship there was no comparison between the two forces . . . The American naval officer has a world-wide reputation for professional knowledge and capacity. The American seaman . . . is intelligent, brave, and resourceful." [6] Admiral Cervera, though a brave man, was a defeatist who looked upon the war as lost from the start. His opponent, Admiral Sampson, was described by John D. Long, Secretary of the American Navy, in the following words:

The moment required a man of splendid judgment, quick decision, possessing intimate knowledge of the characteristics of the vessels he would have to use, and the officers and men manning them, and enjoying the esteem and confidence of his subordinates. The consensus of naval opinion was that Sampson had these qualifications.[7]

The relative strength of the two navies on the outbreak of war was as follows:

UNITED STATES

Ship	Displacement	Speed	Main Armament
	Battleships		
Iowa	11,340 tons	16.5 knots	4 12-inch
			4 8-inch
Indiana	10,288 tons	15.5 knots	4 13-inch
			4 8-inch
Massachusetts	10,288 tons	16.0 knots	4 13-inch
			4 8-inch
Oregon	10,288 tons	16.5 knots	4 13-inch
			4 8-inch
	Armored Cruisers		
Brooklyn	9,215 tons	21.0 knots	6 8-inch
			6 5-inch
New York	8,200 tons	21.0 knots	5 8-inch
			6 4-inch
	Second-Class Battleship		
Texas	6,315 tons	17.0 knots	1 12-inch
			4 6-inch

SPAIN

	Battleships		
Pelayo	9,900 tons	16.0 knots	13 guns
	Armored Cruisers		
Emperador Carlos V	9,090 tons	20.0 knots	14 guns
Almirante Oquendo	7,000 tons	20.0 knots	2 11-inch
			5 5.5-inch
Infanta Maria Teresa	7,000 tons	20.0 knots	2 11-inch
			5 5.5-inch
Vizcaya	7,000 tons	20.0 knots	2 11-inch
			5 5.5-inch
Cristobal Colon	6,840 tons	20.0 knots	7 6-inch

Besides the above vessels, the Americans made use of six monitors, fourteen protected cruisers, fifteen torpedo boats, and forty-eight other craft;[8] the Spaniards of five protected cruisers, twenty-nine torpedo boats, six torpedo-boat destroyers, and forty-six miscellaneous vessels.

At the outbreak of the war the *Oregon* was stationed at San Francisco, from where, on March 19, she sailed by way of Cape Horn for the West Indies. After a remarkable voyage of 14,700 miles, she arrived in perfect condition off Jupiter Inlet, Florida, on May 24.[9]

As for the land forces, on April 1 the Regular Army in the United States numbered 2,143 officers and 26,040 men. The second figure was increased to 41,934 by May and to 56,365 by August. In addition, 200,000 Volunteers were called for. The whole force was in the process of being organized into eight corps of three divisions each when the war ended. This work was carried out by General R. A. Alger, Secretary of War, assisted by Major General Nelson A. Miles, commander of the army.

Though mobilization was rapid, administration, to say the best of it, was indifferent. Tropical uniform, ambulances, medical stores, and transport were lacking. Theodore Roosevelt tells us that ". . . conditions in the large field hospitals were so bad, that as long as possible we kept all of our sick men in the regimental hospital at the front." And again: ". . . it was curious that when war came we should have broken down precisely on the business and administrative side, while the fighting edge of the troops certainly left little to be desired."[10] Rifles were short. The regular troops were armed with the .300 Krag Jorgensen magazine rifle but the Volunteers received the .450 Springfield, firing black powder, as did also the American guns, which, as we shall see, was an enormous drawback.

It is not possible to state definitely how many Spanish soldiers were stationed in Cuba. Sargent says 196,820,[11] and Chadwick says 140,005 regulars and 80,504 volunteers. "Of the regulars, about 31,500 formed the garrison in and about Havana, with some 17,000 at Matanzas . . . 34,000 were in the province of Santiago, of whom 9,430 were in the city of Santiago de Cuba and vicinity, 8,364 at Holguin, and 8,668 at Manzanillo."[12] These men were well supplied with small arms and smokeless powder cartridges, as Roosevelt notes: "Smokeless powder, and the thick cover in our front, continued to puzzle us . . ." and "As the Spaniards used smokeless powder, their artillery had an enormous advantage over ours, and, moreover, we did not have the best type of modern guns, our fire being slow."[13]

Such, in brief, were the forces which were to operate in an immense theater of war, with one extremity in the Philippines and the other in Cuba and Puerto Rico.

Though the chaotic condition of Cuba was the cause of the war, the first blow was struck in the Philippines. Ten days after the destruction of the *Maine*, Admiral George Dewey, on the Asiatic Station, was ordered to hold his squadron in readiness to attack the Spanish naval forces, commanded by Admiral Don Patricio Montojo, should war be declared. Meanwhile, Montojo, instead of retiring to remote parts of the archipelago, which would have been his wisest course of action, decided to hold Manila Bay, a pear-shaped inlet of water some thirty nautical miles in length, defended by 226 guns, 164 of which were old muzzle-loaders. The only really effective armament consisted of four 9.45-inch guns and eight of 4.7-inch.

The two opposing fleets were as follows:

AMERICAN

Ship	Tons	Speed	8 in.	6 in.	5 in.	6-pdr.	Torp. Tubes
Olympia	5,870	21	4		10	14	6
Baltimore	4,413	20	4	6		4	
Boston	3,000	15	2	6			
Raleigh	3,213	19		1	10	8	4
Concord	1,710	16		6		2	
Petrel	892	12		4			
	19,098		10	23	20	28	10

SPANISH

Ship	Tons	Speed	6.3 in.	5.9 in.	4.7 in.	3 and 2.24 in.	Torp. Tubes
Reina Cristina	3,520	14	6			3	5
Castilla	3,260	13		4	2	2	2
Isla de Cuba	1,045	14			4	2	3
Isla de Luzon	1,045	14			4	2	3
D. Juan de Austria	1,159	14			4	1	2
D. Antonio de Ulloa	1,160	12			4	1	2
Marques del Duero	500	10	1		2		
	11,689		7	4	20	11	17

A glance at these two tables is sufficient to show that in every respect, except in torpedoes, Montojo's squadron was outclassed.

When Dewey received his orders he was at Hong Kong with the *Olympia* and *Petrel,* but the remaining vessels of his squadron were scattered, the *Boston* and *Concord* off Korea, the *Raleigh* in the Indian Ocean, and the *Baltimore* at Honolulu. Hastily they were called in, and, having coaled, sailed eastward on April 25.

Meanwhile, Montojo, instead of anchoring his ships under Manila's powerful batteries, took them to Cavite Bay, several miles south of the city, where the land protection was indifferent. The reason for this move was to save Manila from bombardment, but it was a fatal mistake.

Once he had left Hong Kong, Dewey had to proceed more or less by guesswork, for he had no certain information as to which harbor his enemy was sheltering in. Making for Subig Bay, he reconnoitered it early on April 30, and then steamed toward the main entrance to Manila Bay, completely ignoring the possibility of mine fields. Lieutenant Calkins says, "there was no dragging or dodging to eliminate the danger." [14] Though the shore batteries opened an ineffectual fire, the fleet met no enemy warships. At length, as night deepened, the lights of Manila were seen twinkling in the distance.

When May 1 dawned, the battle flags were broken at every masthead, but there were still no enemy warships to be seen. Then, at 5 A.M., "a line of grey and white vessels" became visible off Sangley Point, and a little later the Spanish battery opened an innocuous fire. A moment later the Americans could readily make out Montojo's flagship, the *Reina Cristina.* Thereupon, at a range of 5,400 yards, the battle opened and continued for a little over two hours. Then Dewey withdrew his ships, but at 10.45 A.M. once again engaged the enemy and within two hours completely annihilated them. H. W. Wilson describes the battle as "a military execution rather than a real contest," which is true; for not only did Montojo lose the whole of his squadron, but also 167 men killed and 214 wounded, whereas not a single American ship was seriously damaged and of the 1,743 officers and men engaged, but two officers and six men of the *Baltimore* were slightly wounded.

Directly the battle was over, Manila was blockaded and eventually occupied. Thus, quite unexpectedly, a great archipelago was added to the United States, a fact which gave not only a new aspect to this war, but to those States themselves as a world power.

Meanwhile, in the main theater of the war,—strategically, though not politically, the more important—Admiral Cervera was also having his troubles.

On April 8, having been given no plan of campaign, he had stood out from Cadiz for the Cape Verde Islands and had put into Porto Grande on the 14th. There his troubles began, as we are informed in a letter he wrote five days later to the Minister of Marine: "The boilers of the *Ariete* are practically unserviceable, so that this vessel, instead of being an element of power, is the nightmare of the fleet." [15] On the 22d he received instructions to protect Puerto Rico, to which he replied: "I beg your Excellency to permit me to insist that the result of our voyage to America must be disastrous for the future of our country," and added that nothing could be expected of such an expedition "except the total destruction of the fleet or its hasty and demoralized return." [16] His protests proving vain, on the 29th he set out for Martinique.

In the meantime, on the 21st, Admiral Sampson, then at Key West and in command of all U. S. forces on the North Atlantic Station, had received orders to blockade the north coast of Cuba from Cardenas to Bahia. His most important objective was Havana, the capital, which he approached on the 23d and which he erroneously believed could be captured by direct attack. But on the 29th the whole situation changed, for news was received in Washington that Admiral Cervera had that day sailed from Cape Verde, and it was not possible to know whether his objective was Puerto Rico, Cuba, or the coast of the United States. Nevertheless, Sampson at once made up his mind. Estimating that Cervera would arrive in the West Indies about May 8, and that he would be short of coal, Sampson decided that he would probably put into the port of San Juan, on the northern side of Puerto Rico. His judgment later proved to be right. So he set out on May 4 at 5 P.M., and on the 11th approached his destination, the lights of San Juan becoming visible through the darkness at 2.30 the next morning. He bombarded the port during the day, but as he could obtain no news of Cervera's fleet—the object of his expedition—he reluctantly decided to return to Havana, from where he proceeded to Key West.

While this hit-and-run expedition was in progress, Cervera sent the *Terror* and *Furor* ahead to Martinique to obtain coal. However, none was available there, so on the 12th, learning of Sampson's proximity to Puerto Rico, he assembled his captains and decided to go to Curaçao instead of to San Juan, as it would be madness, he said, to proceed to the latter without a sufficiency of coal. He arrived at Curaçao on the 14th and, unable to obtain more than six hundred tons, set out again on the following day for Santiago, as he supposed San Juan, Havana, and Cienfuegos to be guarded. He steamed into port on the dawn of the 19th, and at once telegraphed General Blanco, the governor general: "Have

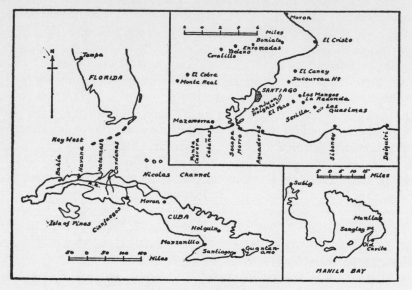

25. Map of Cuba, 1898

cast anchor in this harbor, whence whole squadron sends you greeting, desirous of co-operating in the defence of the country." [17]

The selection of Santiago as his destination and base was a fatal mistake. "Nothing could have been more fortunate for the Americans," writes Sargent, "than Cervera's entrance into Santiago Harbour. His going there transferred the determining centre of war from Havana to Santiago, eliminated from the contest that portion of the Spanish army occupying Western Cuba and caused the decisive struggle to take place where the Spaniards were especially weak." [18]

The port he should have made for was Cienfuegos, because, as Admiral D. Bonamico points out, there he would have been in railway communication with Havana, whence he could have received coal. Further:

"The whole of the military resources could have been concentrated at Cienfuegos with sufficient rapidity, and it can be unhesitatingly affirmed that a force of 50,000 men would have been found insufficient to reduce the place; and since the Union did not have any such force the result for Cervera would have been the security of the squadron, the possibility of holding in until the hurricane season, and for Sampson, the necessity of forcing the port, with gravest dangers, or of bombarding Havana *à outrance,* which would have been impolitic, in order to force the Spanish squadron to battle or to try another solution of the war more odious and less efficacious." [19]

The day Cervera put into Santiago, Commodore Schley sailed with the *Brooklyn, Massachusetts, Texas,* and *Scorpion,* under orders to block-ade Cienfuegos. Later that day, a rumor having been received that Cer-vera was at Santiago, the *Iowa* was sent after him with instructions to make that port instead. Schley received the order on the 21st—the day he reached Cienfuegos—but not satisfied that the Spanish squadron was not hiding in the harbor, he remained there until the 23d. Then, learn-ing definitely that the Spaniards were in Santiago he set sail eastward on the following day, taking with him the *Brooklyn, Iowa, Massachu-setts, Texas, Marblehead, Vixen, Eagle,* and the collier *Merrimac,* and arrived off Santiago on the 31st. Meanwhile Sampson had been ordered to follow him. Reaching Santiago on June 1 with his flagship *New York* and the battleship *Oregon,* accompanied by an armed yacht, the *May-flower,* and a torpedo boat, the *Porter,* he at once assumed personal command.

General Arsenio Linares was in command of the Spanish land forces. Shortly after Cervera arrived, it was decided that directly his squadron had coaled it should sail for San Juan, Puerto Rico. But on the 24th, doubting the wisdom of this move, Cervera assembled a council of war which voted against this plan. Later that day, General Blanco telegraphed to Linares that Schley's Flying Squadron was proceeding to Santiago. Cervera, convinced by this telegram and by the presence of the *Minne-apolis* and three auxiliary cruisers—the *Harvard, Yale,* and *St. Paul*—that he was already blockaded, the next day telegraphed the Minister of Marine:

We are blockaded. I qualified our coming here as disastrous for in-terests of country. Events begin to show I was right. With disparity of forces any effective operations absolutely impossible. We have provisions for one month.[20]

Lastly, on the same day, he wrote to Linares: "It is much to be re-gretted that the squadron did not go out yesterday while it had all the fires lighted . . . owing to the scarcity of our coal, I ordered three-fifths of the fires to be put out . . . If another opportunity presents itself, I intend to try and take advantage of it, but as I cannot hope with these scant forces to attempt any definite operations, it will only be a matter of changing this harbor for another where we would also be blockaded." Then, on the 26th, he called together a second council of war, which unanimously decided that the squadron should at once spread fires and be ready to leave for San Juan at 5 P.M. that day. But at 2 P.M. the semaphore signaled the presence of three enemy ships—the *Minneapolis, Yale,* and *St. Paul*—and the council was again hastily assembled. Some fear was expressed that the prevailing swell might ground the *Colon,* whose draught was 24.9 feet, on "a flat rock" in the water off Point Morrillo, where the water is only twenty-seven and a half feet deep, and five out of the eight officers present voted not to go out until the swell subsided.[21] This fatal recommendation was accepted by Cervera, in spite of the fact that his two ablest captains, Bustamante and Concas, dissented from it. Thus they missed the last chance of escape.

Very different was the action of the enemy. Directly Admiral Sampson arrived off Santiago at 6.30 A.M. on June 1, Schley reported to him, and they immediately decided to block the entrance of the harbor by sinking athwart it the collier *Merrimac.*

The locality selected was opposite Estrella Point, where the channel is no more than 350 feet wide. The enterprise was entrusted to Assistant Naval Constructor Richmond P. Hobson of the U. S. Navy.[22] In bright moonlight he set out at about 3.30 o'clock on the morning of the 3d, steering straight for the Morro, which, as he approached, opened a heavy fire on his ship. Nothing daunted, he continued his course to Estrella Point and there ordered the demolition charges to be fired. Unfortunately, several of the electrical wires had been cut and the steering gear damaged by the enemy's gunfire, and though the *Merrimac* began to sink, the tide swept her beyond the narrow channel into deep water where she settled to the bottom, the entrance remaining unobstructed.

As in so many really desperate adventures, not a single man was killed, and two of the crew were only slightly wounded. It is pleasant to record that the chivalrous Cervera himself, in his steam launch, rescued Hobson and his men whom he found in the water clinging to a catamaran. Later in the day, under a flag of truce, he sent a message to Admiral Sampson "extolling the bravery of the crew in an unusual manner."[23]

While this gallant endeavor was being prepared and attempted, the entrance to the harbor was blockaded by the two squadrons, which were stationed around it in a semicircle of four miles radius. At night time this semicircle was contracted and a searchlight kept playing on the narrow entrance commanded by the old Morro castle. The order regarding its use, writes Admiral Chadwick, "was among the most important of the war; to it more than to any other one circumstance is due the capture of the Spanish squadron. It made it, in the opinion of the Spanish commander, out of the question for the ships to leave the harbor at night with the entrance lighted so brilliantly that it was impossible for any movement to be made in it which would not be noticed. This action removed, too, any fear whatever of torpedo attack. . . . The torpedo-boat henceforth was entirely ignored as a danger." [24]

The blockade having been established, at 7.30 A.M. on the 6th the Americans bombarded the Socapa and Morro batteries as well as Fort Aguadores. Immediately following this action, Sampson, in order to establish a base for repairs and coaling as well as to gain a refuge against hurricanes, turned his attention to Guantanamo Bay, one of the finest of Cuban harbors. On the 9th, with the assistance of the insurgents, he occupied the port.

These various actions placed General Linares in an increasingly difficult situation. Although, topographically, his position at Santiago was strong, its defenses were obsolete, many of the guns protecting the bay dating from between 1718 and 1783. Furthermore, the troops in the province of Santiago, 36,000 strong, were scattered over an all but roadless area of 12,000 square miles; rations were short; [25] the men unpaid. Worst of all there was no unity of command between Linares and Cervera who, realizing the hopelessness of his position at sea, should have dismounted every gun he could from his ships and placed them and his entire force at the disposal of Linares. His blindness to his tactical position was only exceeded by that of his government which, on June 3, telegraphed Blanco to order Cervera at once to dispatch "all the ships . . . that can get out of Santiago" to the Philippines! "This movement would be only temporary, and as soon as object is attained in Philippines the squadron would return to Cuba without loss of time and strongly reinforced." [26] It was, as Admiral Chadwick comments: ". . . one of the most amazing propositions ever made by a minister of state." [27]

Because the Spaniards' supplies were short, blockade alone would almost certainly have forced the surrender of Santiago. Nevertheless, as it could not be occupied and held by Sampson's crews, on May 24 he had been warned by the Navy Department to prepare to convoy an army to Cuba. On the day of his arrival at Santiago, he had received a dispatch informing him that some 25,000 men were then embarking at Tampa, Florida, and would sail for Santiago directly information was received that the whole of Cervera's squadron was bottled in the harbor. Lastly, on June 7, having established the blockade, Sampson telegraphed the Navy Department: ". . . If ten thousand men were here, city and fleet would be ours in forty-eight hours. Every consideration demands immediate army movement. If delayed city will be defended more strongly by guns taken from fleet." [28] Upon receipt of this message, General Shafter, then in command of the training and mobilization camp at Tampa, was asked when he could sail. He replied, "on the following morning."

Major General William R. Shafter, a Civil War veteran then in his sixty-fourth year, was an immensely corpulent man, weighing over 300 lbs. On April 21 he had been assigned the command of New Orleans, and eight days later had been ordered to Tampa to prepare an expeditionary force to assist the Cuban rebels. His position was no easy one, because as yet there was no plan of campaign beyond a suggestion that, since Cuba's rainy season was due in May and likely to last until September, to avoid fever it was advisable to postpone active operations until the autumn. When, on May 24, it was decided to make ready at once, Shafter wisely recommended that all the regular regiments be formed into one corps, so that the initial blow might be delivered by fully trained men.[29]

A week later he received orders from the adjutant general to proceed to Santiago,[30] whereupon he immediately set to work amidst no little confusion. If Colonel Theodore Roosevelt is not exaggerating, the embarkation itself resembled a battle. He writes:

I happened to find out by accident that the transport *Yucatan* had also been allotted to the Second Infantry and the Seventy-first New York [as well as to his Rough Riders] and I ran down to my men and left a guard and took the rest and rushed them down to the dock and got on the *Yucatan,* holding the gang plank against the Second Infantry and the Seventy-first New York, and then letting aboard only the Second Infantry, as there was no room even for all of them; and I understand the Seventy-first spent the next two nights on the train. We ultimately kept four companies of the Second Infantry aboard with us, but we had the *Yucatan.*[31]

Then, suddenly, on the 8th, sailing was postponed on the strength of a report that stated that a Spanish squadron had been sighted in the Bahama Channel.[32] Though this soon proved to be a mere canard—probably originated by sympathizers of Spain—it was not until the 14th that the expedition set out, convoyed by the *Indiana* and several smaller ships. In all it consisted of 32 transports, carrying 16,058 officers and enlisted men, 409 civilians, 89 newspaper correspondents, 11 foreign naval and military attachés, as well as 2,295 horses and mules. The expedition was organized as follows:

First Division, Brigadier General J. F. Kent, commanding: 1st Brigade, Brigadier General H. S. Hawkins; 2d Brigade, Colonel E. W. Pearson; 3d Brigade, Lieutenant Colonel C. A. Wikoff.

Second Division, Brigadier General H. W. Lawton, commanding: 1st Brigade, Colonel J. J. Van Horn; 2d Brigade, Colonel E. Miles; 3d Brigade, Brigadier General A. D. Chaffee.

Cavalry Division (Dismounted), Major General J. Wheeler, commanding: 1st Brigade, Brigadier General S. S. Sumner; 2d Brigade, Brigadier General S. B. M. Young.

Independent Brigade, Brigadier General J. C. Bates, commanding: 3d and 20th Infantry and one squadron 2d Cavalry.

Field Artillery: a light battery of 4 guns each, 1 Hotchkiss revolving cannon; 2 pneumatic dynamite guns, 4 Gatling guns; 4 5-inch siege guns, 4 5-inch howitzers, and 8 3.6-inch field mortars.

On the 20th, Shafter and his expedition arrived off Santiago. The following morning, he, Sampson and the insurgent general, Calixto Garcia, who commanded some 5,000 rebels, met on board the *New York* and decided that, while Garcia made a feint attack on Cabañas, Lawton was to disembark his division at Daiquiri on the 22d. This was successfully accomplished, 6,000 men landing before nightfall.[34] No opposition was met with. Why, it is difficult to say, because the beach could have been rendered all but impregnable had the ridges above Daiquiri been held.

Lawton was ordered to push on to Siboney, seven miles to the west, early on the next morning and to clear that spot in order that Kent's division might land there. He set out at 4 A.M. and, as he approached its garrison, some 600 strong, fired a few long-range shots and bolted. The First Division then began to land.

Colonel Roosevelt, who advanced with the Second Division, says:

It was a hard march, the hilly jungle trail being so narrow that often we had to go in single file . . . It was long after nightfall when we tramped through the darkness into the squalid coast hamlet of

Siboney . . . Black thunder-clouds were gathering. Before they broke the fires were made and the men cooked their coffee and pork, some frying the hard-tack with the pork. The officers, of course, fared just as the men did. Hardly had we finished eating when the rain came, a regular tropic downpour. We sat about, sheltering ourselves as best we could, for the hour or two it lasted; then the fires were relighted and we closed around them, the men taking off their wet things to dry them, so far as possible, by the blaze.[34]

The terrain of the present theater of war though limited in size—tactically it included but a fraction of the province of Santiago—was exceedingly difficult. Around the capital the country was hilly, the mesa-like ridges rising to an elevation of one hundred and fifty to two hundred and fifty feet above sea level. These ridges were covered with tropical trees and dense jungle, and were traversed by narrow eroded trails cut by unbridged streams. In short, the whole country was by nature a strongly defensive one, and was now rendered more so since the rains had broken.

To hold it, as already mentioned, General Linares had at his disposal some 36,000 men. But around Santiago itself he had no more than 9,430, the remainder being split up in detachments—2,666 at El Cristo, Songo, Moron, Dos Caminos, San Luis, and Palma Soriano; 5,992 at Guantanomo; 8,668 at Manzanillo; 8,364 at Holguin; 742 at Baracoa and 720 at Sagua de Tanamo. Besides these, he had a detachment of about 1,000 of Cervera's sailors.

His plan of defense was based on three lines of observation rather than of resistance; the first, along the coast from Punta Cabrera to Daiquiri; the second, north of the city, from Palma Soriano by way of San Luis, Dos Caminos, Moron, El Cristo, and Songo to Socorro; and the third, west of the harbor, from Punta Cabrera by Monte Real to El Cobre and thence via Coralillo, Yseleno, Enramados, and Boniato to El Cristo. As war became imminent the landside of the city was fortified by a 4,000-yard-long system of trenches running along the ridges. Of it, Colonel Sargent writes:

The fieldworks [consisted] generally of two or three lines of trenches and breastworks protected in front by barbed-wire entanglements, occupied the crests of the hills and ridges immediately surrounding the city, and formed a fortified district with its two extremities resting on the bay. The trenches were dug deep with perpendicular sides, and in many cases the excavated dirt had been carried away, so that at a distance of four or five hundred yards no sign of the work on the hilltops was visible.[35]

Knowing nothing of the country, the enemy or his defenses, on the night of the 23d General Wheeler, hearing that the Spaniards who had retired from Siboney had occupied a ridge near Sevilla, ordered Young and his brigade forward. At 5.45 the following morning Young set out

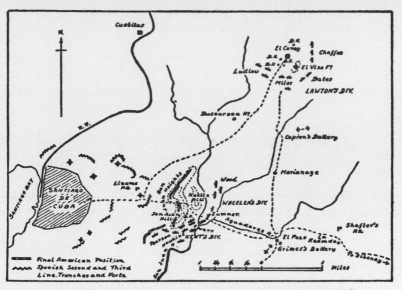

26. Battle of El Caney–San Juan Hill, July 1, 1898

and at 7.30 A.M. came into contact with the enemy at Las Guasimas. A sharp action took place, in which the Spaniards were outflanked by the Rough Riders and compelled to retire. In this first land action of the campaign the Americans engaged 1,141 officers and men against the enemy's 1,500, the former losing 68 officers and men killed and wounded and the latter 36.

On the following day, Sevilla was occupied. Shafter decided to assemble his army there to await the collection of supplies and transport before pushing on against Santiago. The 2d Division and the Cavalry Division occupied La Radonda and Los Mongos, from where a trail ran north to El Caney, while the 1st Division bivouacked at Sevilla. Thus the advanced posts of the invading army were within one and a half miles of San Juan Hill, and no more than three and a half from the eastern outskirts of the capital.

Both El Caney and San Juan Hill had been fortified. On El Caney were a few palm-thatched houses, six wooden blockhouses, a stone church, and a stone fort, called El Viso, surrounded by trenches, rifle pits and wire entanglements. This position was a strong one, but it was meagerly garrisoned, its defenders numbering but 520 all told. San Juan Hill was approached by a track following the Aguadores River and running south of Kettle Hill and thence across the northern end of San Juan Hill into Santiago. On the first of these two hills stood a fortified ranch, and on the second there was a heavy loopholed brick blockhouse; both were entrenched and protected by elaborate entanglements. A thousand yards to the west of this hill ran a second line of trenches. The garrison of these two hills was 1,197 officers and men, of whom 521 held .the first line.

On the 20th, a sufficiency of supplies having by then been collected, General Shafter personally reconnoitered his enemy's position. He writes:

The position of El Caney . . . was of great importance to the enemy as holding the Guantanamo road, as well as furnishing shelter for a strong outpost that might be used to assail the right flank and rear of any force operating against San Juan Hill. In view of this, I decided to begin the attack next day at El Caney with one division, while sending two divisions on the direct road to Santiago, passing by El Pozo House, and, as a diversion, to direct a small force against Aguadores from Siboney, along the railroad by the sea, with a view of attracting the attention of the Spaniards in the latter direction, and of preventing them from attacking our left flank or going to the support of Santiago garrison.[36]

Assembling his divisional commanders, he explained his plan as follows:

Lawton's division, assisted by Capron's light battery, was ordered to move out during the afternoon towards El Caney, to begin the attack there early the next morning. After carrying El Caney, Lawton was to move by the Caney road towards Santiago and take position on the right of the line. Wheeler's division of dismounted cavalry, and Kent's division of infantry, were directed on the Santiago road, the head of the column resting near El Pozo. Toward these heights Grimes's battery moved on the afternoon of the 30th, with orders to take position thereon early the next morning and, at the proper time, to prepare the way for the advance of Wheeler and Kent on San Juan Hill. The attack at this point was to be delayed until Lawton's guns were heard at El Caney and his infantry fire showed that he had become well engaged.[37]

Whether Shafter was right to include El Caney in his frontage of attack has been doubted;[38] but that he was right in pressing his attack at the earliest opportunity is beyond doubt. His reasons were:

(1) The deadliness of the climate demanded the earliest possible termination of the campaign.

(2) Should the hurricane season break, his store ships might be driven to sea.

(3) General Escario with 8,000 reinforcements was reported en route from Manzanillo, and was expected within a few days.

That evening he wrote to Admiral Sampson asking him to bombard the works at Aguadores early on July 1, in order to support the demonstration he had planned against that place. Simultaneously Lawton moved his advanced troops through the jungle and bivouacked them a little over a mile from El Caney.

Next morning, between four and five o'clock, Lawton again advanced, Chaffee's brigade moving on the northern flank of the hamlet and Ludlow's on its southwestern, making use of the Santiago road. Miles's brigade was held in reserve, with two regiments at the Ducoureau House and two with Capron's battery, one and a quarter miles to the south of the objective. Bates's brigade was still in the rear. In all, Lawton had under his command 6,653 men—that is approximately thirteen times the strength of his enemy, who were commanded by General Joaquin Vara de Rey.

At 6.30 A.M. the attack was opened by Capron's battery, and almost immediately after Chaffee's and Ludlow's brigades began to fire. So deadly was the Spanish reply that both brigades were compelled to halt within 600 yards of their enemy. Then followed a rifle duel lasting from four to five hours, during which Lawton's men crawled and crept, yard by yard, toward the Spaniards. "I have never seen," said one of General Vara de Rey's staff officers, "anything to equal the courage and dash of those Americans, who, stripped to the waist, offered their naked breasts to our murderous fire, literally threw themselves on our trenches —on the very muzzle of our guns [rifles]. We had the advantage of position, and mowed them down by hundreds; but they never retreated or fell back an inch. As one man fell, shot through the heart, another would take his place, with grim determination and unflinching devotion to duty in every line of his face. Their gallantry was heroic." [39] Nevertheless, vastly outnumbered though they were, the Spaniards bravely held on to their trenches, pouring volley after volley into their slowly advancing foe.

The fight continued until after noon, when Lawton ordered Miles's brigade up on Ludlow's right, and Bates's on Chaffee's left. An hour later Capron's battery also advanced, coming into action some 1,000 yards to the south of El Caney.

The walls of El Viso having been partially battered down, at 3 o'clock Chaffee ordered the 12th Regiment to charge. Bates's and Miles's brigades, seeing the Twelfth move forward, rushed the hill, drove the Spaniards out of the fort, and won it. However, the battle continued round the blockhouses and the church until five o'clock, when the Spaniards were forced to retire. Chadwick rightly says of this fight: "No men, victors or vanquished, ever played better their parts. Small as were the military results, ill-advised as was the attack itself, the battle of El Caney should be held in pride by both peoples as an unsurpassed example of manly courage and military devotion." [40]

On the American side, 81 officers and men were killed and 360 wounded, or about 7 per cent of the numbers engaged, while the Spanish lost 235 in killed and wounded, and 120 were captured, their gallant general and both his sons falling on the field of honor. Their losses in killed and wounded represent nearly half the total engaged.

It will be remembered that, according to Shafter's plan, this attack was to be subsidiary to the main operation against San Juan Hill, the idea being that Lawton would rapidly deal with El Caney and then move south. As this move was delayed, Shafter, apparently recognizing his mistake in including El Caney in his attack, sent Lawton the following message, which he received at 1.30 P.M.:

I would not bother with the little block-houses. They can't harm us. Bates's brigade and your division and Garcia should move on the city and form the right of the line, going on the Sevilla road. Line is now hotly engaged. [41]

At the time, this was impossible. Not until immediately after the position was won did Bates's weary brigade turn south. Lawton fell back on Ducoureau's House, giving his battle-worn division two to three hours to collect its wounded. There he rested his men until 3 A.M. on July 2, when once again they set out.

As the battle was launched, Linares became aware that his enemy was simultaneously massing his forces on the eastern flank of the San Juan heights. Moving his headquarters near to the junction of the El

Caney and El Pozo roads, he ordered forward two Krupp guns and brought the garrison of his first line up to 521 men and that of his second to 411. Why he did not call to his assistance the 3,000 effective regulars, sailors, and volunteers then in the capital, it is impossible to say. He had ample time since, due to Lawton's delay, the attack on the heights did not take place until 1 P.M. Had he done so, the battle would almost certainly have ended in an American repulse.

The attack was carried out by Wheeler's and Kent's divisions, the former for the time being under the command of Brigadier General Sumner. Sumner was directed to advance along the El Pozo–Santiago road, which traversed a dense jungle, to cross the Aguadores stream, and then turn right until his left rested on the road, with Kettle Hill as his objective. Kent, in his rear, was to turn to the left and deploy to attack San Juan Hill, his right linking up with Sumner's left.

At 8.20 A.M. Grimes's battery, in position a little to the south of El Pozo, came into action and, because of the black powder used, at once drew the Spanish fire.[42] Under cover of this ineffective bombardment Sumner's division advanced, and at about 10 A.M. forded the Aguadores. "First came the Cubans in the order of formation (a little further down the lane they branched off to the right and disappeared for the day); then came the cavalry . . . ; then the balloon led by a rope; then the infantry . . . Two men were in the car of the balloon; two men held it down by a cross bar, and two men walked in front holding stays or guyropes like the stays of a Foresters' banner."[43]

As it was the sole thing the Spaniards could see, shells and volleys of bullets were fired at it, "just above the trees, as savages might fire in a frenzy at a portent in the sky."[44] At length it was brought down and drifted away.

Sumner's division now turned off the track to the right and took up a position directly in front of Kettle Hill. Kent's leading brigade, under Hawkins, followed suit on the left, but was driven back in disorder under a devastating fire. Kent then sent back for Wikoff's and Pearson's brigades, but because of the confusion in the rear it was not until 12.30 P.M. that Wikoff appeared. Three-quarters of an hour later he was killed as his leading regiment was wading the stream. His place was taken by Lieutenant Colonel Worth who, under a terrific fusillade, began to deploy. Then he was wounded and Lieutenant Colonel Liscum, who succeeded him, met the same fate, the command of the brigade devolving on Lieutenant Colonel Ewers. Meanwhile, under a devastating fire, Hawkins pushed up on Ewers's left. Within ten minutes he lost a quarter of his leading troops, and withdrew his brigade to a sunken road in the rear.

As the men were falling fast and as no news was received from Lawton, Ewers turned to Lieutenant Miley, one of General Shafter's staff officers, and suggested an immediate advance. Miley agreed, whereupon Hawkins moved off supported on his right by the 9th Cavalry and the Rough Riders, now under the command of Colonel Roosevelt.[45]

Sargent describes the attack and assault on Kettle Hill as follows:

Crawling along the ground, taking advantage of every shelter, here and there rushing forward, the troopers steadily pushed on in the face of a galling fire. As they advanced the support pushed forward to the main line, and many of the companies and some of the regiments became mixed; but, regardless of formation, they quickened their pace, rushed across the open field, tore through the thick undergrowth and wire entanglements at the foot of the slope, waded the San Juan River, and charged up the hill. Before they reached the summit the Spaniards had fled towards San Juan Heights.[46]

As this assault was made, Lieutenant John H. Parker moved forward three of the four Gatling guns over most difficult country to a clump of trees across the ford, some 600 yards from the enemy's position, from where he opened a very effective fire. Colonel Roosevelt writes: "Suddenly, above the crackling of the carbines, rose a peculiar drumming sound, and some of the men cried, 'the Spanish machine guns!' Listening I made out that it came from the flat ground to the left, and jumped to my feet, smiting my hand on my thigh, and shouting aloud with exultation, 'It's the Gatlings, men, our Gatlings!' "[47]

The effect of this fire was such that, within five minutes, some of the Spaniards were seen running from their trenches on San Juan Hill. Hawkins's leading troops rushed forward followed by Ewers's on their right. "The valley was soon alive with a multitude of cheering, struggling men advancing in the face of terrific volleys, some halting to fire, some rushing forward, all with eyes intently fixed upon the Spanish block-house and entrenchments crowning San Juan Hill. In the lead was that intrepid veteran, General Hawkins. With his erect figure and white hair, he made an inspiring presence as he charged at the head of those two brave regiments [6th and 16th Infantry], swinging his hat and calling out 'Come on! come on!' "[48]

All but simultaneously, the dismounted cavalry on Kettle Hill rushed the northern slope of San Juan Hill, while Kent's men carried the south of it.[49]

It was half-past one when the hill was carried; then Best's battery and the Gatlings were brought forward to open fire on the enemy's second line.

As no news could be obtained from Lawton, and as by now all reserves had been exhausted, Shafter's men began to consolidate their position, which ran from 300 to 800 yards from the enemy's second line. While this was being done, Captain Bustamante, a naval officer, attempted a counterattack, and was mortally wounded. It was the sole Spanish offensive movement of the campaign.

July 1 closed leaving the victors in a position of no little anxiety which was somewhat relieved by the arrival of General Bates, who was directed to march his brigade to the extreme left of the line. This he succeeded in doing by midnight. Meanwhile Lawton with the remainder of his command was instructed to take up a position on the right of Wheeler's division. This movement was accomplished by noon on the 2d. That evening, Shafter, now a sick man, wrote to Admiral Sampson:

"Terrible fighting yesterday but my line is now strongly entrenched about three-quarters mile from town. I urge that you make effort immediately to force the entrance to avoid future losses among my men, which are already very heavy. You can now operate with less loss of life than I can." [50]

Nevertheless the position of the Americans was no less precarious than that of the Spaniards. The city's water supply had been cut and Escario's column, 3,600 officers and men, which had left Manzanillo on June 22 for Santiago, had not yet appeared.

On the 2d no attacks were made; in fact, what seventeen years later was designated as trench warfare had now set in and with it stalemate. What with the rain, the mud-churned roads, the knowledge of the approach of Escario's column, which Shafter supposed to be 8,000 strong, and the report that 10,000 of the enemy were at Holguin and 7,000 near Guantanamo,[51] the American commander in chief lost his nerve. On the 3d, after vainly summoning General José Toral—the successor of Linares, who had been wounded—to surrender the city, he sent the following despairing telegram to the Secretary of War:

We have the town well invested on the north and east, but with a very thin line. Upon approaching it we find it of such a character and the defences so strong it will be impossible to carry it by storm with my present force, and I am seriously considering withdrawing about five miles and taking up a new position on the high ground between the San Juan River and Siboney . . .[52]

He received the following reply: "Of course you can judge the situation better than we can at this end of the line. If, however, you could hold your present position, especially San Juan Heights, the effect upon the country would be much better than falling back."[53] To which he replied: "I shall hold my present position."

The battle of El Caney–San Juan Hill cost the Americans 225 officers and men killed, 1,384 wounded,[54] and 72 men missing, the Spanish losses numbering 593 in all.

This battle was won not by generalship, but by hard fighting against a brave and stubborn enemy. Of the 13,096 soldiers in the vicinity of Santiago, Linares concentrated barely 13 per cent on the battlefield and less than 5 per cent of the total in the Santiago Province. Yet, as Sargent writes: "It may be said without exaggeration that one soldier behind the intrenchments of El Caney or of San Juan Hill was equal in fighting power to six or eight soldiers advancing to attack him."[55] Such was the power of the magazine rifle on the defense.

Shafter's mistake was similar though not so great. Had he concentrated the whole of his 15,065 men against San Juan Hill instead of only 8,412, his losses would have been less considerable. And not only would the El Caney position have been turned, but the probabilities are that the city of Santiago would have been entered on the 1st, and Admiral Cervera forced to capitulate.

It is not necessary here to discuss the vacillations of Cervera's policy from the time he was blockaded until he was ordered to meet his fate. Suffice it to say that, although on June 24 a council of war had unanimously decided that to escape was "absolutely impossible," he received a direct order from General Blanco late at night on July 1, after the fall of San Juan Hill, that a sortie should be made before the enemy could seize and occupy the harbor entrance. Thereupon, on the 2d, Cervera called in such ships' crews as were ashore, but in order to rest them decided to postpone his desperate adventure until the 3d, when all ships which escaped destruction were to run for Cienfuegos or Havana.

On Sunday morning, the 3d, at about a quarter-past nine the squadron got under way, the flagship, the *Infanta Maria Teresa,* leading. Her commander, Captain Victor M. Concas y Palan, writes:

We had just finished making the turn at Diamond Bank, amidst death-like silence, everybody awed by the magnificent spectacle of the ships issuing from the narrow passage between the Morro and Socapa. It was a solemn moment, capable of making the calmest heart beat faster. From outside the conning tower, which I did not want to enter, in order, if I should fall, to set an example to my defenceless crew, I asked leave of the Admiral and with that gave the order to fire. The bugle gave the signal to begin the battle, an order repeated to all the batteries and followed by a murmur of approbation·from all those poor sailors and marines who were anxious to fight; for they did not know that those warlike echoes were the signal which hurled their country at the feet of the victor, since they were to deprive Spain of the only power still of value to her, without which a million soldiers could do nothing to serve her . . .

My bugles were the last echo of those which history tells were sounded in the taking of Granada; it was the signal that the history of four centuries of greatness was ended and that Spain had passed into a nation of the fourth class.[56]

The Americans had not expected that Admiral Cervera would attempt a daylight sortie,[57] and the American flagship *New York,* under the command of Captain Chadwick, was steaming for Siboney when, at 9.35 A.M., the *Iowa,* stationed immediately opposite the entrance to the harbor, saw the *Maria Teresa* slowly moving down the narrow channel. The *Iowa* promptly fired a shotted gun and hoisted the signal "Enemy's ships coming out."

Following the *Maria Teresa,* at intervals of several minutes, came first the *Vizcaya,* then the *Cristobal Colon* and the *Oquendo,* and lastly the *Pluton* and *Furor.* Meanwhile the *New York* put about and the other American ships began to close, their fire being concentrated on the *Maria Teresa.* The Spanish ship replied wildly, many of her gun crews having never fired their pieces before.

Soon the sea was obscured by clouds of smoke. "We might as well have had a blanket tied over our heads," writes Captain Philip of the *Texas.* Then "Suddenly a whiff of breeze and a lull in the firing lifted the pall, and there, bearing down on us and across our bows, turning on her port helm, with big waves curling over her bows and great clouds of black smoke pouring from her funnels, was the *Brooklyn.* She looked as big as half-a-dozen *Great Easterns* and seemed so near it took our breath away." [58] Fortunately a collision was avoided, otherwise one of these two ships would most certainly have been sunk.

Shortly after this narrow escape, two 12-inch shells from the *Iowa* struck the *Maria Teresa* and broke some of the engine piping, putting her pumps out of action. "At the same time," writes Cervera, "I was informed that the after-deck and chart house were burning, while the fire that had commenced in my cabin was spreading with great rapidity to the centre of the ship, and, as we had no water, it made rapid headway, and we were powerless to fight it. I realized that the ship was doomed, and cast about for a place where I could run her aground . . . I therefore steered for a small beach west of Punta Cabrera, where we ran aground just as the engine stopped." [59]

Still everything was obscured by the smoke. "It got in our ears, noses, and mouths, blackened our faces, and blinded our eyes," writes Captain Philip. "Often for minutes at a time, for all we could see, we might as well have been down in the double bottoms as on the bridge. One had the sensation of standing up against an unseen foe . . ." [60] Then, as it began to clear—it was now a little after ten o'clock—the *Texas, Iowa, Oregon,* and *Indiana* turned their secondary batteries on to the Spanish destroyers as they passed on westward down the coast, leaving it to the *Gloucester* to finish off the *Furor,* which immediately after blew up "with a crash that sounded high above the roar of battle." "There was a great gush of black smoke, and a sheet of flame seemed to leap above the tops of the hills under which the doomed craft lay," writes Philip.[61] Meanwhile the *Pluton* ran on the rocks and blew up.

Pressing on, the four American battleships gave chase to the *Oquendo, Vizcaya,* and *Cristobal Colon.* A tremendous fire was opened on the *Oquendo,* several 8-inch shells striking her and causing frightful havoc; then under a hail of smaller projectiles, she, like the *Maria Teresa,* turned landward and ran ashore. At 11.24 A.M. she hoisted the white flag.

The *Brooklyn* now joined the *Indiana, Iowa, Texas,* and *Oregon,* and all five opened fire upon the *Vizcaya,* while the *Cristobal Colon* was rapidly increasing distance. Then it was seen that the *Vizcaya* was on fire and that her surrender was but a question of time. A little after 11 o'clock she veered toward the shore, and as her "nose touched the beach two tremendous explosions in succession literally shook her to pieces," throwing perpendicularly into the air a cloud of smoke "quite a thousand feet in height."

While the *Iowa* went to her assistance, the *Oregon, Brooklyn, Texas, New York,* and *Vixen* took up the pursuit of the last remaining Spanish ship. As they gained on her they opened fire, and it soon became clear that her doom was sealed. At 1.15 P.M., she hauled down her colors, turned inshore, and ran on the beach off the mouth of the Tarquino river, fifty-four miles west of Santiago Harbor. "Thus," as Sargent writes, "ended one of the most remarkable battles in naval history."

This is an accurate appraisal, for not only was every Spanish ship either sunk or put out of action, but the casualties of the contending sides were totally disproportionate, the Spaniards losing 323 killed and 151 wounded [62] to the Americans' one killed and one wounded. This was due not only to the vastly superior position of Sampson's fleet at the opening of the battle, but also to the greater weight of metal it could fire and the greater efficiency of its gunners.

Though this battle sealed the fate of the Spanish West Indies, the war in Cuba continued until July 16, when fortunately for the American army, now in the grip of fever, General Toral informed General Shafter that his government had approved a capitulation. It was signed at 6 P.M. that day, when it was agreed that the Spaniards would march out of Santiago with the honors of war and with as little delay as possible be transported to Spain.

By now more than half Shafter's corps were down with malaria, dysentery, typhoid, and yellow fever. On August 3 the situation was so bad that ten of his senior commanding officers addressed a letter to him stating: "This army must be moved at once or it will perish." [63] The re-embarkation of the Fifth Corps began on the 7th and was completed by the 25th, when Shafter sailed home with the last contingent. Meanwhile, in the East Indies, Manila had surrendered on August 13, and the campaign in Puerto Rico was suspended on the following day.

On October 1 the commissioners for the treaty of peace met in Paris and sat until December 10, the day the treaty was signed. All claims of Spanish sovereignty over Cuba were relinquished, the U. S. A. taking over temporary control of the island. Puerto Rico and the other Spanish islands were ceded to the United States, which also purchased the Philippines for $20,000,000.

The treaty was ratified by the United States Senate on February 6, and by the Queen Regent of Spain on March 19, 1899.

Insignificant though this war may seem when compared to such stupendous struggles as the War of the Revolution and the Civil War, it must nevertheless take its place beside them. It was, in a way, their coping stone. But before I examine its political significance, I will turn to its strategical lessons. In this respect the Spanish-American War marked the tactical turning point from old methods of warfare to new.

First, steam power at sea was put to its first practical test, though it had, in face of immense opposition, begun to transform naval warfare some forty-odd years earlier. Secondly, bullet power on land, though centuries old, reinforced by the use of the magazine rifle and smokeless powder, began to transform the traditional tactics of the nineteenth century.

The naval actions of this war conclusively proved the overwhelming importance of *matériel,* granted normally efficient command, discipline, and training. Unlike an army, which when even indifferently armed and equipped can put up a stubborn fight, a fleet similarly situated is helpless. In other words, in speed, endurance, armor, and gun power it must be equal or superior to its adversary. Without this equality or superiority, however able its command and high its discipline and skill may be, it has no place in a naval battle. This was less true in sailing ship days.

Secondly, the war showed that the supreme function of the fleet was twofold: to blockade and to command the sea. While the purpose of the second function is defensive—to maintain or establish freedom of movement on the high seas; the purpose of the first is offensive—to strangle the enemy economically.

The lessons to be learned from the land fighting in this war are, in spite of its brevity, so numerous that I can mention only a few.

It proved, in the first place, that in spite of the enhanced power of rifle and gun on the defensive, offensive action is still the dominant factor in war. Not only does it energize the will to win, but it enables a general to follow his own plan instead of conforming to his enemy's. Furthermore, it is offense and not defense which offers decisive results. Offensive action is therefore a positive factor, whereas defensive is negative; it is the difference between pressure and resistance.

Secondly, the war showed that because of the ever-increasing power of the defensive, the strength of offensive action depends more and more on quality rather than quantity, and when weapon power is equal, then on chance, discipline, or generalship.

Thirdly, it proved, as Sargent says, that: "Military resources should never be confounded with military strength." [64] This supremely important lesson certainly was not learnt.

Examining the political and international results of this war, we find that it both ends and opens an epoch. "The war," writes Admiral Chadwick, "was the final act in the struggle for supremacy between Anglo-Saxons and men of the Latin race in North America, in which Philip, Elizabeth, Drake, Howard, Chatham, Vernon, Wolfe, Montcalm, Washington had, all, a part. The expedition of the Great Armada; the murderous early struggles in Carolina and Florida; the seven years which drove France from the American continent, were but acts in the drama the culmination of which, in 1898, left the Anglo-Saxon and American in Mexico masters of the whole of the northern continent. It was the end of a race struggle which had lasted full three hundred years." [65]

Yet it was more than all this. It raised the United States from a continental to an intercontinental power; for it handed over to the Americans the great archipelago of the Philippines, and simultaneously it wiped out, as no peaceful event could have done, most of the remaining differences between North and South. Shoulder to shoulder Northerners and Southerners had stormed San Juan Hill and trained their guns on Cervera's ships. They had fought side by side in Cuba, Puerto Rico, and Manila and in their fighting had rounded off the jagged edges of their Civil War. Now, hand in hand, as a united nation, they could step onto the world's stage.

The date of the victory of Manila marks the entry of the United States upon her imperial course, and the voyage of the *Oregon,* by pointing to the imperative necessity of a canal across the Isthmus of Panama, persuaded the Americans to link together the greatest of the oceans.

REFERENCES

[1] *Lessons of the War with Spain,* Alfred T. Mahan, p. 186.

[2] *Recent History of the United States,* Frederic L. Paxson, p. 246.

[3] *Report of Bureau of Navigation, 1898,* Appendix 27, quoted by Rear-Admiral French Ensor Chadwick, in *The Relations of the United States and Spain. The Spanish-American War,* vol. II, pp. 58–59.

[4] "On March 27 Cervera gives the total number of projectiles available as 1,905 (but about a fifth of the number used by Sampson's squadron on July 3), and, on April 2, he writes from Cadiz, where the squadron had gone:

'My fears are realized, for the conflict is approaching at a rapid rate and the *Colon* does not have her heavy guns; the *Carlos V* has not been delivered, and her 3.94-inch armament is not mounted; on the *Pelayo* the redoubt is not completed, and I believe she lacks her secondary battery; the *Vitoria* is without armament, and of the *Numancia* we had better not speak.'" (Chadwick, vol. II, p. 107.)

[5] ". . . a writer in a Spanish magazine has told the following incident: A little more than a year ago we visited General Cervera in La Carraca [the Cadiz

arsenal], and we said to him: 'You appear to be indicated by professional opinion, for command in the squadron in case war is declared.' 'In that case,' he replied, 'I shall accept, knowing, however, that I am going to a Trafalgar.' 'And how could that disaster be avoided?' 'By allowing me to expend beforehand fifty thousand tons of coal in evolutions and ten thousand projectiles in target practice. Otherwise we shall go to a Trafalgar. Remember what I say.'" (Quoted by *Mahan*, p. 86.)

[6] *The Downfall of Spain*, Herbert W. Wilson, pp. 67–68.

[7] *The New American Navy*, John D. Long, vol. I, p. 211.

[8] Including thirteen single-turret monitors of the Civil War period.

[9] See "The Voyage of the Oregon," Lieut. W. H. Allen, *The American-Spanish War, A History by the War Leaders*, chap. VIII.

[10] *The Rough Riders*, Theodore Roosevelt, pp. 200, 185.

[11] *The Campaign of Santiago de Cuba*, Herbert H. Sargent, vol. I, pp. 79–80.

[12] Chadwick, vol. II, p. 54.

[13] Theodore Roosevelt, pp. 98, 118.

[14] *"A History by the War Leaders,"* p. 112.

[15] Chadwick, vol. II, p. 114.

[16] *Ibid.*, vol. II, p. 121.

[17] *Ibid.*, vol. II, p. 261.

[18] Sargent, vol. I, p. 203.

[19] *Insegnamenti della Guerra Ispano-Americano*, pp. 74–75.

[20] Cervera, *Documents*, 91. Quoted by Chadwick, vol. II, p. 313.

[21] Cervera, *Documents*, 95, 96. *Ibid.*, vol. II, p. 315.

[22] See his book *The Sinking of the Merrimac*, and Francis Kelly's account in *A History by the War Leaders*, chap. V.

[23] See Sampson's dispatch No. 113, Chadwick, vol. II, p. 345.

[24] Chadwick, vol. II, pp. 363–364.

[25] Admiral Chadwick, quoting Müller y Tejeiro and Nuñez, writes: "'Had it not been for the arrival of the German steamer *Palaria*, which, fortunately, left at Santiago 1,700 sacks of rice intended for Havana, there would have been an absolute lack of provisions, as neither the merchants nor anyone else attempted to import them.' The last vessel to arrive with provisions was the *Mortera*, April 25, with 180,000 rations of flour, 197,000 of rice, 149,000 of garbanzos (chick-peas), 79,000 of kidney beans, 96,000 of wine, and 150 head of cattle. As about 360,000 rations a month were needed for the army alone, apart from the needs of the population of a town of 30,000 people, and as nothing of importance could be drawn from the neighboring country, the inadequacy of supplies is apparent" (vol. III, pp. 40–41):

[26] Cervera, *Documents*, 100. Quoted by Chadwick, vol. II, p. 353.

[27] Chadwick, vol. II, p. 353.

[28] *Ibid.*, vol. III, p. 17.

[29] *Ibid.*, vol. III, p. 12.

[30] *Ibid.*, vol. III, pp. 12–13.

[31] *Investigation of the Conduct of the War with Spain*, vol. V, cols. 2257–2258. See also Lieutenant John D. Miley's (of General Shafter's staff) *In Cuba with Shafter*, pp. 22–24 and 27.

[32] Sampson was ordered to make certain that all of Cervera's ships were actually at Santiago. This led to a remarkably bold reconnaissance by Lieutenant Blue, who landed on the mainland and after a detour of seventy miles was taken by a party of insurgents to a position from where he was able to count the Spanish ships. For his report, see Chadwick, vol. II, pp. 378–379.

[33] It is interesting to note that, according to General Orders No. 18, "All troops

will carry on the person the blanket roll (with shelter tent and poncho), three days' field rations (with coffee ground), canteen filled and 100 rounds of ammunition per man." (*A History by the War Leaders*, p. 182.)

[34] Theodore Roosevelt, pp. 77–79.
[35] Sargent, vol. II, p. 52.
[36] *A History by the War Leaders*, p. 185.
[37] *Ibid.*, pp. 185–186.
[38] See Chadwick, vol. III, p. 75, and Sargent, vol. II, pp. 144–145.
[39] Quoted by Sargent, vol. II, p. 104.
[40] Chadwick, vol. III, p. 81.
[41] Quoted from *ibid.*, vol. III, p. 80. What is meant by "going on the Sevilla road" is difficult to say, as the El Caney–Santiago road is the obvious one to march by.
[42] Roosevelt (pp. 117–118) writes: "Immediately our guns opened, and at the report great clouds of white smoke hung on the ridge crest . . . As the Spaniards used smokeless powder, their artillery had an enormous advantage over ours . . ."
[43] *The War in Cuba*, p. 123.
[44] *Ibid.*, pp. 124–125.
[45] Theodore Roosevelt, pp. 121–122.
[46] Sargent, vol. II, pp. 117–118.
[47] Theodore Roosevelt, p. 135. He also says: "It was the only sound which I ever heard my men cheer in battle."
[48] Sargent, vol. II, p. 119. Parker, in his report, writes: "Inspired by the friendly rattle of the machine-guns, our own troops rose to the charge, while the enemy, amazed by our sudden and tremendous increase of fire, first diverted his fire to my battery and then, unable to withstand the hail of bullets, augmented by the moral effect of our battery fire and the charging line, broke madly from his safe trenches, and was mercilessly cut by the fire of these guns during his flight." (Chadwick, vol. III, p. 93.)
[49] *The Cuban and Puerto Rican Campaigns*, R. H. Davis, pp. 220–223. Miley, ending his account of this battle and that at El Caney says: "Much has been written about them, but no description can convey to the reader a just appreciation of the gallantry and heroism displayed by officers and men alike" (*In Cuba with Shafter*, John D. Miley, p. 118).
[50] Chadwick, vol. III, p. 106.
[51] See *The Spanish-American War*, R. A. Alger, p. 175.
[52] Chadwick, vol. III, p. 109.
[53] *Ibid.*, vol. III, p. 110.
[54] The American ambulance and medical organization proved quite inadequate to deal with so great a number. (See *Campaigning in Cuba*, George Kennan, pp. 135–136.) Roosevelt writes: "We found all our dead and all the badly wounded. Around one of the latter the big, hideous land-crabs had gathered in a grewsome ring, waiting for life to be extinct. One of our own men and most of the Spanish dead had been found by the vultures before we got at them; and their bodies were mangled, the eyes and wounds being torn" (pp. 104–105).
[55] Sargent, vol. II, p. 135.
[56] Quoted by Chadwick, vol. III, pp. 127–128.
[57] A night sortie was considered by Cervera, and, because of the searchlights, turned down. Admiral Sampson writes: "The great difficulty in a night attempt was our dazzling search-light. A search-light shining direct in one's eyes prevents him absolutely from seeing anything else; it is as though he were looking at the sun: and it was that effect upon them, taken in connection with the necessity of

seeing their way out of the channel, that made them hesitate." (See Chadwick, vol. III, p. 185; also *A History by the War Leaders*, p. 162.)

[58] Chadwick, vol. III, p. 136. The *Great Eastern* was built in 1858. She was a vessel of 32,160 tons displacement. In size nothing approached her until 1899, when the White Star liner *Oceanic* with a displacement of 26,100 tons was launched.

[59] *Ibid.*, vol. III, pp. 138–139.

[60] *Ibid.*, vol. III, p. 139.

[61] *Ibid.*, vol. III, p. 141.

[62] These are Captain Concas's figures. Chadwick (vol. III, p. 177) says "the loss by gun-fire and by drowning was but 264." Captain Robley D. Evans (*A History by the War Leaders*, p. 161) places the killed at 400. "The number of wounded will never be known," he writes, "as a great many of them were burned with their ships."

[63] Sargent, vol. III, p. 47.

[64] *Ibid.*, vol. III, p. 95.

[65] Chadwick, vol. I, p. 587.

1899–1917

SYNOPSIS OF BACKGROUND EVENTS

T HE Spanish-American War left the United States in a dilemma: whether to pursue a policy of isolation or world co-operation. Although the first alternative was immensely attractive, since the causes of war in North America had by now all but been eliminated, the growing power of international trade and finance relentlessly drew the Americans toward bellicose Europe, and in consequence into the next great conflict.

In 1899, Mr. H. G. Wells, then at the apex of his imaginative life, sensed this impending doom in his book *When the Sleeper Wakes,* which coincided with the first of the purely financial wars—the British-Boer War in South Africa. In this book he foretold a society entirely dominated by organized finance.

Out of this age in America emerged the great Captains of Industry and the Money Barons, such as Andrew Carnegie, John D. Rockefeller, and J. Pierpont Morgan, who followed in the footsteps of those of Great Britain and Germany. It was an age of advancing materialism, and, therefore, of cultural and spiritual decline. Under the magic wand of gold, vitalized by an insatiable greed, wealth was piled up in trusts and monopolies which carried with them ever-increasing political power. Simultaneously, yet less directly, profit-seeking both stimulated and exploited the inventive genius of man. From the point of view of war, the three most fateful inventions were motor traction, flight, and wireless telegraphy. Collaterally, as science advanced, printing became a vastly cheaper and speedier process. The new journalism of thrill and flavor, introduced by William Randolph Hearst, drew pennies out of the peoples' pockets as never before, but did more to atrophy than to enlighten public opinion. Then, writes an American—Frederick L. Paxson—"Fiction was brought into the ranks to serve the muck-rakers. Cut-throat speculation furnished the theme for Frank Norris's *Octopus* (1901); the offences of the meat-packers inspired Upton Sinclair's *Jungle* (1906), while the political intrigues of railroads and big business were used by Winston Churchill in *Coniston* (1906)." Next, he continues:

The worship of success with which the critics had reproached American opinion in the nineties was transmuted into suspicion and social hatred . . . "What we have been witnessing," declared the venerable Washington Gladden, "is a new Apocalypse, an uncovering of the iniquity of the land . . . We have found that no society can march hellward faster than a democracy under the banner of unbridled individualism."

Meanwhile, as plutocracy and mobocracy joined hands, the religious spirit shriveled into hysterical emotionalism. Such men as Phillips Brooks and Henry Ward Beecher gave way to Billy Sunday and other hot-gospellers. Much the same kind of change took place in politics, for since the Civil War industry had grown more rapidly than the theory of government. Consequently, Congress, possessing little technical economic knowledge, became more and more incapable of solving and controlling the problems of an ever-growing economic civilization.

Such, within and without America, were the general symptoms of world decay when the United States took its place among the world powers, and by becoming one of them was inevitably drawn into their quarrels.

In 1900, President McKinley was elected for a second time, with Colonel Theodore Roosevelt—the popular hero of the recent war—as vice-president. Big business looked forward to a future of ever-increasing prosperity. Then, in September the following year, McKinley was assassinated in Buffalo, whereupon Roosevelt automatically succeeded him.

Already, during McKinley's brief second term, Manifest Destiny had, through the Boxer Rebellion of 1899, brought United States troops from the Philippines to China, not only to protect her legation in Peking, but also to maintain the "open-door" policy. When, in June, 1900, a small expedition was sent to Peking under General Chaffee, there was at once some friction with the German contingent, which Chaffee accused of looting.

Two years later came another international clash, this time with Great Britain, Germany, and Italy, who, to enforce certain claims, set out to blockade the ports of Venezuela. This agitated the United States not so much because it might be interpreted as a violation of the Monroe Doctrine, but because in 1900, after much trouble, she had finally succeeded in reversing the Clayton Bulwer treaty of 1850, by which it had been agreed that, should a canal be cut across the Isthmus of Panama, neither Great Britain nor the United States would obtain or maintain for itself exclusive control. Freed now from this shackle, which had been forged to check British colonial expansion, in 1903 the United States signed an agreement with Colombia authorizing the United States to take over the French concession at Panama, and to control the region through which the canal was to be dug. Though this agreement, known as the Hay-Herran Treaty, was ratified by the U. S. Senate in March, the Colombian Congress delayed so long that Roosevelt urged the State of Panama to secede from Colombia and negotiate directly with the United States. The independence of Panama was proclaimed in November, after a bloodless revolt and American naval forces were sent there to prevent the landing of Colombian troops. A few days later the Republic of Panama was recognized by Washington; on November 18 it conceded to the United States the rights in question; and early in 1904 work on the canal was begun.

Simultaneously with this great project came the outbreak of the Russo-Japanese War which drew the United States still further into world affairs, for it was terminated through the influence of Roosevelt by the Treaty of Portsmouth, signed on September 5, 1905. The president thus rose to the position of moderator between East and West, and in the following year was awarded the Nobel prize, "for his services in the cause of peace."

The next event hardly bore out this conclusion. Toward the close of 1907 a fleet of American battleships stood out from Hampton Roads to circumnavigate the world. Its aim presumably was to overawe Japan, an act of moral persuasion which lost nothing when four dreadnoughts were laid down during the following year. The first one was commissioned in 1910. By 1916 thirteen of these warships had been built, while four others were on the stocks.

The year 1908 saw the completion of Roosevelt's second term and the election of William Howard Taft as president, and brought another dispute with Great Britain over the Declaration of London, which covered the questions of blockade, contraband, and search in wartime. Though never ratified, it was accepted as a statement of the general trend of international maritime law.

Thus the first decade of the new century passed amidst the rumblings, if not of war, yet of many deep-seated discontents, more especially in Europe, where an armament race was in full and rapid progress. Meanwhile in the United States, Oklahoma had been admitted as a state in 1907, an event which marked the disappearance of the old Indian country. With the admission of Arizona and New Mexico in 1912, the period of Territories came to an end.

That year Woodrow Wilson was elected as a minority president, for though the Republicans and Progressives cast 7,500,000 votes, the Democrats polled only 6,291,000 for Wilson. It was an unfortunate circumstance, for the Agadir incident in 1911 had brought Europe to the boiling point. 1911 also saw the outbreak of the Italo-Turkish War in Libya, and the following year witnessed the war in the Balkans. Serbia, Bulgaria, Greece, and Montenegro, ranged against Turkey, ended by quarreling among themselves. Simultaneously, the fall of Porfirio Diaz in Mexico brought Francisco Madero to the fore. In February, 1913, he was murdered and Victoriano Huerta became dictator. Amidst these crumblings and crashings a minority president was difficultly placed.

Nevertheless, in America the dove of peace continued to flutter, and, in 1913, thanks to the munificence of Andrew Carnegie (1837–1919) a temple was opened for her at the Hague. This event was accepted "as an indication that the world was through with its great wars." Then, the following year, while the celebration of the hundred years peace between the United States and Great Britain was in preparation, Huerta arrested an American officer and a party of marines at Tampico, and a military and naval demonstration was at once prepared against Vera Cruz. On April 20, 1914, President Wilson announced to Congress: "We seek to maintain the dignity and authority of the United States only because we wish always to keep our great influence unimpaired for the uses of liberty, both in the United States and wherever else it may be employed for the benefit of mankind."

But in spite of peace palaces and noble words, the pent-up animosities, jealousies, greeds, and fears in Europe, like a boil, had come to a head; all that was now required to cause it to burst was a slight outside pressure. This was supplied on June 28, 1914, when the Archduke Francis Ferdinand of Austria and his wife were assassinated in Sarajevo. At the moment the international situation was highly involved: Great Britain was on the verge of civil war in Ireland; Germany was bellicose and in the process of reopening the enlarged Kiel Canal; France was in a

state of political decay; Russia appeared to be on the point of revolution, and the U. S. A. was nearing war with Mexico. On July 23 came
Austria's ultimatum to Serbia, and five days later the Austrian guns
thundered against Belgrade.

"The course for the United States to take in this war," writes Paxson,
"had long been established by precedent and theory. The modern doctrine of neutrality was an American idea that Washington had conceived
and Jefferson phrased in 1793. The American Neutrality Act of 1794
was the foundation of all such acts wherever they existed, and the progress of international law thereafter was due largely to the insistence
of neutral states, generally under American leadership and demanding
that belligerents respect their rights and property, and leave them alone."

From now onward until April, 1917, the United States not only led,
but represented neutral opinion.

President Wilson's position was difficult. There were some 9,000,000
Germans or half-Germans in the United States, and as naturally many
of these people sympathized with the German cause, a violent internal
propaganda campaign was opened. However, the bulk of his countrymen, like himself, wanted nothing but neutrality.

The two groups of belligerents, *vis-à-vis* the United States, were also
in a difficult position. Both wanted her good will and her trade; yet for
strategical reasons it was as essential for Great Britain to blockade Germany as it was for Germany to maintain contact with the outer world.
In no way could this blockade become complete unless the imports of
neutral countries, such as Denmark and Holland, were kept at their
prewar figures. But when this was attempted considerable friction arose
between Great Britain and the United States. Further still, on February 4, 1915, the German government, having already protested that the
United States had failed to compel the Allied Powers to respect the
American neutrality laws, announced a war zone around Great Britain,
within which from February 18 onward "every enemy merchant ship
. . . even if it is impossible to avert dangers which threaten the crew
and passengers," would be sunk. In other words, unrestricted submarine
warfare was proclaimed.

Though such action was contrary to international law, this was largely
due to the fact that international lawyers had never troubled to consider it; hence the objection was, from the point of view of common
sense—action adapted to circumstances—little more than a quibble. Nor
could it be condemned on moral grounds, because sinking ships at sight

was no more barbarous than placing an entire nation under blockade. If morally it is justifiable to reduce millions of men, women, and children to starvation and through underfeeding ruin the physical constitution of a nation for several generations, it is equally justifiable to drown a comparatively small number of sailors without warning. Such was the German point of view, and strategically it was the correct one, though politically it might alienate the United States.

Inevitably, that happened when, on May 7, 1915, the British liner, *Lusitania,* bound for Liverpool, was torpedoed off the south coast of Ireland, carrying to the bottom with her 1,200 passengers, among whom were 114 American men, women, and children. Though Theodore Roosevelt declared this sinking to be "an act of piracy," its most important repercussion was that it impelled the national Administration to consider the possibilities of war and in consequence to prepare for it.

At almost the same time, certain peace-loving Americans, among whom was ex-President Taft, launched in Independence Hall, Philadelphia, on June 17, the idea that the prevention of war was better than its cure, and that it could be attained by the establishment of a League to Enforce Peace. Though this substitute for war differed little from Sully's "Grand Design" and the perpetual peace schemes of William Penn, Jean Jacques Rousseau, and Immanuel Kant, as well as of the Holy Alliance, it seized upon the American imagination, and, in 1916, was accepted by Wilson as a workable project. Then, in May of that year, unrestricted submarine warfare having once again been proclaimed by Germany, the *Sussex* was sunk with a loss of two American lives. Wilson at once presented the following ultimatum to the German government:

Unless the Imperial German Government should now immediately effect and declare an abandonment of its present methods of warfare against passenger and freight-carrying vessels, this Government can have no choice but to sever diplomatic relations with the Government of the German Empire altogether.

Thereupon Germany recanted.

Meanwhile national defense was pushed forward. In June a bill was passed "providing an authorized strength for the regular army of 223,-000; the total to be reached in five years," and also for a National Guard of 450,000 officers and men, while an immense sum was appropriated for the building of ten more dreadnoughts and six battle cruisers.

In November Woodrow Wilson was re-elected president. A month later Germany, acting through the United States government, made an offer of peace to her enemies which was rejected. Next, on January 22, 1917, Wilson addressed Congress upon the terms of peace, stating that it should be "a peace without victory," and not one which was dictated by the victor; but, instead, "constructed for the purpose of establishing world peace"—in other words, a League of Nations.

Ten days after this address, the German government withdrew the pledges it had given after the sinking of the *Sussex,* and announced the resumption of unrestricted submarine warfare. Consequently, on February 3, Count von Bernstorff, the German ambassador at Washington, was handed his passports, and, on the 26th, Wilson appeared before Congress "to ask for specific power to defend merchant ships in case they should be attacked." The following month, Tsar Nicholas II having been deposed, the United States welcomed the new Russian Republic.

At length, on April 2, Wilson delivered to Congress an address in which, having recited the grievances of the United States against the German government, he called for a declaration of a state of war with "this natural foe of liberty."

"We are glad," he declared, "now that we see the facts with no veil of false pretense about them, to fight thus for the ultimate peace of the world and for the liberation of the peoples, the German people included; for the rights of nations, great and small, and the privilege of men everywhere to choose their way of life and of obedience. The world must be made safe for democracy." Four days later, on April 6, the war resolution was passed, declaring that the United States were at war with Germany.

CHAPTER XI

THE BATTLE OF THE MEUSE–ARGONNE, 1918

ON the day the United States threw in her lot with the Allied Powers, the war in Europe was already two years and eight months old. Except for the revolution in Russia, now in its initial phase, victory seemed as distant from both sides as it had been at any time since the Battle of the Marne. Summarizing this long period of slaughter and destruction, elsewhere I have written:

> The war opened on sound, traditional lines . . . Millions of men would sweep forward and, like immense clouds of locusts, would gain victory by sheer weight of numbers . . . Nevertheless, this carefully planned war was within a few weeks of its declaration smashed to pieces by fire-power; fire-power so devastating that as armies could no longer live upon the surface of the battlefield there was no choice but to go under the surface; consequently trenches five hundred miles long were dug, and armies went to earth like foxes. Then, in order to secure these trenches from surprise attacks, each side turned itself into an immense spider, and spun hundreds of thousands of miles of steel web around its entrenchments. Thus, after a few weeks of *real* warfare, the *offensive à outrance,* that high gospel of the pre-war manuals, was reduced to a wallowing defensive among shell holes and barbed wire. Armies, through their own lack of foresight, were reduced to the position of human cattle. They browsed behind their fences and occasionally snorted and bellowed at each other.[1]

The reasons for this stalemate were faulty strategy and faulty tactics. As regards the first, gigantic battles, such as the battle of the Somme and Verdun, had been waged with no further object than to ram a zone of earthworks. As early as September, 1915, it became clearly apparent to me that the strategy of the Western Front was not understood;

as is usually the case, it was governed by topography. I was certain that victory would have to be sought in the triangle of ground—Arras-Namur-Rheims, and not in Flanders or in the Verdun or Vosges areas. At the time I wrote:

The German western armies form a huge zigzag running from near Ostend to Noyon, from Noyon to Verdun, and from Verdun to near Basle, the upper half of which constitutes an extensive salient with its apex pointing towards Paris, and the lower a re-entrant with its apex towards Metz. The northern extremity of the salient rests on the sea and the Flanders marshes, the southern on the Ardennes, flanked on one side by Verdun and on the other by Metz. The Ardennes are an obstacle, and though several railways cross them, the natural lines of communications, as far as Germany is at present concerned, run between their northern edge and the Dutch frontier, a small gap, with Liège as its centre. From this point the railways and roads splay fan-shaped westwards. The result of this is that the Germans have every facility communications and security can give them. Further, they can reinforce any position in this salient against a single attack more rapidly than can the French and British reinforce a single attacking army. Should, however, a dual attack be made, one from the direction of Arras eastwards towards Namur, and one from near Rheims north-eastwards towards that same place, the communications in the angle formed by the lines of advance of these attacks will be severed one after another, with the result that the German armies between Arras and Rheims must either fight or fall back. If the latter course is adopted, the continual shifting from one line of supply to another will create such overwhelming confusion that the falling back alone will probably mean to Germany a loss of between three and four hundred thousand men.[2]

On the lines of this strategy a dual attack was launched by the British and the French, the former advancing from Arras eastward on April 9, 1917, and the latter from between Rheims and Soissons northward on April 16. In its initial stage the first attack was successful, but the second was almost immediately shattered and with such disastrous results to France that the morale of her soldiers never fully recovered from this defeat. Both attacks, however, were foredoomed to failure, because all chance of surprise had been bartered away for methodical preparation and lengthy preliminary artillery bombardments, which, like gongs, summoned the enemy to these carnivals of death. It was at this critical moment that the United States entered the war, not a day too soon to save the Allied cause from ruin.

If the situation in which the British and the French now found themselves was serious, that facing the Americans was deplorable. In November, 1916, President Wilson had been re-elected for keeping his country out of the war; therefore it is not surprising that, when less than six months later a war fever swept the States from the Atlantic to the Pacific, few preparations had been made. The Army was without organization, or rather was organized purely for police work. Army Corps had lapsed with the Civil War, and, in 1917, not even a divisional organization existed, and very few officers had ever handled any formation greater than a regiment. The General Staff, created after the Spanish-American War, was still but a small body of amateurs.[3] Munitions were sorely lacking. For issue, no more than 285,000 Springfield rifles, 400 light field guns, and 150 heavy field guns were in store.[4] Although, in 1916, $12,000,000 had been allotted for the construction of machine guns, less than 1,500 had been produced, and those were of four types. Of gun ammunition, excepting 3-inch, there was only enough for a nine hours' battle. Concerning aviation:

The situation . . . was such that every American ought to feel mortified to hear it mentioned. Out of 65 officers and about 1000 men in the Air Service of the Signal Corps, there were 35 who could fly. With the exception of five or six officers, none of them could have met the requirements of modern battle conditions and none had any technical experience with aircraft guns, bombs or bombing devices.

We could boast some 55 training planes in various conditions of usefulness, all entirely without war equipment and valueless for service at the front. Of these 55 planes . . . 51 were obsolete and the other 4 obsolescent. We could not have put a single squadron in the field, although it was estimated later that we should eventually need at least 300 squadrons, each to be composed on the average of some 24 officers, 180 men and 18 aeroplanes, besides a large reserve of planes for replacements.[5]

To tackle this situation many men were required, first and foremost a commander in chief, clear-sighted enough to see what was wanted and energetic enough to get what he considered necessary. The choice fell upon Major General John J. Pershing, who had recently been in command of a punitive expedition operating against Francisco Villa in Mexico. Pershing, at the time, was in command of the Southern Department, with his headquarters at Fort Sam Houston, San Antonio, Texas. He assumed his office as commander in chief on the 26th of May, having meanwhile selected Major General James G. Harbord as his chief of staff.

Born on September 13, 1860, Pershing was in rank the junior of all the major generals except one. He had seen much service in Mexico and the Philippines, and had taken part in the Sioux War of 1890 as well as the Cuban war, having been present at the Battle of San Juan Hill. Later he was appointed military attaché in Tokio, and in 1904 accompanied the Japanese to Manchuria.

Though not an imaginative soldier, Pershing was painstaking, immensely hard-working, and stubborn. His problem was to raise, organize, train, and fight a horde army. The new tank [6] and air warfare did not concern him. Men and more men was his sole concern. For instance, on June 23, 1918, he cabled to the War Department: "To win the victory in 1919, it is necessary to have a numerical superiority which can only be obtained by our having in France in April 80 American divisions and in July 100 divisions." [7] Yet by then tanks had more than proved their usefulness. Pershing and Haig certainly had much in common.

Once appointed to the supreme command, he received the following instruction:

In military operations against the Imperial German Government, you are directed to co-operate with the forces of the other countries employed against that enemy; but in so doing the underlying idea must be kept in view that the forces of the United States are a separate and distinct component of the combined forces, the identity of which must be preserved. [8]

He sailed for Liverpool on May 28 in S.S. *Baltic;* landed there on June 8, and four days later proceeded to France.

Although in Paris he and his staff were received with enthusiasm, there was no disguising the fact that, whereas the morale of the British was still high, that of the French was exceedingly low. On this point Pershing writes:

"The French situation gave me the gravest concern. Pacifist sentiment was prevalent in France and in many quarters there was talk of a peace parley. Old political feuds were revived and the influence of defeatism was openly charged against the ministry." [9]

Nor did French morale rise, for toward the close of this year General Bullard's opinion was: "Whatever may be the spirit or complexion of the Government, France is not going to fight (offensively) any more in this war. They have finished unless forced by Germany." [10]

Bullard thought that the reason why the British could go on fighting whereas the French could not was a matter of discipline. Though this may be true, a better reason is that the French are more imaginative than the British, and though imagination is essential to a general, it frequently unbalances the lower ranks by magnifying dangers.

It was within this depressing moral atmosphere that Pershing had to work. Directly to reinforce the French would be to risk the contamination of his own troops, and to reinforce the British would not directly assist the French. Therefore the only course was for the Americans to build up an offensive right wing while the British formed the offensive left wing of the line of battle. Not only would this distribution of force enable a dual attack to be launched against the flanks of the great salient but, by pushing the French toward its apex, it would relieve them of the severest fighting; for, should a successful dual attack be made, all they would have to do would be to follow up the enemy as he retired from before their front.[11]

Pershing, therefore, cast his eye toward the right flank, and in his *Final Report* he writes:

To the east the great fortified district east of Verdun and around Metz, menaced central France, protected the most exposed portion of the German line of communications, that between Metz and Sedan, and covered the Briey iron region, from which the enemy obtained the greater part of the iron required for munitions and material. The coal fields east of Metz were also covered by these same defences. A deep advance east of Metz, or the capture of the Briey region, by threatening the invasion of rich German territory in the Moselle Valley and the Saar Basin, thus curtailing her supply of coal and iron, would have a decisive effect in forcing a withdrawal of German troops from northern France. The military and economic situation of the enemy, therefore, indicated Lorraine as the field promising the most fruitful results for the employment of our armies.[12]

Moreover, as he points out, by selecting this area he could base his army on the western French ports and so avoid the northern which were crowded by the British, and simultaneously establish his main supply depots well to the south of Paris, and in consequence avoid interfering with the French. Therefore, every consideration—strategical, tactical, and administrative—pointed toward the right flank as the correct position for his operations. Once having decided on the location, on July 6, he cabled Washington: "Plans should contemplate sending over at least 1,000,000 men by next May." Five days later he supplemented this demand by: "Plans for the future should be based, especially in reference to the manufacture of artillery, aviation, and other material, on three times this force—i.e., at least 3,000,000 men."[13]

Because no divisional organization existed, one had to be devised. It consisted of 2 brigades of 2 regiments each "of about treble their original size," 3 regiments of artillery, 14 machine gun companies, 1 engineer regiment, 1 signal battalion, 1 troop of cavalry, and administrative units, making a total strength of 28,256 men. In fact, an American division was nearly as strong as a French or British army corps, and, in my opinion, was cumbersome in the extreme, as it lacked an army corps' elasticity. Not only did its size delay enrollment, equipping, and training, but when moved by rail it required no less than fifty-eight French trains and two days to complete its entrainment.

In all, 4,000,000 men were enlisted [14] and some 200,000 officers commissioned. Since within eighteen months of the American declaration of war approximately half this immense mass was organized, partially trained, and dispatched to France, the frequently heard complaint that American mobilization was slow is directly contradicted. It is true that by February, 1918, there was not a single American-made airplane in France,[15] and that, by the close of the war, only 109 75-mm. guns, 24 8-inch howitzers, and 1,379 airplanes had been shipped from America.[16] Nevertheless, considering that everything started from scratch, the output, in my opinion, was not unduly slow.

General Pershing rightly decided from the start that all training should encourage the offensive spirit, and in October he issued the following instruction:

All instructions must contemplate the assumption of vigorous offensive. This purpose will be emphasized in every phase of training until it becomes a settled habit of thought.[17]

Difficult as was the problem of raising and training an army, vastly more difficult was the political situation which faced the American commander in chief. There was no unity of idea or of plan between the three major Allied Powers. Wilson—rather than America—wanted to smash Germany in order to establish a society of democratic nations; England wanted to divide them in order to maintain her Empire and commercial position; and France wanted European hegemony in order to guarantee her own security.

No strategical conception bound them to a common plan, and though, on November 7, at the Rapallo Conference they had agreed to establish a Supreme War Council, it was little more than a superdebating club. Its members were General Foch (France), General Sir Henry Wilson

(Great Britain), General Cadorna (Italy), and General Bliss (America). Pershing wrote to the Secretary of War early in February: "I think the arrangement for unity of command all that could be desired without one supreme commander, which ideal is apparently considered by all concerned as impossible." [18] Why? Because the British did not trust the French, the French did not trust the British, and both did not trust either the generalship of Pershing or the statecraft of Wilson.

What the French and British wanted was men and men only, in order to balance their extravagant expenditure of human life. Attrition was their policy, and this grim Moloch demanded more and more flesh and blood. On December 2, Mr. Lloyd George, the British prime minister, set the ball rolling by forwarding to Lord Reading, British ambassador at Washington, a letter for Colonel House urging the necessity of mixing American troops with British. Clemenceau did likewise, with the result that Mr. Newton D. Baker, Secretary of War, urged the suggestion on Pershing. Fortunately for the Allied cause Pershing declined to consider this proposal. As was to be expected, an intrigue was set on foot against him, the object of which was to discredit him at Washington. Pershing, however, knew his man—Clemenceau—and after administering a sharp rap on his knuckles, persuaded Lloyd George to agree that this suggested mixing was undesirable since it would rouse hostility in the United States as well as friction between the Allied Powers.[19] Although this was obviously true, his refusal was not accepted as final by either the British or French.

The Allied position was certainly a gloomy one. The French, though by now somewhat revived, were still half out of the war; Great Britain had lost 390,000 men in the swamps around Ypres and 71,000 at Cambrai; the Italians had been routed at Caporetto with a loss of over 300,000 men and 3,000 guns; and fighting on the Russian front had ceased. On December 22 negotiations were opened between the Bolshevik and German governments, to drag on until March 3, 1918, when the signing of the Treaty of Brest-Litovsk brought peace to the Eastern Front.

As 1917 closed, no more than 176,665 American troops had arrived in France, and it was not until January 19 that their 1st Division took over a sector of the trenches north of Toul.[20] Then, in February, the 26th Division went to the Soissons front and the 42d to the Luneville, and in March the 2d Division went to Verdun. Meanwhile Major General

Hunter Liggett opened the First Corps Headquarters at Neufchâteau on January 20. The plan to create an independent America sector on the Lorraine front was beginning to take shape.

Having settled with the Russians, the German higher command forthwith decided to settle also with the British and French. The plan was to strike a blow at the juncture of their armies, roll up the British northward on to the Channel ports, there either destroy or contain them, and then turn on the French. This great attack was launched on March 21 on a frontage of nearly seventy-four miles stretching from near Lens to La Fère. It was so successful that within a week the British Fifth Army was driven back forty miles to a little east of Amiens; then the German attack petered out through lack of supplies.

So desperate did the situation become that, on the 26th, a Conference was assembled at Doullens under President Poincaré, which was attended by M. Clemenceau, M. Loucheur, Lord Milner, Field-Marshal Sir Douglas Haig, General Sir Henry Wilson, and General Foch. It was decided that Foch should be charged with co-ordinating the action of the Allied armies on the Western Front. Two days later Pershing motored over to Clermont-sur-Oise to see him and spoke to him as follows:

I have come to tell you that the American people would consider it a great honour for our troops to be engaged in the present battle. I ask you for this in their name and in my own.

At this moment there are no other questions but of fighting.

Infantry, artillery, aviation, all that we have are yours; use them as you wish. More will come, in numbers equal to requirements.

I have come especially to tell you that the American people will be proud to take part in the greatest battle of history.[21]

Surely, no man could have done more.

On April 3, another important Conference was held, this time at Beauvais, to decide on the functions of General Foch. Largely at the suggestion of General Pershing, the following agreement was arrived at:

Gen. Foch is charged by the British, French and American Governments with the co-ordination of the action of the Allied Armies on the western front . . . To the same end, the British, French and American Governments confide in Gen. Foch the strategic direction of military operations.

The Commanders-in-Chief of the British, French, and American Armies will exercise to the fullest extent the tactical direction of their armies.[22]

It will be seen that this agreement definitely recognized the independence of the American Army.

Six days later the second great German offensive was launched, this time north and south of Armentières on the river Lys. Once again the British were forced back and the Portuguese routed. This attack lasted until April 26. The following day, Foch unsuccessfully attempted to persuade General Pershing to request his government to transport to France during May, June, and July "only infantry and machine gun units." Had Pershing agreed to this, it would have been impossible, as he pointed out, for him to have formed an army at all.[23]

This radical difference in views led to a Conference at Abbeville on May 5, attended by the entire hierarchy. It was a veritable thieves' kitchen in which Pershing was the sole honest man. Clemenceau presided; openly discussed the Americans as if they were loot to be divided equally between the French and the British, and then incensed Lord Milner, British Secretary of State for War, by accusing him of attempting to obtain more than his share. Turning to Pershing, Foch exclaimed: "You are willing to risk our being driven back to the Loire?" and Lloyd George said: "Can't you see that the war will be lost unless we get this support?" To which Pershing replied with the greatest possible emphasis: "Gentlemen, I have thought this programme over very deliberately and will not be coerced." [24] On this incident he writes in his *Experiences:* "There was at the same time a very distinct impression in my mind, and in the minds of many of our officers familiar with the arguments on both sides, that the Allies, while greatly in need of assistance, were especially inclined to press the plea for amalgamation as a means of keeping us in a subordinate role." [25] This was no doubt true, yet it was equally true that they did not believe in the fighting capacity of American troops under American leadership.

The test as to the validity of this belief was soon to come. On May 27 the Germans launched their third great attack, completely surprising the French between the Oise and Berry-au-Bac, and by the 31st had captured Soissons and penetrated to Château-Thierry on the Marne, a distance of thirty miles. In this attack they inflicted on their enemy a loss of 60,000 prisoners and 650 guns. At once panic swept Paris and hundreds of thousands of its inhabitants fled to southern and western France.

On the 30th, Pétain called upon Pershing for assistance. Already, on the 28th, the 1st American Division had carried out a very successful attack at Cantigny. Now the 2d and 3d were hurried forward to Château-Thierry in order to stem the German onrush, which they succeeded in doing between June 4 and 6.

Meanwhile, on June 1, yet another Conference was assembled, this time at Versailles, and once again the question of splitting up the American forces was raised. Finally it was agreed that for June six divisions were to be dispatched from the U. S. A. and for July four, all without artillery, ammunition trains, and supply trains.[26] Thus, in part at least, did the French and British gain their object.

These unceasing conferences were little more than a repetition of the old-fashioned Councils of War. There was no unity of command, no directing head, but solely a Hydra. As Pershing writes of this last conference: "The whole discussion was very erratic, as one of the Allies would take exception to nearly every statement made by the other." Mr. Lloyd George said "that he could not understand why all the losses fell to the Allies and none to the Germans." [27] The obvious answer was that politicians were attempting to direct the strategy of the war.

Pershing's views were noted down by General Dawes on June 23.

The General . . . feels that he must fight vigorously all along the line, utilizing against a worn foe the fresh and eager army which he commands . . . He desires to keep the war one of movement as far as possible. He believes in a constant harassing by raids in the intervals between larger attacks, thus in every way keeping the enemy nervous and on the defensive. Therefore he has determined to demand that America continue until next April a schedule of shipment of 250,000 troops per month, which by April will give him an army of 3,000,000 (or more exactly 2,850,000 men).[28]

How sound these views were events soon proved, for on July 4 the perfect little battle of Hamel was fought by the British in the vicinity of Amiens, four companies of the 33d American Division taking part in it. Then, on the 15th, was launched the fourth and last of the great German offensives, this time on the Champagne front. When this attack failed, General Pétain decided to counterattack the Marne Salient. The assault, on the 18th, was heralded by a large number of French Renault tanks. The 1st and 2d American Divisions greatly distinguished themselves, and at various phases of the battle the 4th, 26th, 28th, 32d, 42d, and 77th Divisions also took part. Though the Germans fought desperately, this counterattack, which pinched out the Salient, was the turning point from defeat to victory, for henceforth the Germans were thrown on the defensive.

On the 24th a Conference was held at Chaumont, at which the following offensive operations were considered:

The release of the Paris-Avricourt railroad in the Marne region as
the minimum result of present (Franco-American) operations;

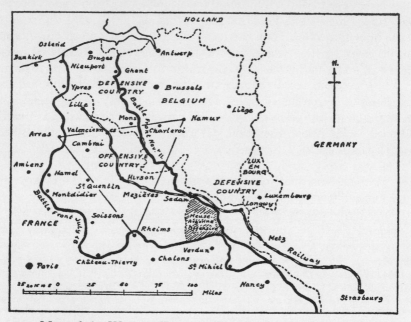

27. Map of the Western Front in France, July to November, 1918

The freeing of the Paris-Amiens railroad by a concerted action of
the British and French;

The release of the Paris-Avricourt railroad in the region of Com-
mercy by the reduction of the St. Mihiel salient by the American Army.
By thus reducing the front, it would bring the Allies within reach of
the Briey region and permit action on a larger scale between the Meuse
and Moselle.[29]

The second of these attacks was launched by the British and the French
on August 8. The British put 415 tanks into the field and crashing
through the Amiens Salient set a strategic limit to the war, because from
that day on it became clear to the German higher command that it had
lost.

The Amiens Salient having been wiped out, to all intents and pur-

poses the Western Front was straightened out, except for the Salient
of St. Mihiel. The reduction of this salient was now entrusted to the
First American Army, which came into being on August 10.[30] Pershing,
taking personal command of it, opened his headquarters at La Ferté-
sous-Jouarre but shortly after moved to Ligny-en-Barrois, some twenty-
five miles southwest of St. Mihiel.

He immediately decided that the First, Fourth, and Fifth Corps
should carry out this attack and set about collecting his scattered divisions,[31] the 26th being the only one in the St. Mihiel area at that time.
It was a prodigious undertaking, because in all 550,000 troops had to
be assembled and most of the movements had to be made at night. As
these troops consisted mainly of infantry, artillery[32] and aviation[33] were
supplied by the French and British. Two hundred and sixty-seven tanks
were borrowed from the French, the British being unable to spare any.

The object of this attack was:

(1) To free the railroad leading through St. Mihiel to Verdun.
(2) To establish a base for further operations against the vital'y
    important Metz-Sedan-Mezières railway and the Briey Iron
    Basin.

The general plan [writes Pershing] was to make simultaneous attacks against the flanks of the salient. The ultimate objective was tentatively fixed as the general line Marieulles (east of the Moselle)—heights
south of Gorze-Mars la Tour-Etain. The operation contemplated the use
on the western face of 3 or 4 American divisions, supported by the attack of 6 divisions of the Second French Army on their left, while 7
American divisions would attack on the southern face, and 3 French
divisions would press the enemy at the tip of the salient.[34]

When, at the Conference of July 24, it was decided to carry out this
attack, there was no idea that the then forthcoming British attack east
of Amiens would be so successful, or that the war could be terminated
in 1918. Therefore all these operations were looked upon as preparation
for 1919. But now that the British were advancing rapidly, on August
30 Foch visited Pershing at Ligny-en-Barrois to discuss the possibilities
of extending these operations. To Pershing's consternation he proposed
that the St. Mihiel operations should be limited to an attack on the southern face only, and that upon its completion "two other operations be
undertaken by combined Americans and French," a number of the
American divisions to go *"under French command."*

The conversation which followed is worth quoting, if only to show how difficult it was to co-operate with the French.[35]

When Pershing pointed out that, "to make an attack in the salient with limited objectives would cost little less than to carry out the original idea," Foch replied:

"That is true, but the fate of the 1918 campaign will be decided in the Aisne region and I wish to limit the Woëvre (St. Mihiel) attack so that the Americans can participate in the Meuse offensive, which will produce still greater results."

"But," said General Pershing, "Marshal Foch, here on the very day that you turn over a sector to the American Army, and almost on the eve of an offensive, you ask me to reduce the operation so that you can take away several of my divisions and assign some to the French Second Army and use others to form an American army to operate on the Aisne in conjunction with the French Fourth Army, leaving me with little to do except hold what will become a quiet sector after the St. Mihiel offensive. This virtually destroys the American Army that we have been trying so long to form."

There can be little doubt that this was the hidden reason for the change; now that things were going well, French vainglory reasserted itself and would brook no rival.

"Marshal Foch then said," writes Pershing, " 'Do you wish to take part in the battle?' I replied, 'Most assuredly, but as an American Army and in no other way.' He argued that there would not be time, whereupon I said, 'If you will assign me a sector I will take it at once.' He asked, 'Where would it be?' I replied, 'Wherever you say.' He then referred to our lack of artillery and other auxiliary troops. I reminded him that the French had insisted on our shipping to France only infantry and machine gun units . . ."

Foch still objecting, Pershing at length said:

"Marshal Foch, you have no authority as Allied Commander-in-Chief to call upon me to yield up my command of the American Army and have it scattered among the Allied forces where it will not be an American Army at all."

Foch, now furious, answered: "I must insist upon the arrangement," to which Pershing replied: "Marshal Foch, you may insist all you please, but I decline absolutely to agree to your plan. While our army will fight wherever you may decide, it will not fight except as an independent American army."[36]

This was not only a victory for Pershing, but also for the Allied cause, for had the readjustment proposed by Foch been agreed upon, the Americans would have been sacrificed to the glory of France, and in all probability the war would have continued into 1919.[37]

On September 2 another Conference was held, at which it was decided to take advantage of the favorable situation and employ all the Allied

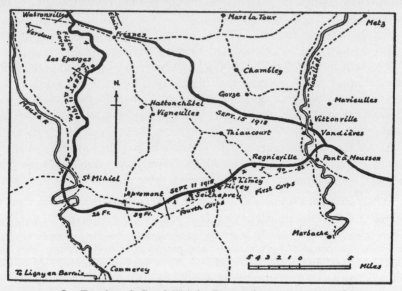

28. Battle of St. Mihiel, September 11–15, 1918

armies in a converging action. "The British armies, supported by the left of the French armies, were to pursue the attack in the direction of Cambrai; the center of the French armies, west of Rheims, would continue the actions, already begun, to drive the enemy beyond the Aisne; and the American Army, supported by the right of the French armies, would direct its attack on Sedan and Mezières." [38]

As the choice between the sectors east of the Aisne, including the Argonne Forest or Champagne, was left to Pershing, and as the attack was to be launched not later than September 25, the depth of the St. Mihiel operation was limited to the line Vigneulles-Thiaucourt-Régnéville. "The number of divisions to be used was reduced to four French and fifteen American, six of which would be in reserve."

The salient to be attacked, which lay between the rivers Meuse and

Moselle, had been peacefully held by the Germans since 1914. Though now practically a fortress, it was not strongly manned; for only seven weak divisions were in line and two in reserve.

On the night of September 11 the attacking forces were deployed as follows:

Southern Flank: On right the First Corps (Liggett), consisting of the 82d, 90th, 5th, and 2d Divisions; on the left the Fourth Corps (Dickman)—89th, 42d, and 1st Divisions.

Center: French Second Colonial Corps, composed of the 39th and 26th Divisions and 2d Dismounted Cavalry Division.

Northern Flank: The Fifth Corps (Cameron) comprising the 26th Division, part of the 4th, and the French 15th Colonial Division.

Reserves: For First Corps—78th; For Fourth Corps—3d, and for Fifth Corp, part of 4th; Army Reserve—35th, 91st, and 80th Divisions.

At 5 A.M., on September 12, the attack was launched after an artillery bombardment of four hours, in which "twenty-nine hundred guns participated, eight hundred and thirty-one of these being on the First Corps Front." [39]

The sky over the battlefield [writes Pershing], both before and after dawn, aflame with exploding shells, star signals, burning supply dumps and villages, presented a scene at once picturesque and terrible. The exultation in our minds that here, at last, after seventeen months of effort, an American Army was fighting under its own flag was tempered by the realisation of the sacrifice of life on both sides, and yet fate had willed it thus and we must carry through. Confidence in our troops dispelled every doubt of ultimate victory. [40]

This confidence was amply rewarded, for by the afternoon of September 13 all objectives had been reached and the Salient had ceased to exist. In all 16,000 prisoners and 443 guns were captured and at small loss, the American casualties totalling less than 7,000.

After the battle, Pershing would have preferred to have pushed forward from the front gained—that is, between Vandières and Watronville—toward Metz and the Briey iron fields. However, on September 2 Marshal Foch had decided [41] in favor of Sir Douglas Haig's plan for a dual and converging attack on Cambrai and Mézières. As the attack on the Meuse-Argonne front was to be launched on September 26, the First American Army had less than a fortnight to shift from one battlefield to another. Since behind the new front there were only three railways and three main roads, and since before half-a-million Americans could occupy it a quarter of a million Frenchmen had to be withdrawn from it, the staff work entailed was most intricate.[42]

The object of the attack was the Carignan-Sedan-Mézières-Valenciennes-Lille railroad. If it could be cut before the German armies facing the French and British could withdraw to the east of it, the problem of supply would be so difficult that their retirement might easily be turned into a rout. As General Pershing says: "The Carignan-Sedan-Mézieres line was essential to the Germans for the rapid strategical movement of troops. Should this southern system be cut by the Allies before the enemy could withdraw his forces through the narrow neck between Mézières and the Dutch frontier the ruin of his armies in France and Belgium would be complete." [43]

From the Meuse-Argonne front the distance to this railway was, as the crow flies, about thirty miles. Nevertheless, as General Harbord writes:

The area . . . to be gained by the Americans was as though the Almighty had designed it as a barrier against the passage of an invader . . . Lying between the unfordable Meuse, and the rough wooded hills of the Forest of Argonne, it was a defile varying from fifteen miles in width measured west from Verdun to twenty-five on an approximately east and west line through Buzancy to Dun-sur-Meuse. The heights of the Meuse commanded the valley to the west as easily as they looked into the broad Woëvre plain on the east. They gave observation and positions from which the enemy could deliver oblique fire on the west bank of the Meuse. The river Aire skirted the Argonne, fordable in a few places. The eastern edge of the Argonne dominated its valley. Batteries there located could cover the German right flank and cross their fire with that of the batteries on the east bank of the Meuse. The watershed between the Meuse River and the Argonne Forest was a great hogback which ran from southeast to northwest in the general line Montfaucon-Romagne-Buzancy. The heights of Montfaucon, Romagne, Cunel, and the wood of Barricourt were natural strong points along or near this axis. Not only could the entire open country south from the German lines be seen from their elevation, but the hogback divided the twenty-mile front into two parts, giving crossfire both ways. The problem which the Americans faced on September 26th was practically the forcing of two defiles.[44]

This naturally formidable area was traversed from east to west by four strong lines of entrenchments, the whole forming a powerfully fortified zone. These were:

(1) First Position, from near Regnéville on the Meuse via Béthincourt and Boureuilles to near Vienne-le-Château at the southern end of the Argonne Forest.

(2) The Giselher Stellung, from Sivry via Montfaucon and Apremont across the Argonne Forest to Autry on the Aisne.

(3) The Kriemhilde Stellung, from Breiulles via Romagne to Grandpré on the Aire north of the Argonne.

(4) The Freya Stellung, from Dun-sur-Meuse via Bayonville and beyond Buzancy. This line was unfinished.

When the battle opened these defenses were held by ten divisions in line with an equal number in reserve.[45]

Pershing opened his General Headquarters at Souilly, to the southwest of Verdun. His plan of attack was as follows: While the Fifth Corps in the center assaulted the hogback, the Third on its right was to advance up the left of the Meuse Valley, and the First up the Valley on its left. By this means it was hoped to outflank Montfaucon. From right to left the order of battle read:

Third Corps (Bullard) with the 33d Division nearest the Meuse, the 80th in the center, and the 4th on the left, with the 3d in reserve.

Fifth Corps (Cameron) with the 79th Division facing Montfaucon, the 37th and 91st on its left, and the 32d in reserve.

First Corps (Liggett) with the 35th Division on the right, the 28th next, and the 77th facing the Argonne, with the French 5th Cavalry Division and the 92d Division (colored) in reserve.

Army Reserve, the 1st, 29th, and 82d Divisions.

On the right of the Third Corps stood the Seventeenth French Corps and on the left of the First Corps the Fourth French Army.

Zero hour was fixed at 5.30 A.M. on September 26, and was to be preceded by an artillery bombardment of three hours' duration.

To appreciate in full the effects of the battle which was to be fought during the next forty-seven days and which absorbed no less than 1,200,-000 men, it should be remembered that it was but one detail in a vastly greater scheme—the engagement of and the driving in of the flanks of the great salient, Ypres-Noyon-Verdun, the chord of which was the Carignan-Sedan-Mézières-Valenciennes-Lille railway. This scheme was, in its turn, but part of a still greater enterprise, which embraced all fronts. On September 21, General Franchet d'Espérey had launched his attack on the Macedonian front, the Bulgarian government asking for an armistice on the 25th; on the 19th, General Allenby, in Palestine, had assailed the Turks and occupied Damascus on October 1; on the 25th, in Italy, General Diaz had completed his preparations for the battle of Vittorio Veneto;[46] on the 26th, Generals Pershing and Gouraud

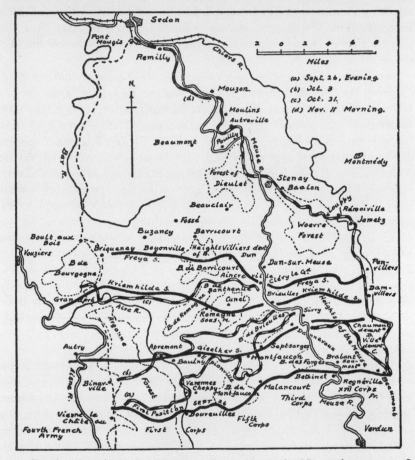

29. Battle of the Meuse-Argonne, September 26—November 11, 1918

struck from the Meuse to the river Suippe; on the 27th the First and Third British Armies attacked the Hindenburg Line between Gouzeaucourt and the Sensée river, and on the 28th their advance was extended southward by the attack of the Fourth British Army and by the First French Army, while simultaneously, to the north, the Second British Army and the Belgian Army attacked in Flanders.

Taking their assigned part in this great plan, under the covering fire of 2,700 guns and supported by 821 airplanes and 189 Renault tanks,[47] at 5.30 A.M. on September 26, the 108,000 first line infantry of the nine attacking American divisions moved forward, the axis of their advance being the line Montfaucon-Romagne-Buzancy. At the same time the Fourth French Army (General Gouraud) advanced west of the Argonne.

The Third Corps carried the enemy's second position before dark, storming the Bois de Forges and occupying the Bois Juré, while the 4th Division advanced east of Montfaucon. Meanwhile the Fifth Corps took Malancourt and pushed west of Montfaucon, and the First Corps took Cheppy, part of Varennes, but was hung up at Champ Mohaut. The next day steady progress was made and Montfaucon was captured by the 79th Division. By the evening of the 28th a maximum advance of eleven kilometers had been made, Baulny, Epinonville, Septsarges, and Dannevoux being captured. Only on the extreme left, in the Argonne, was the advance checked, a region, as General Harbord says, "littered by the debris of many storms, natural and man-made . . . a region forgotten when level ground was being created. Guns could not be driven through it. No man's horizon was more than a few yards away. It curtained unnumbered points of resistance . . ."[48] Fighting here must have closely resembled that experienced by Grant and Lee in the Wilderness in 1864.

On the 29th the Germans threw in six new divisions, and about a mile south of Apremont they vigorously counterattacked the 28th and 35th Divisions. By nightfall, writes Pershing, the First Army front ran as follows: "Bois de la Côte Lemonet-Nantillois-Apremont-southwest across the Argonne. Many divisions, especially those in the center, that were subjected to cross fire of artillery, had suffered heavily. The severe fighting, the nature of the terrain over which they attacked, and the fog and darkness sorely tried even our best divisions."[49] The first phase of the battle was in fact nearing its close. That night the 37th and 79th Divisions, which had suffered a severe setback, were relieved by the 32d and 3d, and the following night the 1st Division relieved the 35th.

The critical problem now was not so much to advance as to restore the communications over no man's land. There were only four available roads, all more or less destroyed by shell fire, while "The whole terrain in front of the enemy's first line was one continuous area of deep shell holes."[50] Moreover, the Americans again had to depend on the French for transport. Harbord writes: "The Services of Supply was stripped of trucks, seriously interfering with work at the base ports, with construction projects at many points, and with the movement of troops in general. The shortage of ambulances to move the sick and wounded was critical. Fifteen American ambulances had to be recalled from Italy. The S.O.S. was reduced to eight hundred horses for its entire service—a telegram having been sent ordering to the front half of its animals, netted the commander in chief four hundred, where the shortage of the combat organizations was fifty thousand." [51] Then again, and it is no disparagement to say so, the Americans were as yet very green in running battles. [52]

On the northern flank of the great salient, the French took St. Quentin on October 1, and the British were rapidly pushing on toward Cambrai. But when on the morning of the 4th the American First Army renewed its attack, now against sixteen German divisions, it encountered such desperate resistance that it made little progress.

This general attack having failed, four specific attacks were carried out between the 7th and 11th:

(1) October 7th. The I Corps, employing the 82nd Division between the 1st and 28th Divisions, attacked the eastern edge of the Argonne Forest.

(2) October 8th. The French XVII Corps, reinforced by the American 33rd and 29th Divisions, attacked east of the Meuse on the front Beaumont-Brabant sur Meuse, with the object of seizing the heights there.

(3) October 9th. The V Corps, reinforced by including within its front the 1st Division, to which was attached a brigade from the 91st Division, attacked the heights of the Bois de Romagne.

(4) October 10th–11th. A general attack was made on the 20-mile front from Beaumont west to the Aire River. [53]

On the whole these attacks were successful, the I Corps reaching Romagne and the French XVII Corps occupying the villages of Beaumont and Haumont, so that by the night of the 11th the line was advanced to Molleville Farm—Bois de la Côte Lemont—part of Bois de Forêt—south of Côte Dame Marie—Sommerance—Grandpré.

This stiff fighting, resulting as it did in heavy casualties, brought the question of reinforcements to the fore. Between September 26 and October 11, 75,000 men had been killed and wounded and thousands of men were down with influenza, [54] yet no more than 45,000 reinforcements were available by November 1. The result was that infantry companies had to be cut down from 250 to 175 men. Considering the reorganization this entailed and the fact that over 1,000,000 men were now in the battle area, on or behind a front of some 75 miles, Pershing decided to split this mass into two armies. Therefore, on the 12th, he formed all troops on the front from Port-sur-Seille, east of the Meuse, to Fresnes-en-Woëvre, southeast of Verdun, into the Second American Army [55] and placed it under the command of Lieutenant General Robert L. Bullard. On the 16th he transferred the rest to Lieutenant General Hunter Liggett.

The next attack was based on the following general plan:

(a) The French XVII Corps under American Command was to continue its offensive east of the Meuse River.

(b) The III and V Corps, with fresh divisions (the 5th and 42nd), were to drive salients through the hostile positions on both flanks of the Bois de Romagne and the Bois de Bauthenville.

(c) The I Corps was to hold the enemy on its left flank while advancing its right in conjunction with the left of the V Corps.

(d) The French Fourth Army [which had come up on the left of the I Corps], and held the south bank of the Aire and the west bank of the Aisne as far as Vouziers, was ordered by General Pétain to attack on the same day, so as to outflank the enemy opposing [the left of the I corps].[56]

During this attack, launched on the 14th, the stronghold on Côte-Dame Marie was captured as well as Cunel and Romagne sous Montfaucon. Nevertheless, the maximum penetration effected since the initial attack on September 26 was but a little over ten miles—that is approximately half a mile a day.

During the remainder of the month the fighting was local. Grandpré was carried on the 16th, and between the 18th and 23d the Kriemhilde Stellung—the objective on September 26—was penetrated at Bois-de-Blantheville.

There could be little doubt that the end was now approaching, in spite of the fact that the Germans were fighting as staunchly as ever. The Franco-British advance was sweeping onward towards Valenciennes. On the 17th, Ostend, Lille, and Douai were regained. On the 24th the Italians opened the battle of Vittorio Veneto, which led to the collapse of Austria. On the next day the Serbians reached the Danube and on the 30th an armistice was concluded with Turkey. In these circumstances it was imperative that the enemy should be given no rest on the Meuse-Argonne front.

Discussing the general situation of the Americans, General Liggett writes: "The condition of the First Army was such that it was imperative to rehabilitate our Divisions, get necessary replacements into condition for action, gather up a mass of stragglers and return them to their proper commands, and, while keeping up pressure on the enemy, prepare for a powerful well-considered effort." [57] The main difficulties, as throughout the battle, were transport and communications. The latter had to be maintained unceasingly, frequently under all but impossible circumstances.[58]

Nevertheless, difficult though the situation of the American First Army was, that of their enemy was getting desperate. "His divisions," writes Pershing, "had been thrown into confusion by our furious assaults, and his morale had been reduced until his will to resist had well-nigh reached the breaking point. Once a German division was engaged in the fight, it became practically impossible to effect its relief. The enemy was forced to meet the constantly recurring crises by breaking up tactical organizations and sending hurried detachments to widely separated portions of the field." [59]

Meanwhile the foundations were being laid for the most mortifying betrayal in military history, compared to which the breaking of the terms of the Convention of Saratoga appears but an episode. Having been informed on October 3 by Field Marshal von Hindenburg that there was no longer a possible hope of forcing a peace on the enemy, on the 6th the Imperial Chancellor, Prince Max von Baden, telegraphed President Wilson that the German government was willing to accept the program set forth by him in his message to Congress on January 8 and in his later addresses [60] as a basis of peace negotiations.

On the 23d, Wilson replied that he could not consider peace negotiations, but solely surrender. Thereupon, on the 27th the German government asked for an armistice.

The president's messages were forthwith transmitted to the Allied governments, and upon receipt of their replies, the following note was sent to the German government:

The Allied Governments have given careful consideration to the correspondence which has passed between the President of the United States and the German Government. Subject to the qualifications which follow [relating to the freedom of the seas and restoration of the invaded territories and losses by land, sea, and air], they declare their willingness to make peace with the German Government on the terms of peace laid down in the President's address to the Congress of January, 1918, and the principles of settlement enunciated in his subsequent addresses.[61]

While these terms were being discussed and the Germans were carrying out one of the most skillfully directed retreats in the whole history of war, the last phase of America's greatest battle was initiated on October 21 by the following order, addressed by General Pershing to General Liggett:

1. The Allied Armies in Flanders are to advance on Brussels. The British Armies are to advance toward the line of the Meuse, north of Givet.

The French Fourth, Fifth, Tenth and First Armies are to operate south of the line Froid-Chapelle, Phillipeville, Agimont (north of Givet).

The immediate task of the First American and Fourth French Armies is to turn the enemy's position on the Aisne by reaching the region of Buzancy-Le Chesne.

2. The First Army will prepare to launch a general attack on October 28th, with the object of securing control of Buzancy and the heights immediately east of that place . . .

The operations of your left flank will be conducted in the closest liaison with the right of the French Fourth Army.[62]

This attack was, however, postponed until November 1, as the Fourth French Army required four days more wherein to make ready.

At once every effort was made to move the artillery forward and to establish dumps of ammunition and supplies. So confident was General Liggett that orders for the pursuit were issued to corps commanders before the attack started.[63]

This final phase of the Battle of the Meuse-Argonne may be divided into three distinct operations: the attack on November 1; the pursuit, and the crossing of the river Meuse.

The American order of battle was as follows:

Right Wing: Third Corps (Hines), composed from right to left of the 5th and 90th Divisions. Objective—the Barricourt ridge at Villers-devant-Dun.

Center: Fifth Corps (Summerall), with the 89th and 2d Divisions. Objective—ridge west of Barricourt and Fosse. In reserve the 1st and 42d Divisions.

Left Wing: First Corps (Dickman), consisting of the 80th, 77th, and 78th Divisions. Objective—Boult-aux-Bois.

This order formed a huge wedge, the cutting-edge of which was to drive towards Beaumont, and so rend the German front in two.

At 3.30 on the morning of November 1 an intense barrage of high explosive and mustard gas shells was directed at the German position. Two hours later, the greatest army America has ever sent to war moved forward to the attack. "Squadrons of swift-flying combat planes drove the enemy planes from the air and fired on the hostile infantry, while the bombing squadrons harassed important points behind the enemy's lines. The attack went forward with precision, gaining momentum with every mile. For the first time, the enemy's lines were completely broken through." [64] Of this attack General Harbord writes: "That was the day when with a proper quota of tanks we might have cut off a hundred thousand prisoners." [65]

Though, on the left, the First Corps was partially held up, by evening the Fifth Corps had taken the heights of Barricourt, while the Third had reached the Meuse, north of Brieulles, and captured Cléry-le-Grand. The French Fourth Army was less successful, as it was unable to advance beyond the line of the Aisne River.

Resisting stubbornly, the Germans fell back. On the 2d and 3d the attack was continued, the Third Corps pushing the enemy beyond the Meuse as the Fifth drove them back towards Beauclair, capturing the high ground east and north of La Fosse. On the 4th, the Germans, covered by numerous machine gun detachments, were in full retreat. During the day their pursuers reached La Neuville and the outskirts of Beaumont. The 5th Division crossed the Meuse, establishing bridge-heads south of Dun-sur-Meuse.

The general direction of the advance was now toward Sedan and Mézières, neither of which was in the American sector. Nevertheless, as the First Army was in advance of the French Fourth Army, on the afternoon of the 5th Pershing issued the following order to the First and Fifth Corps:

General Pershing desires that the honor of entering Sedan should fall to the First American Army. He has every confidence that the troops of the First Corps, assisted on their right by the Fifth Corps, will enable him to realize this desire.[66]

Notwithstanding Pershing's instructions, the Fifth Corps Commander ordered the 1st Division to accomplish this task. Setting out, the 1st Division cut across the line of advance of the First Corps and threw its units into such confusion that, early on the 7th, the war nearly ended in a battle between these two corps.[67]

As the German main line of communications was now within range of the machine guns of the First Army, the enemy's position on the Western Front was no longer tenable. Meanwhile, plans were prepared for an advance of the First Army on Longwy and the Second Army toward the Briey Iron Basin. The pursuit was continued until the 11th, when the First Army occupied Stenay, Pouilly-sur-Meuse, Outreville, Baâlon, and Grimaucourt, and the Second, Marimbois Farm, its front line extending from Port-sur-Seille to Fresnes-en-Woëvre.

"At 6:35 A.M.," that day, writes General Liggett, "word was received at my Headquarters that the Armistice had been signed, and would take effect at 11:00 A.M. This information was at once transmitted to the troops. The line of the First Army on November 11th at 11:00 A.M. ran—Fresnes, Grimaucourt, Abacourt, Ville-devant-Chaumont, Chaumont-devant-Damvillers, Penvillers, Jametz, Rémoiville, Louppy, Baâlon, Stenay, the Meuse, Moulins, the Meuse, Pont-Maugis." [68]

The next day General Pershing issued General Orders, No. 203, notifying his troops that the enemy had capitulated. [69]

Thus ended America's greatest battle, greatest in the number of men engaged, yet not the greatest in interest. Like all the major conflicts of the years 1914–1918, it was too great to be personal and in consequence was anonymous—an anonymity symbolically crystallized in the cult of the Unknown Soldier.

I do not intend here, as I have done in former chapters, to conclude the story of this war with a summary of the peace treaty which sealed its end—and for two reasons:

(1) It was not an American peace.

(2) It was not a peace at all.

No sooner was the Armistice of November 11 signed than its terms were scrapped by the Allies. Consequently, the period that followed it was no more than a suspension of arms. Hysteria ruled the day—the black day for Europe. Like Sindbad, the Money Power had released the Jinn—mass emotionalism—from his bottle of brass, and henceforth no reason or unreason could persuade him to return to it.

What did this greatest of American battles cost the First Army? Out of a total strength of 1,031,000 officers and men (including 135,000 French) 117,000 were killed and wounded; it inflicted 100,000 casualties upon the enemy and captured 26,000 prisoners, 874 cannon, and 3,000 machine guns. [70] During the whole war the Americans lost 81,141 killed in action; 35,556 died of wounds; 24,786 died of disease, and 5,669 of other injuries. [71]

In money:

For the period of twenty-five months, from April, 1917, through April, 1919, the War cost the United States considerably more than one million dollars an hour. Treasury disbursements during the period reached a total of $23,500,000,000, of which $1,650,000,000 may be charged to normal expenses which would have occurred in peace. The balance may be counted as the direct money cost of the War to the end of April, 1919, a sum of $21,850,000,000. The figure is twenty times the pre-war national debt . . . In addition to this huge expenditure loans were advanced to the Allies at the rate of nearly half a million of dollars an hour. Congress authorized for this purpose $10,000,000,000 and there was actually paid to various Governments the sum of $8,850,000,000.[72]

What were the lessons and results of this war? As regards the first, there were four that stood head and shoulders above all others:

(1) The increasing necessity of political authority in war.

(2) The increasing necessity of economic self-sufficiency in war.

(3) The increasing necessity of national discipline in war.

(4) And the increasing necessity of mechanization in war.

If in war, then in peace also, because peace is the laboratory of war.

On these four lessons, burnt into their souls by defeat, the vanquished nations set out to build for themselves new political houses to dwell in, whereas the victors, believing that they had won the war because their opponents were in a state of physical collapse and forgetting that no war can be truly won unless it establishes a better peace than the one it broke—like the Bourbons they learned nothing and like them also they forgot nothing. Therefore, once the war was at an end, they attempted to slide back into 1913. Nevertheless, they could not, because the economic and financial foundations of that period had been blown to dust, and they could not be relayed, because the bricks of gold they had been built with had now vanished.

I am not concerned here with their lot, nor with their many bickerings and vain attempts to raise the financial ghost from its tomb, whose golden body, mummified by greed, had been translated to the land of its birth. Here I am concerned only with the United States—its pall bearers. Therefore I will look at this event solely from their angle.

The war which was declared on April 6, 1917, was unlike any the Americans had hitherto waged. It was not to be fought for self-preservation, as were the wars against the French and the Indians: it was not to be fought for liberty, as was the War of Independence: it was not to be fought for unity, as was the Civil War; and it was not to be fought for conquest, as were the wars against the Spaniards. What then was it fought for?

On the face of it, President Wilson supplied the answer: "to make the world safe for democracy." But what is the meaning of that magic word? If, as Lincoln proclaimed, it is the government "of the people, by the people, for the people," then such a form of rule existed solely in the pedagogic imagination of the visionary of Princeton. In any case, no European nation was thus governed. Instead, since the substitution of an industrial for the agricultural order of society and the conquest of the industrial by the financial, the government of the Western nations, whether monarchical or republican, had passed into the invisible hands of a plutocracy, international in character and grasp.

It was, I venture to suggest, this semioccult power which, automatically, rather than calculatedly, pushed the mass of the American people into the cauldron. In other words, as this was an economic-financial age, and as the United States had during their two and a half years of neutrality reaped and garnered a golden harvest, they could not risk an Allied defeat, because the Allied Powers were their more important debtors.

Let us glance back on these thirty-odd months:

With the outbreak of the war American foreign trade rapidly dwindled; but this loss was made good by orders from the Allied nations, and heavy loans were raised in the United States by Great Britain, France, and Russia in order to meet their cost. Then the favorable balance of trade rose from $690,000,000 in 1913 to $3,000,000,000 in 1916.

This enormous debit was balanced by securities and gold sent to America in the approximate amount of three billion dollars, besides two billion dollars in foreign war bonds. The demand for foodstuffs raised the price of grain and other farm produce. The high cost of living became an issue in politics. The great munition factories offered high wages and drew many thousands of laborers into the temporary factory towns. Hundreds of thousands of men called home for war left America for Europe. The net immigration fell from 1,200,000 in 1914 to 300,000 in 1916.[73]

And, when all was over, "The Federal Excess Profits Tax for corporations alone, for the years 1917–1919, was over five and a half billions of dollars." [74]

How was this hidden government of great financial interests to attain its ends? Through the infinite credulity of the masses, their infinite hopes, their infinite attraction toward the wonderful, the better, and the Best.

The vision of saving civilization gripped the imaginations of men as had once the desire to regain the Holy Sepulcher. For Americans, this war assumed the nature of a crusade, and mysticism, fundamental in human nature, was stoked and fired by propaganda: the art of illuminating the masses and inducing them to see things which do not exist.

The spirit of adventure was awakened in every young American's heart. War promised a change from drudgery and the commonplace: war revealed what was essential in man and in woman too—the urge to destroy and to create.

But, when their task was done and the Americans returned home, they brought with them the corpse of a dead epoch, which was to fester and putrefy in the cradle of a new-born age.

The Spanish gold hunt in the Americas had been the forerunner of the Reformation, which had led to attempts to mix the new economics with the old religion. Similarly, the American gold hunt in Europe simultaneously closed the door of that period and opened the door of a new; under the sway of Wall Street, efforts were made to force the old economics down the throat of a new-born political world.

This I believe to be the most powerful effect of the war—a clash between two systems, incompatible and hostile, which, as in the sixteenth and seventeenth centuries, could be settled only by force of arms. This effect, or precipitate, I believe to be the occult architect of the Second World War. As I write, the Second World War is still being waged; when it ends, we shall see either a more perfect peace established or yet another brief suspension of arms. Let it be remembered that the wars of the Reformation—the so-called Wars of Religion— endured for well over a hundred years, and that in the end it was not those who held fast to the past, but those who had faith in the future who were triumphant.

On the plinth of General Sherman's statue in Washington are inscribed these words:

"THE LEGITIMATE OBJECT OF WAR IS A MORE PERFECT PEACE." In them lives the secret of every victory. Should a more perfect peace be established, this present war will be truly won; if not, it will be morally lost. Therefore may the countries now at war remember these ten words, and when the time comes live up to them, so that the period of economic wars may come at last to an end.

REFERENCES

[1] *War and Western Civilization, 1832–1932,* J. F. C. Fuller, pp. 227–228.

[2] "The Principles of War with Reference to the Campaigns of 1914–1915," *Journal of the Royal United Service Institution,* February, 1916. Also see: *Memoirs of an Unconventional Soldier,* J. F. C. Fuller, pp. 55–56.

[3] General John J. Pershing, in *My Experiences in the World War,* p. 145, writes: "Our staff officers generally have little conception of problems involved in directing armies . . . or of strategic questions involved . . ."

[4] By the end of the War there were in France 1,761,000 rifles, 2,106 75-mm. field guns, and 1,485 heavy guns. Nearly all of the guns were of French or British manufacture.

[5] Pershing's *Experiences,* p. 37.

[6] One of his few remarks on tanks is thoroughly conventional: ". . . the British (heavy) Mark VI [really Mark IV], a tank of thirty tons, appeared to be useful according to circumstances . . ." (*Experiences,* p. 156).

There was however a major (? by name Palmer or Parker) in the American Army who held ultramodern views. In August, 1917, he showed me a paper marked "Very Secret" in which he had set forth his "tactical concept." He wrote:

"The operation works out this wise:

"(a) A cloud of fighting avions at high altitude, to clear the air.

"(b) A cloud of observation avions at low altitudes, just in front of the line of tanks, dropping bombs and using machine guns on the trenches.

"(c) Our long-range artillery blocking the German artillery.

"(d) Our light artillery barraging the front to prevent escape of the Germans in their front lines.

"(e) Our mobile machine guns following up the tanks at about 500 *yards,* covering them with *canopy* fire, step by step.

"(f) OUR DIVISIONAL JITNEY COMPANIES OF MACHINE GUNS driving in 'Hell-Bent' after the tanks and *widening the breach.*

"(g) Our cavalry riding through the breach as soon as it is opened for them, and swinging out, *à la* Jeb Stuart around McClellan's Army. Sacrificed? Of course; but winning results worth the sacrifice.

"(h) Jitney- or truck-transported infantry following as fast as gasoline can carry it to support the success and make our foothold sure.

"(i) Truck-transported—or tank-transported—artillery following 'Hell for leather.'

"I BELIEVE SUCH A PLAN WILL WIN. FRITZ HAS NOT THE RESOURCES TO ADOPT SUCH A PLAN. WE HAVE. WE SHOULD DO IT AND DO IT now as fast as preparation goes in material. It will take time to get ready." (*Memoirs of an Unconventional Soldier,* p. 158.)

It certainly did, for it was not put into practice until 1939, and then by the Germans in Poland, when it became known as *"Blitzkrieg."*

[7] Pershing's *Experiences,* p. 461.

[8] *Ibid.,* p. 46.

[9] *Ibid.,* pp. 76, 96, and 98.

[10] *Personalities and Reminiscences of the War,* Robert Lee Bullard, pp. 240–241. This is true, but the battlefield selected by Haig was the worst possible for an offensive. As a matter of fact this offensive destroyed the British Army before the Americans could develop their strength, and therefore was misplaced. General Dawes writes on November 30, 1917: "France is 'fed up' with war. Only the

entrance of the United States into war prevented her from going to pieces before this" (p. 58).

[11] To those interested, "The Tactics of Penetration" are fully discussed in Chapter III of my book *On Future Warfare*. See more especially Section 7— "The Tactics of Dual Penetration"—in which the attack on a salient is dealt with.

[12] *Final Report of Gen. John J. Pershing*, pp. 9–10.

[13] *Ibid.*, p. 8.

[14] 27.4 per cent of all examined were rejected as unfit; another 24 per cent were defective and accepted for partial military service, and tests showed "47.3 per cent of the white draft were of a mental age of 13–15 years; while the average mental age of the black draft was 10.1." (Harbord, p. 27.)

[15] Pershing's *Experiences*, p. 298.

[16] Pershing's *Final Report*, pp. 75–76.

[17] *Ibid.*, pp. 14–15.

[18] Pershing's *Experiences*, pp. 281–282.

[19] See *ibid.*, p. 277.

[20] The first American unit which participated in active fighting was the Eleventh Engineers, attached to the British Third Army during the Battle of Cambrai in November, 1917.

[21] Pershing's *Experiences*, p. 324.

[22] Pershing's *Final Report*, p. 31.

[23] See Pershing's *Experiences*, pp. 362–365.

[24] *Ibid.*, pp. 379–380.

[25] *Ibid.*, p. 385.

[26] Pershing's *Final Report*, p. 30.

[27] Pershing's *Experiences*, p. 421.

[28] Dawes' *Journal*, pp. 127–128.

[29] Pershing's *Experiences*, p. 505.

[30] The order creating the First Army was issued on July 24, to take effect on August 10.

[31] The 27th and 30th were left to support the British Fourth Army then operating east of Amiens.

[32] Pershing writes: "We had 3,010 artillery guns of all calibres, none of which were of American manufacture. Of the total, 1,681 were manned by Americans and 1,329 by French. Before the attack 40,000 tons of ammunition were placed in dumps" (*Experiences*, p. 581).

[33] The aviation force consisted of nearly 1,400 planes, "the strongest that had been assembled up to that time." It included the British Independent Bombing Squadrons, under General Trenchard, and a French division of 600 planes. (Pershing's *Experiences*, p. 582.)

[34] Pershing's *Final Report*, p. 39. The French placed at his disposal numbered 110,000 officers and men.

[35] The French are adepts at changing their minds and prefer paper plans above all things as they can so easily be torn up. A typical case is quoted by General Harbord. When Pershing took over Ligny-en-Barrois, "The French General and his Chief of Staff turned out in the peace-time uniform of blue tunic and red trousers [and] delivered to General Pershing two volumes, each of perhaps a hundred and fifty pages. One was the Plan for the Defense of St. Mihiel; the other an offensive Plan. The American Staff had prepared plans corresponding to those now handed over with such ceremony; they were respectively of eight and six pages" (p. 415). I have seen several such plans and have always found that the more there is on paper, the less there is on the ground.

[36] Pershing's *Experiences*, pp. 568–571.

[37] Most fortunately, in 1914, Lord Kitchener refused to place the British Expeditionary Force under the command of General Joffre; most unfortunately, in 1939, Mr. Chamberlain handed it over to General Gamelin.

[38] Pershing's *Final Report*, p. 40. He writes: "It should be recorded that although this general offensive was fully outlined at the conference no one present expressed the opinion that the final victory could be won in 1918."

[39] *Commanding an American Army*, Hunter Liggett, p. 64.

[40] Pershing's *Experiences*, p. 588.

[41] *Memoirs of Marshal Foch*, p. 391.

[42] Figures regarding supplies, etc. are given by General Harbord, see pp. 429–430.

[43] Pershing's *Final Report*, p. 44.

[44] Harbord, p. 432.

[45] Pershing's *Final Report*, p. 45.

[46] For various reasons the attack was postponed until October 24.

[47] The Renault (7-ton) tank was far inferior to the British Mark V (27-ton) machine. It could cross no trench of any width without infantry assistance, and consequently had to advance behind instead of in front of the infantry (see *The History of the A.E.F.* Shipley Thomas, Captain 26th U.S. Infantry, 1st Division, A.E.F., p. 244).

[48] Harbord, p. 437.

[49] Pershing's *Final Report*, pp. 46–47.

[50] Pershing's *Experiences*, p. 617.

[51] Harbord, p. 442.

[52] *Our Greatest Battle* (*The Meuse-Argonne*), Frederick Palmer, p. 139.

[53] Pershing's *Experiences*, p. 642.

[54] "Influenza in the Army had assumed very serious proportions, over 16,000 cases additional having been reported during the week ending October 5th. Large number of cases were brought in by our troopships. The total number of cases of influenza treated in hospitals was nearly 70,000, of whom many developed a grave form of pneumonia. The death rate from influenza rose to 32 per cent of cases for the A.E.F., and was as high as 80 per cent in some groups." (Pershing's *Experiences*, p. 640.)

[55] It consisted of the 26th, 78th, and 89th Divisions.

[56] Pershing's *Experiences*, pp. 649–650.

[57] Liggett, p. 102.

[58] Bullard, p. 271.

[59] Pershing's *Final Report*, p. 50.

[60] On February 11, 1918, President Wilson had said before Congress: "There shall be no annexations, no contributions, no punitive damage . . . Self-determination is not a new phrase. It is an imperative principle of action statesmen will henceforth ignore at their peril."

[61] Quoted from Pershing's *Experiences*, p. 657.

[62] Liggett, pp. 100–101.

[63] *Ibid.*, p. 112.

[64] Pershing's *Experiences*, p. 681.

[65] Harbord (quoting Colonel George C. Marshall), p. 453.

[66] *Ibid.*, p. 455.

[67] See *ibid.*, pp. 458–459.

[68] Liggett, p. 120.

[69] Pershing's *Experiences*, pp. 693–694.

[70] See *ibid.*, p. 602, and Liggett, p. 123.
[71] Pershing's *Final Report*, p. 77.
[72] *The War with Germany*, Ayres, p. 131.
[73] Harbord, p. 6.
[74] *Ibid.*, p. 21.

INDEX

Other DA CAPO titles of interest

Available at your bookstore

OR ORDER DIRECTLY FROM

DA CAPO PRESS, INC.

1-800-321-0050